Selections from Virgil's *Aeneid* Books 7–12

Selections from Virgil's *Aeneid* Books 7–12

A Student Reader

Ashley Carter

BLOOMSBURY ACADEMIC
LONDON • NEW YORK • OXFORD • NEW DELHI • SYDNEY

BLOOMSBURY ACADEMIC
Bloomsbury Publishing Plc
50 Bedford Square, London, WC1B 3DP, UK
1385 Broadway, New York, NY 10018, USA
29 Earlsfort Terrace, Dublin 2, Ireland

BLOOMSBURY, BLOOMSBURY ACADEMIC and the Diana logo are trademarks of
Bloomsbury Publishing Plc

First published in Great Britain 2021

For legal purposes the Preface on p. vi constitutes an extension of this copyright page.

Cover design: Terry Woodley
Cover image: Aeneas cured by lapis before Aphrodite and Ascanium. Album / Alamy Stock Photo.

Bloomsbury Publishing Plc does not have any control over, or responsibility for,
any third-party websites referred to or in this book. All internet addresses given in this
book were correct at the time of going to press. The author and publisher regret
any inconvenience caused if addresses have changed or sites have ceased to exist,
but can accept no responsibility for any such changes.

A catalogue record for this book is available from the British Library.

Library of Congress Cataloging-in-Publication Data
Names: Virgil, author. | Carter, Ashley, editor.
Title: Selections from Virgil's Aeneid books 7–12 : a student reader / [edited by] Ashley Carter.
Other titles: Aeneis. Liber 7–12. Selections
Description: London : Bloomsbury Academic, 2021. | Includes bibliographical references and index. |
Text in Latin, with introduction and commentary in English. | Summary: "This reader of Virgil's text features
passages from the second half of the Aeneid and is designed to help students understand and appreciate
Virgil's poem, as well as improve their Latin reading skills. Each Latin passage is accompanied by running
vocabulary, on-page commentary notes and targeted questions. The book can be used as a source of
one-off unseen passages or as a reader for students working through individual books or the whole poem.
The commentary notes explain references to characters, places and events, provide linguistic and grammatical
help on more challenging Latin phrases, and point out stylistic features. The questions test students'
comprehension of the characters and storyline, and give them practice in handling literary terms. The
passages are linked by summaries of the continuing plot, so students can grasp the progression of the
poem as a whole. An introduction sets the story of the Aeneid in its mythological, literary and historical
context and includes a glossary of literary devices and essays explaining the principles of Virgil's word order
and metre. At the end of the book is a complete alphabetical vocabulary list"– Provided by publisher.
Identifiers: LCCN 2020040458 (print) | LCCN 2020040459 (ebook) | ISBN 9781350136250 (paperback) |
ISBN 9781350136267 (epub) | ISBN 9781350136274 (ebook)
Subjects: LCSH: Virgil. Aeneis. | Latin language–Readers. | LCGFT: Poetry.
Classification: LCC PA6802.A9 C37 2021 (print) | LCC PA6802.A9 (ebook) | DDC 873/.01—dc23
LC record available at https://lccn.loc.gov/2020040458
LC ebook record available at https://lccn.loc.gov/2020040459

ISBN: PB: 978-1-3501-3625-0
         ePDF: 978-1-3501-3627-4
         eBook: 978-1-3501-3626-7

Typeset by RefineCatch Limited, Bungay, Suffolk
Printed and bound in Great Britain

To find out more about our authors and books visit www.bloomsbury.com
and sign up for our newsletters.

CONTENTS

PREFACE

The purpose of this book is to provide a source of selections from Books 7–12 of Virgil's *Aeneid*. Each of these books has contributed around 250 lines of text, sufficient to provide comprehensive coverage of the storyline and principal characters.

Virgil's great work has inevitably been dipped into many times over the years. The intention behind this set of selections is to provide the kind of layout and help appropriate to the needs of students with only a few years of study behind them. The book is suitable as a reader for its own sake or to act as a prescribed text for examination. The characters and storyline are summarised in the Introduction; students reading a single book should read this summary first. Significant gaps between Latin passages are summarised in Italics.

The principle behind the glossing of words is that all except for the commonest words are glossed, with meanings appropriate to the context. When a word is repeated in the same book, it is not glossed again, unless the meaning has changed. Verbs are given two principal parts if they are used with the present stem, otherwise three or four parts; following the principle used in a number of current text books, the perfect participle passive replaces the supine as the fourth principal part. Since students are likely to focus on one book, full glossing recommences at the start of each book. At the end of the book is a complete alphabetical wordlist.

The Introduction aims to set the story of the *Aeneid* into its mythological, literary and historical context. Students preparing for GCSE or similar examinations will need little of the information provided there, but those progressing beyond the boundaries of a single book may find at least some of the detail helpful. Metre and style are also covered. Those who wish to explore further will find the long-established editions of Williams or Page helpful.

The notes aim to help students to understand references to characters, places and events, though only at a basic level. Teachers may wish to expand these references in class. The notes also help students to cope with more challenging linguistic items, and point out some stylistic features.

The questions test students' comprehension of the characters and storyline, and give them practice in handling literary terms. The Introduction contains a list of the commonest literary devices, which are generally considered appropriate for students at this level of study.

The text is that of Williams (1972 and 1996), with the following exceptions: all accusative plural endings in -*is* have been changed to -*es*, and the lower case is used for initial letters of paragraphs.

Line numbers alongside the text are the standard line numbers from the complete books, following Williams where the manuscripts are unclear.

I am grateful to Bloomsbury for the encouragement given and for authorising the use of Williams' text. Their editorial staff have been most helpful.

Introduction

1. Virgil and the *Aeneid*

Virgil began composing the *Aeneid* in about 30 BC, continuing to work on it until his death at the age of 50 in 19 BC. He was commissioned to write the work by Octavian, who in 31 BC had defeated Mark Antony and Cleopatra at the Battle of Actium, thereby gaining supreme power in Rome. Octavian devoted the next four years to making his power secure, with the result that, in 27 BC, he became the first emperor, with the title Augustus. Although he was popular with many sections of Roman society from the moment of his triumph over Antony, he was anxious to avoid the same fate as his adoptive father, Julius Caesar, who, in similar circumstances, had been assassinated in 44 BC by a group of senators.

One means available to Octavian of securing his position was self-publicity. Among the various methods regularly used by statesmen of the time was glorification through poetry; in fact it was entirely fashionable for successful and wealthy statesmen to pay poets within their patronage to write poems of various lengths extolling the virtues and achievements of their patron. The poets Horace, Propertius and Virgil were in turn invited to produce an epic poem with Octavian, later Augustus, as its hero. All at first refused, deterred no doubt by the conflicting demands of historical distortion and artistry. Then Virgil changed his mind, having devised a way of combining the positive presentation of Octavian and his victory with the need of all true poets for creative self-expression. And so the *Aeneid* was born.

By the time of Virgil, the tradition of epic poetry was at least 700 years old. Many poets of the classical, Hellenistic and Roman periods produced a wide range of epic poems of very varying quality. None came close to achieving the status accorded by general consent to Homer, the first of the surviving epic poets, who composed the *Iliad* and *Odyssey* probably during the late 8th century BC. Homer's works were widely known and read in Virgil's Rome, much as Shakespeare is in today's society.

Virgil took upon himself the delicate task of composing an epic similar enough to the *Iliad* and *Odyssey* for the two poets to be directly compared, but different enough for Virgil to avoid charges of plagiarism. The *Aeneid* would combine a conventional epic tale of heroic endeavour (the story of Aeneas), the ancestry of Rome and its leaders, glorification of Rome and the Augustan regime, and an example of the social and moral responsibilities that a *pius* or dutiful leader ought to be prepared to shoulder.

Doubtless Virgil's contemporaries would have been surprised by a first reading of this literary cocktail: Augustus and his victory at Actium are barely mentioned; and yet from a closer scrutiny Augustus and his achievements shine forth with more persuasive clarity than any more overt form of flattery could have achieved. Virgil presents his contemporary Rome as the climax of twelve hundred years of history, all foretold and so sanctioned by Jupiter in Book 1; Aeneas' father, Anchises, in Book 6 repeats the prophecy, while the shield made by Vulcan for Aeneas in Book 8 shows the great moments of Roman history.

That Augustus was satisfied with Virgil's achievement is clear from his veto of the poet's will, in which, dissatisfied with its unfinished condition, he had given orders for the poem to be burned; Augustus demanded publication. He is also said to have been overcome with emotion when listening to the recitation of parts of the poem.

The conclusion may therefore be drawn that, at least as far as Virgil's patrons were concerned, the *Aeneid* was successful in terms of its glorification of Rome and its leader. But what of the heroic dimension? Aeneas undergoes adventures parallel to those of Homer's Odysseus, and fights battles every bit as bloody as those of the heroes of the *Iliad*. But Homer's heroes lived and fought for the present, with responsibilities only to their own heroic status and to their fellow-heroes. Aeneas, in contrast, in addition to these still-important considerations, has a destiny to fulfil, a destiny which demands his absolute *pietas*. This destiny is nothing less than the transfer of the spirit and survivors of Troy to a new homeland, from which will spring Rome and ultimately Augustus.

Aeneas earns a place in the ranks of the great heroes of legend, having negotiated his way past all the obstacles to his success; but, unlike the Homeric stereotypes, who exist on a plane somewhere between gods and ordinary mortals, Aeneas is essentially human, with all the weaknesses and flaws of his fellow men and without the constant help and guidance of an Athena. Venus' interventions are infrequent and sometimes of questionable value to him.

2. Synopsis of Books VII–XII of the *Aeneid*

Book VII

The Trojans reach the mouth of the river Tiber, which they recognise as being their destination. Aeneas sends out men to explore the region, known as Latium, and find its principal city and ruler. The king of Latium is Latinus, a fair-minded but weak ruler. His city is Laurentum. He has been told a prophecy that his daughter, Lavinia, should marry a foreigner, and he believes Aeneas to be that man. He therefore promises his daughter's hand to Aeneas. This infuriates her mother, Amata, and Turnus, the leader of the Rutuli (a neighbouring tribe allied to Latinus), to whom Lavinia has already been betrothed. The goddess Juno is also infuriated, because she has been opposed to the Trojans throughout and has done all within her power to thwart their ambitions to sail to their promised land and to found a new city. She sends the Fury, Allecto, to stoke the Italians' hostility to the Trojans. Soon anger flares up between the two peoples, leading to bloodshed and the declaration of war by Turnus. Latinus is powerless to prevent it. Virgil lists the main protagonists on both sides.

Book VIII

Aeneas realises that his army is not strong enough to fight off the combined forces of the Latins and their allies, and so he leaves his men to defend the walls of their newly-built camp, sailing up the Tiber to meet Evander, the king of Pallanteum. This city lies on the site of the future Rome. Evander and his son Pallas welcome Aeneas and promise their support, as the Rutuli are hostile to them too. They conduct Aeneas round their city, pointing out the places of interest, that would later become famous Roman landmarks. Venus, the mother of Aeneas, persuades the blacksmith god, Vulcan, to make a new set of armour for her son. Aeneas happily receives this gift, and admires the shield, on which are depicted all the major events from Rome's future history. These are described in great detail, even though Aeneas does not understand their meaning.

Book IX

Turnus takes advantage of the absence of Aeneas to attack the Trojan camp, at the same time setting fire to the Trojan ships, which are turned by Neptune into sea-nymphs. A young pair of friends, Nisus and Euryalus, conceive a plan to take a message through the encircling enemy camp to Aeneas, urging him to hurry back, as the Trojan camp is severely threatened. In the middle of the night they set off through the midst of the enemy, but get sidetracked into killing as many of the sleeping men as they can. A returning patrol catches sight of them, runs them down and kills them. Next day Turnus returns to the attack and succeeds in forcing his way into the camp, where he is cut off from his fellows and has to jump into the river to escape. During the fight, Ascanius, the son of Aeneas also known as Iulus, makes his first kill.

Book X

On the advice of Evander, Aeneas secures the alliance of the Etruscans, who inhabit the land to the north of Pallanteum. They are hostile to the Rutulians because Turnus has given refuge and support to the Etruscan tyrant, Mezentius, whom his people have driven out and want to punish. The Etruscan leader, Tarchon, promises his support and leads forth his army. Aeneas is also accompanied by an army from Pallanteum, led by the young Pallas. When they reach the Trojan camp by the mouth of the Tiber, they find Turnus and his army waiting for them, and a full-scale battle ensues. During this Pallas enjoys many victories before coming face to face with Turnus, who kills him, stripping his ornamental sword-belt from his body. Then Aeneas kills Mezentius and his young son, Lausus, who bravely tries to defend his father.

Book XI

Aeneas celebrates the Trojan victory over Mezentius but mourns the death of Pallas. The young prince's body is returned to Pallanteum, where king Evander is overcome with grief. A truce is agreed on the battlefield to allow both sides to recover and dispose of their dead. A Latin ambassador, Drances, proposes that the war be decided by single combat between Aeneas and Turnus. Aeneas agrees. Drances returns to Laurentum, where there is already a strong public revulsion against the war. Latinus again proposes a peace treaty with the Trojans, when scouts report that the Trojan army is on the move and closing upon the city. Turnus responds with a call to arms, which is enthusiastically taken up by the young men. As he disposes his forces to protect the city and lay an ambush to trap the Trojans, Camilla, a princess from a neighbouring tribe, commits her forces to the defence. In the fighting that follows, Camilla, after tearing through the Trojan forces, is killed by Arruns, who in turn is killed by the goddess Opis, an assistant of Diana, to whom Camilla had been pledged.

Book XII

Turnus finally agrees to single combat, to the dismay of Amata and Lavinia. When Juno learns of this, she persuades Turnus' sister, the immortal nymph Juturna, to do what she can to ward off his death. She takes the form of one of the Latin leaders and whips up a blood lust among the young warriors, until one hurls his spear and kills a Trojan ally. At once fighting flares up again. Aeneas tries to restore order, but an arrow pierces his thigh, forcing him to withdraw. Turnus, realising that his enemies are now leaderless, charges through the Trojan ranks, killing many. Meanwhile Aeneas is given healing herbs through the intervention of his mother and returns to the battle. Juturna sees him and makes one last attempt to prolong the life of her brother: she takes the form of Turnus' charioteer and drives him away from the fighting, pursued by Aeneas. Aeneas loses his temper and kills many Latins and Rutulians, before wheeling the army against the city. Queen Amata, believing that Turnus is already dead, kills herself. Turnus is informed by a messenger of the tragedy, and orders his sister to desist. Finally the two leaders face each other, and Aeneas wounds Turnus in the thigh. Aeneas is almost persuaded by Turnus' pleas for mercy to spare him; then he spies the sword-belt that Turnus stripped from the body of Pallas, and kills him.

3. Virgil's metre

Every line has the same basic rhythm or metre, called the dactylic hexameter. The word 'dactylic' indicates the nature of the rhythmical unit being used; 'hexameter' tells us that there are six of these units (called 'feet') in each line.

In Latin poetry rhythm is determined by the length of each syllable, either short or long. Scansion involves writing out a line of verse and marking the length of each syllable, by writing above the syllable ∪ if it is short, – if it is long; also the divisions between feet should be marked with a vertical line through the text.

A dactylic hexameter, therefore, consists of six feet, with each foot containing one dactyl (or equivalent). A dactyl consists of one long syllable followed by two short ones, and is marked like this: – ∪ ∪ . To provide variation of rhythm, each dactyl in the line (apart usually from the fifth one) may be replaced by a spondee, which comprises two long syllables, marked – – . The sixth foot always contains two syllables only, either long + short or long + long.

The metrical scheme for a dactylic hexameter therefore looks like this:

$$
\underset{–\,∪\,∪|}{–\,–}\quad \underset{–\,∪\,∪|}{–\,–}\quad \underset{–\,∪\,∪|}{–\,–}\quad \underset{–\,∪\,∪|}{–\,–}\quad \underset{–\,∪\,∪|}{–\,–}\quad \underset{–\,∪.}{–\,–}
$$

There are fairly precise rules for determining whether a syllable is short or long. The following are always long:

- diphthongs (in Latin *ae* and *au* are the commonest; also *oe* and, in proper names, *eu* and sometimes *ei*);
- vowels followed by two or more consonants, whether in the same word or the next. An exception to this rule is when the second of two consonants is *l* or *r*, in which case the syllable may be short or long;
- vowels that are long by nature (such as ablative singular endings of the first and second declensions). Where the vowel appears in the stem of a word, dictionaries generally indicate its length.

The following syllables are short:

- single vowels that are followed by a single consonant, or by another vowel that does not form a diphthong, so long as they are normally pronounced as short (dictionaries here too are useful guides).

Scanning a line can be a very useful indicator of which part of a word is being used; e.g. *puellă* must be nominative or vocative, while *puellā* must be ablative.

Some further rules that need to be mastered are:

- *qu-* and *-gu* before a vowel count as a single consonant (i.e. the *u* is ignored) – e.g. *sanguis*;

- *x* and *z* always count as double consonants (and so the vowel before them is always scanned long);
- *i* when followed by another vowel sometimes becomes a consonant (e.g. *iam*, which has one syllable, not two, and *cuius*, which has two syllables); at other times it is treated as a separate vowel (e.g. *audiet. ierat*);
- a vowel at the end of a word elides before a vowel at the start of the next word; when scanning such a line, you should place brackets round the elided vowel and ignore it when scanning the rest of the line;
- there is one other type of syllable that elides in the same way: any word ending in *-am*, *-em*, *-im*, *-om* or *-um* before a word starting with a vowel should be bracketed and then ignored;
- *h-* at the start of a word should be ignored;
- every dactylic hexameter has a natural pause around the middle; this is known as a caesura (a Latin word with the literal meaning 'cutting'); the caesura is marked by a double vertical line through the verse; in most verses the caesura comes after the first syllable of the third foot, as long as it coincides with the end of a word; if that is not possible, the caesura may be placed in the second or fourth foot, again after the first syllable.

It should be noted that the above rules are slightly simplified, but are sufficient for the needs of anyone reading this book. For a more detailed treatment, other sources of information are available (see 7. Further Reading, p. 16).

Here are some examples:

  – ∪∪|– – |– ∪ ∪|–‖ –| –∪ ∪| – –
sed variis portenta deum terroribus obstant (VII.58)

  – ∪∪| – – | – ‖∪∪|–   –|– ∪∪|– –
expedi(am), et primae revocab(o) exordia pugnae (VII.40)

It can be seen from the above examples that each line is slightly different; in this way variation is introduced. Poets capitalized on this by sometimes making lines strongly dactylic or strongly spondaic. Dactylic rhythm was considered fast, while spondaic rhythm was thought of as slow. This convention allowed poets to match the rhythm to the subject matter: rapid action or excitement could be emphasized by the abundant use of dactyls, while inactivity, solemnity, sadness or awe could be enhanced by the use of spondees. An example of the former is IX, line 422:

  – ∪ ∪| – ∪∪|–‖∪ ∪|– ∪∪ |– ∪ ∪| – –
'tu tamen interea calido mihi sanguine poenas (IX.422)

Here Volcens quickly puts an end to the life of Euryalus. This contrasts with the previous line, in which he stands over his victim searching in vain for signs of Euryalus' friend Nisus:

  – –|–   – | –‖ – | – – – |– ∪∪|– ∪
auctorem nec quo s(e) ardens immittere possit. (IX.421)

4. Virgil's word order

The word order in verse is very different from that in prose. The most obvious difference is that words that belong together in sense are often separated from each other. An example can be seen under *synchysis* in the following section, but examples are so frequent that they rarely call for comment. One major determining factor for word placement is the fact that the beginning and end of a line are seen as places for emphasis, and so very often, but not always, key words are placed there; see also *enjambement* in the next section. Where the poet wishes to achieve sound effects with e.g. *alliteration*, he places words together for their sound qualities rather than because they form a discrete phrase. The requirements of rhythm are the other main reason for words being apparently jumbled; very often there is only one place in a line where a particular word will fit the metre.

Students will need to develop the habit of glancing through whole sentences to see how they fit together, keeping an eye out for subjects, verbs and objects; other words can then be slotted in around these. An example is VII.124–7:

> cum te, nate, fames ignota ad litora vectum
> accisis coget dapibus consumere mensas,
> tum sperare domos defessus, ibique memento
> prima locare manu molirique aggere tecta.

For translation, the order is *cum, nate, fames coget te, vectum ad ignota litora, dapibus accisis, consumere mensas, tum defessus memento sperare domos, ibique locare prima tecta manu molirique aggere*. It will be seen that the sentence begins with a *cum* clause; *cum* must mean 'when' because it is followed by a future indicative (*coget*). This *cum* clause must end at *mensas*, because *tum*, the correlative of *cum*, begins the main clause. Inside the *cum* clause are two participial phrases; the first participle is accusative and so agrees with *te*; the second is ablative agreeing with *dapibus* and may be assumed to be an ablative absolute. In the main clause are three infinitives (*sperare, locare, moliri*), leaving *memento* as the only contender for main verb, upon which the infinitives must be dependent. Also resembling an infinitive is *aggere*, but no such verb exists; it must therefore be an ablative singular noun.

Some teachers may prefer a different approach, relying more on intuition to take each word as it comes and place it into its context within the sentence.

5. Stylistic features

The *Aeneid* is a rich treasure-house of stylistic features, which, just like the storyline, characters and metre, are integral to the poetry. Indeed, it can be argued that it is the liberal and intelligent use of these features that turns ordinary poetry into great poetry.

It is almost impossible to find a line of the *Aeneid* that does not contain at least one identifiable stylistic feature; many contain several. So many are there, indeed, that it would be impractical to identify them all in the commentary. Instead, only the most significant features are mentioned. Readers are encouraged to familiarise themselves with all the commonest features so that they can identify them as they meet them.

To help readers to achieve this, a list of the commonest and most important features is given below. This is not an exhaustive list; rather the most frequently-met ones are listed. Although some scholars would argue that we cannot know Virgil's purpose in using any given stylistic feature, because he is not around to be asked, it is legitimate to discuss the effect it has on the reader. For a modern reader, the only way to achieve expertise in this is through frequent exposure to them through reading and regular analysis and evaluation of their usage.

Alliteration

The use of the same letter to start two or more adjacent words, usually, but not always, in the same line. Occasionally the alliterated words may be separated by another word. At its most basic level, the effect is simply to draw attention to the words alliterated or to give a pleasing sound. Some letters can have more particular effects. For example a and m are regularly used by Virgil to express high emotion, usually fear, horror, sadness or anger; s can represent hissing, whether of serpents, the sea, sleep or to express anger (see also Sibilance); hard consonants can represent harsh events, while l or m can suggest softness or calm. For example:

> aut pugnam aut aliquid iamdudum invadere **magnum**
> **mens** agitat **mihi**, nec placida contenta quiete est. (IX.186–7)

Anaphora

The repetition of a word to introduce two or more parallel statements. The effect is to increase the importance of that word and to emphasise the parallel nature of two or more objects or actions. This feature is much used in oratory. For example:

> **ter** totum fervidus ira
> lustrat Aventini montem, **ter** saxea temptat
> limina nequiquam, **ter** fessus valle resedit. (VIII.230–2)

Antithesis

The inclusion of opposite or contrasting words or phrases within a line or sentence. The effect, to heighten the contrast, is further enhanced if the contrasting words or phrases are juxtaposed, i.e. placed next to each other. For example:

> fidite ne **pedibus. ferro** rumpenda per hostes
> est via. (X.372–3)

Apostrophe

Literally a 'turning away' from the general audience or reader to address a person, place or abstract idea that is not present. This is used to express heightened emotion by giving a dramatic twist to a narrative or speech. For example:

> sternitur Arcadiae proles, sternuntur Etrusci
> **et vos, o Grais imperdita corpora, Teucri.** (X.429–30)

Assonance

The repetition of the same sound, usually a vowel, in adjoining words. The effect is usually to project some emotion: assonance of u often indicates surprise or sadness, while a regularly (like alliteration of m) reflects a more visceral emotion. For example:

> dicam acies actosque animis in funera reges (VII.42)

Asyndeton

The omission of conjunctions in a sequence of parallel words or phrases. The effect may be no more than to focus attention on the parallel ideas; it may also be to emphasise the rapidity of a sequence of events. For example:

> *terrorem ingeminat: Teucros in regna **vocari**,*
> ***stirpem** admisceri Phrygiam. se limine pelli.* (VII.578–9)

Chiasmus

A group of usually four words that together form a symmetry about a central point. Examples are *verb, noun / noun, verb*; *adjective, noun / noun adjective*; *nominative, accusative / accusative, nominative*. Any two parallel pairs of words, where the order of the second is reversed, is chiastic. A single word may provide a central pivot, while conjunctions may be ignored. The effect of a chiasmus is to draw attention to the words and to emphasise the parallel importance of the two pairs. Very rarely three pairs of words may form a chiasmus. NB the sequence *adjective, noun / adjective noun* is not chiastic. A superb example of a triple chiasmus, including alliteration, is:

> *puberibus caulem foliis et flore comantem*
> *purpureo;* (XII.413–14)

Consonance

The repetition of a consonant within neighbouring words. This is similar to **alliteration**, and is usually used in conjunction with it. For example:

> *ingentem gemitum tunsis ad sidera tollunt* (XI.37)

Enclosing word-order

A phrase in which two or more words relating to one object, action or state enclose one or more words relating to a second object, action or state, in such a way that they reflect the sense of the phrase. For example, *in medio stat foro* has the verb enclosed within *in medio foro*, reflecting what is actually happening. For example:

> *alba solo recubans, **albi circum ubera nati**.* (VIII.45)

Enjambement

The carrying over of sense to the beginning of the next line. The effect is to place extra emphasis on the word that is carried over. For example:

> *quisquis honos tumuli, quidquid solamen humandi est,*
> *largior.* (X.413–14)

Hendiadys

The separation of an adjective-plus-noun phrase into two parallel nouns linked by a conjunction. It is used to give greater emphasis to the words. For example:

*exitio. passim **somno vinoque** per herbam*
corpora fusa vident, arrectos litore currus, (IX.316–17)

Hypallage *or* Transferred Epithet

The transfer of an adjective from the noun to which it logically belongs to another noun in the same phrase. For example *primi sub lumina solis*: 'just before the light of the first sun', i.e. 'just before the first light of the sun'. For example:

circum omnis famulumque manus Troianaque turba
*et **maestum** Iliades **crinem** de more solutae.* (XI.34–5)

Hyperbole

Exaggeration, used to emphasise a point. For example:

maxima ter centum totam delubra per urbem. (VIII.716)

Litotes

A double negative, making a strong affirmative. For example:

nec non *mediis in milibus ipsi*
ductores auro volitant ostroque superbi (XII.125–6)

Metaphor

The use of a word with a meaning different from its literal or normal one. Whereas a simile says that one thing is *like* another (e.g. 'the world is like a stage'), a metaphor says one thing *is* another (e.g. 'the world is a stage'). For example:

accendamque animos *insani Martis amore*
undique ut auxilio veniant; ***spargam arma*** *per agros.'* (VII.550–1)

Metonymy

Calling something not by its own name but by the name of something related to it. For example:

*quo **thalamum** eripiat Teucris **taedasque** moretur.* (VII.388)

Onomatopoeia

A word that sounds like what it means. For example:

> *consurgunt gemitu Rutuli totusque* **remugit**
> *mons circum et vocem late nemora alta remittunt.* (XII.928–9)

Polyptoton

The repetition of a noun, verb, adjective or pronoun with different endings (closely related to **anaphora**). For example:

> *numina nulla premunt,* **mortali** *urgemur ab hoste*
> **mortales;** *totidem nobis animaeque manusque.* (X.375–6)

Polysyndeton

The repeated use of conjunctions (usually 'and') in quick succession to join words or phrases; sometimes more are used than necessary. The effect may be to give a sense of rapidity to a sequence, or it may stress the number of items in the sequence. For example:

> *regem adit et regi memorat* **nomenque genusque** (X.149)

Prolepsis

The anticipation of a future act or state by treating it as if it already existed. For example:

> *invadit sociosque incendia poscit* **ovantes** (IX.71)

Rhetorical question

A question (often in a series) asked, not to elicit a reply, but as a stronger alternative to a statement. For example:

> **quem** *telo primum,* **quem** *postremum, aspera virgo,*
> *deicis? aut* **quot** *humi morientia corpora fundis?* (XI.664–5)

Sibilance

Alliteration of the letter *s*, or the repetition of *s* within adjacent words. For effects, see **alliteration**. For example:

> *ceu septem surgens sedatis amnibus altus*
> *per tacitum Ganges aut pingui flumine Nilus* (IX.30–1)

Simile

A comparison of one thing, event or scene with another one. A simple simile is generally introduced by the prepositional 'like' or 'as'. Like Homer, Virgil most often uses extended or 'epic' similes, often several lines long; they are introduced by some part of *qualis* ('just as') or *ut cum* ('just as when'), or *velut* ('just as'), where the following *haud secus* or *haud aliter* ('no differently'), relates the simile to the narrative episode. There are other occasional variants, for example:

> **non secus ac si** qua penitus vi terra dehiscens
> infernas reseret sedes et regna recludat
> pallida, dis invisa, superque immane barathrum
> cernatur, trepident immisso lumine Manes. (VIII.243–6)

Synchysis

An interlocking of the word order of two pairs of words, so that the words that belong syntactically together are separated. For example the order may be adjective – noun – adjective – noun, where the first adjective defines the second noun; or it may be adjective – adjective – noun – noun (this variety, with the verb in the middle, is known as a 'golden line'). For example:

> *ora virum* **tristi** *pendebant* **pallida tabo**. (VIII.197)

Synecdoche

The substitution of a part of something for the whole thing. For example:

> *triginta* **capitum** *fetus enixa iacebit* (VIII.44)

Tautology

Saying the same thing twice using different words. For example:

> *posse viam ad* **muros et moenia** *Pallantea*. (IX.196)

Zeugma

Here a verb is given two objects, each requiring a different meaning of the verb. For example:

> *ille humilis supplexque* **oculos dextramque** *precantem*
> **protendens** *'equidem merui nec deprecor' inquit* (XII.930–1)

6. List of names of people and places

Abaris	An Italian killed by Euryalus
Abas	An Etruscan killed by Lausus
Achates	Aeneas' arms bearer and loyal friend
Acheron	One of the five rivers of the underworld
Achilles	Most famous and powerful warrior in the Greek army that fought at Troy; he killed Hector
Acoetes	An old squire of Evander
Actium	Site of the sea battle of 31 BC, in which Octavian defeated Antony and Cleopatra; after this Octavian became emperor
Aeneas	The leader of the Trojan survivors, son of Venus and Anchises
Aetnaeus	Of Mount Etna, an active volcano in Sicily
Agylla	City in Etruria, better known as Caere
Alba Longa	City of Latium, to be founded by Aeneas' son, Ascanius
Alcides	Hercules, who was forced to carry out Twelve Labours
Allecto	One of the three avenging Furies of Greek mythology
Alpes	The Alps
Amastrus	Trojan or ally killed by Camilla
Amata	Wife of Latinus and mother of Lavinia
Amathus	Place in Cyprus where Venus was worshipped
Amazon	A member of a mythical race of female warriors, noted for their archery
Amphytrionides	Son of Amphytrion, i.e. Hercules
Anchises	Father of Aeneas and lover of Venus
Apollo	God of prophecy, medicine, etc., born on the island of Delos
Arcades	Arcadians, inhabitants of Arcadia; hence citizens of Pallanteum
Arcadia	A region of Greece from which Evander came
Ardea	A town about 20 miles south of Rome, traditionally the capital of the Rutuli and so the home of Turnus
Argos	A city in the Greek Peloponnese, supposedly founded by Inachus; a centre for the worship of Juno
Argolicus	Of Argos, i.e. Greek
Arruns	Etruscan who killed Camilla
Ascanius	Son of Aeneas and Creusa, also known as Iulus
Asilas	Prominent Trojan leader
Assaracus	Grandfather of Anchises
Augustus	The first emperor (previously Octavian), who commissioned Virgil to write the *Aeneid*
Aurora	Dawn, often personified as a goddess
Ausonia	Southern Italy
Ausonidae	Female inhabitants of Ausonia
Ausonius	Ausonian, i.e. Italian
Aventinus	The Aventine Hill is one of the seven hills of Rome; the traditional site of the monster Cacus' cave
Bacchus	God of wine, called by the Greeks Dionysus
Bellona	Sister of Mars and goddess of war
Cacus	Monster which lived on the Aventine Hill; killed by Hercules
Caesar	Julius Caesar, Roman general and statesman; adoptive father of Octavian; assassinated in 44 BC
Caicus	A Trojan ship's captain
Camilla	Volscian princess; ally of Turnus; killed by Arruns
Capitolium	The Capitoline Hill in Rome, which housed the temple of Jupiter

Cassandra	Trojan daughter of Priam and Hecuba, gifted with prophecy but cursed to be believed by no one
Ceres	Goddess of Corn; called by the Greeks Demeter
Chromis	Trojan ally killed by Camilla
Cisseis	Daughter of Cisseus, i.e. Hecuba, queen of Troy
Clonus	Artist who decorated the sword-belt of Pallas
Clytius	Father of Eunaeus, who was killed by Camilla
Cretaeus	Of Crete, a Greek island, noted for archers and its main centre, Knossos
Cybebe	The Asiatic goddess Cybele, also called 'the Great Mother'
Cyclops	One-eyed giant blinded by Odysseus in Homer's *Odyssey*
Cymodocea	One of the nymphs that had once been Trojan ships
Cythera	An island off the south coast of Greece where Venus was worshipped
Dardania	Another name for Troy, after Dardanus
Dardanidae	Dardanian, i.e. Trojan
Dardanus	A founder of Troy; brother of Iasius; both came originally from Italy
Daunus	Father of Turnus
Demophoon	Trojan ally killed by Camilla
Drances	Latin elder and orator, who opposed Turnus
Erato	The Muse of love poetry
Erinys	A Fury, one of three sisters of Greek mythology
Etruria	The region to the north of Latium, inhabited by the Etruscans
Etruscus	Etruscan; the Etruscans were allies of the Trojans
Euandrus	Evander, king of Pallanteum and father of Pallas; ally of Aeneas
Eunaeus	Son of Clytius; killed by Camilla
Eurus	The East Wind
Euryalus	Young Trojan warrior and friend of Nisus
Eurytus	Father of Clonus
Fadus	Italian warrior killed by Euryalus
Fama	Personification of Rumour, perceived as a monstrous, many-mouthed goddess
Faunus	Father of Latinus
Fortuna	Personification of fortune or luck, which might be good or bad
Ganges	River of Northern India
Geryones	Three-bodied monster killed by Hercules as one of his labours
Gorgoneus	Of the Gorgons, three sisters with snakes in their hair, like the Fury Allecto
Grai	The Greeks
Harpalycus	Trojan ally killed by Camilla
Hector	Son of Priam and Hecuba; the greatest warrior in the Trojan army; killed by Achilles
Herbesus	Italian warrior killed by Euryalus
Hesperia	The Western Land, i.e. Italy; the Trojans' final destination
Hippotes	Father or ancestor of Amastrus
Hisbo	Ally of the Latins killed by Pallas
Hyrtacus	Father of Nisus
Iapyx (1)	South Italian
Iapyx (2)	A Trojan healer, who treated Aeneas' thigh wound
Iasius (1)	Brother of Dardanus; both sailed from Italy to found Troy
Iasius (2)	Imagined father of Iapyx (2)
Ida	One of two mountains: one near Troy and one in Crete
Idalia	A centre of the worship of Venus
Ignipotens	'Mighty with Fire', an epithet of the god Vulcan (in Greek Hephaestus)
Iliacus	Trojan
Iliades	Trojan women

Ilioneus	An elderly companion of Aeneas
Inachus	Traditional founder of the Greek city of Argos
Italia	Italy
Italis	An Italian woman
Italus	Italian; an Italian man
Iulus	Cognomen of Ascanius, the son of Aeneas; thus became the founder of the Julian *gens*
Iuturna	Juturna, an immortal nymph who was the sister of Turnus
Karthago	Carthage, a city on the North African coast ruled by Dido
Lagus	Italian warrior killed by Pallas
Lamus	Italian warrior killed by Nisus
Lamyrus	Italian warrior killed by Nisus
Larina	Companion of Camilla
Latinus (1)	Latin, i.e. of the region or kingdom of Latium, to the south of the river Tiber
Latinus (2)	King of the city of Laurentum and the region of Latium
Latium	The region of Italy lying to the south of the Tiber
Latonia	Daughter of Latona, i.e. the goddess Diana (in Greek Artemis)
Laurens	Of or from the city of Laurentum
Laurentum	City of Latium, seat of Latinus
Lausus	Son of Mezentius; killed by Aeneas
Lavinia	Daughter of Latinus, betrothed to Turnus but destined to marry Aeneas
Leucate	A headland near Actium off the west coast of Greece
Liris	Trojan ally killed by Camilla
Lydius	Lydian, i.e. of Lydia, a kingdom of Asia Minor, possibly the original home of the Etruscans
Maeonia	Another name for Lydia
Mars, Marvors	Mars, God of war; named by the Greeks Ares; sometimes the personification of war
Messapus	A Latin leader, a son of Neptune, who could not be killed by fire or iron
Mezentius	An Etruscan tyrant thrown out by his people for cruelty; killed by Aeneas
Mnestheus	A Trojan commander
Neptunius	Of Neptune, i.e. son of Neptune, i.e. Messapus
Nilus	The river Nile
Nisus	Young Trojan warrior; friend and protector of Euryalus
Notus	The South Wind
Oceanus	The Sea, thought to encircle the Earth; sometimes personified
Olympus	Mountain in Northern Greece; home of the gods
Opis	Immortal assistant of the goddess Diana; killed Arruns
Oricius	Of Oricum, a town in Northern Greece, where the terebinth tree grew
Ornytus	Etruscan ally of the Trojans, killed by Camilla
Pachynus	A promontory on the SE corner of Sicily
Paeonius	Of Paeon; *Paeon* was an epithet of Apollo as healer-god
Pagasus	A Trojan ally killed by Camilla
Pallanteum	City founded by Evander on the site of the future Rome
Pallas	The son of Evander and ally of the Trojans; killed by Turnus
Pandarus	Trojan who rashly challenged Turnus and was killed by him
Paphus	Paphos: a town in Cyprus where Venus was worshipped
Parcae	The Fates, three sisters of Greek mythology
Paris	Son of Priam and Hecuba; abducted Helen; caused the Trojan War
Parrhasius	Of Parrhasia, a town in Arcadia in Greece, from where Evander came
Pergama	The citadel or fortified central high point of Troy
Phoebe	Goddess of the Moon, identified with Diana

Phoebus	Apollo, brother of Diana or Phoebe
Phryges	Inhabitants of Phrygia, one of the kingdoms of Asia Minor
Phrygius	Phrygian, of Phrygia
Priamus	King of Troy
Remulus	Brother-in-law of Turnus
Remus (1)	Brother of Romulus (founder of Rome)
Remus (2)	Italian killed by Nisus
Rhamnes	Rutulian chieftain killed by Nisus
Rhoetus	Rutulian warrior killed by Euryalus
Romanus	Roman
Rutulus	Rutulian, i.e. of the tribe of Rutuli, ruled by Turnus
Sabellus	Sabine; the Sabines were a race that lived to the east of Rome
Saturnia	Of Saturn, i.e. daughter of Saturn, i.e. Juno
Saturnus	Father of Jupiter, Juno and other gods
Serranus	Italian warrior killed by Nisus
Siculus	Sicilian
Sila	Mountain range in Southern Italy
Simois	River that flowed close to Troy
Sirius	The Dog Star; its rising heralded the hottest time of the year
Sol	The Sun or the Sun god
Stymonius	Of the Strymon, a river in NE Greece, where cranes overwintered
Taburnus	Mountain range in Southern Italy
Tarchon	Etruscan king and leader of the Etruscan alliance with the Trojans
Tarpeia	Companion of Camilla
Tartara	Tartarus, the part of the underworld reserved for the damned
Tereus	Trojan ally killed by Camilla
Teucri	One of the names of the Trojans; named after Teucer, a founder
Thracius	Of Thrace, part of N. Greece, including the northern shore of the Aegean Sea
Thybris	The Tiber, the river that flows through Rome; also the god of the river
Tiburtus	Son of the founder of Tibur near Rome; brother of two Latin commanders
Tirynthius	Of Tiryns in Greece, i.e. Hercules, who lived there
Troia	Troy, a city on the southern shore of the Hellespont; ruled by Priam with his queen, Hecuba; sacked by the Greeks
Troianus	Trojan
Troiugena	Trojan
Troius	Trojan
Tros	Trojan
Tulla	A companion of Camilla
Turnus	Leader of the Rutulian tribe, allied to Latinus
Tyrius	Of Tyre (in the Lebanon), i.e. Carthaginian; Tyre was the original home of Dido before she emigrated to North Africa
Tyrrhenus	Etruscan
Tyrrhidae	The two sons of Tyrrheus (a Latin), whose pet stag was killed by Ascanius, so sparking warfare
Venus	Goddess of love and beauty; mother of Aeneas; supported the Trojans; in Greek Aphrodite
Vesta	Goddess of the hearth, fire and home; in Greek Hestia
Volcanus	Vulcan, the god of fire and blacksmithery; in Greek Hephaestus
Volcens	Latin commander who killed Euryalus before being killed by Nisus
Volsci	A tribe living near the southern borders of Latium, to which Camilla belonged
Xanthus	River that flowed close to Troy
Zephyrus	The West Wind

7. Further reading

There have been three Penguin translations, by W.F. Jackson Knight (1963), David West (2003) and Robert Fagles (2012). There is also a Loeb version.

General editions consulted in the preparation of this book are those of T.E. Page (*The Aeneid of Virgil, Books I–VI*, Macmillan, 1960); R.D.Williams (*Virgil, Aeneid I–VI*, Bristol Classical Press, 1972 and 2005)

Also of interest are K. Quinn, *Virgil's Aeneid*, Routledge & Kegan Paul, 1968; W.A. Camps, *An Introduction to Virgil*, Oxford University Press, 1969; S.E. Winbolt, *The Latin Hexameter*, Blackie and Son Ltd, 1906; D.S. Raven, *Latin Metre: An Introduction*, Faber and Faber, 1965. Editions of individual books by Gould and Whiteley have been reprinted and are useful for less-experienced readers.

Book 7

On their way north, along the west coast of Italy, Aeneas had to stop to bury his dead nurse, Caieta. Then they sailed on past the island of the witch Circe, coming at last to the mouth of the river Tiber, their final destination.

nunc age, qui reges, Erato, quae tempora rerum,	37
quis Latio antiquo fuerit status, advena classem	
cum primum Ausoniis exercitus appulit oris,	
expediam, et primae revocabo exordia pugnae.	40
tu vatem, tu, diva, mone. dicam horrida bella,	
dicam acies actosque animis in funera reges,	
Tyrrhenamque manum totamque sub arma coactam	
Hesperiam. maior rerum mihi nascitur ordo,	
maius opus moveo. rex arva Latinus et urbes	45
iam senior longa placidas in pace regebat.	46
filius huic fato divum prolesque virilis	50
nulla fuit, primaque oriens erepta iuventa est.	

age, agite	come now	*rex, regis* m.	king
rex, regis m.	king	*Tyrrhenus, -a, -um*	Etruscan
Erato (nom. only) f.	Erato	*manus, -us* f.	hand, band of
tempus, -oris n.	time		men
res, rei f.	thing, matter	*totus, -a, -um*	the whole of
Latium, -i n.	Latium	*sub* + acc.	under
antiquus, -a, -um	ancient	*arma, -orum* n.pl.	arms
status, -us m.	state	*cogo, -ere, coegi, coactus*	I gather, force
advena, -ae m/f.	foreign	*Hesperia, -ae* f.	Hesperia
classis, -is f.	fleet	*nascor, -i, natus sum*	I am born
primum	first	*ordo, -inis* m.	sequence
Ausonius, -a, -um	Italian	*opus, -eris* n. 45	work
exercitus, -us m.	army	*moveo, -ere*	I move, begin
appello, -ere, -puli, -pulsus	I bring (to)	*arvum, -i* n.	field, land
ora, -ae f.	shore	*Latinus, -i* m.	Latinus
expedio, -ire 40	I relate	*urbs, urbis* f.	city
revoco, -are	I recall	*senex, -is*	old
exordium, -i n.	beginning	*longus, -a, -um*	long
pugna, -ae f.	fight	*placidus, -a, -um*	peaceful
vates, -is m/f.	prophet, poet,	*pax, pacis* f.	peace
	prophetess	*rego, -ere*	I rule, deal with
diva, -ae f.	goddess	*filius, -i* m. 50	son
moneo, -ere	I advise	*fatum, -i* n.	fate
dico, -ere	I tell (of)	*divus, -i* m.	god
horridus, -a, -um	dreadful	*proles, -is* f.	child
bellum, -i n.	war	*virilis, -e*	male
acies, -ei f.	battle, army	*nullus, -a, -um*	no
ago, -ere, egi, actus	I drive	*orior, oriri, ortus sum*	I rise
animus, -i m.	mind, spirit, fury	*eripio, -ere, eripui, ereptus*	I snatch away
funus, -eris n.	death	*iuventa, -ae* f.	youth

37–40 The first three lines are dependent on *expediam*, which should be taken first. **qui reges:** supply *fuerint* from 38, as also with *tempora rerum*. The kings are those that ruled in Latium at the time of the Trojans' arrival. **Erato:** the Muse of love poetry, perhaps invoked here in a more general sense, as the only love theme relevant to Books VII to XII is the one involving Lavinia, but that rarely surfaces. **tempora rerum:** 'the times of things', i.e. 'the sequence of events'. **Latio antiquo:** i.e. in the period following the Trojan War. **cum primum:** to be taken first. **advena . . . exercitus:** 'a foreign (i.e. Trojan) army'. **Ausoniis . . . oris:** 'to the shores of Italy' (dative of goal of motion); Ausonia was an ancient name for Italy. **primae . . . pugnae:** i.e. the outbreak of war between the Trojans and the Latins.

41 **diva:** i.e. Erato. **vatem mone:** 'advise your poet'.

42 Note the heavy <u>assonance</u> of *a* in this line, showing the deeply emotional tone of the line. **actosque animis:** 'and (kings) driven by their violent passions'.

43–4 **Tyrrhenamque manum:** these are the Etruscans, who lived to the north of Rome, who allied themselves with the Trojans under the leadership of Tarchon. **totamque . . . Hesperiam:** 'the whole of the West', i.e. the whole of Italy. Hesperia was the first clue Aeneas was given about his destination (by Creusa at the end of Book II); as he continued his journey, 'the West' became gradually defined as 'Ausonia' or 'Italy'.

44–5 **maior rerum . . . ordo:** 'a greater sequence of events', i.e. greater than the events of Books I–VI; Virgil is saying that the warfare of Books VII–XII is of greater consequence, or greater epic merit, than the wanderings of the Trojans. **maius opus:** this repeats the same idea; these two words have often been quoted by scholars to support the idea that Virgil favoured the traditional epic theme of heroic engagement in war (as in Homer's *Iliad*) over the more *Odyssey*-like adventures of Books I–VI.

45–6 **Latinus:** an elderly, peace-loving king of all the Latins and living in Laurentum. **longa . . . in pace:** 'in a long period of peace'.

50–1 **filius . . . prolesque virilis nulla:** 'no son, no male child'; the <u>tautology</u> emphasises that it was male heirs that Latinus lacked; he did have a daughter. **fato divum:** 'by the decree of the gods'; *divum* = *deorum*. **primaque . . . iuventa:** 'for (his son) was snatched away in his first youth', i.e. in his earliest childhood. **oriens:** this agrees with *proles* and repeats the idea of *iuventa*: 'just beginning to grow up'. **erepta . . . est:** this also agrees with *proles*. The idea is that Latinus had at least one son, who died in early childhood, snatched away by fate.

Questions

1 What adventures have Aeneas and the Trojans had on their way to the Tiber?

2 Why do you think Virgil appeals to Erato?

3 What do you think is Virgil's purpose in lines 37–44?

4 What is the emotional content of these same lines?

5 Why might Virgil have considered the warfare books to be a *maius opus*?

6 Find out all you can about Latinus.

sola domum et tantas servabat filia sedes
iam matura viro, iam plenis nubilis annis.
multi illam magno e Latio totaque petebant
Ausonia; petit ante alios pulcherrimus omnes   55
Turnus, avis atavisque potens, quem regia coniunx
adiungi generum miro properabat amore:
sed variis portenta deum terroribus obstant.
laurus erat tecti medio in penetralibus altis
sacra comam multosque metu servata per annos.   60
huius apes summum densae (mirabile dictu)   64
stridore ingenti liquidum trans aethera vectae   65
obsedere apicem, et pedibus per mutua nexis
examen subitum ramo frondente pependit.
continuo vates 'externum cernimus' inquit
'adventare virum et partes petere agmen easdem
partibus ex isdem et summa dominarier arce.'   70

solus, -a, -um	alone, only	*penetralia, -um* n.pl.		innermost part
domus, -us f.	house, home	*altus, -a, -um*		high
tantus, -a, -um	so great	*sacer, sacra, sacrum*	60	sacred
servo, -are	I look after	*coma, -ae* f.		foliage, hair
filia, -ae f.	daughter	*metus, -us* m.		fear, awe
sedes, -is f.	home, palace	*annus, -i* m.		year
maturus, -a, -um	ripe, ready	*apis, -is* f.		bee
vir, viri m.	man, husband	*summus, -a, -um*		the top of, highest
plenus, -a, -um	full			
nubilis, -e	ready for marriage	*densus, -a, -um*		dense
		mirabilis, -e		amazing
annus, -i m.	year	*dico, -ere, dixi, dictus*		I say, tell
peto, -ere	I seek	*stridor, -oris* m.	65	buzzing
Ausonia, -ae f.	55 Italy	*liquidus, -a, -um*		clear
ante + acc.	before	*trans* + acc.		across
pulcher, -ra, -rum	beautiful, handsome	*aether, -eris* (acc. *-era*) m.		air
		veho, -ere, vexi, vectus		I convey, carry
Turnus, -i m.	Turnus	*obsideo, -ere, -sedi, -sessus*		I occupy
avus, -i m.	grandfather	*apex, -icis* m.		top, crown
atavus, -i m.	ancestor	*pes, pedis* m.		foot
potens, -entis	powerful	*per mutua*		together
regius, -a, -um	royal	*necto, -ere, nexui, nexus*		I join together
coniunx, -iugis f.	wife	*examen, -inis* n.		swarm
adiungo, -ere	I join, unite	*subitus, -a, -um*		sudden
gener, -eri m.	son-in-law	*ramus, -i* m.		branch
mirus, -a, -um	wondrous	*frondens, -entis*		leafy
propero, -are	I hasten	*pendeo, -ere, pependi*		I hang
amor, -oris m.	love	*continuo*		at once
varius, -a, -um	various	*externus, -a, -um*		foreign
portentum, -i n.	portent, omen	*cerno, -ere*		I see
terror, -oris m.	terror	*advento, -are*		I arrive
obsto, -are	I block the way	*pars, partis* f.	70	part, direction
laurus, -i f.	laurel tree	*agmen, -inis* n.		army
tectum, -i n.	building, house	*dominor, -ari, -atus sum*		I reign, rule
medium, -i n.	middle	*arx, arcis* f.		citadel

52–3 sola . . . filia: 'a single daughter'. Her name was Lavinia; in contrast to Dido in Book IV, she is kept by Virgil in the background, her only function being to serve as a replacement wife for Aeneas and then the mother of his second son, Silvius Aeneas. **servabat:** either 'lived in' or 'preserved the future lineage of'. **iam matura viro:** 'now ripe for a husband'. **plenis . . . annis:** 'being fully of age'.

54 petebant: 'used to seek in marriage'. Note the change of tense in the next line to *petit*: previously there were many suitors, now only the one; *petit* is historic present.

55–7 ante alios pulcherrimus omnes: in effect a double superlative. **Turnus:** note the enjambement, building suspense. **avis atavisque:** his power and authority stemmed 'from his grandfathers and previous generations'; since Turnus' mother was a nymph, the probability is that at least one grandparent was a deity, although Virgil does not go into such detail. Certainly his sister was the nymph Juturna, who plays a significant role in later books. **regia coniunx:** i.e. *regina*; the queen was Amata, as strong a character as her husband was weak. She strongly supported Turnus in his suit, and was a major obstacle to the acceptance of the Trojans. **generum:** 'as her son-in-law'. **properabat:** an unusual usage: she 'hastened' in the sense of 'was keen to bring about (the joining)'. **adiungi:** the object of *properabat*.

58 deum: = *deorum*.

59–67 Virgil interrupts the main narrative to give an example of the terrifying portents.

59–60 tecti medio: in prose this would be *in medio tecto*. Virgil probably is thinking of the central courtyard that featured in most Greek houses in his day. **in penetralibus altis:** repeats the idea of the laurel's central position, to emphasise that the tree was sacred, so making the portent all the more shocking and significant. **sacra comam:** 'sacred with respect to its foliage', and so 'its foliage sacred'; the accusative, of respect, is modelled on Greek usage. **metu:** 'with religious awe'.

61–3 These omitted lines describe the origin of the laurel tree.

64–6 huius . . . summum . . . apicem: 'the topmost crown of the tree'. **dictu:** the second supine, used after a neuter adjective to express surprise: '(amazing) to relate'. **obsedere:** = *obsederunt*.

66–7 pedibus . . . nexis: ablative absolute. **ramo:** local ablative.

68–70 cernimus: plural because the prophet speaks as a member of a sacred order. **externum . . . virum:** he means, of course, Aeneas. **partes . . . easdem:** 'the same places (as the bees have done)'; that is, the foreigners will make for the centre of the palace, threatening its sacred core. **partibus ex isdem:** '(coming) from the same direction (as the bees)'; presumably the bees appeared from the direction of the sea, as will the Trojans. **dominarier:** an archaic form of the deponent infinitive. **summa . . . arce:** 'over the top of the citadel'; the citadel was the central, highest part of the ancient city, and the laurel tree was at its core; if the Trojans take control of that core, they will possess the whole city. Note the alliteration of *p*.

Questions

1 In lines 55–58, how does Virgil make his description of Lavinia interesting?

2 Find out all you can about Turnus and Amata.

3 What is the portent that the Latins witness?

4 Explain the interpretation of the portent that the prophet gives.

5 How does the prophet's use of words strengthen his interpretation?

praeterea, castis adolet dum altaria taedis,
et iuxta genitorem astat Lavinia virgo,
visa (nefas) longis comprendere crinibus ignem
atque omnem ornatum flamma crepitante cremari,
regalesque accensa comas, accensa coronam   75
insignem gemmis; tum fumida lumine fulvo
involvi ac totis Volcanum spargere tectis.
id vero horrendum ac visu mirabile ferri:
namque fore inlustrem fama fatisque canebant
ipsam, sed populo magnum portendere bellum.   80

Alarmed by these portents, Latinus visited a local oracle, sacred to his father, Faunus, to seek further clarification. After making the due sacrifices, a voice was suddenly heard.

'ne pete conubiis natam sociare Latinis,   96
o mea progenies, thalamis neu crede paratis;
externi venient generi, qui sanguine nostrum
nomen in astra ferant, quorumque a stirpe nepotes
omnia sub pedibus, qua Sol utrumque recurrens   100
aspicit Oceanum, vertique regique videbunt.'

praeterea	furthermore	*horrendus, -a, -um*	dreadful
castus, -a, -um	unblemished	*fero, ferre*	I speak of
adoleo, -ere	I sacrifice at	*namque*	for
altaria, -ium n.pl.	altar	*inlustris, -e*	illustrious
taeda, -ae f.	pine wood	*fama, -ae* f.	repute, renown
iuxta + acc.	next to	*cano, -ere*	I sing, prophesy
genitor, -oris m.	father	*populus, -i* m. 80	people
asto, -are	I stand	*portendo, -ere*	I portend
Lavinia, -ae f.	Lavinia	*conubium, -i* n. 96	marriage
virgo, -inis f.	maiden	*nata, -ae* f.	daughter
nefas n. indecl.	monstrous thing	*socio, -are*	I unite, join
comprendo, -ere	I catch	*Latini, -orum* m.pl.	the Latins
crinis, -is m.	hair	*progenies, -ei* f.	child
ignis, -is m.	fire	*thalamus, -i* m.	bedroom,
ornatus, -us m.	apparel		wedding
flamma, -ae f.	flame	*neu*	and do not
crepito, -are	I crackle	*credo, -ere* + dat.	I trust
cremo, -are	I consume by fire	*paro, -are, -avi, -atus*	I prepare
regalis, -e 75	regal, royal	*sanguis, -inis* m.	blood
accendo, -ere, -ndi, -nsus	I set on fire	*nomen, -inis* n.	name
corona, -ae f.	garland, crown	*astrum, -i* n.	star
insignis, -e	distinguished	*stirps, -is* f.	lineage
gemma, -ae f.	jewel	*nepos, -otis* m.	descendant
fumidus, -a, -um	smoking	*Sol, Solis* m. 100	the Sun
lumen, -inis n.	light, eye	*uterque, utraque, utrumque*	both
fulvus, -a, -um	deep yellow	*recurro, -ere*	I run back
involvo, -ere	I envelop	*aspicio, -ere*	I observe, see
Volcanus, -i m.	fire	*Oceanus, -i* m.	Ocean
spargo, -ere	I scatter	*verto, -ere*	I overturn, turn
vero	indeed		

71 praeterea: introduces a second portent. **adolet:** the subject is probably Lavinia rather than Latinus. **castis ... taedis:** in sacrifices it was important to ensure that every element was pure.

73–5 visa: supply *est*. **nefas:** an interjection. **longis ... crinibus:** local ablative. **ornatum:** her decorative head-dress; the accusative is one of respect, similar to *comam* in 60 and *comas* and *coronam* in 75; in translation it is easier to make these accusatives the subjects. **accensa:** supply *esse*, dependent on *visa (est)*: '(and she seemed) to have been set on fire', i.e. 'her royal hair seemed to have been set on fire'; the repetition of *accensa* is stronger than another simple conjunction.

76–7 involvi, spargere: also dependent on *visa (est)*. **lumine fulvo:** the colour of flames. **Volcanum:** fire personified as the god of fire. **totis ... tectis:** 'throughout the whole palace', local ablative; note the <u>enclosing</u> word order, reflecting what was happening. Note also the slow rhythm of 77, suggesting that the portent lasted some time. Clearly Lavinia was not harmed by the flames.

78 id: the portent. **ferri:** historic infinitive: 'was spoken of (by the prophets) as being ...'. **visu:** second supine, identical in usage to *dictu* in 64. Note the strong elisions here, and also in the preceding lines, perhaps reflecting awe at the events being described, as does the spondaic rhythm.

79–80 canebant: lit. 'they (the prophets) sang'; since oracles were delivered in verse form, this verb is also used of prophecies. **ipsam:** 'Lavinia herself'; the <u>enjambement</u> makes this emphatic; it also strengthens the contrast with *populo*. **fama fatisque:** ablatives of respect, linked also by the <u>alliteration</u>. **portendere:** it is easiest to supply *id* (from 78) as the subject.

96 ne pete ... sociare: in prose this would be *noli petere ut socies*. **conubiis ... Latinis:** 'with any Latin marriages'.

97 progenies: the voice is that of Faunus. **thalamis ... paratis:** 'the marital bedrooms you have prepared'; the plural, like *conubiis*, gives the oracular response a general force.

98–9 generi: the plural continues the idea of a general statement, even though there will be only one son-in-law, Aeneas. **sanguine:** 'with their blood', i.e. by joining their bloodlines. **nostrum nomen:** i.e. the Latin name. **ferant:** subjunctive either of purpose or to express a generic idea.

99–101 quorum a stirpe nepotes: 'and the descendants of (lit. 'from') their bloodline'. **omnia ... videbunt:** 'will see everything', i.e. all the lands. **qua:** 'where'. **recurrens:** 'in his repeated journey (across the sky)'. **utrumque ... Oceanum:** 'both oceans', i.e. the one to the West and the one to the East; the Romans believed that a single ocean, often personified, surrounded all the known lands; the reference here is to the eastern and western branches of the ocean, as witnessed by the Sun in his daily travels. **vertique regique:** 'both overthrown and ruled'; i.e. Rome will first defeat all the other countries and then rule them.

Questions

1 What happens to Lavinia?

2 How does Virgil show that this was an unnatural event?

3 What two interpretations are made of the portents?

4 What does Faunus urge Latinus not to do?

5 How does Faunus make his prophecy palatable to Latinus?

Aeneas primique duces et pulcher Iulus   107
corpora sub ramis deponunt arboris altae,
instituuntque dapes et adorea liba per herbam
subiciunt epulis (sic Iuppiter ipse monebat)   110
et Cereale solum pomis agrestibus augent.
consumptis hic forte aliis, ut vertere morsus
exiguam in Cererem penuria adegit edendi,
et violare manu malisque audacibus orbem
fatalis crusti patulis nec parcere quadris: 115
'heus, etiam mensas consumimus' inquit Iulus,
nec plura, adludens. ea vox audita laborum
prima tulit finem, primamque loquentis ab ore
eripuit pater ac stupefactus numine pressit.
continuo 'salve fatis mihi debita tellus   120
vosque' ait 'o fidi Troiae salvete penates:
hic domus, haec patria est. genitor mihi talia namque
(nunc repeto) Anchises fatorum arcana reliquit:

dux, ducis m.	leader	*fatalis, -e*	115 fateful
Iulus, -i m.	Iulus	*crustum, -i* n.	pastry
corpus, -oris n.	body	*patulus, -a, -um*	spreading, broad
depono, -ere	I lay down	*parco, -ere* + dat.	I spare
arbos, -oris f.	tree	*quadra, -ae* f.	square, table
instituo, -ere	I make ready	*heus!*	hey!
daps, dapis f.	meal	*mensa, -ae* f.	table
adoreus, -a, -um	made of spelt	*adludo, -ere*	I jest
libum, -i n.	pancake	*vox, vocis* f.	voice
herba, -ae f.	grass	*labor, -oris* m.	work, toil
subicio, -ere	110 I place under	*finis, -is* m.	end
epulae, -arum f.pl.	feast, meal	*loquor, -i, locutus sum*	I speak
Iuppiter, Iovis m.	Jupiter	*os, oris* n.	mouth, face
Cerealis, -e	of Ceres, corn	*stupefactus, -a, -um*	astonished
solum, -i n.	ground, earth	*numen, -inis* n.	divine will
pomum, -i n.	fruit	*premo, -ere, pressi, pressus*	I press, stop
agrestis, -e	wild	*continuo*	120 at once
augeo, -ere	I increase, pile up	*salve, salvete*	hail
consumo, -ere, -mpsi, -mptus	I consume	*debeo, -ere, -ui, -itus*	I owe
forte	by chance	*tellus, -uris* f.	land
morsus, -us m.	bite, tooth	*aio* (defective verb)	I say
exiguus, -a, -um	thin	*fidus, -a, -um*	loyal, faithful
Ceres, Cereris f.	Ceres, corn	*Troia, -ae* f.	Troy
penuria, -ae f.	need, lack	*penates, -ium* m.pl.	penates
adigo, -ere, -egi, -actus	I drive	*patria, -ae* f.	homeland
edo, -ere	I eat	*talis, -e*	such
violo, -are	I violate	*repeto, -ere*	I recall
manus, -us f.	hand	*Anchises, -ae* m.	Anchises
mala, -ae f.	jaw	*arcanus, -a, -um*	secret
audax, -acis	rash, bold	*relinquo, -ere, -liqui, -lictus*	I leave
orbis, -is m.	circle, disc		

107–8 Following the account of the portents in the Latin city, Virgil now turns to a parallel portent among the Trojans, who have only just disembarked from their ships. **deponunt:** historic present, the normal narrative tense used by Virgil; translate as past.

109–10 **dapes, epulis:** normally used of extravagant feasts, these two words must be used ironically here. **adorea liba:** 'pancakes of spelt' (an inferior form of wheat); *liba* were often used in sacrifices, and Virgil uses the word to add an air of seriousness to what otherwise would have been simply an amusing event. **subiciunt:** they placed the pancakes 'underneath' the feast, i.e. they used them as plates or tables. **epulis:** dative after the compound verb. **sic Iuppiter ipse monebat:** Virgil does not explain this; perhaps he is simply suggesting that the idea came into their heads and, as often believed in the past, such an idea had to have a cause outside of themselves; *monebat* is perhaps best translated as 'inspired'.

111 **Cereale solum:** 'the base made of corn'; corn is personified as Ceres, the goddess of corn. **augent:** 'they increase', i.e. 'pile up'.

112–13 **hic:** 'then'. **aliis:** = *ceteris*. **ut:** 'when'. **penuria ... edendi:** 'the lack of (something) to eat', i.e. 'the lack of food'; clearly the food supplied for the 'banquet' was insufficient. **adegit:** supply *eos* as object. **vertere morsus:** 'to turn their bites', i.e. 'begin to eat instead'. **Cererem:** another personification, meaning no more than 'corn'.

114–15 **et violare ... orbem:** 'and violate the disc(s)'; the discs are 'violated' because, insofar as the pancakes had a religious connotation, it would be considered a sacrilege to damage them. **audacibus:** to be taken with both *manu* and *malis*; these are 'rash' because they dare to violate the sacred pancakes. **fatalis crusti:** the pastry pancakes are 'fateful' because eating them fulfils a prophecy (see below). **nec:** to be taken first. **patulis ... quadris:** 'the broad tables'.

112–15 Virgil has put together an amazing concentration of rich and unusual vocabulary, all designed to shine a spotlight on this episode, which is a pivotal moment in the main storyline. This is because in Book III, lines 250ff., Celaeno the Harpy queen prophesied to Aeneas that the Trojans would not find a homeland until they were forced by hunger to eat their tables; now the prophecy has been fulfilled, and the Trojans know that their years of wandering are over.

116–17 **nec plura:** supply *dixit*.

117–19 **ea vox audita:** 'that voice, once heard', i.e. 'those words, once heard'. **prima ... primamque:** the <u>polyptoton</u> is a rhetorical flourish to emphasise the rapidity of Aeneas' reaction. **loquentis:** 'of the speaker'. **ab ore eripuit:** 'snatched (the words first) from the mouth (of the speaker)'; the idea of *eripuit* is that Aeneas seized upon the words. **numine:** 'by the (manifestation of) divine will'. **pressit:** 'stopped' (Iulus from saying more).

120–1 **fatis:** the land is owed to him 'by the fates' because of the prophecy. **tellus:** vocative. **fidi ... penates:** in Book II the ghost of Hector entrusted the penates (guardian spirits) of Troy to Aeneas for safe-keeping; then in Book III in a dream Aeneas saw the spirits, which promised the Trojans this home.

122–3 **hic:** 'here'. **genitor:** either Virgil or Aeneas has forgotten that it was Celaeno, not Anchises, who delived the prophecy. **namque:** to be taken first. **fatorum arcana:** 'the secrets of fate'.

Questions

1 Describe the feast.

2 In lines 112–115, how is Virgil's language unusual?

3 Explain the portent, including details from Book III.

4 What is Aeneas' mood when he speaks? How do we know?

"cum te, nate, fames ignota ad litora vectum
accisis coget dapibus consumere mensas,   125
tum sperare domos defessus, ibique memento
prima locare manu molirique aggere tecta."
haec erat illa fames, haec nos suprema manebat
exsiliis positura modum.   130
quare agite et primo laeti cum lumine solis
quae loca, quive habeant homines, ubi moenia gentis,
vestigemus et a portu diversa petamus.
nunc pateras libate Iovi precibusque vocate
Anchisen genitorem, et vina reponite mensis.'

*Aeneas offered prayers, which were answered by three peals of thunder. The Trojans,
delighted to learn that they had reached their destination, renewed the feast. Next morning
they split up to explore the local area, discovering Laurentum, the town of Latinus. Aeneas
began building a camp and sent a hundred ambassadors with gifts to the city. Latinus
welcomed them to his magnificent palace, which also served as a temple to the native gods.
Latinus spoke first.*

'dicite, Dardanidae (neque enim nescimus et urbem   195
et genus, auditique advertitis aequore cursum),
quid petitis? quae causa rates aut cuius egentes
litus ad Ausonium tot per vada caerula vexit?
sive errore viae seu tempestatibus acti,
⌈qualia multa mari nautae patiuntur in alto,⌉   200

natus, -i m.	son	*portus, -us* m.	harbour
fames, -is f.	hunger	*diversus, -a, -um*	different
ignotus, -a, -um	unknown	*patera, -ae* f.	bowl
litus, -oris n.	shore	*libo, -are*	I offer, pour
veho, -ere, vexi, vectus	I convey	*prex, precis* f.	prayer
accido, -ere, -cidi, -cisus 125	I use up	*voco, -are*	I call
spero, -are	I hope, hope for	*repono, -ere*	I put back
defessus, -a, -um	weary	*Dardanidae, -arum* m.pl. 195	Trojans
ibi	there	*nescio, -ire*	I do not know
memini, -isse	I remember	*genus, -eris* n.	race, people
loco, -are	I place	*adverto, -ere*	I direct
molior, -iri, -itus sum	I build	*aequor, -oris* n.	sea
agger, -eris m.	rampart	*cursus, -us* m.	course
supremus, -a, -um	last, greatest	*causa, -ae* f.	cause, reason
maneo, -ere	I await	*ratis, -is* f.	boat
exsilium, -i n.	exile	*egeo, -ere* + gen.	I lack, need
pono, -ere, posui, positus	I place	*tot*	so many
modus, -i m.	end	*vadum, -i* n.	sea
quare	and so	*caerulus, -a, -um*	dark blue
laetus, -a, -um 130	glad, happy	*sive . . . seu*	whether . . . or
locus, -i m. (pl. *loca*)	place	*error, -oris* m.	mistake
homo, -inis m.	person, man	*via, viae* f.	road, way
moenia, -ium n.pl.	city walls, city	*tempestas, -atis* f.	storm
gens, gentis f.	people, race	*qualis, -e* 200	such as
vestigo, -are	I investigate	*patior, -i, passus sum*	I suffer, allow

124–5 The order is *cum fames coget te, nate, vectum ad ignota litora, consumere mensas dapibus accisis*. **dapibus accisis:** a rare usage of *accidere*: 'when their feast had been used up'.
126–7 **memento:** imperative, governing *sperare, locare* and *moliri*. **defessus:** 'though you are weary'. **prima . . . tecta:** 'the first buildings' of the new city. **manu:** 'by hand', i.e. 'by your own efforts'. **aggere:** 'with a rampart' for protection.
128–9 **haec nos suprema manebat:** 'this was the final (challenge) that awaited us'. **positura:** 'destined to put (an end)'. Line 129 is one of many incomplete lines in the *Aeneid*; probably Virgil would have completed the line had he lived to revise the work.
130–2 **vestigemus:** to be taken first; the subjunctive expresses an exhortation. **quae loca:** supply *sint*: 'what places there are'. **ubi moenia gentis:** supply *sint*: 'where is the city of the people'. **diversa:** 'different targets'; he is suggesting that they split up.
133–4 **pateras libate:** 'pour (wine from) the bowls', as an offering to Jupiter. **vina reponite:** 'put wine back on the tables', i.e. renew the feast.

195–6 **neque . . . nescimus:** the double negative makes this a strong affirmative. **et urbem et genus:** 'both your city (i.e. Troy) and your race (i.e. Trojan)'. Wherever Aeneas has led the Trojans, news of the Trojan War has got there first. **auditi:** 'having (already) been heard of'. **aequore:** 'across the sea'.
197–8 **quae causa . . . vexit:** 'what cause has conveyed', i.e. 'what purpose has brought'. **aut cuius egentes:** supply *vos*, parallel to *rates*: 'or (you) needing what?'; it is best left until the end as a separate question.
199–200 **errore viae:** 'as a result of a mistake of route'. **qualia multa:** 'like the many that . . .'. **mare . . . in alto:** 'far out at sea'.

Questions

1 What is the prophecy that Aeneas attributes to Anchises?

2 What does Aeneas believe Anchises ordered him to do when the prophecy was fulfilled?

3 Find two examples of alliteration from lines 124–127 and discuss their effect.

4 In lines 128–134, what is Aeneas' mood? How does his language show this?

5 What is Latinus' first concern when he speaks to the Trojan ambassadors?

6 What two explanations does he suggest for their arrival in Italy?

fluminis intrastis ripas portuque sedetis,
ne fugite hospitium, neve ignorate Latinos
Saturni gentem haud vinclo nec legibus aequam,
sponte sua veterisque dei se more tenentem.'   204
dixerat, et dicta Ilioneus sic voce secutus: 212
'rex, genus egregium Fauni, nec fluctibus actos
atra subegit hiems vestris succedere terris,
nec sidus regione viae litusve fefellit: 215
consilio hanc omnes animisque volentibus urbem
adferimur pulsi regnis, quae maxima quondam
extremo veniens sol aspiciebat Olympo.
ab Iove principium generis, Iove Dardana pubes
gaudet avo, rex ipse Iovis de gente suprema: 220
Troius Aeneas tua nos ad limina misit.   221
dis sedem exiguam patriis litusque rogamus   229
innocuum et cunctis undamque auramque patentem.   230
non erimus regno indecores, nec vestra feretur
fama levis tantique abolescet gratia facti,
nec Troiam Ausonios gremio excepisse pigebit.'

'Oracles have sent us here; now we bring you gifts from Troy.'

flumen, -inis n.	river	*consilium, -i* n.	plan
intro, -are, -avi, -atus	I enter	*adfero, -ferre*	I bring to
ripa, -ae f.	bank	*pello, -ere, pepuli, pulsus*	I drive
sedeo, -ere	I sit	*regnum, -i* n.	kingdom, realm
fugio, -ere	I flee (from)	*quondam*	once, sometimes
hospitium, -i n.	hospitality	*extremus, -a, -um*	furthest
ignoro, -are	I do not know	*aspicio, -ere*	I look upon
Saturnus, -i m.	Saturn	*Olympus, -i* m.	Olympus
haud	not	*principium, -i* n.	beginning
vinclum, -i n.	chain, bond	*Dardanus, -a, -um*	Trojan
lex, legis f.	law	*pubes, -is* f.	people
aequus, -a, -um	equal, just	*gaudeo, -ere*	220 I rejoice
sponte	204 by one's will	*Troius, -a, -um*	Trojan
vetus, veteris	old	*limen, -inis* n.	threshold
mos, moris m.	custom, habit	*mitto, -ere, misi, missus*	I send
teneo, -ere	I hold, keep	*exiguus, -a, -um*	229 small
dictum, -i n.	212 word	*patrius, -a, -um*	native
Ilioneus, -i m.	Ilioneus	*innocuus, -a, -um*	230 harmless
sequor, sequi, secutus sum	I follow	*cunctus, -a, -um*	all
egregius, -a, -um	outstanding	*unda, -ae* f.	wave, water
Faunus, -i m.	Faunus	*aura, -ae* f.	air
fluctus, -us m.	wave	*patens, -entis*	open, available
ater, atra, atrum	black, dark	*indecoris, -e*	shameful
subigo, -ere, -egi, -actus	I force	*levis, -e*	light
hiems, hiemis f.	storm	*abolesco, -ere*	I decay, vanish
succedo, -ere + dat.	I approach, go to	*gratia, -ae* f.	gratitude
sidus, -eris n.	215 star	*gremium, -i* n.	bosom, lap
regio, -onis f.	region, direction	*excipio, -ere, -cepi, -ceptus*	I welcome
fallo, -ere, fefelli, falsus	I deceive	*piget, -ere*	it causes regret

201 **fluminis**: the Tiber. **intrastis**: = *intravistis*. **portu**: local ablative.

202–4 **ne fugite**: in prose this would be *noli fugere*. **neve ignorate**: 'and know full well'; the <u>litotes</u> makes a strong affirmative. **Latinos**: supply *esse*, so that *gentem* becomes the complement. **gentem Saturni**: the god Saturn was believed by the Romans to have presided over a golden age in their prehistory. **gentem . . . aequam**: 'a race that is righteous'. **haud . . . nec**: 'neither . . . nor'. **vinclo**: the bonds of tyranny, and so 'compulsion'. **se . . . tenentem**: 'controlling itself'. **sponte sua**: 'by its own free will', contrasted with *vinclo*. **veterisque dei . . . more**: 'and according to the custom of the old god', i.e. Saturn; this phrase is contrasted with *legibus*.

205–11 Latinus recounts the legend of Dardanus, who supposedly sailed from Italy to Troy.

212 **dixerat**: Virgil regularly uses the pluperfect of this verb to mark the end of a speech; translate 'he finished speaking'. **Ilioneus**: an elderly companion of Aeneas. **secutus**: supply *est*.

213–15 **genus**: here 'son'. The order is *nec atra hiems subegit (nos), actos fluctibus, succedere vestris terris*; Ilioneus is answering Latinus' queries in line 199. **regione viae**: 'in the direction of our route' (ablative of respect). **fefellit**: supply *nos* again. His argument is that they have made no navigational mistake through misreading the stars or wrongly identifying landmarks along the coast.

216–18 **consilio**: emphatic by position: 'by plan', i.e. 'deliberately'. **hanc . . . urbem**: accusative of goal of motion. **animisque volentibus**: i.e. 'willingly', parallel to *consilio*. **regnis**: 'from the kingdom' (i.e. Troy). **quae maxima**: 'the greatest (kingdom) which'; the superlative is attracted into the relative clause. **extremo . . . Olympo**: 'from the furthest reaches of the heavens'; in verse *Olympus* occasionally substitutes for *caelum*.

219–20 **ab Iove**: supply *est*; King Priam of Troy was the great-grandson of Jupiter. **Iove . . . avo**: 'in their ancestor, Jupiter' (causal ablative), i.e. 'they rejoice to have Jupiter as their ancestor'. **rex ipse**: supply *est*; Aeneas was the son of Venus and so the grandson of Jupiter.

229–30 **dis . . . patriis**: 'for our native gods', i.e. the penates (see note on line 121). **litusque . . . innocuum**: either 'that will bring us no harm' or 'that will cause no harm'; opinions are equally divided. They need the coastline because the Trojans are a sea-faring people. **cunctis . . . patentem**: 'freely availabe to all'.

231–3 **regno . . . indecores**: 'shameful to your kingdom', i.e. 'we shall not bring shame to your kingdom'. **feretur**: 'will (not) be said to be'. **abolescet gratia**: 'nor will our gratitude diminish'. **tanti . . . facti**: 'for so great a deed (of kindness)'. **pigebit**: an impersonal verb that takes an accusative of the person who will feel the regret (i.e. the Italians).

Questions

1 What picture of his kingdom does Latinus draw?

2 How welcoming of the Trojans is Latinus?

3 How does Ilioneus' reply match the speech of Latinus point by point?

4 How does Ilioneus make his speech persuasive?

Latinus thought deeply about the oracle concerning his daughter's marriage, and decided that Aeneas must be the intended foreign groom.

tandem laetus ait: 'di nostra incepta secundent	259
auguriumque suum! dabitur, Troiane, quod optas.	260
munera nec sperno: non vobis rege Latino	
divitis uber agri Troiaeve opulentia deerit.	
ipse modo Aeneas, nostri si tanta cupido est,	
si iungi hospitio properat sociusque vocari,	
adveniat, vultus neve exhorrescat amicos:	265
pars mihi pacis erit dextram tetigisse tyranni.	
vos contra regi mea nunc mandata referte.	
est mihi nata, viro gentis quam iungere nostrae	
non patrio ex adyto sortes, non plurima caelo	
monstra sinunt; generos externis adfore ab oris,	270
hoc Latio restare canunt, qui sanguine nostrum	
nomen in astra ferant. hunc illum poscere fata	
et reor et, si quid veri mens augurat, opto.'	

Latinus chose gifts of horses for all the Trojan ambassadors and for Aeneas.

ecce autem Inachiis sese referebat ab Argis	286
saeva Iovis coniunx aurasque invecta tenebat,	
et laetum Aenean classemque ex aethere longe	
Dardaniam Siculo prospexit ab usque Pachyno.	

inceptum, -i n.	undertaking	*mandatum, -i* n.	instruction
secundo, -are	I favour	*refero, -ferre*	I take back,
augurium, -i n.	260 prophecy		reply
opto, -are	I wish	*adytum, -i* n.	shrine, sanctuary
munus, -eris n.	gift	*caelum, -i* n.	sky, heaven
sperno, -ere	I reject	*monstrum, -i* n.	270 portent, monster
dives, -itis	rich	*sino, -ere*	I allow
uber, uberis n.	fruitfulness	*adsum, -esse*	I am present
opulentia, -ae f.	wealth	*resto, -are*	I remain
desum, -esse	I am lacking	*posco, -ere*	I demand
modo	only	*reor, reri, ratus sum*	I think
cupido, -inis f.	desire	*verus, -a, -um*	true
iungo, -ere	I join	*mens, mentis* f.	mind
propero, -are	I hasten	*auguro, -are*	I prophesy
advenio, -ire	265 I come	*ecce*	286 see, look
vultus, -us m.	face	*Inachius, -a, -um*	of Inachus
exhorresco, -ere	I am frightened of	*Argi, -orum* m.pl.	Argos
amicus, -a, -um	friendly	*saevus, -a, -um*	cruel
dextra, -ae f.	right hand	*invehor, -i, -vectus sum*	I ride, go into
tango, -ere, tetigi, tactus	I touch	*Dardanius, -a, -um*	Trojan
tyrannus, -i m.	ruler	*Siculus, -a, -um*	Sicilian
contra	on the other	*prospicio, -ere, -exi, -ectus*	I look out
	hand, opposed, in	*usque*	all the way
	reply	*Pachynus, -i* m.	Pachynus

259–60 **di . . . secundent:** the subjunctive expresses a wish. **suum:** 'their own', because the portent of the bees must have been sent by the gods. Note the <u>chiastic</u> word order across the two lines: *nostra incepta . . . auguriumque suum.* **quod:** = *id quod.*

261–2 The order is *Latino rege, uber divitis agri opulentiave Troiae non deerit vobis.* **Latino rege:** ablative absolute. His promise is that the Trojans will not miss the fruitfulness of the fields of Troy nor its wealth: he will ensure they enjoy the same level of prosperity.

263–5 **Aeneas:** the subject of *adveniat.* **nostri:** objective genitive after *cupido:* 'the desire to meet us'. **neve:** to be taken first.

266 **pars . . . pacis:** 'part of a peace', i.e. 'a condition of a peace treaty'. **dextram tetigisse:** 'to have touched the right hand', i.e. 'to have shaken the hand'. **tyranni:** used in a neutral sense of any ruler, good or bad, here referring to Aeneas. Note the double <u>alliteration</u>.

267 **vos contra:** this marks the transfer of attention from Latinus himself to the ambassadors.

268–70 **nata:** Lavinia. **iungere:** 'join in marriage'. **patrio ex adyto:** his father Faunus' oracle. **plurima monstra:** <u>hyperbolic</u>, as he is referring to the two portents of Lavinia and the bees.

270–2 **generos adfore:** plural for singular; indirect statement dependent on *canunt.* **hoc . . . canunt:** 'this is what they prophesy'. **Latio restare:** 'is in store for Latium'. **qui . . . ferant:** a direct quote of the oracle's words (lines 98–99).

272–4 **hunc illum:** an abbreviated indirect statement which in full would be something like *(reor) hunc (virum) esse illum quem fata poscant.* **et reor et . . . opto:** 'I both think and wish'. **si quid veri:** partitive genitive: 'if . . . anything of truth', i.e. 'if anything true'.

286–7 The scene suddenly switches from the human plane to the divine. **Inachiis . . . Argis:** 'Argos of Inachus'; Argos was a city in the Peloponnese, of ancient origin and supposedly founded by Inachus; it was a centre for the worship of Juno. **sese referebat:** 'was returning'. **Iovis coniunx:** Juno. **aurasque . . . tenebat:** 'and was keeping to the air'. **invecta:** 'riding', i.e. in a chariot pulled by winged horses, as frequently in Greek mythology.

288–9 **laetum Aenean:** note the strong contrast with the parallel *saeva Iovis coniunx* in the line above. The two adjectives set the tone for the whole episode: Juno is *saeva* precisely because she sees that Aeneas is *laetus.* **ab usque** = *usque ab*: 'all the way from'. **Siculo Pachyno:** 'Sicilian Pachynus'; Pachynus was a promontory on the SE corner of Sicily; if Juno was flying directly from Argos to her other centre of worship in Carthage, she would have passed over Pachynus; Virgil shows a remarkable grasp of geography.

Questions

1 What promise does Latinus make?

2 How welcoming is Latinus in these lines?

3 What does Latinus want?

4 How does Latinus interpret the portents and oracle?

5 How does Virgil introduce Juno? What suggests that she will prove hostile to the Trojans?

moliri iam tecta videt, iam fidere terrae,   290
deseruisse rates: stetit acri fixa dolore.

*Juno spoke to herself: 'Oh hated race of Troy! Have I lost my power? They have avoided
all my efforts to destroy them. Other gods have destroyed whole races, while I, queen of
the gods, have been defeated by Aeneas. Well, if I am too weak, I can still call on others for
help.'*

'flectere si nequeo superos, Acheronta movebo.   312
non dabitur regnis, esto, prohibere Latinis,
atque immota manet fatis Lavinia coniunx:
at trahere atque moras tantis licet addere rebus,   315
at licet amborum populos exscindere regum.
hac gener atque socer coeant mercede suorum:
sanguine Troiano et Rutulo dotabere, virgo,
et Bellona manet te pronuba. nec face tantum
Cisseis praegnas enixa iugales;   320
quin idem Veneri partus suus et Paris alter,
funestaeque iterum recidiva in Pergama taedae.'
haec ubi dicta dedit, terras horrenda petivit;
luctificam Allecto dirarum ab sede dearum
infernisque ciet tenebris, cui tristia bella   325
iraeque insidiaeque et crimina noxia cordi.

fido, -ere + dat.	290	I trust	*tantum*		only
desero, -ere, -serui, -sertus		I abandon	*Cisseis, -idis* f.	320	Hecuba
acer, acris, acre		sharp, bitter	*praegnas, -atis*		pregnant
figo, -ere, fixi, fixus		I fix, pierce	*enitor, -i, enixus sum*		I give birth to
dolor, -oris m.		pain, grief	*iugalis, -e*		nuptial
flecto, -ere	312	I change	*quin*		no
nequeo, -ire		I cannot	*partus, -us* m.		child, offspring
superi, -orum m.pl.		the gods	*Paris, -idis* m.		Paris
Acheron, -ontis m. (acc. *-a*)		river Acheron	*alter, -era, -erum*		a second
esto		let it be so	*funestus, -a, -um*		deadly
prohibeo, -ere		I ban	*iterum*		again
immotus, -a, -um		unmoved	*recidivus, -a, -um*		returning
traho, -ere	315	I prolong	*Pergama, -orum* n.pl.		Pergama, Troy
mora, -ae f.		delay	*taeda, -ae* f.		torch
licet, -ere		it is allowed	*luctificus, -a, -um*		causing grief
addo, -ere		I add	*Allecto* f.		Allecto
res, rei f.		thing, affair	*dirus, -a, -um*		dreadful
ambo, -ae, -o		both	*infernus, -a, -um*	325	of the underworld
exscindo, -ere		I destroy	*cieo, -ere*		I summon
socer, -eri m.		father-in-law	*tenebrae, -arum* f.pl.		darkness
coeo, -ire		I come together	*tristis, -e*		sad, grim
merces, -edis f.		payment, price	*ira, -ae* f.		anger
Rutulus, -a, -um		Rutulian	*insidiae, -arum* f.pl.		treachery
doto, -are		I give as dowry	*crimen, -inis* n.		crime, charge
Bellona, -ae f.		Bellona	*noxius, -a, -um*		harmful
pronuba, -ae f.		brideswoman	*cor, cordis* n.		heart, pleasure
fax, facis f.		torch			

290–1 moliri . . . videt: supply *eum*. **fidere terrae:** 'trusting the land', i.e. trusting that he had found the promised land. **deseruisse rates:** <u>asyndeton</u> (supply *et*).

312 Acheronta movebo: the Acheron was one of the five rivers of the underworld, used here to refer to the underworld as a whole. Note the all-dactylic rhythm and <u>chiastic</u> word order.
313–14 non dabitur: 'it will not be permitted (to me)'. **esto:** 'granted'. **prohibere:** supply *eum*. **immota . . . fatis:** 'unmoved by the fates'; she means that the fates will not block the marriage of Lavinia and Aeneas.
315–16 at . . . licet, at licet: the emphatic repetition marks what her powers will allow her to do, in contrast with *non dabitur*, what she cannot do. **trahere:** 'to draw out', i.e. prolong the process of settlement and marriage. **tantis . . . rebus:** 'to such important matters'. **excindere:** a strong word; she intends that the foundation of the Trojans' new city and alliance with the Latins will only happen when she has brought about the deaths of great numbers of both races. Her basic argument is that, although she cannot alter fate, according to which Aeneas will found Lavinium and marry Lavinia, she can turn it from a triumph into a misery for all concerned.
317 coeant: 'let them unite' to make a single people. **hac . . . mercede suorum:** 'at this price of their people', i.e. 'at this cost in terms of their people's lives'. Note the emphatic position of *hac*.
318 dotabere, virgo: 'your dowry, maiden, will be . . .'. She addresses Lavinia as if she were there, an example of <u>apostrophe</u>.
319–20 Bellona: the sister of Mars and goddess of war. **pronuba:** 'as the brideswoman'; at Roman weddings, the *pronuba* was generally an older woman who assisted the bride; Juno as goddess of marriage was often invoked for such a role. Here because of her hatred Juno promises that warfare will attend the wedding. **nec . . . tantum Cisseis:** 'and the daughter of Cisseus (i.e. Hecuba) was not the only one who . . .'. Hecuba was the wife of king Priam. According to one myth she dreamt that she was pregnant with a torch, before she gave birth to Paris. Torches were religious objects carried at both weddings and funerals. **enixa:** supply *est*. Juno is saying that, because Paris, through his marriage to Helen, brought about the deaths of countless Greeks and Trojans, so Aeneas will do the same. The idea is amplified in the next two lines.
321–2 Veneri partus suus: 'her own son born to Venus', i.e. 'Venus' own son'. **idem:** supply *erit:* 'will be the same' (as Paris). **funestae . . . taedae:** 'funeral torches'; supply some verb such as 'will consume'. **recidiva in Pergama:** '(against) Troy reborn'.
323 horrenda: a strong word to describe the intensity of Juno's implacable hatred of the Trojans.
324–6 luctificam Allecto: 'Allecto, the architect of grief'; *Allecto* is accusative here; she was one of the three avenging Furies (*dirarum dearum*) of Greek mythology. **ab sede:** their home was in the cave at the entrance to the underworld, as described in Book VI. **infernisque . . . tenebris:** 'and from the darkness of the underworld'. **cui:** supply *sunt*. **cordi:** 'to whom (wars, etc.) are a source of pleasure'; *cordi* (lit. 'to the heart') as a predicative dative has a special meaning.

Questions

1 In lines 290–291, what causes Juno to be 'pierced by grief'?

2 What are the main arguments of Juno's speech?

3 What makes this speech one of the most powerful in the *Aeneid*?

4 Why does Juno call upon Allecto for help?

5 How is Allecto described?

Allecto was a monster hated by her sisters and father. Black snakes sprouted from her hair. Juno ordered her to destroy the pact between Aeneas and Latinus.

exim Gorgoneis Allecto infecta venenis	341
principio Latium et Laurentis tecta tyranni	
celsa petit, tacitumque obsedit limen Amatae,	
quam super adventu Teucrum Turnique hymenaeis	
femineae ardentem curaeque iraeque coquebant.	345
huic dea caeruleis unum de crinibus anguem	
conicit, inque sinum praecordia ad intima subdit,	
quo furibunda domum monstro permisceat omnem.	
ille inter vestes et levia pectora lapsus	
volvitur attactu nullo, fallitque furentem	350
viperam inspirans animam; fit tortile collo	
aurum ingens coluber, fit longae taenia vittae	
innectitque comas et membris lubricus errat.	
ac dum prima lues udo sublapsa veneno	
pertemptat sensus atque ossibus implicat ignem	355
necdum animus toto percepit pectore flammam,	
mollius et solito matrum de more locuta est,	
multa super nata lacrimans Phrygiisque hymenaeis:	

exim	341 then	*attactus, -us* m.	touch
Gorgoneus, -a, -um	of the Gorgons	*furens, -entis*	mad, raging
inficio, -ere, -feci, -fectus	I infect, taint	*vipereus, -a, -um*	of a snake
venenum, -i n.	poison	*inspiro, -are*	I breathe into
Laurens, -entis	of Laurentum	*anima, -ae* f.	spirit
celsus, -a, -um	high, lofty	*fio, fieri, factus sum*	I become
tacitus, -a, -um	silent	*tortilis, -e*	twisted
Amata, -ae f.	Amata	*collum, -i* n.	neck
super + abl.	at, upon	*aurum, -i* n.	gold
adventus, -us m.	arrival	*taenia, -ae* f.	band, ribbon
Teucri, -orum m.pl.	Trojans	*vitta, -ae* f.	head-band
hymenaeus, -i m.	marriage	*innecto, -ere*	I mingle with
femineus, -a, -um	345 womanly	*membrum, -i* n.	limb
ardeo, -ere	I burn	*lubricus, -a, -um*	slippery
cura, -ae f.	anxiety, care	*erro, -are*	I wander
coquo, -ere	I torment	*lues, -is* f.	pest, blight
anguis, -is m.	snake	*udus, -a, -um*	damp, moist
conicio, -ere	I throw	*sublabor, -i, -lapsus sum*	I slip under
sinus, -us m.	bosom	*pertempto, -are*	355 I pervade
praecordia, -orum n.pl.	heart	*sensus, -us* m.	sense
intimus, -a, -um	innermost	*os, ossis* n.	bone
subdo, -ere	I send into	*implico, -are*	I entangle
furibundus, -a, -um	mad	*necdum*	and not yet
permisceo, -ere	I confuse	*percipio, -ere, -cepi, -ceptus*	I perceive
vestis, -is f.	clothes	*mollis, -e*	soft
pectus, -oris n.	breast	*solitus, -a, -um*	usual
labor, -i, lapsus sum	I glide	*lacrimo, -are*	I cry, weep
volvo, -ere	350 I coil	*Phrygius, -a, -um*	Trojan

341 **Gorgoniis . . . venenis:** the three Gorgon sisters, the most monstrous of whom was Medusa, had venomous snakes entwined in their hair. In this respect Allecto is like the Gorgons.

342–3 **principio:** ablative of time. **tacitum . . . limen:** Amata's threshold is 'silent' for two possible reasons: either because Amata herself is silently brooding over her anxieties, or because there is no sound as Allecto enters her apartment. **obsedit:** a military word used of an army laying siege to a town, here it creates a strong image of the way Allecto takes over the palace; note the change from historic present to perfect: 'she has (already) taken over'.

344–5 Note the chiasmus in line 344, linking the Trojans' arrival with the wedding of Turnus. **femineae:** to be taken with both *curae* and *irae*. **ardentem:** agrees with *quam* and explained by *super . . . hymenaeis*. **coquebant:** a strong word, used metaphorically here.

346–7 **huic:** 'at her'. **conicit, subdit:** the snake is invisible to humans and cannot be felt directly. It enters Amata's heart without her knowing. The image of the fury that infects a person and warps her mind is a standard method used by epic poets to explain sudden and uncontrolled passions.

348 **quo:** this replaces *ut eo* to introduce a purpose clause: 'so that (driven mad) by this (monstrosity) she might . . .'. **domum . . . omnem:** note the enclosing word order.

349–50 **ille:** the snake. **attactu nullo:** 'with no touch', i.e. 'without being felt'.

350–1 **fallit:** supply *eam*. **furentem:** probably proleptic: 'maddening her'. **inspirans:** 'breathing into her'. Notice the continuing alliteration of *f*, representing the hissing of the snake.

351–3 **fit . . . fit:** the *ingens coluber* 'becomes' the gold necklace and the ribbon of the headband, either in the sense of replacing them or occupying them with its presence; both items would be snake-like in appearance, one being twisted and the other wrapped round Amata's head. **collo:** local ablative. **longae . . . vittae:** the *vitta* was a ceremonial headband worn by priests and others who took a leading part in ceremonies. The whole sentence emphasises how completely the snake took over every part of Amata's being.

354–5 **prima lues:** 'the first blight', i.e. ' the blight when it first began'. **udo . . . veneno:** 'with its liquid poison'. **ossibus implicat ignem:** 'entangles fire in her bones', i.e. 'fills her bones with fire'; the fire is that of unbridled passion; *ossibus* is dative after the compound verb.

356 **percepit:** 'perceived' in the sense that she had not yet become aware of the full extent of the passion gripping her.

357 **mollius:** 'more softly' than she would later. **de more:** 'in the (usual) manner'.

358 **multa:** 'many tears'. **super:** 'over' in the sense of 'because of'.

Questions

1 In lines 341–343, how does Virgil give a dramatic account of Allecto?

2 Why is Amata likely to be an easy victim for Allecto?

3 In lines 344–345, how does Virgil use sound effects to enliven his narrative?

4 What impression are we given of the snake? How does Virgil achieve this?

5 In lines 356–358, which consonant is dominant? What is the effect of this?

6 How does Virgil imbue this whole passage with a sense of horror?

'Latinus, have you no pity for your daughter or for me? What of your promise to Turnus?
Turnus can trace his ancestry back to Greece; does he not count as a foreigner?'

his ubi nequiquam dictis experta Latinum
contra stare videt, penitusque in viscera lapsum
serpentis furiale malum totamque pererrat,   375
tum vero infelix ingentibus excita monstris
immensam sine more furit lymphata per urbem.
ceu quondam torto volitans sub verbere turbo,
quem pueri magno in gyro vacua atria circum
intenti ludo exercent – ille actus habena   380
curvatis fertur spatiis; stupet inscia supra
impubesque manus mirata volubile buxum;
dant animos plagae: non cursu segnior illo
per medias urbes agitur populosque feroces.
quin etiam in silvas simulato numine Bacchi   385
maius adorta nefas maioremque orsa furorem
evolat et natam frondosis montibus abdit,
quo thalamum eripiat Teucris taedasque moretur.

Amata called upon the other mothers of Latium to join her in the forests, where they
practised Bacchic revels. Allecto, satisfied that she had turned Laurentum against the
Trojans, now turned her attention to Ardea, the city of Turnus. She chose the middle of
the night to visit him, changing her appearance to that of Calybe, an aged servant of Juno's
temple. She spoke to him.

nequiquam	in vain	exerceo, -ere	I keep spinning
experior, -iri, -pertus sum	I try to move, test	ago, -ere, egi, actus	I drive, harass
penitus	deep inside	habena, -ae f.	whip, rein
viscera, -um n.pl.	insides	curvatus, -a, -um	curved
serpens, -entis f.	375 snake	spatium, -i n.	course
furialis, -e	fearful	stupeo, -ere	I am amazed
malum, -i n.	evil	inscius, -a, -um	unaware
pererro, -are	I wander through	supra	above
infelix, -icis	unhappy	impubes, -is	youthful
excio, -ire, -ivi, -itus	I rouse	miror, -ari, -atus sum	I marvel at
immensus, -a, -um	vast, huge	volubilis, -e	spinning
furo, -ere	I rave, rage	buxum, -i n.	boxwood
lympho, -are, -avi, -atus	I drive mad	plaga, -ae f	blow
ceu	just like	segnis, -e	slow
torqueo, -ere, torsi, tortus	I spin, turn	ferox, -ocis	fierce
volito, -are	I fly to and fro	simulo, -are, -avi, -atus	385 I pretend
verber, -eris n.	whip	Bacchus, -i m.	Bacchus
turbo, -inis m.	whipping top	adorior, -iri, -ortus sum	I venture upon
puer, pueri m.	boy	ordior, -iri, orsus sum	I begin
gyrus, -i m.	circle	furor, -oris m.	madness
vacuus, -a, -um	empty	evolo, -are	I dash forth
atrium, -i n.	hall	frondosus, -a, -um	leafy
circum + acc.	around	mons, montis m.	mountain
intentus, -a, -um + dat.	380 intent upon	abdo, -ere	I hide
ludus, -i m.	game	moror, -ari, -atus sum	I delay

373–4 **ubi**: this is picked up by *tum vero* in 376. **contra stare**: supply *eum*: 'that he stood firm against her'.

374–5 The order is *furialeque malum serpentis lapsum (est) penitus in viscera pererratque (eam) totam*. **totamque pererrat**: 'and pervaded her whole being'.

376–7 **ingentibus . . . monstris**: 'by the huge monsters', i.e. 'by the vastness of the demonic possession'. **immensam . . . urbem**: note the <u>enclosing word order</u>; the city is described as 'immense' to emphasise that Amata visited every part of it in her madness. **sine more**: 'wildly'.

378 **ceu**: this word is one of several used by Virgil to introduce an <u>extended simile</u>; here Amata is compared to a child's toy, a whipping top. This simile is one of the longest and most unusual in the *Aeneid*. **quondam**: here the less common 'sometimes'. **torto . . . sub verbere**: 'under the spun whip', i.e. 'under the lash of the whip'.

379–80 **circum**: to be taken before *vacua atria*. Note the slow rhythm of line 380, perhaps to underline the length of time the boys keep the top spinning.

380–2 **ille**: the top. **curvatis . . . spatiis**: 'in circular courses'. **supra**: 'over it'. **inscia**: like *impubes* this agrees with *manus*, the group of boys; they are 'unaware' of the world outside the moving top. **buxum**: an example of <u>metonymy</u>, in which the top is referred to by the name of the wood from which it is made.

383–4 **dant animos plagae**: 'the blows give (the top) impetus'. **non cursu segnior illo**: '(Amata), no slower than that course', i.e. 'every bit as fast as the course of the top'. **urbes**: plural for singular. **populosque feroces**: the citizens of Laurentum are described as fierce either because they object to Amata's wild behaviour, or because they have been infected by her madness. Note the <u>chiasmus</u> in line 384.

385–6 **quin etiam**: these words introduce an escalation of wild behaviour. **simulato numine Bacchi**: 'pretending to be under the power of Bacchus'; she is behaving like a Bacchante, a female worshipper of Bacchus, notorious for wild and improper behaviour. She hopes that other women will join her if she claims to be under the control of Bacchus. **maius . . . nefas**: 'a greater sin', explained in line 387. **maioremque orsa furorem**: this repeats the same idea as the first half of the line; Amata's *furor* reflects that of Dido in Book IV. **montibus**: local ablative.

388 **quo**: used instead of *ut* to introduce a purpose clause; cf. line 348. **thalamum, taedas**: both are examples of <u>metonymy</u>, using the name of a part for the whole: *thalamus* is strictly the bridal bed chamber, while *taeda* is the torch carried at a wedding procession; both stand for the wedding as a whole. **Teucris**: dative of disadvantage, and centrally positioned to belong to both verbs. Amata's purpose is to delay and if possible prevent the marriage of Lavinia and Aeneas.

Questions

1 Why do you think Latinus refuses to listen to Amata's arguments?

2 How does Virgil show the power of the snake inside Amata in lines 374–377?

3 Why do you think Virgil chooses to introduce an extended simile here?

4 How effective and appropriate is the simile? Find as many points of similarity as you can.

5 Why does Amata pretend to be under the power of Bacchus?

6 How does Virgil emphasise the madness of Amata in these lines?

'Turne, tot incassum fusos patiere labores,   421
et tua Dardaniis transcribi sceptra colonis?
rex tibi coniugium et quaesitas sanguine dotes
abnegat, externusque in regnum quaeritur heres.
i nunc, ingratis offer te, inrise, periclis;   425
Tyrrhenas, i, sterne acies, tege pace Latinos.
haec adeo tibi me, placida cum nocte iaceres,
ipsa palam fari omnipotens Saturnia iussit.
quare age et armari pubem portisque moveri
laetus in arma para, et Phrygios qui flumine pulchro   430
consedere duces pictasque exure carinas.
caelestum vis magna iubet. rex ipse Latinus,
ni dare coniugium et dicto parere fatetur,
sentiat et tandem Turnum experiatur in armis.'
hic iuvenis vatem inridens sic orsa vicissim   435
ore refert: 'classes invectas Thybridis undam
non, ut rere, meas effugit nuntius aures;
ne tantos mihi finge metus. nec regia Iuno
immemor est nostri.
sed te victa situ verique effeta senectus,   440
o mater, curis nequiquam exercet, et arma
regum inter falsa vatem formidine ludit.
cura tibi divum effigies et templa tueri;

incassum		in vain	
fundo, -ere, fudi, fusus		I pour	
transcribo, -ere		I transfer	
sceptrum, -i n.		sceptre	
colonus, -i m.		settler	
coniugium, -i n.		marriage	
quaero, -ere, -sivi, -situs		I seek, win	
dos, dotis f.		dowry	
abnego, -are		I deny, refuse	
externus, -a, -um		foreign	
heres, heredis m.		heir	
ingratus, -a, -um	425	ungrateful	
offero, -ferre		I expose	
inrideo, -ere, -risi, -risus		I ridicule	
periclum, -i n.		danger	
sterno, -ere		I overthrow	
tego, -ere		I protect	
adeo		indeed	
iaceo, -ere		I lie	
palam		openly	
for, fari, fatus sum		I say, speak	
omnipotens, -entis		all-powerful	
Saturnia, -ae f.		Juno	
iubeo, -ere, iussi, iussus		I order	
quare		therefore	
armo, -are	429	I arm	
consido, -ere, -sedi, -sessus		I settle	
pingo, -ere, pinxi, pictus		I paint	
exuro, -ere		I burn down	
carina, -ae f.		hull, ship	
caelestis, -is m.		god	
vis, vim, vi f.		power	
pareo, -ere + dat.		I obey, consent	
fateor, -eri, fassus sum		I admit	
sentio, -ire		I feel	
iuvenis, -is m.	435	young man	
orsa, -orum n.pl.		beginnings	
vicissim		in turn	
Thybris, -is m.		river Tiber	
effugio, -ere		I escape	
nuntius, -i m.		message, news	
auris, -is f.		ear	
fingo, -ere		I invent	
immemor, -oris		forgetful	
vinco, -ere, vici, victus	440	I overcome	
situs, -us m.		inactivity	
effetus, -a, -um		worn out	
senectus, -utis f.		old age	
falsus, -a, -um		false	
formido, -inis f.		dread	
ludo, -ere		I delude	
effigies, -ei f.		statue	
templum, -i n.		temple	
tueor, -eri, tuitus sum		I look after	

421 **incassum fusos:** 'poured forth in vain', i.e. 'wasted'. **patiere:** = *patieris* (future). **labores:** the reference in line 426 suggests that Turnus has been helping Latinus to fight the Etruscans.
422 **tua . . . sceptra:** the sceptre is that of Latinus, which would eventually pass to Turnus if he married Lavinia.
423–4 **quaesitas sanguine dotes:** 'your dowry won by blood'; by helping Latinus against the Etruscans, he has earned the king's friendship and the promise of a large dowry.
425 **i nunc:** sarcastic. **ingratis . . . periclis:** 'to ungrateful dangers', i.e to dangers that will bring you no gratitude from the king.
426 **i:** the repetition redoubles the sarcasm. **tege pace Latinos:** 'protect the Latins with peace', i.e. the peace that you will win when you have defeated the Etruscans.
427–8 The order is *omnipotens Saturnia ipsa iussit me palam fari haec adeo tibi, cum iaceres placida nocte.* **Saturnia:** Juno was the daughter of Saturn. **palam:** probably to be taken with *fari*, though some editors have taken it with *ipsa iussit.* **placida . . . nocte:** ablative of time.
429–31 **armari pubem . . . para:** 'prepare the men to be armed'; *pubes* is used by Virgil to mean grown men of sufficient youth to be enrolled in an army. **portis:** 'out of the gates' (ablative of separation). **in arma:** 'to arms', i.e. 'to war'. **flumine:** local ablative. **consedere:** = *consederunt.* **exure:** 'burn down (the leaders and the ships)', i.e. destroy them by fire. **carina:** synecdoche.
432–4 **ni:** = *nisi.* **dare coniugium:** supply *tibi.* **dicto parere:** 'to obey his word', i.e. 'keep his promise'. **sentiat, experiatur:** 'let him feel and let him experience (Turnus)', i.e. let him know the consequences of his betrayal.
435–6 **sic orsa vicissim ore refert:** A singularly Virgilian expression: '(he) returned beginnings from his mouth in turn thus', i.e. 'he spoke the following words in reply'.
436–7 The order is *nuntius classes invectas (esse) undam Thybridis non, ut rere (= reris) effugit meas aures.* **classes invectas (esse):** indirect statement. **Thybridis undam:** 'the river Tiber'.
438–9 **mihi:** an 'ethic' dative; translate as 'I pray you'. **nostri:** 'of me'.
440 **te:** the object of *exercet.* **victa situ:** her old age is 'overcome by inactivity', i.e. 'grown weak through inactivity'. **verique effeta:** 'and worn out in relation to the truth', i.e. 'no longer capable of discerning the truth'.
441–2 **mater:** a term of respect for an older woman. **arma regum inter:** = *inter arma regum*; the argument is that in matters of warfare her prophecies are useless. **vatem ludit:** the subject is again *senectus*: 'deludes a prophet'.
443 **cura:** supply *est*: 'your responsibility is . . .'.

Questions

1 What are the *labores* (line 421) that Turnus has been occupied with? Why would they be wasted?

2 What news does 'Calybe' bring Turnus?

3 What tone does she use in lines 425–426? How appropriate do you think this is?

4 Why does she mention Saturnia (Juno) in line 428?

5 In lines 429–431, how does her tone change?

6 How does Virgil make Allecto's speech effective and dramatic?

7 How does Turnus respond to 'Calybe'? How sensible is he being?

bella viri pacemque gerent quis bella gerenda.'
talibus Allecto dictis exarsit in iras.   445
at iuveni oranti subitus tremor occupat artus,
deriguere oculi: tot Erinys sibilat hydris
tantaque se facies aperit; tum flammea torquens
lumina cunctantem et quaerentem dicere plura
reppulit, et geminos erexit crinibus angues,   450
verberaque insonuit rabidoque haec addidit ore:
'en ego victa situ, quam veri effeta senectus
arma inter regum falsa formidine ludit.
respice ad haec: adsum dirarum ab sede sororum,
bella manu letumque gero.'   455
sic effata facem iuveni coniecit et atro
lumine fumantes fixit sub pectore taedas.
olli somnum ingens rumpit pavor, ossaque et artus
perfundit toto proruptus corpore sudor.
arma amens fremit, arma toro tectisque requirit: 460
saevit amor ferri et scelerata insania belli.

Turnus called his men to arms, and marched to Laurentum to confront Latinus. Meanwhile Allecto darted away to the Trojan camp. Iulus was out hunting with his hounds, and Allecto infected them with madness, causing them to chase after a stag, which happened to be a pet belonging to a high-ranking Latin called Tyrrhus. Iulus shot the stag, which, mortally wounded, limped back to Tyrrhus and his family. They were so incensed that they called for help from all the locals, who took up arms and ran after Iulus, who retreated back towards his camp. The Trojans rushed out to protect him, and a battle ensued. There were many casualties on both sides. Allecto, satisfied that she had accomplished her purpose, left Latium and reported back to Juno.

gero, -ere	444	I wage	*en*	see!
exardesco, -ere, -arsi, -arsus		I am roused	*respicio, -ere*	I take notice of
oro, -are		I beg	*soror, -oris* f.	sister
tremor, -oris m.		trembling	*letum, -i* n.	455 death
occupo, -are		I seize	*effor, -fari, -fatus sum*	I speak out
artus, -us m.		limb	*fumo, -are*	I smoke
derigesco, -ere, -rigui		I become fixed	*somnus, -i* m.	sleep
oculus, -i m.		eye	*rumpo, -ere*	I break off
Erinys, -os f.		a Fury	*pavor, -oris* m.	terror
sibilo, -are		I hiss	*perfundo, -ere*	I drench
hydrus, -i m.		serpent	*prorumpo, -ere, -rupi, -ruptus*	I break out
facies, -ei f.		face	*sudor, -oris* m.	sweat
aperio, -ire		I open, reveal	*amens, -entis*	460 mad
flammeus, -a, -um		flaming	*fremo, -ere*	I shout for
cunctor, -ari, -atus sum		I hesitate	*torus, -i* m.	bed
repello, -ere, -ppuli, -pulsus		I thrust back	*requiro, -ere*	I look for
geminus, -a, -um	450	twin, two	*saevio, -ire*	I rage, rave
erigo, -ere, erexi, erectus		I raise	*ferrum, -i* n.	iron, weapon
insono, -are, -ui		I make to sound	*sceleratus, -a, -um*	vicious
rabidus, -a, -um		raving	*insania, -ae* f.	insanity

444 quis bella gerenda: *quis* = *quibus*; supply *sunt* or *erunt* with *gerenda*. Turnus is telling the old woman to leave matters of war and peace to the men, whose responsibility they are.
445 exarsit: almost 'exploded'.
446–7 iuveni oranti: 'to the young man as he spoke', i.e. while he was still speaking. Sometimes *oro* carried the meaning 'speak' rather than 'beg'. The dative is one of disadvantage, but may be translated as 'his limbs while he spoke'. **deriguere:** = *deriguerunt*.
447–8 tot . . . hydris: 'with so many snakes'. **tantaque facies:** 'and so much of her face'; *facies* could mean either her 'face' or her 'true appearance'.
448–50 torquens: 'turning (her eyes) upon him'. **cunctantem . . . reppulit:** 'thrust him back as he hesitated'. **quaerentem:** 'and trying'. **crinibus:** local ablative.
451 verberaque insonuit: 'and cracked her whip'.
452–3 She throws his insults (lines 440–2) back at him almost word for word for maximum effect. **en:** the effect of this is 'look: you can see how old I am'.
454–5 dirarum ab sede sororum: repeated from line 324. **gero:** 'I deal out'.
456–7 facem, taedas: these are the metaphysical torches from the underworld, in contrast with the real wedding torches mentioned previously. Presumably Virgil imagines them spreading terror. **iuveni:** 'at the young man', dative of goal of motion. **atro lumine:** an amazing oxymoron, but appropriate because blackness was the colour always associated with the underworld.
458–9 olli: an archaic form of *illi*, a dative of disadvantage, but translatable as 'his'. Note the slow rhythm of line 459, reflecting the lasting horror felt by Turnus. **toto . . . corpore:** local ablative.
460 arma amens . . . arma: the <u>assonance</u> and repetition make a vivid picture of his terror and confusion. **toro tectisque:** local ablatives.
461 amor ferri: 'his thirst for weapons'. Virgil regularly uses *ferrum* to mean 'weapons' (usually swords), which in his day were made of iron; he was probably unaware that the events he describes took place in the Bronze Age (assuming that the traditional chronology is correct), when iron was a rarity and certainly not used for making entire weapons. **insania belli:** 'his mad desire for war'. Note the variety of words implying madness: *amens, saevit, insania*.

Questions

1 Why is Turnus' final comment likely to enrage Allecto?

2 How effectively does Virgil show the effect upon Turnus of Allecto's anger?

3 What methods does Allecto use to terrify Turnus besides speaking?

4 What makes Allecto's words effective?

5 How does Virgil effectively show the growing madness of Turnus in lines 458–461?

'en, perfecta tibi bello discordia tristi;   545
dic in amicitiam coeant et foedera iungant.
quandoquidem Ausonio respersi sanguine Teucros,
hoc etiam his addam, tua si mihi certa voluntas:
finitimas in bella feram rumoribus urbes,
accendamque animos insani Martis amore   550
undique ut auxilio veniant; spargam arma per agros.'
tum contra Iuno: 'terrorem et fraudis abunde est:
stant belli causae, pugnatur comminus armis,
quae fors prima dedit sanguis novus imbuit arma.   554
te super aetherias errare licentius auras   557
haud pater ille velit, summi regnator Olympi.
cede locis. ego, si qua super fortuna laborum est,
ipsa regam.' tales dederat Saturnia voces.   560

*Allecto returned to her underworld home, while Juno orchestrated the war. All the herdsmen
returned from the battle to the city, carrying the dead and appealing to Latinus.*

Turnus adest medioque in crimine caedis et igni   577
terrorem ingeminat: Teucros in regna vocari,
stirpem admisceri Phrygiam. se limine pelli.
tum quorum attonitae Baccho nemora avia matres   580
insultant thiasis (neque enim leve nomen Amatae)
undique collecti coeunt Martemque fatigant.
ilicet infandum cuncti contra omina bellum,
contra fata deum perverso numine poscunt.

perficio, -ere, -feci, -fectus	I complete	*imbuo, -ere*	I stain
discordia, -ae f.	545 quarrel	*super* + acc.	over, through
amicitia, -ae f.	friendship	*aetherius, -a, -um*	of the upper
coeo, -ire	I come		world
	together	*licenter*	freely
foedus, -eris n.	peace treaty	*regnator, -oris* m.	ruler
quandoquidem	since	*cedo, -ere*	559 I withdraw
respergo, -ere, -rsi, -rsus	I spatter	*supersum, -esse*	I am left
certus, -a, -um	certain, sure	*fortuna, -ae* f.	chance
voluntas, -atis f.	will, wish	*caedes, -is* f.	577 slaughter
finitimus, -a, -um	neighbouring	*ingemino, -are*	I redouble
rumor, -oris m.	rumour	*admisceo, -ere*	I mingle, mix
insanus, -a, -um	550 insane, mad	*attonitus, -a, -um*	580 astonished
Mars, Martis m.	Mars, war	*nemus, -oris* n.	grove
undique	from all sides	*avius, -a, -um*	pathless
auxilium, -i n.	help	*insulto, -are*	I leap upon
ager, agri m.	field, land	*thiasus, -i* m.	Bacchic dance
fraus, fraudis f.	treachery	*colligo, -ere, -legi, -lectus*	I gather
abunde	in abundance	*fatigo, -are*	I weary
pugno, -are	I fight	*ilicet*	straightaway
comminus	hand to hand	*infandus, -a, -um*	unspeakable
fors, fortis f.	554 chance	*omen, -inis* n.	omen
novus, -a, -um	new	*perversus, -a, -um*	perverse

545 **perfecta:** supply *est*.

546 **dic:** in prose this would be *impera eis ut coeant*. She is using heavy irony, similar to that she used when speaking to Turnus. She is almost defying Juno to try undoing her work.

548 **hoc etiam his addam:** 'to these (deeds) I shall also add this'. **certa voluntas:** supply *est*.

549 **in bella feram:** 'I shall bring into the war'. **rumoribus:** 'by means of rumours', i.e. she will ensure that rumours about the hostilities that have broken out reach the neighbouring cities.

550–1 **Martis:** 'of war'. **auxilio:** dative of purpose: 'to help'. **spargam arma per agros:** a vivid metaphor.

552 **Iuno:** supply *respondit* or *dixit*. **abunde est:** a rare equivalent of *satis est* + genitive: 'there is enough (of)'.

553 **stant belli causae:** 'the reasons for war are established'. **pugnatur:** impersonal passive of the intransitive verb: 'there is fighting'. **comminus armis:** 'hand to hand with weapons'; *armis* adds little to the sense. Note the slow rhythm.

554 **quae fors prima dedit:** '(the arms) which chance first gave'; the argument is that chance brought about the first use of arms (i.e. when Iulus killed the stag), but now human bloodshed has stained the arms, meaning that they will be used again deliberately for revenge.

557–8 The order is *ille pater, regnator summi Olympi, haud velit te errare licentius super aetherias auras.* **super:** 'up among'. **aetherias . . . auras:** i.e. in the upper world, as opposed to the underworld, where Allecto normally resides. Juno is suggesting that there is a danger that Allecto, if given free rein, could cause mayhem across the world. **pater ille:** 'the father on high'.

559–60 **cede locis:** 'withdraw from (these) places'. **si qua super fortuna laborum est:** 'if there is any chance of work left', i.e. 'if chance requires any further work to be done'. **ipsa regam:** 'I shall take care of it myself'. **tales . . . voces:** 'such words'.

577–8 **Turnus adest:** i.e. in Laurentum. **medioque in crimine:** 'in the midst of the charges', i.e. those made by the returning herdsmen. **igni:** ablative; supply *in medio* again: 'and in the midst of the fire of passion', that is the outrage felt by the citizens. **terrorem ingeminat:** he does this with the arguments that follow.

578–9 Supply a verb such as *dixit* to introduce the indirect speech. **admisceri:** 'was being mixed (with their own)'. **se limine pelli:** 'that he was being driven from the door', in the sense that he was not being allowed to marry Lavinia. Note the asyndeton, indicating perhaps that these were a series of charges that he continued to make.

580–2 Now the families of the women, the third target of Allecto's mischief-making, arrive to join the other two targets. **quorum:** supply *ei*: 'those people whose (mothers)'. **attonitae Baccho:** 'frantically inspired by Bacchus' (dative of the agent after the passive participle). **nemora avia . . . insultant thiasis:** 'leap about in the pathless groves doing the Bacchic dances'. **Martemque fatigant:** 'and weary Mars', i.e. 'keep calling for war'.

583–4 The same idea is repeated with *contra omina, contra fata* and *perverso numine*; Virgil is giving his own judgement on the war to come. Note the alliteration, which strengthens his comments. **perverso numine:** 'because the will of the gods was against them', referring to Juno and Allecto.

Questions

1 How does Allecto show her powerful and destructive nature in her words to Juno?

2 What arguments does Juno use to drive Allecto away?

3 What makes lines 577–584 an effective introduction to the war about to break out?

At first Latinus resisted the pressure to renounce his treaty with the Trojans.

verum ubi nulla datur caecum exsuperare potestas	591
consilium, et saevae nutu Iunonis eunt res,	
multa deos aurasque pater testatus inanes	
'frangimur heu fatis' inquit 'ferimurque procella!	
ipsi has sacrilego pendetis sanguine poenas,	595
o miseri. te, Turne, nefas, te triste manebit	
supplicium, votisque deos venerabere seris.	
nam mihi parta quies, omnisque in limine portus	
funere felici spolior.' nec plura locutus	
saepsit se tectis rerumque reliquit habenas.	600

Latinus could not bring himself to open the Gates of War on the temple of Janus, as his people asked him to do. Juno herself, therefore, came down and thrust them open; thus war was formally declared upon the Trojans. All over Italy foundries worked to forge new weapons and armour. Many were the kings that led forth their armies to fight in support of the Latins. First of all was Mezentius with his son Lausus. There followed a host of others, and finally Turnus himself, accompanied by the Amazon-like Camilla.

verum	but	*poena, -ae* f.	penalty, punishment
caecus, -a, -um	blind		
exsupero, -are	I overpower	*miser, -era, -erum*	wretched, poor
potestas, -atis f.	power	*supplicium, -i* n.	punishment
nutus, -us m.	nod, will	*votum, -i* n.	vow
testor, -ari, -atus sum	I call as witness	*veneror, -ari, -atus sum*	I venerate
inanis, -e	empty, useless	*serus, -a, -um*	late
frango, -ere	I break	*pario, -ere, peperi, partus*	I accomplish
heu!	alas!	*felix, -icis*	happy
procella, -ae f.	storm, violence	*spolio, -are*	I rob, deprive
sacrilegus, -a, -um	595 sacrilegious	*saepio, -ire, -psi, -ptus*	600 I enclose, shut
pendo, -ere	I pay		

591–2 datur: supply *ei*. **caecum . . . consilium:** the 'plan' or 'intention' is that of his people, to declare war on the Trojans; it is 'blind' because the people do not see the dangers ahead or the sacrilege they are committing by ignoring the prophecies. **nutu Iunonis:** 'at the nod of Juno', i.e. 'by the will of Juno'. **eunt res:** 'matters were proceeding'.

593 multa: accusative of respect: 'in many things', and so 'repeatedly'. **aurasque . . . inanes:** 'and the empty air'; he appeals to both the gods and the air, as it is the air that carries prayers to heaven; for Latinus, the air fails to do this, and so is 'empty'.

594 frangimur: 'we are broken', like a ship in a storm. **ferimurque procella:** 'and we are carried along by the storm', continuing the <u>metaphor</u> of the ship.

595 ipsi: emphatic by position; he is addressing the whole nation. **has. . . poenas:** 'these penalties', meaning 'penalties for doing this'. **sacrilego . . . sanguine:** 'with (your) sacrilegious blood'; this is an example of <u>hypallage</u>, since it is the people who are sacrilegious, not their blood.

596–7 te, te: the repetition suggests pointing a verbal finger of blame at Turnus; also the position of the first *te* matches that of *ipsi*, to provide a strong contrast between the two targets of his anger. **nefas:** most editors take this to be parallel to *supplicium*, i.e. also a subject of *manebit*; however, the <u>asyndeton</u> would be harsh and Turnus' 'sin' or 'crime' is hardly going to await him, as he is already committing it. The word can be used as an interjection, meaning 'oh what horror!', which would be more appropriate here; a further usage, to refer to a person as a 'wicked man', is also possible, especially as there would then be two vocatives together. **triste . . . supplicium:** the 'grim punishment' will be meted out by the gods in return for his sacrilege. **votis . . . seris:** 'with late vows'; i.e. his vows to make atonement for his sin will be too late to save him from the anger of the gods. **venerabere:** = *veneraberis*.

598–9 parta: supply *est*: he has won his rest from his responsibilities. **mihi:** dative of the agent after the perfect passive; it parallels *ipsi* and *te*. **omnis:** most editors and translators seem to ignore this word, as it is difficult to construe; as a genitive with *portus* it would give no sense; therefore it can only be nominative, describing himself; there is one poetic usage of the word used in this way, to mean 'wholly' or 'completely', which gives adequate sense here; thus *omnis spolior* would mean 'I am completely deprived'. **in limine portus:** 'on the threshold of the harbour'; there are two possible interpretations of this: either *portus* is used entirely metaphorically to mean the haven of death (as some editors take it); or it continues the <u>metaphor</u> of the ship in the storm (line 594), meaning that he, like the ship, is right at the point of salvation when death strikes. **funere felici:** ablative dependent on *spolior*: 'deprived of a happy death'. The <u>alliteration</u> and position of these words as the climax of his speech give them extra weight; he is saying, not that he is being deprived of death, but rather that the death that will inevitably come will not be a happy one.

600 tectis: local ablative: 'in his palace'. **rerum . . . habenas:** 'the reins of government'.

647–817 The last section of Book VII comprises a catalogue of armies and their leaders that came to the aid of the Latins. This list is modelled on the Catalogue of Ships in Book II of Homer's *Iliad*. Many of the characters named here reappear in later books.

Questions

1 In lines 591–593, what is Latinus' state of mind? What actions does he take?

2 How cleverly constructed is Latinus' speech?

3 How does Latinus show his dismay?

4 Who do you think is responsible for the outbreak of war in Book VII?

5 How well does Virgil portray the personalities of the main characters in Book VII?

Book 8

Turnus and the other Latin leaders prepared for full-scale war. They also sent an ambassador to Diomede, a Greek hero from the Trojan War, to ask for his help, on the assumption that he would still be hostile to the Trojans. In the Trojan camp, Aeneas was weighed down with anxieties about how to prosecute the war. After he fell asleep on the bank of the river Tiber, the god of the river, Tiberinus, appeared to him in a dream. He spoke to Aeneas.

'o sate gente deum, Troianam ex hostibus urbem	36
qui revehis nobis aeternaque Pergama servas,	
exspectate solo Laurenti arvisque Latinis,	
hic tibi certa domus, certi (ne absiste) penates.	
neu belli terrere minis; tumor omnis et irae	40
concessere deum.	
iamque tibi, ne vana putes haec fingere somnum,	
litoreis ingens inventa sub ilicibus sus	
triginta capitum fetus enixa iacebit,	
alba solo recubans, albi circum ubera nati.	45
ex quo ter denis urbem redeuntibus annis	47
Ascanius clari condet cognominis Albam.	

satus, -a, -um	sown, sprung	*vanus, -a, -um*	vain, empty
gens, gentis f.	race	*puto, -are*	I think
deus, -i m.	god	*fingo, -ere*	I make
Troianus, -a, -um	Trojan	*litoreus, -a, -um*	on the shore
hostis, -is m.	enemy	*ingens, -entis*	huge
urbs, urbis f.	city	*invenio, -ire, -veni, -ventus*	I find
reveho, -ere	I bring back	*sub* + abl.	under
aeternus, -a, -um	eternal	*ilex, ilicis* f.	holm-oak tree
Pergama, -orum n.pl.	Pergama, Troy	*sus, suis* f.	sow
servo, -are	I save, protect	*triginta*	thirty
exspecto, -are, -avi, -atus	I await	*caput, -itis* n.	head
solum, -i n.	soil, ground	*fetus, -us* m.	litter
Laurentum, -i n.	Laurentum	*enitor, -i, enixus sum*	I give birth to
arvum, -i n.	field	*iaceo, -ere*	I lie
Latinus, -a, -um	Latin	*albus, -a, -um*	white
hic	here	*recubo, -are*	I lie
certus, -a, -um	certain, sure	*circum* + acc.	around
domus, -us f.	house, home	*uber, uberis* n. 45	udder
absisto, -ere	I depart, give up	*natus, -i* m.	son, offspring
penates, -ium m.pl.	penates	*ter*	thrice
neu	and do not	*denus, -a, -um*	ten
bellum, -i n. 40	war	*redeo, -ire*	I return
terreo, -ere	I frighten	*annus, -i* m.	year
mina, -ae f.	threat	*Ascanius, -i* m.	Ascanius
tumor, -oris m.	swelling	*clarus, -a, -um*	famous
omnis, -e	all	*condo, -ere*	I found
ira, -ae f.	anger	*cognomen, -inis* n.	name
concedo, -ere, -cessi, -cessus	I subside	*Alba, -ae* f.	Alba Longa
iam	now		

36–7 o sate: 'o you (who are) sprung', i.e. 'descended'. **gente deum:** (*deum = deorum*) 'from the race of gods'; Aeneas was the son of the goddess Venus, herself the daughter of Jupiter. The order for the next part is *qui revehis nobis urbem Troianum ex hostibus servasque Pergama aeterna.* **ex hostibus:** i.e. the Greeks who captured Troy. **revehis:** Aeneas is 'bringing back' Troy in the sense that he is going to re-establish the city in the Italian province of Latium; the prefix *re-*, together with *nobis*, is to remind the reader that, according to one legend, Dardanus, the founder of Troy, originally came from Italy. **aeternaque Pergama:** 'Pergama for ever'; the use of *aeterna* is <u>proleptic</u>; Pergama was the central citadel of Troy, and Virgil often uses the name of the part for the whole (<u>synecdoche</u>). The citadel was the heart of the city, the home of its main buildings and the royal family; these are symbolised and protected by the *penates*, guardian gods of the home and the city, which Aeneas has taken great care to bring with him from Troy, so that they will extend their protection to the new city he founds.

38 exspectate: vocative of the perfect participle: 'you who have been awaited'. **solo, arvisque:** local ablatives; Aeneas is 'awaited' there because of the prophecy that a foreigner would arrive and claim the king's daughter, Lavinia, in marriage (see Book VII). **Laurentum:** the Latin city ruled over by Latinus.

39 hic: i.e. in Latium. **certa domus:** supply *erit:* 'you will have an assured home'. **ne absiste:** 'do not give up'; in prose this would be *nole absistere.* **certi . . . penates:** 'a sure place for your gods'.

40–1 neu . . . terrere: passive imperative: 'and do not be frightened'. **tumor . . . et irae:** 'the swelling and anger', i.e. 'the swelling anger', an example of <u>hendiadys</u>. **concessere:** = *concesserunt.* **deum:** = *deorum.* The unfinished line is one of many in the *Aeneid*, evidence that Virgil died before he had time to revise his work.

42–4 tibi: dative of the agent with *inventa.* **ne . . . putes:** 'lest you think', followed by accusative and infinitive. **vana . . . haec fingere somnum:** 'that sleep creates these words (to be) empty', i.e. that sleep has caused him to imagine the god's words. The order then is *ingens sus, inventa tibi, iacebit sub litoreis ilicibus, enixa fetus triginta capitum.* **litoreis . . . sub ilicibus:** 'under coastal holm-oak trees'. **triginta capitum fetus:** 'a litter of thirty heads'; *capitum* is an example of <u>synecdoche</u>, the part standing for the whole animal.

45 alba, albi: repeated to strengthen the link to *Albam* in line 48. **solo:** local ablative. **albi . . . nati:** note the <u>enclosing word order</u>: the white piglets surround the udders.

46 This line does not appear in most mss and all editors condemn it.

47–8 ex quo: probably 'from this moment in time'; alternatively 'in accordance with this (portent)'. **ter denis . . . annis:** 'thirty years', ablative absolute. **redeuntibus:** 'coming round again'; the whole means 'after the passage of thirty years'. **Ascanius:** Aeneas' son, also called Iulus. **urbem . . . Albam:** 'the city of Alba'; the city's full name was Alba Longa. The legend is that, thirty years after Aeneas has founded his new city of Lavinium, his son will found his own city, Alba Longa, which will be ruled over by his descendants until finally Romulus and Remus move away and found Rome. **clari . . . cognominis:** genitive of description: '(a city) with a famous name'; it will be named 'Alba' after the white sow. Note the double <u>alliteration</u> and <u>chiastic</u> order.

Questions

1 In lines 36–41, what is the tone of Tiberinus' words? How do we know this?

2 What is Tiberinus' prophecy?

3 How does Virgil make Tiberinus' words powerful and vivid?

haud incerta cano. nunc qua ratione quod instat
expedias victor, paucis (adverte) docebo.   50
Arcades his oris, genus a Pallante profectum,
qui regem Euandrum comites, qui signa secuti,
delegere locum et posuere in montibus urbem
Pallantis proavi de nomine Pallanteum.
hi bellum adsidue ducunt cum gente Latina;   55
hos castris adhibe socios et foedera iunge.
ipse ego te ripis et recto flumine ducam,
adversum remis superes subvectus ut amnem.
surge age, nate dea, primisque cadentibus astris
Iunoni fer rite preces, iramque minasque   60
supplicibus supera votis. mihi victor honorem
persolves. ego sum pleno quem flumine cernis
stringentem ripas et pinguia culta secantem,
caeruleus Thybris, caelo gratissimus amnis.
hic mihi magna domus, celsis caput urbibus exit.'   65

haud	not	*ripa, -ae* f.	bank
incertus, -a, -um	uncertain	*rectus, -a, -um*	straight
cano, -ere	I sing, prophesy	*flumen, -inis* n.	river
ratio, -ionis f.	means	*adversus, -a, -um*	against
insto, -are	I threaten	*remus, -i* m.	oar
expedio, -ire 50	I settle	*supero, -are*	I overcome
victor, -oris	victorious	*subveho, -ere, -vexi, -vectus*	I convey up
pauci, -ae, -a	few	*amnis, -is* m.	river
adverto, -ere	I take note, direct	*surgo, -ere, surrexi, -rectus*	I arise
doceo, -ere	I teach	*age*	come on
Arcades, -um m.pl.	Arcadians	*dea, -ae* f.	goddess
ora, -ae f.	shore	*primus, -a, -um*	first
genus, -eris n.	race, type, kind	*cado, -ere, cecidi, casus*	I fall, set
Pallas, -antis m.	Pallas	*astrum, -i* n.	star
proficiscor, -i, -fectus sum	I set out, originate	*Iuno, Iunonis* f. 60	Juno
rex, regis m.	king	*rite*	duly
Euandrus, -i m.	Evander	*prex, precis* f.	prayer
comes, -itis m.	companion	*supplex, -icis*	humble
signum, -i n.	sign, standard	*votum, -i* n.	vow
sequor, -i, secutus sum	I follow	*honos, -oris* m.	honour
deligo, -ere, -legi, -lectus	I choose	*persolvo, -ere*	I pay, offer
locus, -i m.	place	*plenus, -a, -um*	full
pono, -ere, posui, positus	I place	*cerno, -ere*	I see, watch
mons, montis m.	mountain	*stringo, -ere*	I skim
proavus, -i m.	great-grandfather	*pinguis, -e*	rich, fertile
nomen, -inis n.	name	*cultum, -i* n.	farmland
Pallanteum, -i n.	Pallanteum	*seco, -are*	I cut, cleave
adsiduus, -a, -um 55	constant	*caeruleus, -a, -um*	dark blue
castra, -orum n.pl.	camp	*Thybris, -is* m.	the Tiber
adhibeo, -ere	I add	*caelum, -i* n.	sky, heaven
socius, -i m.	ally	*gratus, -a, -um*	pleasing
foedus, -eris n.	treaty	*celsus, -a, -um* 65	high, lofty
iungo, -ere	I join, make	*exeo, -ire*	I emerge

49–50 **haud incerta cano**: 'these are no uncertain prophecies I make'; the <u>litotes</u> makes a strong affirmative. **qua ratione**: 'how'. **quod instat expedias**: 'you may resolve the threats against you'. **victor**: 'victoriously'. **paucis**: supply *verbis*.

51–4 **Arcades**: the Arcadians had come from a city, possibly also called Pallanteum, in Arcadia, in southern Greece. **his oris**: local ablative. **genus**: in apposition to *Arcades*. **a Pallante**: 'from Pallas', i.e. the grandfather of the current king, Evander. **qui . . . secuti**: supply *sunt*: 'who followed'. **comites**: 'as his companions'. **signa**: like *regem* the object of *secuti*; the standards are the emblems carried into battle. **delegere**: = *delegerunt*; *posuere* is similar; these contractions are so common in verse that they will not be commented upon again. **locum**: to be taken closely with *his oris*. **in montibus**: i.e. the seven hills of Rome. **Pallanteum**: 'named Pallanteum', in apposition to *urbem*. The legend of Pallanteum provided an origin for the Palatine Hill in Rome.

55 **hi . . . ducunt**: 'these people (i.e. the people of Pallanteum) are conducting'.

56 **hos castris adhibe socios**: 'add them to your camp as allies'. **foedera iunge**: 'make an alliance with them'.

57–8 **ripis et recto flumine**: 'past my banks and directly upstream'; ablatives of route taken. **adversum . . . amnem**: 'the river even though it will be flowing against you'. **remis**: instrumental ablative, qualifying *subvectus*.

59–60 **nate dea**: 'goddess-born', i.e. 'son of a goddess'; *dea* is ablative of origin. Aeneas was the son of Venus. **primisque cadentibus astris**: ablative absolute, indicating a time just before dawn.

60–61 **iram minasque**: 'her anger and threats (against you)'. Juno's hostility to the Trojans was implacable, ever since Venus won the goddesses' beauty contest, judged by Paris, a son of king Priam of Troy. Every book of the *Aeneid* features her attempts to destroy the Trojan exiles or prevent their settling in Italy. Now Tiberinus suggests that vows properly made might win her favour.

61–2 **victor**: 'when you have won'. It was customary for people to worship a deity that was thought to have given them help.

62–4 **ego sum . . . quem . . . cernis**: 'I am the one whom you see'. **pinguia culta secantem**: 'cutting through rich farmland'. **Thybris, amnis**: these are the complements of *sum*.

65 **hic**: supply *est*: 'here is'. **mihi magna domus**: 'my great home'; there have been many interpretations of this: he could be referring to the river mouth, which is where Aeneas is sleeping; or to Latium in general, as opposed to any other part of Italy; or he could be thinking ahead to the foundation of Rome, where he will be honoured with a temple. **caput**: the 'head' of the river is its source. **celsis . . . urbibus**: these are the lofty cities of Etruria, which lies to the north of Rome.

Questions

1 In lines 49–50, how does the god reassure Aeneas?

2 Who are the Arcadians? Why would they agree to support the Trojans?

3 How likely do you think it is it that Juno will be placated by any prayers that Aeneas makes to her?

4 How does the river god show his self-importance?

5 If you were Aeneas, how would you feel alfter hearing the river god's words?

Aeneas awoke from his sleep and prayed. Then he prepared two ships and set crews on board.

ecce autem subitum atque oculis mirabile monstrum,	81
candida per silvam cum fetu concolor albo	
procubuit viridique in litore conspicitur sus:	
quam prius Aeneas tibi enim, tibi, maxima Iuno,	
mactat sacra ferens et cum grege sistit ad aram.	85
Thybris ea fluvium, quam longa est, nocte tumentem	
leniit, et tacita refluens ita substitit unda,	
mitis ut in morem stagni placidaeque paludis	
sterneret aequor aquis, remo ut luctamen abesset.	
ergo iter inceptum celerant rumore secundo:	90
labitur uncta vadis abies; mirantur et undae,	
miratur nemus insuetum fulgentia longe	
scuta virum fluvio pictasque innare carinas.	
olli remigio noctemque diemque fatigant	
et longos superant flexus, variisque teguntur	95
arboribus, viridesque secant placido aequore silvas.	

ecce	see	*sterno, -ere, stravi, stratus*	I flatten, cover
subitus, -a, -um	sudden	*aequor, -oris* n.	flat expanse
oculus, -i m.	eye	*aqua, -ae* f.	water
mirabilis, -e	wonderful	*luctamen, -inis* n.	struggle
monstrum, -i n.	portent, monster	*absum, -esse*	I am absent
candidus, -a, -um	white	*ergo* 90	therefore
silva, -ae f.	wood	*iter, itineris* n.	journey
concolor, -oris	of the same colour	*incipio, -ere, -cepi, -ceptus*	I begin
procumbo, -ere, -cubui, -itus	I lie down	*celero, -are*	I speed up
viridis, -e	green	*rumor, -oris* m.	approval
litus, -oris n.	shore	*secundus, -a, -um*	favourable
conspicio, -ere	I see	*labor, -i, lapsus sum*	I glide
prius	first	*ungo, -ere, unxi, unctus*	I caulk
macto, -are 85	I sacrifice	*vadum, -i* n.	shallow water
sacrum, -i n.	sacred object, rite	*abies, -etis* f.	fir-wood
grex, gregis m.	litter	*miror, -ari, -atus sum*	I am amazed at, admire
sisto, -ere	I place	*nemus, -oris* n.	grove
ara, arae f.	altar	*insuetus, -a, -um*	unaccustomed
fluvius, -i m.	river	*fulgeo, -ere*	I gleam
longus, -a, -um	long	*scutum, -i* n.	shield
nox, noctis f.	night	*pingo, -ere, pinxi, pictus*	I paint
tumeo, -ere	I swell	*inno, -are*	I sail upon
lenio, -ire, -ii, -itus	I calm	*carina, -ae* f.	hull, ship
tacitus, -a, -um	silent	*remigium, -i* n.	rowing
refluo, -ere	I flow back, recoil	*dies, -ei* m.	day
subsisto, -ere, -stiti	I stand still	*fatigo, -are*	I weary, tire
unda, -ae f.	wave, water	*supero, -are* 95	I overcome, pass
mitis, -e	gentle	*flexus, -us* m.	bend
mos, moris m.	custom, manner	*varius, -a, -um*	various
stagnum, -i n.	pool	*tego, -ere*	I cover
placidus, -a, -um	peaceful	*arbos, -oris* f.	tree
palus, -udis f.	marsh		

81 **subitum ... monstrum:** this is accusative dependent on *ecce*.

82–3 **candida ... sus:** the huge separation of adjective from noun is designed to create suspense and build to a climax. **per silvam:** this could be taken with *candida* ('appearing white through the woods') or with *conspicitur*. **concolor:** strictly speaking this is redundant, because both the sow and her litter are described as 'white' (and note the position of the two 'white' words); but the prophecy made it clear that the colour of the sow and her piglets was important, and so Virgil cleverly inserts the word between *fetu* and *albo* to emphasise the point. **procubuit:** because *conspicitur* is an historic present, *procubuit* must have its full perfect meaning: 'has lain down'. Note the careful word order throughout these lines, designed to reflect the observer's experience: first something white, seen through the woods; then the piglets appear, also white; it is seen that the mother has lain down; it is on the shore; it is – a sow!

84–5 **tibi, tibi:** repeated to emphasise the surprising fact that Aeneas is sacrificing the sow to Juno of all deities, the one who was so hostile to him. This is also an example of <u>apostrophe</u>. **enim:** here 'even'. **sacra ferens:** 'carrying the sacred objects', i.e. those used in making a sacrifice. **ad aram:** 'at the altar'. **sistit:** probably the sow and her litter would have been placed on the altar before being slaughtered, in which case Virgil has reversed the sequence of events (a device called *hysteron proteron*). The altar would probably have been a wooden table brought into service for this special event.

86–7 **ea:** ablative of time, as the metre requires, and agreeing with *nocte*. **quam longa est:** 'as long as it is', the full meaning being 'for the whole duration of that night'. **refluens ita substitit:** 'reversing his flow, he brought the river so fully to a halt that ...'. **tacita ... unda:** 'with his water silent'.

88–9 **ut:** to be taken first. **in morem:** 'in the manner of', followed by two genitives phrases. **aequor aquis:** 'the flat expanse of water'; *aquis* is an ablatave of description, literally 'the level surface with its water'. **remo:** a collective singular, best translated as plural.

90 **celerant:** the subject is the Trojan sailors.

91–3 **vadis:** local ablative. **abies:** an example of <u>synecdoche</u>, the material standing for the whole ship or ships. **et:** 'also'. **mirantur undae:** an example of personification, as though the waves were sentient beings; similarly *nemus*. The <u>polyptoton</u> of *mirantur, miratur* stresses how unusual the sight was. **insuetum:** the grove is 'unaccustomed' to the sight of the ships. **virum:** = *virorum*. **fluvio:** local ablative, belonging with *innare*. **carinas:** another example of <u>synecdoche</u>, standing for the whole ships.

94 **olli:** an archaic form of *illi* (the Trojans). **remigio:** 'with their rowing' (instrumental ablative). **fatigant:** <u>metaphorical</u>: they 'wear out both a day and a night', i.e. they consume them. The distance they had to row was about 25 miles or 40 kilometres. **longos ... flexus:** 'the long meanders' of the river. **teguntur:** 'they are sheltered'. **secant:** <u>metaphorical</u>: 'they cut through'. **aequore:** local ablative.

Questions

1 In lines 81–83, how does Virgil make the appearance of the sow and its litter dramatic?

2 What does the river god do to help the Trojans?

3 How does Virgil make the journey seem both interesting and exotic?

sol medium caeli conscenderat igneus orbem
cum muros arcemque procul ac rara domorum
tecta vident, quae nunc Romana potentia caelo
aequavit, tum res inopes Euandrus habebat.   100
ocius advertunt proras urbique propinquant.
forte die sollemnem illo rex Arcas honorem
Amphytrioniadae magno divisque ferebat
ante urbem in luco. Pallas hic filius una,
una omnes iuvenum primi pauperque senatus   105
tura dabant, tepidusque cruor fumabat ad aras.
ut celsas videre rates atque inter opacum
adlabi nemus et tacitos incumbere remis,
terrentur visu subito cunctique relictis
consurgunt mensis. audax quos rumpere Pallas   110
sacra vetat raptoque volat telo obvius ipse,
et procul e tumulo: 'iuvenes, quae causa subegit
ignotas temptare vias? quo tenditis?' inquit.
'qui genus? unde domo? pacemne huc fertis an arma?'

sol, solis m.	sun	cruor, -oris m.	spilt blood
medius, -a, -um	middle (of)	fumo, -are	I smoke, reek
conscendo, -ere, -ndi, -nsus	I ascend to	ratis, -is f.	boat
igneus, -a, -um	fiery	inter + acc.	between, among
orbis, -is m.	orbit, disc	opacus, -a, -um	shady, dark
murus, -i m.	wall	adlabor, -i, -lapsus sum	I glide
arx, arcis f.	citadel	incumbo, -ere + dat.	I lean on, lean
procul	far away	visus, -us m.	sight
rarus, -a, -um	scattered	cunctus, -a, -um	all
tectum, -i n.	roof, building	relinquo, -ere, -liqui, -lictus	I leave
Romanus, -a, -um	Roman	consurgo, -ere	110 I rise together
potentia, -ae f.	power	mensa, -ae f.	table
aequo, -are, -avi, -atus	100 I make level	audax, -acis	bold
res, rei f.	thing, realm	rumpo, -ere	I break off
inops, -opis	poor, meagre	veto, -are	I forbid
ocior, -ius	swifter	rapio, -ere, rapui, raptus	I seize
prora, -ae f.	prow	volo, -are	I fly, dash
propinquo, -are + dat.	I approach	telum, -i n.	weapon
forte	by chance	obvius, -a, -um	to meet
sollemnis, -e	customary	tumulus, -i m.	mound
Arcas, -adis	Arcadian	causa, -ae f.	cause, reason
Amphytrioniades, -ae m.	Hercules	subigo, -ere, -egi, -actus	I compel, induce
divus, -i m.	god	ignotus, -a, -um	unknown
ante + acc.	before	tempto, -are	I try
lucus, -i m.	grove	via, viae f.	road, way
una	together	tendo, -ere	I go, head
iuvenis, -is m.	105 young man	unde	from where
pauper, -eris	poor	pax, pacis f.	peace
senatus, -us m.	senate	huc	to here
tus, turis n.	incense	an	or
tepidus, -a, -um	warm	arma, -orum n.pl.	arms, war

97 **medium orbem caeli**: 'the middle of its orbit across the sky'; i.e. it was midday.

98–9 **cum . . . vident**: indicative as it is an inverse-*cum* clause.

99–100 **quae**: this refers to all the structures mentioned rather than just *tecta*. **nunc**: a rare instance of Virgil referring openly to his own time. **res inopes**: 'a meagre realm', in apposition to a second *quae*, to be supplied as the object of *habebat*.

101 **advertunt proras**: supply some such word as *illuc* ('to there').

102–4 **die . . . illo**: ablative of time. **rex Arcas**: i.e. Evander. **Amphytrioniadae**: Hercules was the son of Jupiter, who took the form of Amphytrion to seduce Alcmene, Amphytrion's wife. Hercules was worshipped as a god after his death, and there was an annual festival in Rome in his honour; Virgil imagines that the ceremony mentioned here is the origin of the later festival.

104–6 **una**: 'together with him'. **iuvenum primi**: 'the leaders of the young men'. **dabant**: the subject is threefold: *Pallas*, *primi* and *senatus*. **pauper senatus**: Virgil imagines that the senate of his own day had its origin in Evander's settlement; it is 'poor' to show that, in contrast with the senate of his own day, Evander's senate prized material poverty above wealth. **tepidus cruor**: this is the blood of the sacrificed animal, still warm. **ad aras**: 'on the altar'.

107–8 **ut videre**: 'when they saw'; this has a direct object (*celsas rates*) and introduces two indirect statements. **adlabi**: 'and that they were gliding'. **tacitos**: supply *viros*.

109–10 Note the slow rhythm of line 110.

110–11 **quos**: the connecting relative, referring to those attending the ceremony; translate as 'them'. **sacra**: 'the sacred rites'. In Virgil's day it was a bad omen if sacred rites were interrupted. **obvius**: 'to meet them'.

112–13 **procul**: 'while still a long way off (from the ships)'. **subegit**: supply *vos*. **qui genus**: supply *estis*: 'who are you in terms of race?', i.e. 'of what race are you?'; *genus* is accusative of respect. **unde domo**: lit. 'from where from home?', i.e. 'from what home (have you come)?'

Questions

1 How do we know it was midday?

2 What contrasts does Virgil make between Evander's time and his own time?

3 Why do the Trojans increase their speed (*ocius*)?

4 Why would Virgil's contemporaries be interested to read of the festival in honour of Hercules?

5 Why do you think Virgil repeats *una* (lines 104–105)?

6 What alarms Evander's people?

7 Virgil emphasises the word *audax* (line 110) by placing it first in the sentence; in what ways does Pallas deserve this description?

tum pater Aeneas puppi sic fatur ab alta   115
paciferaeque manu ramum praetendit olivae:
'Troiugenas ac tela vides inimica Latinis,
quos illi bello profugos egere superbo.
Euandrum petimus. ferte haec et dicite lectos
Dardaniae venisse duces socia arma rogantes.'   120
obstipuit tanto percussus nomine Pallas:
'egredere o quicumque es,' ait 'coramque parentem
adloquere ac nostris succede penatibus hospes.'
excepit manu dextramque amplexus inhaesit.
progressi subeunt luco fluviumque relinquunt.   125

*Aeneas addressed the king with friendly words, claiming that their families were once
related, and requesting an alliance against the common enemy. Evander replied that as a
child he had met and admired Aeneas' father, Anchises. He agreed to Aeneas' request and
invited the Trojans to join him in honouring Hercules. Food was quickly brought out and
all enjoyed a banquet. When they had finished, Evander explained that their worship of
Hercules was because he had saved them from a cruel fate.*

'iam primum saxis suspensam hanc aspice rupem,   190
disiectae procul ut moles desertaque montis
stat domus et scopuli ingentem traxere ruinam.

pater, -tris m.	father, senator	*aio* (defective verb)	I say
puppis, -is f.	115 stern	*coram*	face to face
for, fari, fatus sum	I speak	*parens, -entis* m.	parent
altus, -a, -um	high	*adloquor, -i, -locutus sum*	I speak to
pacifer, -fera, -ferum	peace-bearing	*succedo, -ere* + dat.	I approach
manus, -us f.	hand	*hospes, -itis* m.	guest, host
ramus, -i m.	branch	*excipio, -ere, -cepi, -ceptus*	I welcome
praetendo, -ere	I hold out	*dextra, -ae* f.	right hand
oliva, -ae f.	olive	*amplector, -i, -plexus sum*	I embrace
Troiugena, -ae m.	a Trojan	*inhaereo, -ere, -haesi, -sum*	I cling to
inimicus, -a, -um	hostile	*progredior, -i, -gressus sum*	I proceed
profugus, -a, -um	exiled	*subeo, -ire* + dat. 125	I approach
ago, -ere, egi, actus	I drive	*saxum, -i* n. 190	rock
superbus, -a, -um	arrogant, proud	*suspensus, -a, -um*	raised
peto, -ere	I seek	*aspicio, -ere*	I look at
lego, -ere, legi, lectus	I choose	*rupes, -is* f.	crag, cliff
Dardania, -ae f.	120 Troy	*disiectus, -a, -um*	split off
dux, ducis m.	leader	*moles, -is* f.	mass, boulder
socius, -a, -um	allied	*desertus, -a, -um*	abandoned
rogo, -are	I ask for	*sto, stare*	I stand
obstipesco, -ere, -stipui	I am amazed	*scopulus, -i* m.	rock, crag
tantus, -a, -um	so great	*traho, -ere, traxi, tractus*	I drag
percutio, -ere, -cussi, -cussus	I strike	*ruina, -ae* f.	ruin,
egredior, -i, egressus sum	I come out		destruction
qui-, quae-, quodcumque	whoever, whatever		

115–16 **pater Aeneas:** Virgil often calls Aeneas *pater*, as he was in effect the father of his people. **paciferae . . . olivae:** an olive branch was symbolic of peace throughout antiquity.
117–18 **quos:** the antecedent is *Troiugenas*. **illi:** the Latins. **egere:** 'have driven out'. **profugos:** '(making us) exiled', and so 'into exile'; the fact that they are already exiles from Troy is irrelevant here; the point Aeneas is making is that they are being driven into a second exile. **bello . . . superbo:** 'in an arrogant war', i.e. 'by arrogantly declaring war'.
119–20 **ferte haec:** either 'take this olive branch' or 'report these words'. **lectos . . . duces:** 'chosen leaders', his point being that he has selected men of rank specially for this embassy.
121 **tanto . . . nomine:** i.e. Dardania, that is, Troy; the city was supposedly well-known throughout the ancient world.
122–3 **nostris . . . penatibus:** i.e. 'come under the protection of our guardian deities'. **hospes:** 'as a guest'.
124 **dextramque amplexus inhaesit:** 'having clasped his right hand, he clung to it', emphasising his friendliness.
125 The sequence is reversed.

190 Evander now begins the story of the monster Cacus and Hercules, a story also told by the historian Livy. This is a parenthetical narrative of a type found frequently in Homer, and has the purpose of explaining the origin of the worhip of Hercules in Rome. **suspensam saxis:** 'raised over the rocks', i.e. 'that rises up above the rocks'.
191–2 **ut:** 'how'. **disiectae:** supply *sunt*; the boulders have been torn from the cliff. **procul:** i.e. far from the cliff. **montis . . . domus:** 'a home of a mountain', i.e. 'a mountain home', that is, a cave. **scopuli:** i.e. 'falling rocks'. **traxere:** 'have dragged', i.e. 'have caused as they fell'.

Questions

1 How does Aeneas make it clear that he is not hostile?

2 How does Aeneas design his speech to be brief but effective?

3 What mainly persuades Pallas to welcome the Trojans?

4 How does Pallas show his welcome?

5 Describe the cliff that begins Evander's narrative.

hic spelunca fuit vasto summota recessu,
semihominis Caci facies quam dira tenebat
solis inaccessam radiis; semperque recenti　　　　　　195
caede tepebat humus, foribusque adfixa superbis
ora virum tristi pendebant pallida tabo.
huic monstro Volcanus erat pater: illius atros
ore vomens ignes magna se mole ferebat.
attulit et nobis aliquando optantibus aetas　　　　　　200
auxilium adventumque dei. nam maximus ultor
tergemini nece Geryonae spoliisque superbus
Alcides aderat taurosque hac victor agebat
ingentes, vallemque boves amnemque tenebant.
at furiis Caci mens effera, ne quid inausum　　　　　　205
aut intractatum scelerisve dolive fuisset,
quattuor a stabulis praestanti corpore tauros
avertit, totidem forma superante iuvencas.
atque hos, ne qua forent pedibus vestigia rectis,
cauda in speluncam tractos versisque viarum　　　　　210
indiciis raptos saxo occultabat opaco;

spelunca, -ae f.	cave	*adventus, -us* m.	arrival
vastus, -a, -um	huge	*ultor, -oris* m.	avenger
summoveo, -ere, -ovi, -otus	I remove	*tergeminus, -a, -um*	three-bodied
recessus, -us m.	recess	*nex, necis* f.	slaughter
semihomo, -inis	half-human	*Geryones, -ae* m.	Geryon
Cacus, -i m.	Cacus	*spolia, -orum* n.pl.	spoils
facies, -ei f.	form, shape	*Alcides, -ae* m.	Hercules
dirus, -a, -um	dreadful	*adsum, adesse*	I am present
teneo, -ere	I occupy	*taurus, -i* m.	bull
inaccessus, -a, -um 195	not reached	*vallis, -is* f.	valley
radius, -i m.	ray	*bos, bovis* m/f.	bull, cow
recens, -entis	fresh	*furia, -ae* f. 205	fury, frenzy
caedes, -is f.	slaughter	*mens, mentis* f.	mind
tepeo, -ere	I am warm	*efferus, -a, -um*	savage
humus, -i f.	ground	*inausus, -a, -um*	undared
foris, -is f.	door	*intractatus, -a, -um*	untried
adfigo, -ere, -fixi, -fixus	I fix, nail (to)	*scelus, -eris* n.	crime
os, oris n.	mouth, face	*dolus, -i* m.	trickery
tristis, -e	sad, grim	*stabulum, -i* n.	stall
pendeo, -ere	I hang	*praestans, -ntis*	outstanding
pallidus, -a, -um	pale	*corpus, -oris* n.	body
tabum, -i n.	corruption, decay	*averto, -ere, averti, aversus*	I lead away
Volcanus, -i m.	Vulcan	*totidem*	the same number
ater, atra, atrum	black	*forma, -ae* f.	beauty
vomo, -ere	I spew out	*iuvenca, -ae* f.	heifer
ignis, -is m.	fire, flame	*pes, pedis* m.	foot
adfero, -re, attuli, -latus 200	I bring to	*vestigium, -i* n.	tracks, prints
aliquando	at last	*rectus, -a, -um*	right
opto, -are	I wish, choose	*cauda, -ae* f. 210	tail
aetas, aetatis f.	age, time	*indicium, -i* n.	sign, trace
auxilium, -i n.	help	*occulto, -are*	I hide

193 **vasto summota recessu:** lit. 'removed in a huge recess', i.e. 'reaching back into a huge space'.

194–5 **quam:** to be taken first; the antecedent is *spelunca*. **semihominis Caci facies:** 'the (dreadful) form of the half-human Cacus', a poetic way of saying 'Cacus of half-human shape'. **inaccessam:** this agrees with *quam*, i.e. the cave.

195–7 **recenti caede:** causal ablative. **foribus . . . superbis:** 'the proud doorway (of the cave)'; this is an example of <u>hypallage</u>, in that it is Cacus who was arrogant, not his doorway; Virgil imagines the doorway being proud to bear the trophies of his crimes. **ora . . . tristi . . . pallida tabo:** this is an example of <u>synchysis</u>; **tristi . . . tabo:** probably qualifies *pallida*: 'pale from the sad decay'.

198–9 **Volcanus:** the Roman god of fire. **illius:** i.e. of Vulcan; the word is emphatic because it begins the clause, and so should be translated not as 'his flames' but 'his were the flames that'. **atros . . . ignes:** the flames were 'black' because they were accompanied by black smoke. **magna se mole ferebat:** 'he carried himself with great bulk', i.e. 'he moved his great bulk around'.

200–201 The order is *aetas aliquando attulit et nobis optantibus auxilium adventumque dei.* **et nobis:** 'even to us'. **optantibus:** 'wishing (for help)', i.e. 'in answer to our prayers'. **dei:** the god in question is Hercules, as soon made clear. Note the strong <u>assonance</u> of *a*, suggesting high emotion.

201–4 **maximus ultor:** 'the greatest avenger'; Hercules is called this because he was portrayed in legend as the greatest righter of human wrongs. **tergemini Geryonae:** Geryon was a three-bodied monster who lived in Spain. As his tenth labour, Hercules had been ordered to fetch Geryon's cattle, and to do this he had to kill Geryon. Hercules had to drive the cattle all the way across Europe, calling at Pallanteum on the way. **nece, spoliisque:** dependent on *superbus*: 'proudly returning from the killing . . . and with the spoils'. **hac:** supply *via*: '(by) this way'. **vallemque boves amnemque tenebant:** 'and the cattle were occupying the valley and the river', that is, the low ground at the foot of the Palatine Hill along the river Tiber. In Virgil's day this land was the Forum Boarium, or Cattle Market, where there was also situated the Ara Maxima, established for the worhip of Hercules.

205–6 **furiis . . . effera:** Cacus' mind was 'savage with frenzy'. **ne quid:** 'lest anything'. **scelerisve dolive:** partitive genitives dependent on *quid*: '(lest anything) either of crime or of trickery', i.e. 'lest any crime or trickery'. **fuisset:** 'might prove to have been'.

207–8 **stabulis:** either Hercules had fenced off the ground to create an enclosure, or the word simply refers to the pasture. **praestanti corpore:** ablative of description: '(bulls) of outstanding physical condition'. **forma superante:** this means the same as *praestanti corpore*.

209–11 **ne qua . . . vestigia:** 'lest any tracks'. **pedibus . . . rectis:** 'with the feet pointing the right way'. **cauda:** 'by the tail(s)'. **tractos:** agrees with *hos*. **versisque viarum indiciis:** 'the signs of their path having been reversed'. Cacus tried to fool Hercules by dragging the cattle backwards into his cave, so that no tracks would appear to lead into the cave. **raptos:** this also agrees with *hos*, which in turn is the object of *occultabat*. **saxo . . . opaco:** local ablative.

Questions

1 Describe Cacus.

2 What use does Evander make of <u>hyperbole</u> in his account?

3 How else does he make his story gripping?

4 How clever was Cacus? Give reasons for your answer.

quaerenti nulla ad speluncam signa ferebant.
interea, cum iam stabulis saturata moveret
Amphitryoniades armenta abitumque pararet,
discessu mugire boves atque omne querelis 215
impleri nemus et colles clamore relinqui.
reddidit una boum vocem vastoque sub antro
mugiit et Caci spem custodita fefellit.
hic vero Alcidae furiis exarserat atro
felle dolor, rapit arma manu nodisque gravatum 220
robur, et aërii cursu petit ardua montis.
tum primum nostri Cacum videre timentem
turbatumque oculi; fugit ilicet ocior Euro
speluncamque petit, pedibus timor addidit alas.
ut sese inclusit ruptisque immane catenis 225
deiecit saxum, ferro quod et arte paterna
pendebat, fultosque emuniit obice postes,
ecce furens animis aderat Tirynthius omnemque
accessum lustrans huc ora ferebat et illuc,
dentibus infrendens. 230

quaero, -ere	I seek, search	*timeo, -ere*	I am afraid
interea	meanwhile	*turbo, -are, -avi, -atus*	I trouble
saturo, -are, -avi, -atus	I fill	*fugio, -ere*	I flee
moveo, -ere	I move	*ilicet*	at once
armentum , -i n.	cattle	*ocior, ocius*	swifter
abitus, -us m.	departure	*Eurus, -i* m.	the East Wind
paro, -are	I prepare	*timor, -oris* m.	fear
discessus, -us m.	215 departure	*addo, -ere, -didi, -ditus*	I add
mugio, -ire	I low, moo	*ala, -ae* f.	wing
querela, -ae f.	complaint	*includo, -ere, -si, -sus*	225 I shut in
impleo, -ere	I fill	*immanis, -e*	huge
collis, -is m.	hill	*catena, -ae* f.	chain
clamor, -oris m.	shout, lowing	*deicio, -ere, -ieci, -iectus*	I let fall
reddo, -ere, reddidi, redditus	I return, give back	*ferrum, -i* n.	iron
vox, vocis f.	voice	*ars, artis* f.	skill
antrum, -i n.	cave	*paternus, -a, -um*	of a father
spes, spei f.	hope	*fulcio, -ire, fulsi, fultus*	I secure
custodio, -ire, -ivi, -itus	I guard	*emunio, -ire, -ii, -itus*	I fortify
fallo, -ere, fefelli, falsus	I deceive	*obex, obicis* m/f.	barrier
vero	indeed, however	*postis, -is* m.	door-post
exardesco, -ere, -arsi, -arsus	I am roused	*furens, -entis*	raging
fel, fellis n.	220 bile, gall	*animus, -i* m.	mind, fury
dolor, -oris m.	pain, anger	*Tirynthius, -i* m.	Hercules
nodus, -i m.	knot	*accessus, -us* m.	approach
gravo, -are, -avi, -atus	I make heavy	*lustro, -are*	I scan
robur, -oris n.	oak club	*illuc*	to there
aërius, -a, -um	lofty	*dens, dentis* m.	230 tooth
cursus, -us m.	course, running	*infrendo, -ere*	I gnash the teeth
arduus, -a, -um	steep		

212 **quaerenti:** supply *cuiquam*: 'to anyone searching', i.e. 'to the eyes of anyone searching'.
ferebant: 'led'. Note the heavily spondaic rhythm.
213–14 **stabulis:** ablative of separation. **saturata . . . armenta:** 'his cattle when they had eaten
their fill'.
215–16 **discessu:** 'on their departure', ablative of time. **mugire, impleri, relinqui:** historic
infinitives, as frequently translatable as 'began to . . .'. Virgil has made the last two passive to
give variety of expression, even though logically it was the cattle that did all three actions.
clamore: 'with clamour', i.e. 'amidst lowing', ablative of manner.
217–18 **reddidit . . . vocem:** 'gave back a voice', i.e. 'lowed in response'. **sub:** 'deep inside'.
Caci spem fefellit: 'deceived the hope of Cacus', i.e. 'frustrated Cacus' intentions', that is,
to keep the stolen cattle secret. **custodita:** 'having been guarded', i.e. 'although it had been
guarded'.
219–221 **hic:** 'hereupon'. **furiis, felle, dolor:** all mean more or less the same thing, thus
piling anger upon anger. **furiis:** 'in his fury', possibly an instrumental ablative alongside
felle. **exarserat:** the pluperfect, followed by the historic present (*rapit*), is used to indicate a
rapid sequence of events. **nodisque gravatum robur:** 'and his oak club heavy with knots', i.e.
'his heavily-knotted oak club'. Hercules famously wielded a massive wooden club in all his
exploits; the knots at one end, where in life branches had split off from a main stem, made
that end thicker and heavier and so a more effective weapon. **cursu:** 'at a run'. **ardua:** 'the
steep slopes'.
222–3 Note the heavily spondaic rhythm of line 222: for the first time Cacus froze in fear.
nostri . . . videre . . . oculi: 'our eyes beheld'.
223–4 **petit, pedibus:** <u>alliteration</u> and <u>assonance</u>, accompanied by <u>asyndeton</u>, emphasise the
rapidity of Cacus' actions.
225–6 **ut:** 'when'. **ruptisque catenis:** 'and by breaking the chains'; apparently Cacus had
devised a contraption for blocking the entrance to his cave: a boulder raised and lowered
by chains, like a mediaeval portcullis; in his haste to hide, he broke the chains instead of
running them slowly through his hands.
226–7 **quod:** to be taken first: 'which', referring to *saxum*. **ferro . . . et arte paterna:** 'by
means of iron and his father's skill', i.e. 'with his father's skill with iron', a sort of <u>hendiadys</u>;
his father, Vulcan, was also the blacksmith god; either Vulcan had made the chains, or Cacus
had learned the skill from his father. **fultos . . . emuniit . . . postes:** 'fortified the secured door
posts', i.e. 'secured and fortified the entrance'; Virgil often uses *postes* to mean the whole
doorway, an example of <u>synecdoche</u>. **emuniit:** the subject is *quod*, i.e. the *saxum*.
228–30 **furens animis:** 'raging with fury'. **aderat:** 'was right there'. **Tirynthius:** Hercules had
grown up in Tiryns, near Mycenae in Greece. **omnemque:** the final syllable elides before the
vowel at the start of the next line; it is called a hypermetric syllable; it has the effect of making
the strongly dactylic line appear even faster (in constrast with line 229, which is heavily
spondaic). **ora ferebat:** 'cast his eyes'. **dentibus:** redundant as *infrendens* includes the concept.

Questions

1 What caused Cacus' deception to fail?

2 How does Virgil contrast Hercules with Cacus?

3 How else does he make this story lively?

4 How effectively does Virgil use rhythm to support the narrative?

                         ter totum fervidus ira   230
lustrat Aventini montem, ter saxea temptat
limina nequiquam, ter fessus valle resedit.
stabat acuta silex praecisis undique saxis
speluncae dorso insurgens, altissima visu,
dirarum nidis domus opportuna volucrum.   235
hanc, ut prona iugo laevum incumbebat ad amnem,
dexter in adversum nitens concussit et imis
avulsam solvit radicibus, inde repente
impulit; impulsu quo maximus intonat aether,
dissultant ripae refluitque exterritus amnis.   240
at specus et Caci detecta apparuit ingens
regia, et umbrosae penitus patuere cavernae,
non secus ac si qua penitus vi terra dehiscens
infernas reseret sedes et regna recludat
pallida, dis invisa, superque immane barathrum   245
cernatur, trepident immisso lumine Manes.

ter	230 three times	*impello, -ere, -puli, -pulsus*	I thrust
totus, -a, -um	the whole (of)	*impulsus, -us* m.	pressure, shock
fervidus, -a, -um	burning, seething	*intono, -are*	I thunder
Aventinus, -i m.	the Aventine Hill	*aether, -eris* m.	air
saxeus, -a, -um	rocky	*dissulto, -are*	240 I leap apart
nequiquam	in vain	*exterritus, -a, -um*	terrified
fessus, -a, -um	weary	*specus, -us* m.	cave
resido, -ere, -sedi	I settle back	*detego, -ere, -texi, -tectus*	I reveal, uncover
acutus, -a, -um	sharp	*appareo, -ere, -ui*	I appear
silex, -icis f.	crag	*regia, -ae* f.	palace
praecisus, -a, -um	steep, sheer	*umbrosus, -a, -um*	shady
dorsum, -i n.	back, ridge, rock	*penitus*	deep inside
insurgo, -ere	I rise up	*pateo, -ere, -ui*	I lie open
nidus, -i m.	235 nest	*caverna, -ae* f.	cave, cavern
opportunus, -a, -um	suitable	*secus*	otherwise
volucris, -is f.	bird	*vis*, abl. *vi* f.	force
pronus, -a, -um	leaning forward	*dehisco, -ere*	I gape wide
iugum, -i n.	ridge	*infernus, -a, -um*	of the underworld
laevus, -a, -um	on the left	*resero, -are*	I unlock, reveal
dexter, -tra, -trum	on the right	*sedes, -is* f.	dwelling
nitor, -i, nixus sum	I press (upon)	*regnum, -i* n.	realm, kingdom
concutio, -ere, -cussi, -cussus	I shake	*recludo, -ere*	I open
imus, -a, -um	lowest	*invisus, -a, -um*	245 hated
avello, -ere, avelli, avulsus	I tear off	*super*	from above
solvo, -ere, solvi, solutus	I loosen	*barathrum, -i* n.	abyss
radix, -icis f.	root	*trepido, -are*	I tremble
inde	then	*lumen, -inis* n.	light
repente	suddenly	*Manes, -ium* m.pl.	souls of the dead

230–2 **ter . . . ter. . . ter:** this <u>anaphora</u> is one of Virgil's favourites. **fervidus ira:** 'seething with anger'. **Aventini montem:** the Aventine Hill is one of the seven hills of Rome and was the traditional site of Cacus' cave. **saxea . . . limina:** i.e. the giant boulder Cacus had lowered. **valle:** local ablative.

233–5 **stabat:** 'there stood'. **speluncae dorso insurgens:** either 'rising up from the back of the cave', or 'rising up to the roof of the cave'. The general idea is that there was a pinnacle towering above the cave. **visu:** the second supine: 'to behold'. **dirarum . . . volucrum:** probably vultures, attracted by Cacus' activities. **nidis:** 'for their nests'.

236–9 **hanc:** i.e. the *silex*. **ut:** 'as'. **prona iugo:** 'leaning forward from the ridge'. **laevum . . . ad amnem:** 'towards the river on the left'. **dexter . . . nitens:** 'pushing from the right'. **in adversum:** 'forwards', i.e. towards the river. **imis . . . radicibus:** 'from its deepest foundations' (ablative of separation). **avulsam:** agrees with *hanc*. **impulit:** 'he thrust'; having loosened the pinnacle, he thrust it over into the river.

239–40 **impulsu quo** = *quo impulsu*: 'at this pressure' (causal ablative). **maximus . . . aether:** 'the vastness of heaven'. **exterritus:** an example of personification. The idea is that the falling pinnacle caused a giant wave that spread outwards in all directions, widening the river and pushing the water back upstream.

241–2 **Caci . . . regia:** 'Cacus' palace'; the irony is strengthened by the <u>enjambement</u>. **apparuit:** 'became visible'. Note the <u>chiastic</u> order of *umbrosae . . . cavernae*, enclosing the <u>alliterated</u> words.

243–6 **non secus ac si:** 'not otherwise than if', i.e. 'just as if', introducing a <u>simile</u>; the subjunctive verbs that follow are dependent on *si*, in effect a present unfulfilled condition; the historic present tenses stand for the imperfect in normal prose. **qua penitus vi:** 'as a result of some force deep inside'. **infernas . . . sedes:** i.e. the abodes of the dead in the underworld. **regna . . . pallida:** 'the pale realms', i.e. the underworld, pale because the souls of the dead were thought to be pale and insubstantial. **dis invisa:** '(realms) hated by the gods'. **barathrum:** part of the underworld (called Tartarus) was thought to take the form of a deep abyss (see Book VI.577–9). **immisso lumine:** 'with the admission of light'. In Book VI, Virgil describes only the fields of the blessed as having their own sun; the other half of the underworld was relatively dark.

Questions

1 What is the effect of the repetition of *ter* in lines 230–232?

2 Describe the pinnacle of rock in as much detail as you can.

3 How did Hercules gain access to the cave?

4 How effectively does Virgil descibe Hercules' actions?

5 What is the purpose of the simile?

6 How effective is the simile?

ergo insperata deprensum luce repente
inclusumque cavo saxo atque insueta rudentem
desuper Alcides telis premit, omniaque arma
advocat et ramis vastisque molaribus instat.   250
ille autem, neque enim fuga iam super ulla pericli,
faucibus ingentem fumum (mirabile dictu)
evomit involvitque domum caligine caeca
prospectum eripiens oculis, glomeratque sub antro
fumiferam noctem commixtis igne tenebris.   255
non tulit Alcides animis, seque ipse per ignem
praecipiti iecit saltu, qua plurimus undam
fumus agit nebulaque ingens specus aestuat atra.
hic Cacum in tenebris incendia vana vomentem
corripit in nodum complexus, et angit inhaerens   260
elisos oculos et siccum sanguine guttur.
panditur extemplo foribus domus atra revulsis
abstractaeque boves abiurataeque rapinae
caelo ostenduntur, pedibusque informe cadaver
protrahitur. nequeunt expleri corda tuendo   265
terribiles oculos, vultum villosaque saetis
pectora semiferi atque exstinctos faucibus ignes.'

insperatus, -a, -um		unexpected	*incendium, -i* n.		fire
deprendo, -ere, -ndi, -nsus		I catch unawares	*corripio, -ere*	260	I seize
lux, lucis f.		light	*complector, -i, -plexus sum*		I embrace
cavus, -a, -um		hollow	*ango, -ere*		I strangle
rudo, -ere		I roar	*elido, -ere, -isi, -isus*		I prise out
desuper		from above	*siccus, -a, -um*		dry
premo, -ere		I press, attack	*sanguis, -inis* m.		blood
advoco, -are	250	I call upon	*guttur, -uris* n.		throat
molaris, -is m.		mill-stone	*pando, -ere*		I throw open
fuga, -ae f.		flight	*extemplo*		straightaway
periclum, -i n.		danger	*revello, -ere, -velli, -vulsus*		I tear off
fauces, -ium f.pl.		throat	*abstraho, -ere, -xi, -ctus*		I drag out
fumus, -i m.		smoke	*abiuro, -are, -avi, -atus*		I deny on oath
evomo, -ere		I belch forth	*rapina, -ae* f.		theft
involvo, -ere		I envelop	*ostendo, -ere*		I show
caligo, -inis f.		fog, murk	*informis, -e*		shapeless
caecus, -a, -um		blind, dark	*cadaver, -eris* n.		corpse
prospectus, -us m.		sight, view	*protraho, -ere*	265	I drag forth
eripio, -ere		I snatch away	*nequeo, -ire*		I cannot
glomero, -are, -avi, -atus		I gather into a mass	*expleo, -ere*		I satisfy
			cor, cordis n.		heart
fumifer, -era, -erum	255	smoke-filled	*tueor, -eri, tuitus sum*		I look at
commisceo, -ere, -ui, -xtus		I mix together	*terribilis, -e*		dreadful
tenebrae, -arum f.pl.		darkness	*vultus, -us* m.		face
praeceps, -cipitis		headlong	*villosus, -a, -um*		shaggy
iacio, -ere, ieci, iactus		I throw, hurl	*saeta, -ae* f.		bristle
saltus, -us m.		leap	*pectus, -oris* n.		heart, breast
nebula, -ae f.		mist, pall	*semifer, -eri* m.		half-beast
aestuo, -are		I seethe	*exstinguo, -ere, -nxi, -nctus*		I extinguish

247–9 deprensum: supply *Cacum*, as object of *premit*, of which the subject is *Alcides*. **cavo saxo:** local ablative. **insueta rudentem:** 'roaring unaccustomed things', and so 'bellowing strangely'.

249–50 omnia . . . arma: 'all sorts of weapons'. **advocat:** 'he summoned to his aid'. **molaribus:** lit. 'with mill-stones', and so 'with rocks the size of mill-stones'.

251–4 ille: the subject of *evomit*. **super:** this is an abbreviation for *superest*: 'remains'. **pericli:** 'from danger' (an objective genitive). **faucibus:** 'from his throat'. **dictu:** the second supine, dependent on *mirabile*: 'amazing to relate'. **prospectum eripiens oculis:** 'removing the ability to see from (Hercules') eyes'; *oculis* is a dative of disadvantage, as frequently with a verb of abstraction.

254–5 sub antro: 'down in the cave'. **commixtis igne tenebris:** 'mingling darkness with fire', an example of <u>antithesis</u>.

256–8 non tulit: supply *haec*: 'did not tolerate this'. **animis:** 'in his fury'. **ipse:** this simply reinforces *se*, and can be omitted. **qua:** 'where'. **plurimus undam . . . agit:** 'billowed the thickest'. **nebula . . . atra:** ablative.

259–61 in nodum complexus: 'having embraced him into a knot', and so 'knotting his arms around him'. **inhaerens:** 'maintaining his grip'. **elisos oculos:** lit. '(he strangled) his prised-out eyes'; logically *angit* belongs only with *guttur*, and so *elisos oculos* is generally understood to mean '(he squeezed his throat) until his eyes started from his head'. **siccum sanguine:** 'drained of blood'.

262–5 foribus . . . revulsis: 'the doors having been torn off', that is, the boulder that formed the door having been pushed out from the inside. **abiuratae rapinae:** 'the theft Cacus had sworn he had not committed'. **pedibus:** 'by its feet'. **informe:** Cacus' corpse is 'shapeless' either because Hercules broke his body, or because his body was not human to start with.

265–7 nequeunt: most editors assume the subject to be the onlookers, which forces them to treat *corda* as an accusative of respect: 'they could not be satisfied in (respect to) their hearts'; another possibility is to take *corda* as the subject: 'our hearts could not be satisfied'. **tuendo:** 'by looking at'; the overall meaning is that the onlookers could not get enough of observing the monster. **faucibus:** local ablative.

Questions

1 How did Hercules attack Cacus?

2 How did Cacus resist the attack?

3 How does Virgil use references to colour to make his account more vivid?

4 What other means does Virgil use to enhance his narrative?

5 How did Hercules finally defeat Cacus?

6 How does Virgil make the description of Cacus' corpse vivid?

'Ever since that time we have observed this rite.' Evander ended his account with an invitation to join in the celebration. Priests sang hymns in honour of the god. After the rites came to an end, Evander led the Trojans into his city. In answer to Aeneas' questions, he explained something of the early history of the place, telling how Saturn came to them after being defeated by Jupiter; he gave the people their first laws and named the area 'Latium'. Evander pointed out many landmarks familiar to later Romans. Finally they reached Evander's home as night fell.

at Venus haud animo nequiquam exterrita mater	370
Laurentumque minis et duro mota tumultu	
Volcanum adloquitur, thalamoque haec coniugis aureo	
incipit et dictis divinum aspirat amorem:	
'dum bello Argolici vastabant Pergama reges	
debita casurasque inimicis ignibus arces,	375
non ullum auxilium miseris, non arma rogavi	
artis opisque tuae, nec te, carissime coniunx,	
incassumve tuos volui exercere labores,	
quamvis et Priami deberem plurima natis,	
et durum Aeneae flevissem saepe laborem.	380
nunc Iovis imperiis Rutulorum constitit oris:	
ergo eadem supplex venio et sanctum mihi numen	
arma rogo, genetrix nato.'	

So Venus spoke. Her loving embrace persuaded him to agree. He fell asleep in her arms. In the morning he arose and made his way to Mt Etna in Sicily, where his forge lay deep under the mountain. There he found the Cyclopes already at work forging a thunderbolt for Jupiter, constructing a chariot for Mars, and fashioning an aegis for Minerva, with the Gorgon's severed head in its centre. Vulcan addressed them at once.

Venus, -eris f.	370 Venus	*miser, -era, -erum*	poor, wretched
mater, matris f.	mother	*ops, opis* f.	help, power
Laurens, -entis m.	a Laurentian	*carus, -a, -um*	dear
mina, -ae f.	threat	*incassum*	in vain
durus, -a, -um	hard, harsh	*exerceo, -ere*	I employ
tumultus, -us m.	uprising	*labor, -oris* m.	work, labour
thalamus, -i m.	bed-chamber	*quamvis*	although
coniunx, -iugis m.	husband	*Priamus, -i* m.	Priam
aureus, -a, -um	golden	*fleo, -ere, -evi, -etus*	380 I weep (for)
dictum, -i n.	word	*Iuppiter, Iovis* m.	Jupiter
divinus, -a, -um	divine	*imperium, -i* n.	command
aspiro, -are	I breathe into	*Rutuli, -orum* m.pl.	Rululians
amor, -oris m.	love	*consisto, -ere, -stiti*	I stop, halt
Argolicus, -a, -um	Greek	*supplex, -icis*	humble
vasto, -are	I lay waste	*sanctus, -a, -um*	sacred
debeo, -ere, -ui, -itus	375 I owe	*numen, -inis* n.	divine will, god
ullus, -a, -um	any	*genetrix, -icis* f.	mother

370 **at:** as frequently, Virgil uses this word to introduce a change of subject or scene. The new scene features Aeneas' mother, Venus, who is anxious about her son's safety. She therefore asks her husband, Vulcan, to make a set of armour for him, later described in great detail. **animo:** local ablative. **haud ... nequiquam:** an example of litotes, making a strong affirmative. **Venus ... mater:** the two words neatly enclose the line.

371–2 **mota:** 'impelled by'. **duro ... tumultu:** 'by the hard uprising', i.e. the brutal breaking of the treaty and the attacks on the Trojans. Note the heavy allliteration and consonance of *m*, serving to emphasise Venus' strong emotions.

372–3 **thalamo ... aureo:** local ablative. **haec:** supply *verba*. **dictis:** dative: 'into her words'; Virgil imagines that Venus had the power to infuse her words with irresistible love.

374–5 **Argolici:** this name is modelled on Homer's regular name for the Greeks, Argeioi, from the city of Argos in the NE Peloponnese. **Argolici ... reges:** there were many Greek kings participating in the siege of Troy, including Agamemnon, king of Mycenae, which was a close neighbour of Argos. **Pergama:** see note on line 37. **debita:** 'owed' to the Greeks by fate. **casurasque ... arces:** 'the citadel(s) doomed to fall'; essentially this is the same as *Pergama debita*, as Pergama was the citadel of Troy.

376–8 **auxilium, arma:** both are the objects of *rogavi*. **miseris:** 'for the wretched (Trojans)'. **artis opisque tuae:** (weapons) of (i.e. made by) your skill and power'. **incassum:** such help from Vulcan would have been in vain because even he could not overturn fate.

379–80 **deberem plurima:** 'I owed very much', because Paris had judged her to be the most beautiful goddess in the beauty contest. It was this contest which turned Minerva and particulary Juno so implacably against the Trojans, because they lost that contest. **Priami ... natis:** in particular, of course, Paris. **durum ... laborem:** like Homer's Odysseus, Aeneas had had to endure endless hardships on his way from Troy.

381 **Iovis imperiis:** in Book IV, Jupiter ordered Mercury to command Aeneas to lead his people away from Carthage to a new home in Italy. **oris:** local ablative.

382–3 **eadem ... venio:** 'I, the same woman, come', i.e. 'now I *do* come'. **supplex:** 'humbly'. **sanctum mihi numen:** '(I ask) your divine will, that is sacred to me'. **arma:** a second direct object of *rogo*. **genetrix nato:** 'a mother (asking) for her son'.

Questions

1 How does Virgil make clear Venus' feelings for her son?

2 What comparison does Venus make?

3 Why do you think she makes this comparison?

4 What details can you find about Jupiter's command to Aeneas to travel to Italy?

5 How does Venus make her appeal persuasive?

'tollite cuncta' inquit 'coeptosque auferte labores,   439
Aetnaei Cyclopes, et huc advertite mentem: 440
arma acri facienda viro. nunc viribus usus,
nunc manibus rapidis, omni nunc arte magistra.
praecipitate moras.' nec plura effatus, at illi
ocius incubuere omnes pariterque laborem
sortiti. fluit aes rivis aurique metallum   445
vulnificusque chalybs vasta fornace liquescit,
ingentem clipeum informant, unum omnia contra
tela Latinorum, septenosque orbibus orbes
impediunt. alii ventosis follibus auras
accipiunt redduntque, alii stridentia tingunt   450
aera lacu; gemit impositis incudibus antrum.
illi inter sese multa vi bracchia tollunt
in numerum versantque tenaci forcipe massam.

While this work proceeded, Evander and Aeneas met at dawn. Evander was able to promise the Trojans the support of a powerful nation, for the Trojans' arrival fulfilled a prophecy.

'haud procul hinc saxo incolitur fundata vetusto   478
urbis Agyllinae sedes, ubi Lydia quondam
gens, bello praeclara, iugis insedit Etruscis.   480

tollo, -ere	I get rid of, raise	*impedio, -ire*	I encircle
coepi, -isse	I began	*ventosus, -a, -um*	windy
aufero, -ferre	I set aside	*follis, -is* m.	bellows
Aetnaeus, -a, -um	440 of Mt Etna	*aura, -ae* f.	air
Cyclops, -opis m.	Cyclops	*accipio, -ere*	450 I receive
acer, acris, acre	fierce, valiant	*strideo, -ere*	I hiss
vires, -ium f.pl.	strength	*tingo, -ere*	I dip
usus, -us m. + abl.	need, use	*lacus, -us* m.	lake, tank
magistra, -ae f. adj.	of a master	*gemo, -ere*	I groan
praecipito, -are	I cast aside	*impono, -ere, -posui, -positus*	I place upon
mora, -ae f.	delay	*incus, -udis* f.	anvil
effor, -fari, -fatus sum	I speak out	*bracchium, -i* n.	arm
pariter	equally	*numerus, -i* m.	rhythm, time
sortior, -iri, -itus sum	445 I share out	*verso, -are*	I turn
fluo, -ere	I flow, run	*tenax, -acis*	gripping
aes, aeris n.	bronze	*forceps, -ipis* f.	tongs
rivus, -i m.	stream	*massa, -ae* f.	mass
aurum, -i n.	gold	*hinc*	478 from here
metallum, -i n.	ore, metal	*incolo, -ere*	I inhabit
vulnificus, -a, -um	causing wounds	*fundo, -are, -avi, -atus*	I found
chalybs, -ibis m.	steel	*vetustus, -a, -um*	ancient
fornax, -acis f.	furnace	*Agyllinus, -a, -um*	of Agylla
liquesco, -ere	I melt	*Lydius, -a, -um*	Lydian
clipeus, -i m.	shield	*quondam*	once
informo, -are	I shape	*praeclarus, -a, -um*	480 illustrious
contra + acc.	against	*insido, -ere, -sedi, -sessus*	I settle
septenus, -a, -um	sevenfold	*Etruscus, -a, -um*	Etruscan

439 **coeptos . . . labores:** 'the tasks you have begun'.
440 **Cyclopes:** the Cyclopes were one-eyed giants who worked for Vulcan in his forge
under Mt Etna; the best-known of them was Polyphemus, whose encounter with Odysseus
occupied Book IX of the *Odyssey*; he also features in Book III of the *Aeneid*. **huc:** 'over
here' or 'to me'. **mentem:** 'attention'.
441–2 **facienda:** supply *sunt*. **usus:** supply *est*; *usus est*, like the more familiar *opus est*, takes
an ablative of the thing needed; here there are three ablatives dependent on it. **arte magistra:**
this is a rare usage of the feminine *magistra* as an adjective (though some editors treat it
as a noun in apposition to *arte*, giving inferior sense); it is simplest to take *arte magistra* as
'master-skill'.
443–5 **effatus:** supply *est*. **illi:** the Cyclopes. **incubuere:** 'bent to the task'. **sortiti:** supply *sunt*.
445 **rivis:** 'in streams' (ablative of manner). **aurique metallum:** 'ore of gold', or perhaps 'gold
metal'.
446 **vulnificus:** steel weapons were harder and sharper than ordinary iron ones, and so
prized for their effectiveness. **vasta fornace:** local ablative; the furnaces for producing steel
are known as 'bloomeries', where carbon was added to the iron ore to produce carbon steel.
447–9 **ingentem clipeum:** Virgil embarks on a long description of this shield in line 626.
septenos orbibus orbes impediunt: 'they encircle sevenfold discs on discs', i.e. 'they weld
together seven circular layers (of metal), one to another'.
449–51 **accipiunt redduntque:** 'they draw in and blow back out'. **tingunt:** the quenching of
red-hot iron in water hardens it. **lacu:** local ablative. **impositis incudibus:** 'because of the
anvils placed inside it'.
452–3 **sese:** = *se*. **in numerum:** 'rhythmically'. **tenaci forcipe:** singular for plural. **massam:** the
mass of heated metal.

478–80 **saxo . . . vetusto:** local ablative. **urbis Agyllinae sedes:** 'the site of the city of Agylla';
the city is more commonly known as Caere. **Lydia . . . gens:** 'the Lydian race'; there was a
tradition, now given some support by archaeology, that the Etruscans migrated to Italy from
Lydia in Asia Minor. **bello:** ablative of respect. **iugis . . . Etruscis:** local ablative; Etruria was a
hilly region.

Questions

1 How does Vulcan make clear the urgency for action?

2 How does Virgil show the speed of the Cyclopes' work?

3 What can you learn from this passage about ancient metalwork?

4 Describe the process of working iron or steel.

5 Does Virgil make any use of rhythm to support his narrative?

6 Find out all you can about the Etruscans and their origins.

hanc multos florentem annos rex deinde superbo
imperio et saevis tenuit Mezentius armis.
quid memorem infandas caedes, quid facta tyranni
effera? di capiti ipsius generique reservent!
mortua quin etiam iungebat corpora vivis   485
componens manibusque manus atque oribus ora,
tormenti genus, et sanie taboque fluentes
complexu in misero longa sic morte necabat.
at fessi tandem cives infanda furentem
armati circumsistunt ipsumque domumque,   490
obtruncant socios, ignem ad fastigia iactant.
ille inter caedem Rutulorum elapsus in agros
confugere et Turni defendier hospitis armis.
ergo omnis furiis surrexit Etruria iustis,
regem ad supplicium praesenti Marte reposcunt.   495
his ego te, Aenea, ductorem milibus addam.
toto namque fremunt condensae litore puppes
signaque ferre iubent, retinet longaevus haruspex
fata canens: "o Maeoniae delecta iuventus,
flos veterum virtusque virum, quos iustus in hostem   500
fert dolor et merita accendit Mezentius ira,
nulli fas Italo tantam subiungere gentem:

floreo, -ere	I flourish	*iustus, -a, -um*	just
saevus, -a, -um	cruel	*supplicium, -i* n.	495 punishment
Mezentius, -i m.	Mezentius	*praesens, -entis*	present
memoro, -are	I relate	*Mars, Martis* m.	Mars, war
infandus, -a, -um	unspeakable	*reposco, -ere*	I demand
tyrannus, -i m.	ruler, tyrant		back
gener, -eri m.	son-in-law	*ductor, -oris* m.	leader
reservo, -are	I reserve	*mille*, pl. *milia*	thousand
mortuus, -a, -um	dead	*namque*	for
quin	485 yes indeed	*fremo, -ere*	I grumble, howl
vivus, -a, -um	living, alive	*condensus, -a, -um*	packed together
compono, -ere	I fix together	*iubeo, -ere*	I order
tormentum, -i n.	torture	*retineo, -ere*	I hold back
sanies, abl. *sanie* f.	gore	*longaevus, -a, -um*	long-lived
complexus, -us m.	embrace	*haruspex, -icis* m.	soothsayer
mors, mortis f.	death	*fatum, -i* n.	fate
neco, -are	I kill	*Maeonia, -ae* f.	Maeonia, Lydia
armo, -are, -avi, -atus	490 I arm	*iuventus, -utis* f.	young men
circumsisto, -ere	I surround	*flos, floris* m.	500 flower
obtrunco, -are	I cut to pieces	*vetus, -eris*	old
fastigium, -i n.	roof-top	*virtus, -utis* f.	valour
iacto, -are	I toss	*meritus, -a, -um*	righteous
elabor, -i, elapsus sum	I slip away	*accendo, -ere*	I inflame
confugio, -ere	I seek refuge	*nullus, -a, -um*	no
Turnus, -i m.	Turnus	*fas* n. (indecl.)	law, right
defendo, -ere	I defend	*Italus, -a, -um* (also a noun)	Italian
Etruria, -ae f.	Etruria	*subiungo, -ere*	subdue

481–2 **hanc:** supply *urbem*; it is the object of *tenuit*, with *rex Mezentius* as subject. **deinde:** 'then', i.e. after the long period of flourishing. Note the spondaic rhythm of line 481, supporting the long duration of the city's success. **Mezentius:** the tyrant Mezentius was exiled by his own people because of his cruelty; because Turnus took him in, his people, the Etruscans, were happy to ally themselves with the Trojans in order to see him finally punished. In Book X Mezentius fights fiercely but is eventually killed by Aeneas.

483–4 **quid memorem:** 'why should I relate' (deliberative subjunctive); the verb has two objects, *caedes* and *facta*, with <u>anaphora</u> of *quid* for extra emphasis; the expression is for rhetorical effect, as he does proceed to describe his crimes. **di . . . reservent:** 'may the gods reserve (such wickedness)'. **capiti ipsius:** 'for his own head'. **generique:** lit. 'for his son-in-law'; this causes difficulty because Virgil and the legends drew upon mention only Mezentius' son, Lausus. Most editors assume that Virgil is using the word loosely to mean family members in general, although this usage is not attested elsewhere.

485 **quin etiam:** 'yes indeed, he even . . .'. **vivis:** supply *corporibus*.

486 **manibusque manus:** '(binding together) both hands to hands and . . .'.

487–8 **fluentes:** supply *eos*. **longa . . . morte:** 'in a long-drawn-out death'.

489–90 **infanda furentem . . . ipsumque:** 'both the man himself, raging atrociously' (lit. 'unspeakable things'. Note the spondaic rhythm of both lines, signifying the climax of the story.

491 **ignem:** 'fire' in the form of fire-brands.

492–3 **Rutulorum:** this belongs with *agros*, not *caedem*. **confugere, defendier:** historic infinitives; *defendier* is an archaic form of the passive infinitive. **armis:** 'by the weapons'.

494 **furiis . . . iustis:** 'in righteous fury'.

495 **praesenti Marte:** 'with present war', i.e. 'threatening immediate war'.

496 **his . . . milibus:** i.e. the Etruscans. **ductorem:** 'as leader'.

497–9 **toto . . . litore:** local ablative. **fremunt . . . puppes:** 'the sterns grumble', i.e. 'the ships creak' (because they are packed so tightly together); *puppes* is an example of <u>synecdoche</u>. **iubent:** supply some such word as *milites*. **signa ferre:** 'to carry (forward) the standards', i.e. to initiate a march against the enemy. **retinet:** supply *eos*; the <u>asyndeton</u> calls for the insertion of 'but'.

499–501 **Maeoniae:** see note on line 479. **delecta iuventus:** in the *Aeneid*, young men are frequently 'chosen', because *iuventus* is a collective noun referring to men of military age, and these have been selected by their leaders to fight. **flos veterum . . . virum** (= *virorum*): 'the flower of men of old', implying that these warriors stand comparison with the best of previous generations; note the strong <u>alliteration</u>, helping to make this a remarkable phrase. **merita . . . ira:** 'with justifiable anger'.

502 **nulli fas Italo:** supply *est*: 'it is right for no Italian'. **tantam . . . gentem:** i.e. the Latins and their allies. Only a foreign leader can do this. This is the same prophecy as the one that was delivered to Latinus in Book VII.96 (q.v.).

Questions

1 How does Evander justify his feelings towards Mezentius?

2 How does Virgil show the character of Mezentius?

3 What has caused the Etruscans to rise up in arms?

4 What is the prophecy that caused the soothsayer to hold back the Etruscans?

externos optate duces." tum Etrusca resedit
hoc acies campo monitis exterrita divum.
ipse oratores ad me regnique coronam   505
cum sceptro misit mandatque insignia Tarchon,
succedam castris Tyrrhenaque regna capessam.
sed mihi tarda gelu saeclisque effeta senectus
invidet imperium seraeque ad fortia vires.
natum exhortarer, ni mixtus matre Sabella   510
hinc partem patriae traheret. tu, cuius et annis
et generi fata indulgent, quem numina poscunt,
ingredere, o Teucrum atque Italum fortissime ductor,
hunc tibi praeterea, spes et solacia nostri,
Pallanta adiungam; sub te tolerare magistro   515
militiam et grave Martis opus, tua cernere facta
adsuescat, primis et te miretur ab annis.
Arcadas huic equites bis centum, robora pubis
lecta dabo, totidemque suo tibi nomine Pallas.'

*As soon as Evander finished speaking, there was lightning and thunder, which Aeneas
recognised as a sign from his mother. He sent most of his men on their ships back to the
camp, while he remained with a chosen few. These made ready to ride to the Etruscan army.
Evander made a passionate appeal to the gods to protect his son. When the group neared
the Etruscan camp, Venus appeared to her son, bringing him the armour Vulcan had made.
Aeneas was delighted with the gifts and picked up each in turn to admire it, first the helmet,
then the sword and the breastplate.*

externus, -a, -um	foreign	*traho, -ere*	I draw, drag
acies, -ei f.	army	*indulgeo, -ere* + dat.	I am kind to
campus, -i m.	plain	*posco, -ere*	I demand, call upon
monitum, -i n.	warning		
orator, -oris m.	505 envoy	*ingredior, -i, -gressus sum*	I embark upon
corona, -ae f.	crown	*Teucri, -orum* m.pl.	Trojans
sceptrum, -i n.	sceptre	*fortis, -e*	brave
mando, -are	I entrust	*praeterea*	furthermore
insignia, -ium n.pl.	regalia, insignia	*solacium, -i* n.	consolation
Tarchon, -onis m.	Tarchon	*adiungo, -ere*	515 I attach, join
Tyrrhenus, -a, -um	Etruscan	*tolero, -are*	I endure
capesso, -ere	I take over	*magister, -tri* m.	teacher
tardus, -a, -um	slow	*militia, -ae* f.	military service
gelu, -us n.	cold	*gravis, -e*	heavy, severe
saeclum, -i n.	years, age	*opus, -eris* n.	work
effetus, -a, -um	worn out	*factum, -i* n.	deed
senectus, -utis f.	old age	*adsuesco, -ere*	I become used
invideo, -ere	I begrudge	*eques, -itis* m.	cavalryman
serus, -a, -um	too late	*bis*	twice
exhortor, -ari, -atus sum	510 I urge	*centum*	one hundred
ni	unless	*robur, -oris* n.	strength
misceo, -ere, -ui, mixtus	I mix	*pubes, -is* f.	adult
Sabellus, -a, -um	Sabine	*lego, -ere, legi, lectus*	I choose
pars, partis f.	part	*totidem*	the same number
patria, -ae f.	native land		

503–4 hoc . . . campo: local ablative: 'on this plain', i.e. on the plain where they had assembled. **divum:** = *divorum*.

505–6 The order is inverted: first the direct objects, then two verbs, and finally the subject, *Tarchon*. Tarchon was the leader of the Etruscan alliance. **insignia:** these would be other objects that kings carried or wore as symbols of their rule.

507 succedam, capessam: jussive subjunctives dependent on a verb to be supplied, such as *rogantes*. The extent of Tarchon's offerings, stretching to his entire kingdom, indicates how desperate was his desire to obtain a 'foreign' leader to help him to defeat Mezentius and his Latin allies.

508–9 tarda gelu saeclisque effeta: a good example of a chiasmus; the meaning is 'slowed down by cold and worn out by the years'. **seraeque ad fortia vires:** *vires* is a second subject of *invidet*; his strength is 'too late for valorous deeds', i.e. it is too late in his life for him to find the strength to fight.

510–11 exhortarer: imperfect subjunctive in a present unfulfilled condition; he means he would be urging his son to accept the role of leader. **mixtus matre Sabella:** 'being (of) mixed (blood), as his mother is a Sabine'. The Sabines were a race that lived to the east of Rome, and so this meant that Pallas was half-Greek and half-native; this would preclude him from accepting the role of 'foreign leader'. **hinc:** i.e. 'from here', i.e. 'from Italy'.

511–12 cuius et annis et generi: 'to whose age and race'. **indulgent:** 'are kind to', i.e. 'approve of'.

513–15 ingredere: imperative: 'embark upon (the task)', and so 'accept the role'. **Italum:** = *Italorum*. **hunc tibi . . . Pallanta adiungam:** 'I shall give you Pallas here in addition'. **spes et solacia nostri:** according to strict grammar, *spes* and *solacia* should refer either to Evander himself, if nominative; or to Aeneas, if vocative; however most editors assume that they refer to Pallas. **nostri:** objective genitive, best translated as 'our' (i.e. 'my').

515–17 sub te . . . magistro: 'under you as teacher', i.e. 'under your guidance'. **tolerare:** the infinitive is dependent upon *adsuescat*: 'let him become accustomed'. **miretur:** another 3rd person command: 'let him admire'. **primis et:** = *et primis*.

518–19 Arcadas . . . equites: *Arcadas* has a Greek accusative plural ending, masculine to agree with *equites*. **huic:** 'to Pallas'. **robora pubis lecta:** 'the select strength of our men'. **tibi:** supply *dabit*. **suo . . . nomine:** 'in his own name'; perhaps these were men who had sworn loyalty to Pallas rather than to his father; this would have been a strategy by Evander to accustom his son to command before being called upon to fight.

Questions

1 How does Virgil show the desperation of Tarchon?

2 Why did Evander reject Tarchon's entreaty?

3 Why could Pallas not take up the offer of leadership?

4 How does Evander try to persuade Aeneas to accept leadership?

5 Do you think *spes* and *solacia* (line 514) make more sense taken with *tibi* (i.e. Aeneas) or with Pallas? Give reasons for your answer.

6 How many additional troops will Aeneas take away with him?

tum leves ocreas electro auroque recocto,	624
hastamque et clipei non enarrabile textum.	625
illic res Italas Romanorumque triumphos	
haud vatum ignarus venturique inscius aevi	
fecerat Ignipotens, illic genus omne futurae	
stirpis ab Ascanio pugnataque in ordine bella.	
fecerat et viridi fetam Mavortis in antro	630
procubuisse lupam, geminos huic ubera circum	
ludere pendentes pueros et lambere matrem	
impavidos, illam tereti cervice reflexa	
mulcere alternos et corpora fingere lingua.	

Nearby were depicted many other scenes from Roman history.

in medio classes aeratas, Actia bella,	675
cernere erat, totumque instructo Marte videres	
fervere Leucaten auroque effulgere fluctus.	
hinc Augustus agens Italos in proelia Caesar	
cum patribus populoque, penatibus et magnis dis,	
stans celsa in puppi, geminas cui tempora flammas	680
laeta vomunt patriumque aperitur vertice sidus.	

Opposing him was Mark Antony with his Egyptian ally, Cleopatra, who soon fled in defeat.

lēvis, -e		smooth	*cervix, -icis* f.	neck
ocrea, -ae f.		greave	*reflecto, -ere, -flexi, -flexus*	I bend back
electrum, -i n.		electrum	*mulceo, -ere*	I caress
recoctus, -a, -um		refined	*alternus, -a, -um*	each in turn
hasta, -ae f.	625	spear	*fingo, -ere*	I shape
clipeus, -i m.		shield	*lingua, -ae* f.	tongue, language
enarrabilis, -e		describable	*classis, -is* f.	675 fleet
textum, -i n.		fabric	*aeratus, -a, -um*	bronze-clad
illic		there	*Actius, -a, -um*	of Actium
triumphus, -i m.		triumph	*instruo, -ere, -struxi, -structus*	I equip
vates, -is m.		prophet	*fervo, -ere*	I stir, am aroused
ignarus, -a, -um		ignorant	*Leucate, -es* m. (acc. *-en*)	Leucate
inscius, -a, -um		unaware	*effulgeo, -ere*	I shine
aevum, -i n.		age	*fluctus, -us* m.	wave
Ignipotens, -entis		Mighty with fire	*hinc*	on one side
stirps, -is f.		lineage	*Augustus, -i* m.	Augustus
pugno, -are, -avi, -atus		I fight	*proelium, -i* n.	battle
ordo, -inis m.		sequence, line	*Caesar, -aris* m.	Caesar
fetus, -a, -um	630	newly delivered	*populus, -i* m.	people
Marvors, -ortis m.		Mars	*tempus, -oris* n.	680 temple
lupa, -ae f.		female wolf	*flamma, -ae* f.	flame
geminus, -a, -um		twin	*laetus, -a, -um*	joyful
ludo, -ere		I play	*patrius, -a, -um*	a father's
lambo, -ere		I lick	*aperio, -ire*	I open, reveal
impavidus, -a, -um		fearless	*vertex, -icis* m.	head
teres, teretis		shapely	*sidus, -eris* n.	star

624 ocreas: greaves were shin-guards. **electro auroque:** ablatives of material; electrum is a natural alloy of gold and silver, and is paler than pure gold. **recocto:** 'resmelted', that is, heated in the furnace repeatedly to purify the gold.

625 clipei . . . textum: 'the fabric of the shield', i.e. its structure and manufacture. **non enarrabile:** 'indescribable', referring to the workmanship rather than the subject-matter depicted. The description of the shield's decoration occupies the next 103 lines, and was inspired by Homer's parallel decription of the shield made for Achilles (*Iliad* 18).

626–8 The order is *illic Ignipotens, haud ignarus vatum insciusque venturi aevi, fecerat Italas res Romanorumque triumphos.* **illic:** i.e. on the shield. **Ignipotens:** i.e. Vulcan. **res Italas:** 'the story of Italy'. **haud:** take with both *ignarus* and *inscius*. **vatum:** 'of prophets', i.e. 'of prophecy'. **venturique . . . aevi:** 'and of the future'. The examples of <u>litotes</u> make strong affirmatives.

628–9 illic genus: supply *fecerat*. **genus omne:** 'the whole race', meaning all the generations descended from Ascanius. **in ordine:** 'in sequence', i.e. in chronological order.

630–1 et: 'also'. **fetam . . . lupam:** 'the wolf that had recently given birth' (and so had milk). This is the foundation-myth of Rome, according to which Romulus and Remus, the twin sons of Rhea Silvia and Mars, were cast into the Tiber as babies by their uncle, Amulius, who had usurped the throne of Alba Longa from their grandfather, Numitor. They were found and adopted by a wolf, who suckled them until they were found and raised by a shepherd. When they were fully grown, they killed Amulius and restored Numitor to the throne. Then they set out to found their own city; in a dispute over which had laid the stronger foundations, Romulus killed his brother, and so his city, Rome, grew and prospered. **viridi . . . Mavortis in antro:** 'in the green cave of Mars', which became a shrine called the Lupercal, at the foot of the Palatine Hill. **procubuisse:** dependent on *fecerat*: 'he had depicted her having lain down' (so that she could suckle the infants).

631–3 geminos . . . pueros: Romulus and Remus. **huic:** equivalent to a genitive here. **ludere:** this and the following infinitives, like *procubuisse* dependent on *fecerat*, are also best translated as participles. **matrem:** the object of *lambere*, not its subject, because of what follows.

633–4 illam: the wolf. **tereti cervice reflexa:** ablative absolute. **alternos:** 'them each in turn'. **corpora fingere lingua:** 'shaping their bodies with her tongue', i.e. 'licking them into shape'.

675–6 in medio: i.e. of the shield. **aeratas:** Roman ships had bronze beaks at the front for ramming enemy ships. **Actia bella:** 'the battle of Actium', fought in 31 BC between Octavian on behalf of the Roman senate, and Mark Antony and his Egyptian ally and lover, Cleopatra. It was as a result of his victory in this battle that Octavian became the first emperor of Rome, taking the name Augustus. **cernere erat:** 'it was possible to see', a usage modelled on a Greek idiom.

676–7 totum . . . Leucaten: 'the whole of Leucate' (a headland near Actium off the west coast of Greece). **instructo Marte:** 'with war having been prepared'. **videres:** 'you could see'. **auro:** 'with gold', that is the gold that decorated the ships.

678 Augustus . . . Caesar: i.e. Octavian, whose adoptive father was Julius Caesar. **agens Italos:** Virgil presents Augustus as a patriot, unlike Antony who had Asiatics and Egyptians as allies.

679 cum patribus: 'with the senators', many of whom had accompanied him in his pursuit of Antony. **populo:** supply *Romano*. **magnis dis:** 'with the great gods', meaning either that he had statues of the great gods (Jupiter and the other Olympian gods) with him, or that they were supporting him.

680–1 cui tempora . . . laeta: 'and his joyful temples', and so 'joyfully his temples'. **geminas . . . flammas:** 'twin flames'; these have been interpreted as rays of sunlight reflected off the twin crests of his helmet; or a supernatural portent, like the flames that played around the head of Ascanius in Book II. **patrium sidus:** his father's (i.e. Caesar's) star, perhaps a reference to a comet that appeared soon after Caesar's death. **vertice:** local ablative.

Questions for pages 74–75

1 What events in Rome's future history are depicted on the shield?

2 What effect do you think seeing these images would have had on Aeneas?

3 What effect do you think they would have had on contemporary readers?

4 What effect do you think they would have had on Augustus?

5 Why do you think Virgil devotes so many lines to the description of the shield?

at Caesar, triplici invectus Romana triumpho	714
moenia, dis Italis votum immortale sacrabat,	715
maxima ter centum totam delubra per urbem.	
laetitia ludisque viae plausuque fremebant;	
omnibus in templis matrum chorus, omnibus arae;	
ante aras terram caesi stravere iuvenci.	
ipse sedens niveo candentis limine Phoebi	720
dona recognoscit populorum aptatque superbis	
postibus; incedunt victae longo ordine gentes,	
quam variae linguis, habitu tam vestis et armis.	

Many tribes and races were there.

talia per clipeum Volcani, dona parentis,	729
miratur rerumque ignarus imagine gaudet	730
attollens umero famamque et fata nepotum.	

triplex, -icis	triple	*Phoebus, -i* m.		Phoebus Apollo
inveho, -ere, -vexi, -vectus	I carry into	*donum, -i* n.		gift
moenia, -ium n.pl.	715 city, city walls	*recognosco, -ere*		I review
immortalis, -e	immortal	*apto, -are*		I hang
sacro, -are	I consecrate	*incedo, -ere*		I advance, move
delubrum, -i n.	shrine	*vinco, -ere, vici, victus*		I conquer
laetitia, -ae f.	happiness, joy	*habitus, -us* m.		style
ludus, -i m.	game	*vestis, -is* f.		clothes
plausus, -us m.	applause	*talis, -e*	729	such
templum, -i n.	temple	*imago, -inis* f.	730	representation
chorus, -i m.	band	*gaudeo, -ere*		I rejoice
caedo, -ere, cecidi, caesus	I slaughter	*attollo, -ere*		I lift up
iuvencus, -i m.	bullock	*umerus, -i* m.		shoulder
niveus, -a, -um	720 snow-white	*fama, -ae* f.		repute, fame
candens, -entis	dazzling			

714–5 **invectus . . . moenia**: 'carried into the city', and so 'riding into the city'. **Romana . . . moenia**: 'the city of Rome'. **triplici . . . triumpho**: 'in a threefold triumph'; Octavian had won victories over the rebel forces at Actium, in Dalmatia, and at Alexandria. Victorious generals were awarded a triumph upon their return to Rome; the triumph consisted of a procession through the city, made up of the victorious soldiers, enemy captives and captured arms and loot. **votum immortale**: 'an immortal vow', i.e. a vow that not even death could revoke.

716 The line is in apposition to *votum*, explaining what the vow comprised. **ter centum**: an example of <u>hyperbole</u>: Augustus himself claimed to have restored 82 temples and built 12 new ones. **maxima . . . delubra**: another example of <u>hyperbole</u>: the temples were not especially large.

717 **laetitia, ludis, plausu**: ablatives of manner, defining *fremebant*.

718 Supply *erat*. **omnibus arae**: in full this would be *in omnibus templis erant arae*; since altars were always outside the temples, several metres in front, so that the public could attend sacrifices, *omnibus* is best translated as 'at all the temples'.

719 **stravere**: 'were strewn across'.

720 **ipse**: Augustus. **candentis . . . Phoebi**: 'of the dazzling temple of Apollo'; it was *candentis* because it was covered with white marble. Augustus built this temple in 24 BC.

721–2 **populorum**: i.e. all the subject nations. **superbis postibus**: the temple doorways are 'proud' because they are so resplendent with their new marble; it was customary to hang offerings on temple doorways.

722–3 **incedunt**: they form part of the triumphal procession. **longo ordine**: ablative of manner. **quam . . . tam**: *variae* is to be taken twice: '(they were) as varied in in style of dress and arms as they were in their languages'. Virgil proceeds to list the tribes and nations involved.

729–31 **talia . . . miratur**: 'such were the things he admired'. **per clipeum**: 'all across the shield'. **dona**: in apposition to *talia*. **rerum ignarus**: 'though ignorant of the events (depicted)'; this is important, because despite his ignorance he was both impressed by the gift and fired with a new enthusiasm to complete his destiny, understanding as he did that the events shown on the shield were destined to involve his descendants in centuries to come. In this respect the shield reinforced what he had learned during his visit to the underworld in Book VI. **attollens umero**: he hoisted the shield onto his shoulders, and with it the fame and destiny of his descendants.

Questions for pages 76–77

1 What is being described in lines 714–723?

2 Why do you think Virgil thought this important?

3 How realistic is the description of the shield?

4 How appropriate is this ending for Book VIII?

Book 9

While Aeneas was away from his camp seeking allies, Juno sent Iris, her messenger, to visit Turnus. Iris told him that it would be sensible to attack the Trojan camp while Aeneas was absent. Turnus recognised the goddess and vowed to the gods to do as he was advised.

iamque omnis campis exercitus ibat apertis	25
dives equum, dives pictai vestis et auri;	
Messapus primas acies, postrema coercent	
Tyrrhidae iuvenes, medio dux agmine Turnus:	28
ceu septem surgens sedatis amnibus altus	30
per tacitum Ganges aut pingui flumine Nilus	
cum refluit campis et iam se condidit alveo.	
hic subitam nigro glomerari pulvere nubem	
prospiciunt Teucri ac tenebras insurgere campis.	
primus ab adversa conclamat mole Caicus:	35
'quis globus, o cives, caligine volvitur atra?	
ferte citi ferrum, date tela, ascendite muros,	
hostis adest, heia!'	

iam	25	now	
campus, -i m.		plain, open ground	
exercitus, -us m.		army	
eo, ire		I go	
apertus, -a, -um		open	
dives, -itis		rich	
equus, -i m.		horse	
pingo, -ere, pinxi, pictus		I paint, embroider	
vestis, -is f.		clothes	
aurum, -i n.		gold	
Messapus, -i m.		Messapus	
primus, -a, -um		first	
acies, -ei f.		battle line	
postremus, -a, -um		last	
coerceo, -ere		I enclose, command	
Tyrrhidae, -arum m.pl.		the sons of Tyrrheus	
iuvenis, -is m.		young, young man	
medius, -a, -um		the middle (of)	
dux, ducis m.		leader	
agmen, -inis n.		army, column	
Turnus, -i m.		Turnus	
ceu	30	just like	
surgo, -ere		I rise	
sedatus, -a, -um		calm, tranquil	
amnis, -is m.		river, tributary	
altus, -a, -um		high, deep	
tacitus, -a, -um		silent	
Ganges, -is m.		river Ganges	
aut		or	
pinguis, -e		fertile	
flumen, -inis n.		river	
Nilus, -i m.		river Nile	
refluo, -ere		I flow back	
condo, -ere		I hide, enclose, bury	
alveus, -i m.		river bed	
subitus, -a, -um		sudden	
niger, -gra, -grum		black	
glomero, -are		I mass	
pulvis, -eris m.		dust	
nubes, -is f.		cloud	
prospicio, -ere		I observe	
Teucri, -orum m.pl.		Trojans	
tenebrae, -arum f.pl.		darkness	
insurgo, -ere		I rise	
adversus, -a, -um	35	facing	
conclamo, -are		I shout	
moles, -is f.		embankment	
Caicus, -i m.		Caicus	
globus, -i m.		mass	
civis, -is m.		citizen	
caligo, -inis f.		murk	
volvo, -ere		I roll	
ater, atra, atrum		black	
citus, -a, -um		quick	
ferrum, -i n.		iron, sword	
telum, -i n.		missile, weapon	
ascendo, -ere		I climb onto	
murus, -i m.		wall	
hostis, -is m.		enemy	
adsum, -esse		I am here	
heia!		come on!	

25 **omnis . . . exercitus:** that is the combined forces of the Latins and their allies, mostly neighbouring tribes. **campis . . . apertis:** local ablative: 'across the open plains'.

26 **dives equum:** 'rich in horses'; *equum = equorum*, a genitive of respect, as are the two following genitives. **pictai:** an archaic form of the genitive *pictae*.

27–8 **Messapus:** a son of Neptune, who could not be killed by fire or iron; supply *coercet* as the verb. **postrema:** 'the rear'. **coercent:** this is the first of many historic presents, which are standard throughout Virgil's narrative. **Tyrrhidae iuvenes:** 'the young sons of Tyrrheus'; Tyrrheus had two sons, who were the brothers of Silvia, whose pet stag had been killed by Ascanius (Aeneas' son); it was this action that caused war to break out. **dux . . . Turnus:** supply *erat*. **medio . . . agmine:** local ablative. **Turnus:** the leader of the Rutuli, a neighbouring tribe, he was betrothed to king Latinus' daughter, Lavinia; but when the Trojans appeared in Latium, Latinus remembered a prophecy that his daughter should marry a foreigner, and so offered her to Aeneas. The goddess Juno was able to use this as a lever to persuade Turnus to take up arms against the Trojans (Book VII.323ff.).

29 This line is rejected by most editors, and has been omitted here.

30–1 **ceu:** this word regularly introduces a <u>simile</u>; here the tide of warriors is compared to the onward march of a river. The order is *ceu altus Ganges, septem amnibus sedatis, surgens per tacitum.* **Ganges:** this river rises to the north of India and flows south-eastwards to the Bay of Bengal; thus it was well beyond the boundaries of the Roman Empire; Virgil must have heard accounts of it from merchants who traded with India and beyond. **septem amnibus:** 'because of its seven tributaries'; it is actually said to have six main tributaries; Virgil may have confused them with the seven branches of the Nile in the Delta. **altus:** the river is 'deep' after the seven tributaries have merged. **per tacitum:** this is generally taken to mean simply 'quietly'. Note the strong <u>sibilance</u> and <u>assonance</u>, and the slow rhythm of line 30.

31–2 **pingui flumine:** 'with its fertile river'; it is fertile following the annual flood, which brings rich nutrients down to fertilise the margins and delta in Lower Egypt. **cum refluit campis:** 'when it has flowed back (into its channel) from the open fields'. **alveo:** 'in its (proper) channel'. The point of the double simile is that the rivers have changed: the Ganges has become a single river having accumulated water from many different areas, while the Nile has ended its widespread flood and become a single river again.

33–4 **hic:** 'at this point'. **subitam . . . nubem:** 'a sudden cloud'. **nigro . . . pulvere:** 'of black dust' (ablative of description). **glomerari:** 'massing'. **tenebras insurgere campis:** 'darkness rising up across the plains'.

35 **ab adversa . . . mole:** 'from the embankment (i.e. rampart) facing the enemy'. **Caicus:** the only other mention of him is as a Trojan ship's captain in Book I.

36 **caligine . . . atra:** 'in black murk' (ablative of manner).

37–8 **citi:** best translated as an adverb. **ferrum, tela:** *ferrum* is used of weapons held in the hand, i.e. swords, while *tela* are weapons thrown, usually javelins.

Questions

1 What tribes and regional groups made up the bulk of Turnus' army?

2 How does Virgil make Turnus' army seem more significant?

3 Explain the simile and show how it is appropriate.

4 What causes the alarm to be sounded in the Trojan camp?

                        ingenti clamore per omnes
condunt se Teucri portas et moenia complent.
namque ita discedens praeceperat optimus armis   40
Aeneas: si qua interea fortuna fuisset,
neu struere auderent aciem neu credere campo;
castra modo et tutos servarent aggere muros.
ergo etsi conferre manum pudor iraque monstrat,
obiciunt portas tamen et praecepta facessunt,   45
armatique cavis exspectant turribus hostem.
Turnus, ut ante volans tardum praecesserat agmen
viginti lectis equitum comitatus et urbi
improvisus adest, maculis quem Thracius albis
portat equus cristaque tegit galea aurea rubra,   50
'ecquis erit mecum, iuvenes, qui primus in hostem – ?
en,' ait et iaculum attorquens emittit in auras,
principium pugnae, et campo sese arduus infert.

ingens, -entis	huge	*exspecto, -are*	I wait for
clamor, -oris m.	shout	*turris, -is* f.	tower
porta, -ae f.	gate	*ante*	ahead, forwards,
moenia, -ium n.pl.	walls		before
compleo, -ere	I fill	*volo, -are*	I fly, dash
namque 40	for	*tardus, -a, -um*	slow
discedo, -ere	I depart	*praecedo, -ere, -cessi, -cessus*	I precede
praecipio, -ere, -cepi, -ceptus	I instruct	*viginti*	twenty
arma, -orum n.pl.	arms	*lego, -ere, legi, lectus*	I choose
interea	meanwhile	*equites, -um* m.pl.	cavalry
fortuna, -ae f.	emergency	*comito, -are, -avi, -atus*	I accompany
neu . . . neu	neither . . . nor	*urbs, urbis* f.	city
struo, -ere	I arrange for	*improvisus, -a, -um*	unexpected
	battle	*macula, -ae* f.	spot
audeo, -ere	I dare	*Thracius, -a, -um*	Thracian
acies, -ei f.	battle-line	*albus, -a, -um*	white
credo, -ere + dat.	I trust	*porto, -are* 50	I carry
castra, -orum n.pl.	camp	*crista, -ae* f.	crest
modo	only	*tego, -ere*	I cover, conceal
tutus, -a, -um	safe	*galea, -ae* f.	helmet
servo, -are	I protect, keep	*aureus, -a, -um*	golden
agger, -eris m.	rampart	*ruber, rubra, rubrum*	red
ergo	therefore	*ecquis, ecquae, ecquid*	any one?
etsi	although	*en*	see!
confero, -ferre	I join together	*aio* (defective verb)	I say
manus, -us f.	hand, group	*iaculum, -i* n.	javelin
pudor, -oris m.	shame	*attorqueo, -ere*	I tilt upwards
ira, irae f.	anger	*emitto, -ere*	I throw
monstro, -are	I indicate, show	*aura, -ae* f.	air, breeze
obicio, -ere 45	I close	*principium, -i* n.	beginning
praeceptum, -i n.	command	*pugna, -ae* f.	battle, fight
facesso, -ere	I carry out	*arduus, -a, -um*	towering
armo, -are, -avi, -atus	I arm	*infero, -ferre*	I carry forward
cavus, -a, -um	hollow		

38–9 condunt se: '(they) hide themselves', i.e. those outside the camp 'seek shelter' within. **moenia complent:** 'fill the walls', i.e. 'man the walls', that is the perimeter wall of the camp, which would have been provided with a walkway atop an embankment, defended by a palisade.

40–1 optimus armis Aeneas: 'Aeneas best in arms' (ablative of respect). Note the enjambement, which has the effect of making his name a climax to which the rest of the sentence builds. Like any good general, Aeneas had made provision for a possible enemy attack before he left on his mission to find allies.

41–2 si qua . . . fortuna: 'if any (bad) fortune', and so 'emergency'. **fuisset:** these two lines are to be read as an indirect command, introduced by *praeceperat*; *fuisset* therefore represents the future perfect indicative of direct speech ('if there will have been an emergency, you should . . .'). **neu . . . neu:** these introduce alternative negative indirect commands. **neu credere campo:** 'nor to trust the plain', i.e. 'entrust themselves to the field of battle'.

43 castra: like *muros*, the object of *servarent*. **tutos:** best taken with both *castra* and *muros*: they should protect them with a rampart, i.e. embankment of earth.

44–5 pudor iraque: the two emotional responses to the threat of an attack. **conferre manum:** a military term meaning 'to engage in close combat'. **monstrat:** the indicative marks a return to the narrative; the meaning and syntax are unusual: it is singular despite having two subjects; it takes an infinitive instead of *ut* + subjunctive (for an indirect command); and the meaning, lit. 'show', is here 'indicate' or even 'suggest'. The argument is that, although the men's natural inclination was to fight, they obeyed Aeneas' instructions (*praecepta facessunt*).

46 cavis . . . turribus: 'in the hollow towers' (local ablative); Virgil supposes that, as in his own day, military camps were fortified with towers at intervals along the perimeter walls.

47–50 ut: 'as'. **viginti lectis equitum:** accompanied 'by twenty chosen cavalrymen'; the genitive is partitive, and can be ignored in translation. **et:** some take this to equal *etiam*: 'he actually reached'; but that would leave the main verb *ait* (line 52) with asyndeton, which Virgil does not normally do; perhaps it is simplest to take it as joining *praecesserat* and *adest*: 'he had gone ahead and (now) was present'. **urbi:** dependent on *adest*. **improvisus:** his approach was unexpected because the Trojans had kept their eyes on the main body of enemy troops. **Thracius . . . equus:** Thrace was renowned for its horses and horsemanship. **maculis . . . albis:** ablative of description. **crista . . . rubra:** another ablative of description.

51 equis erit: 'will there be anyone'. **qui primus in hostem:** supply *ibit*; 'who will will be the first (with me) (to go) against the enemy'. Turnus interrupts himself to throw his javelin and never finishes the question.

52 en: he draws his companions' attention to his cast. **attorquens:** Virgil is fond of *torqueo* and its compounds, and they are often difficult to translate; the meaning given opposite gives more sense than 'brandishing' or 'hurling'.

53 principium: this is accusative in loose apposition to the previous line. In Virgil's day the standard way of declaring war was to hurl a javelin into enemy territory. **campo:** dative of goal of motion; a *campus* was any piece of open ground, clear of trees and cultivation; here it refers to the ground that the Trojans would have cleared of shrubs and trees around their camp to give them a clear view of hostile activity. **sese . . . infert:** 'carried himself in(to the plain)', i.e. 'rushed into the open ground'.

Questions

1 How does Virgil make clear Aeneas' leadership qualities?

2 How does Virgil show Turnus' impetuous nature?

clamorem excipiunt socii fremituque sequuntur
horrisono; Teucrum mirantur inertia corda,   55
non aequo dare se campo, non obvia ferre
arma viros, sed castra fovere. huc turbidus atque huc
lustrat equo muros aditumque per avia quaerit.
ac veluti pleno lupus insidiatus ovili
cum fremit ad caulas ventos perpessus et imbres   60
nocte super media; tuti sub matribus agni
balatum exercent, ille asper et improbus ira
saevit in absentes, collecta fatigat edendi
ex longo rabies et siccae sanguine fauces:
haud aliter Rutulo muros et castra tuenti   65
ignescunt irae; duris dolor ossibus ardet.
qua temptet ratione aditus, et quae via clausos
excutiat Teucros vallo atque effundat in aequum?

excipio, -ere	I catch, follow on	*agnus, -i* m.	lamb
socius, -i m.	ally	*balatus, -us* m.	bleating
fremitus, -us m.	roar	*exerceo, -ere*	I carry on
sequor, -i, secutus sum	I follow	*asper, -era, -erum*	cruel
horrisonus, -a, -um 55	dreadful-sounding	*improbus, -a, -um*	reckless
miror, -ari, -atus sum	I am amazed at	*saevio, -ire*	I rage
iners, -rtis	cowardly	*absens, -entis*	absent
cor, cordis n.	heart	*colligo, -ere, -egi, -ectus*	I gather
aequus, -a, -um	level	*fatigo, -are*	I torment
obvius, -a, -um	to meet	*edo, -ere*	I eat
foveo, -ere	I keep to	*longus, -a, -um*	long
huc atque huc	this way and that	*rabies, -ei* f.	rage, fury
turbidus, -a, -um	wild	*siccus, -a, -um*	dry, parched
lustro, -are	I scan	*sanguis, -inis* m.	blood
aditus, -us m.	entrance	*fauces, -ium* f.pl.	jaws
avius, -a, -um	pathless	*haud* 65	not
quaero, -ere	I seek	*aliter*	differently
veluti	just as	*Rutulus, -i* m.	Rutulian
plenus, -a, -um	full	*tueor, -eri, tuitus sum*	I observe
lupus, -i m.	wolf	*ignesco, -ere*	I ignite
insidior, -ari, -atus sum + dat.	I plot against	*durus, -a, -um*	hard
ovile, -is n.	sheep-fold	*dolor, -oris* m.	pain, rage
fremo, -ere	I roar, howl	*os, ossis* n.	bone
caulae, -arum f.pl. 60	enclosure	*ardeo, -ere*	I burn
ventus, -i m.	wind	*tempto, -are*	I try
perpetior, -i, -pessus sum	I endure	*ratio, -ionis* f.	means
imber, -bris m.	rain	*claudo, -ere, -si, -sus*	I shut in
nox, noctis f.	night	*excutio, -ere*	I drive out
super + abl.	at	*vallum, -i* n.	rampart
mater, matris f.	mother	*effundo, -ere*	I pour forth

54–5 clamorem excipiunt: 'take up his cry', i.e. they echo or copy his cry. **horrisono:** a strong adjective made even stronger by the enjambement. **Teucrum:** = *Teucrorum*.

56–7 non . . . dare se: the infinitive (along with *ferre* and *fovere*) serves to give an example of *inertia corda*; all have *viros* as their subject: 'their cowardly hearts: that the men do not give themselves (i.e. entrust themselves) . . .'. **obvia . . . arma:** 'arms to meet (them)', i.e. 'arms against them'. **castra fovere:** lit. 'keep their camp warm'; *fovere* is used derogatively as another accusation of cowardice.

57–8 turbidus: supply *Turnus* and translate as an adverb. **equo:** local ablative. **per avia:** 'through the pathless (areas)'; i.e. he searches for entrances where there are none.

59–61 ac veluti . . . cum: introduces an extended simile. **pleno . . . ovili:** note the enclosing word order, with the wolf already 'inside' the full sheep-fold. **ad caulas:** 'right up to the enclosure'. **nocte super media:** 'at midnight', a rare and virtually redundant use of *super*.

62–4 ille: the wolf. **in absentes:** supply *agnos*: 'against the lambs he cannot reach'. **collecta . . . ex longo rabies:** 'a mad craving, long-gathered'. **edendi:** 'of eating', i.e. 'to eat' (a sort of objective genitive). **fatigat:** singular despite having two subjects; supply *eum*. **siccae sanguine fauces:** 'jaws dry of blood', i.e. 'his jaws deprived of blood' (ablative of separation); note the sibilance.

65–6 haud aliter: 'in just the same way', relating the simile back to the narrative. **Rutulo:** i.e. Turnus; the dative is that of the person interested. **tuenti:** 'as he observed'. **duris . . . ossibus:** 'in his hard bones'; the bones were seen as the core of the being and the seat of the emotions.

67–8 qua . . . ratione: 'by what means'. **temptet . . . aditus:** 'might he try to gain entry'; this is a deliberative question, representing his thought process. **quae via:** 'what approach', introducing another deliberative question. **vallo:** 'from the rampart' (ablative of separation). **in aequum:** 'on to the plain'.

Questions

1 In lines 54–55, how does Virgil show the aggression of the Rutulians?

2 What surprises the Rutulians?

3 Explain the simile and show how it is appropriate.

4 How does Virgil emphasise the anger and frustration of Turnus?

5 What three objectives does Turnus have?

classem, quae lateri castrorum adiuncta latebat,
aggeribus saeptam circum et fluvialibus undis,   70
invadit sociosque incendia poscit ovantes
atque manum pinu flagranti fervidus implet.
tum vero incumbunt (urget praesentia Turni),
atque omnis facibus pubes accingitur atris.
diripuere focos: piceum fert fumida lumen   75
taeda et commixtam Volcanus ad astra favillam.

At this point Cybele, mother of the gods, saved the ships, which had been built of timber cut from forests sacred to her. She turned each ship into a sea nymph. While the rest were terrified by this portent, Turnus claimed that it was the Trojans who had been punished, because they had now lost their ships and so could not escape. His army now laid siege to the camp. The Trojans observed this in trepidation.

Nisus erat portae custos, acerrimus armis,   176
Hyrtacides, comitem Aeneae quem miserat Ida
venatrix iaculo celerem levibusque sagittis;
et iuxta comes Euryalus, quo pulchrior alter
non fuit Aeneadum Troiana neque induit arma,   180
ora puer prima signans intonsa iuventa.

classis, -is f.	fleet	*taeda, -ae* f.	pine-torch
latus, -eris n.	side	*commisceo, -ere, -ui, -xtus*	I mix together
adiungo, -ere, -iunxi, -iunctus	I join to	*Volcanus, -i* m.	Vulcan, fire
lateo, -ere	I lie hidden	*astrum, -i* n.	star
saepio, -ire, -psi, -ptus 70	I enclose, fence	*favilla, -ae* f.	embers, ashes
circum	around	*Nisus, -i* m. 176	Nisus
fluvialis, -e	of a river	*custos, -odis* m.	guard, sentry
unda, -ae f.	wave, water	*acer, acris, acre*	fierce, valiant
invado, -ere	I attack, attempt	*Hyrtacides, -ae* m.	son of Hyrtacus
incendium, -i n.	fire	*comes, -itis* m.	companion
posco, -ere	I demand, ask	*Ida, -ae* f.	Ida
ovo, -are	I rejoice	*venatrix, -icis* f.	huntress
pinus, -us f.	pine-torch	*celer, -eris, -ere*	swift
flagro, -are	I blaze	*levis, -e*	light
fervidus, -a, -um	fiery, violent	*sagitta, -ae* f.	arrow
impleo, -ere	I fill	*iuxta*	alongside
vero	indeed	*Euryalus, -i* m.	Euryalus
incumbo, -ere	I set to work	*pulcher, -ra, -rum*	beautiful, handsome
urgeo, -ere	I encourage		
praesentia, -ae f.	presence	*alter, -era, -erum*	other
fax, facis f.	torch	*Aeneades, -ae* m. 180	follower of Aeneas
pubes, -is f.	men		
accingo, -ere	I arm	*Troianus, -a, -um*	Trojan
diripio, -ere, -ui, -reptus 75	I plunder	*induo, -ere, -ui, -utus*	I put on
focus, -i m.	hearth	*os, oris* n.	face
piceus, -a, -um	(of) pitch	*signo, -are*	I mark
fumidus, -a, -um	smoky	*intonsus, -a, -um*	unshaven
lumen, -inis n.	light	*iuventa, -ae* f.	youth

69–71 classem: this is the object of *invadit* in line 71; it refers to the Trojan fleet. Note the emphatic position of the word. **latebat:** clearly the fleet was not successfully hidden; probably Virgil uses this verb to provide <u>alliteration</u> and <u>assonance</u> with *lateri*. **aggeribus, undis:** instrumental ablatives. **fluvialibus undis:** the fleet was drawn up on the shore between the camp and the river, thus being protected on two sides.

71–2 sociosque incendia poscit: *poscit* takes two direct objects; *incendia* is plural for singular. **ovantes:** an example of <u>prolepsis</u>: the companions rejoice when the plan has been put into operation, not before it. **fervidus:** best translated as an adverb.

73–4 Note the slow rhythm; perhaps the idea, reinforced by *tum vero*, is to emphasise the gravity of the threat to the Trojans. **urget praesentia Turni:** Turnus sets the example for the rest to follow. **accingitur:** 'arm themselves (with)'; the passive replaces the reflexive *se* with the active. **facibus . . . atris:** note the <u>enclosing word order</u>; surprisingly the torches are 'black', either because they are giving off large quantities of smoke or because of the 'dark' work they are about to do.

75–6 These two lines explain the source of the torches. **diripuere:** = *diripuerunt*; the use of the perfect in the midst of so many historic presents has the effect of marking the action as instantaneous. **focos:** the location of these hearths is uncertain; possibly by this time the rest of the Latin army had arrived and set up camp, one of the first actions being to start fires for cooking; the only other possibility is that the Trojans for some reason had built fires outside their camp, only to abandon them when the enemy appeared. **piceum fert fumida lumen taeda:** here are examples of <u>alliteration</u> (*f*), <u>assonance</u> (*um*) and <u>synchysis</u>. **piceum . . . lumen:** i.e. light produced by burning pitch; the pitch would have been obtained from pine trees and would perhaps have formed a standard part of a soldier's kit. **taeda:** singular for plural. **Volcanus:** supply *fert* again; Virgil either personifies the fire or imagines that the god was there in person. **commixtam favillam:** lit. 'ashes mingled together', i.e. ashes mingled with smoke and sparks; it is unclear whether Virgil means the ashes from the burning torches or those from the ships as they began to burn.

176–8 Nisus . . . Hyrtacides: Nisus, along with his young friend Euryalus, has already appeared, in the foot-race described in Book V.294ff., where the nature of their relationship was also in question. **armis:** ablative of respect. **Ida venatrix:** presumably the mother of Nisus. **comitem:** 'as a companion'. **iaculo, sagittis:** ablatives of respect.

179–81 iuxta: supply *erat*. **quo:** 'than whom'. **alter:** 'any other'. **Aeneadum:** genitive plural. **Troiana . . . arma:** note the <u>enclosing word order</u>. **ora . . . intonsa:** 'his unshaven cheeks'. **signans:** lit. 'marking', i.e. 'showing' (his cheeks). **prima . . . iuventa:** 'in his first youth', i.e. 'at the beginning of his manhood'. The poetic image is intended to mean that his cheeks were showing the first evidence of beard growth, but not sufficiently for him to start shaving.

Questions

1 How is the Trojan fleet protected from attack? Why is this inadequate?

2 How does Virgil emphasise the threat to the ships?

3 Explain how torches were made.

4 Read the episode of the foot-race in Book V (in translation) and describe the two young men.

5 How does Virgil here build up the qualities of Nisus and Euryalus? Why does he do this?

his amor unus erat pariterque in bella ruebant;
tum quoque communi portam statione tenebant.
Nisus ait: 'dine hunc ardorem mentibus addunt,
Euryale, an sua cuique deus fit dira cupido?   185
aut pugnam aut aliquid iamdudum invadere magnum
mens agitat mihi, nec placida contenta quiete est.
cernis quae Rutulos habeat fiducia rerum:
lumina rara micant, somno vinoque soluti
procubuere, silent late loca. percipe porro   190
quid dubitem et quae nunc animo sententia surgat.
Aenean acciri omnes, populusque patresque,
exposcunt, mittique viros qui certa reportent.
si tibi quae posco promittunt (nam mihi facti
fama sat est), tumulo videor reperire sub illo   195
posse viam ad muros et moenia Pallantea.'

Nisus wished to go alone, in order not to endanger the life of his friend. But Euryalus insisted on going with him. In the end, Nisus gave way, and the two went off to find Iulus and the other leaders.

amor, -oris m.	love	*vinum, -i* n.	wine
pariter	equally	*solvo, -ere, solvi, solutus*	I relax
bellum, -i n.	war	*procumbo, -ere, -cubui, -itus*	I sink down
ruo, -ere	I rush	*sileo, -ere*	190 I am silent
communis, -e	shared	*late*	far and wide
statio, -onis f.	sentry duty	*locus, -i* m. (pl. *loca*)	place
teneo, -ere	I hold	*percipio, -ere*	I learn, note
deus, -i m.	god	*porro*	besides
ardor, -oris m.	keenness	*dubito, -are*	I consider
mens, mentis f.	mind	*animus, -i* m.	mind
addo, -ere	I add	*sententia, -ae* f.	opinion
an	185 or	*Aeneas, -ae* m. (acc. *-an*)	Aeneas
quisque, quaeque, quidque	each	*accio, -ire*	I summon
fio, fieri, factus sum	I become	*populus, -i* m.	people
dirus, -a, -um	dreadful	*pater, -tris* m.	father, elder
cupido, -inis f.	desire	*exposco, -ere*	I beg
aut . . . aut	either . . . or	*mitto, -ere*	I send
aliquis, -quid	someone,	*certus, -a, -um*	certain, definite
	something	*reporto, -are*	I report
iamdudum	for long now	*promitto, -ere*	I promise
agito, -are	I urge	*factum, -i* n.	deed
placidus, -a, -um	peaceful	*fama, -ae* f.	195 fame
contentus, -a, -um	content	*sat* (indecl.)	enough
quies, -etis f.	rest	*tumulus, -i* m.	mound
cerno, -ere	I see	*videor, -eri, visus sum*	I seem
fiducia, -ae f.	confidence	*reperio, -ire*	I find
res, rei f.	thing, affair	*sub* + abl.	under
rarus, -a, -um	sparse	*via, -ae* f.	way
mico, -are	I shine	*Pallanteus, -a, -um*	of Pallanteum
somnus, -i m.	sleep		

182 his: i.e. for Nisus and Euryalus. **pariter:** i.e. 'side by side'.

183 tum quoque: these two words mark the return to the main narrative. **communi . . . statione:** ablatives either of manner or instrument.

184–5 dine: = *dei-ne*. **hunc ardorem:** 'this thirst (for battle)'. **mentibus:** 'to (our) minds'; he is probably thinking in general terms. **an sua cuique deus fit dira cupido:** 'or does his own terrible desire become for each man a god'; this is a profound idea, asking rhetorically whether a man's lust for fighting is instilled in him by the gods, or whether each man generates his own violent tendencies, conveniently attributing them to a divine source. We may ask these questions about all the main events in the *Aeneid*, and indeed in Homer's works before that.

186–7 The order is *iamdudum mens mihi agitat invadere aut pugnam aut aliquid magnum*. **iamdudum:** 'for a long time now', taking the present instead of the perfect required by English. **mens mihi agitat:** 'my mind has been urging (me)'; *mihi* is effectively a possessive dative. **invadere:** a poetic version of *ut invadam*. **aliquid . . . magnum:** 'some (other) great (undertaking)'. Note the heavy <u>alliteration</u> and <u>consonance</u> of *m*, reflecting the strong passion behind his words. **placida contenta:** scansion will show that *placida* qualifies *quiete*, while *contenta* describes *mens*. He is in effect saying he is a warrior by inclination, not a pacifist.

188 quae Rutulos habeat fiducia: a poetic inversion of the more prosaic *quam fiduciam Rutuli habeant*: here the confidence possesses the Rutuli. **rerum:** confidence 'in things', i.e. 'in their situation'.

189–90 lumina: these are the lights from camp fires; the fact that they are few and far between indicates that most of the Rutuli are asleep. **somno vinoque:** instrumental ablatives. **soluti:** supply *Rutuli*. **procubuere:** note the <u>enjambement</u>. **procubuere:** i.e. they are asleep.

190–1 quid dubitem: not 'why I am hesitating' but 'what I am considering', as shown by the following clause, which amplifies the meaning of this one. **animo:** local ablative.

192–3 Aenean acciri: indirect command dependent on *exposcunt*, poetic for *ut acciatur*. **populusque patresque:** these identify *omnes*; in Virgil's day senators were often called *patres*; he applies this custom to the earlier period. **mittique viros:** another indirect command; note the <u>chiasmus</u> formed with *Aenean acciri*. **qui certa reportent:** *qui* + subjunctive expressing purpose: 'to report the true situation' (to him).

194–6 si . . . promittunt: 'if they (i.e. *populusque patresque*) promise'; the future or future perfect would have been more usual, as his unexpressed thought is 'I shall go to Aeneas'; instead of saying this, he points out where he believes his destination lies; the present tense gives more immediacy to the hoped-for action. **tibi:** Nisus suggests that he will ask for rewards for his bravery, but will request that they be given to Euryalus, as he himself wants only the *facti fama* (glory of the deed), in traditional heroic fashion. **videor reperire . . . posse:** 'I seem to be able to find', i.e. 'I think I can find'. **tumulo . . . sub illo:** 'beneath that mound'; clearly Nisus is pointing to a hill some distance away. **muros et moenia:** an example of <u>tautology</u>, though *moenia* may be translated as 'city'. **Pallantea:** Pallanteum was the city founded by Evander on the site of the future Rome; it is here that Aeneas has gone to seek an alliance with the king (see Book VIII). Note the rare spondaic 5th foot, involving a name, as most commonly.

Questions

1 Summarise the different stages of Nisus' speech.

2 How does Nisus add vividness and emotion to his words?

3 What impression do you get of Nisus from this speech? Give reasons for your answer.

cetera per terras omnes animalia somno   224
laxabant curas et corda oblita laborum: 225
ductores Teucrum primi, delecta iuventus,
consilium summis regni de rebus habebant,
quid facerent quisve Aeneae iam nuntius esset.
stant longis adnixi hastis et scuta tenentes
castrorum et campi medio. tum Nisus et una   230
Euryalus confestim alacres admittier orant;
rem magnam pretiumque morae fore. primus Iulus
accepit trepidos ac Nisum dicere iussit.

*Nisus repeated the arguments he had made to Euryalus. His plan found favour and
Ascanius joined in the praise.*

'immo ego vos, cui sola salus genitore reducto,'   257
excipit Ascanius 'per magnos, Nise, penates
Assaracique larem et canae penetralia Vestae
obtestor, quaecumque mihi fortuna fidesque est,   260
in vestris pono gremiis; revocate parentem,
reddite conspectum: nihil illo triste recepto.'

Ascanius promised lavish rewards to both men and close friendship to Euryalus.

ceteri, -ae, -a	the rest (of)	*immo*	257 yes indeed
animal, -alis n.	animal	*solus, -a, -um*	only, alone
laxo, -are	225 I release, relax	*salus, -utis* f.	safety
cura, -ae f.	care, anxiety	*genitor, -oris* m.	father
obliviscor, -i, oblitus sum	I forget	*reduco, -ere, -duxi, -ductus*	I bring back
labor, -oris m.	work, toil	*Ascanius, -i* m.	Ascanius
ductor, -oris m.	leader	*penates, -ium* m.pl.	penates
deligo, -ere, -legi, -lectus	I choose	*Assaracus, -i* m.	Assaracus
iuventus, -utis f.	young men	*lar, laris* m.	lar
consilium, -i n.	consultation	*canus, -a, -um*	ancient
summus, -a, -um	most important	*penetralia, -ium* n.pl.	shrine
regnum, -i n.	kingdom	*Vesta, -ae* f.	Vesta
nuntius, -i m.	messenger	*obtestor, -ari, -atus sum*	260 I appeal to
sto, stare	I stand, stop	*qui-, quae-, quodcumque*	whoever,
adnitor, -i, -nixus sum	I lean upon		whatever
hasta, -ae f.	spear	*fortuna, -ae* f.	fortune
scutum, -i n.	shield	*fides, -ei* f.	trust
medium, -i n.	230 middle	*vester, -tra, -trum*	your
una	together	*pono, -ere*	I place
confestim	hastily	*gremium, -i* n.	lap
alacer, -cris, -cre	eager, keen	*revoco, -are*	I recall
admitto, -ere	I admit	*parens, -entis* m/f.	parent
oro, -are	I beg	*reddo, -ere*	I restore
pretium, -i n.	price	*conspectus, -us* m.	sight
Iulus, -i m.	Iulus	*nihil* n. (indecl.)	nothing
accipio, -ere, -cepi, -ceptus	I welcome	*tristis, -e*	grim
trepidus, -a, -um	excited	*recipio, -ere, -cepi, -ceptus*	I recover
iubeo, -ere, iussi, iussus	I order		

224–5 somno: 'in sleep' (ablative of instrument). **curas et corda:** both are direct objects of *laxabant*, which is used with two slightly different meanings: 'were releasing (their anxieties) and relaxing (their bodies)'; this is an example of <u>zeugma</u>. **laborum:** *obliviscor* takes a genitive.

226 primi: almost redundant, as it hardly adds to *ductores*. **delecta iuventus:** a favourite expression of Virgil (cf. Book VIII.499); in Virgil's day *iuventus* was regularly used to mean men still qualified by age for military service, after which they became *senes* (at around 50).

228 Supply a verb such as *rogantes* to introduce the two indirect deliberative questions.

229–30 Note the slow rhythm of line 229, reinforcing *stant* and the duration of the discussion. **longis . . . hastis:** *hastae* were longer than *pila* (javelins), as they were used by men in the front ranks to thrust at the enemy when fighting came to close quarters. Clearly the men were in a constant state of readiness for any assault on the camp. **castrorum et campi medio:** 'in the middle of the open space in the camp'; clearly *campo* does not refer to the battleground outside the camp, but to the area in the centre of the camp where soldiers could gather to line up and receive orders, etc. The phrase may be translated as an example of <u>hendiadys</u>.

230–1 alacres: best translated as an adverb. **admittier:** an archaic form of the passive infinitive, here used as a poetical alternative to the *ut admitterentur* of prose.

232 rem magnam: supply *esse*; this is an indirect statement dependent on a verb to be supplied, such as *dixerunt* or *dicunt*. **pretiumque morae fore:** modern editors take this to mean 'and it would be worth the delay', that is the delay to the conference that their entry has caused. *Pretium* can have a good or a bad sense, of which the former provides the above interpretation: lit. 'there would be a (good) price (i.e. reward) for the delay'. The ancient commentator, Servius, however, notes the bad sense: 'there would be a (bad) price for delay', i.e. if the Trojans delayed sending them to fetch Aeneas, there would be a heavy price to pay. This second interpretation, considered 'curious' by Williams, seems to offer excellent sense, showing the impatience of the two young men.

257–60 vos: this is the object of *obtestor* (line 360), brought forward to provide the contrast with *ego*, as so frequently in Latin. **cui:** refers to Ascanius; supply *erit* or *est*. **genitore reducto:** ablative absolute, defining the source of the safety; translate 'whose safety depends entirely upon the return of my father'. **excipit Ascanius:** 'Ascanius followed on', i.e. followed the previous speaker in welcoming Nisus and Euryalus. **magnos . . . penates:** the penates were the household gods, worshipped in the form of figurines at shrines in every household in Roman times. Here they are described as 'great' because Ascanius is referring to the penates of the whole nation, symbolised by the statues given to Aeneas to convey to a new city, which they would protect in the same way that the ordinary penates protected each home. **Assaracique larem:** the lares were another type of household gods, worshipped in the same way as the penates; here the lar is thought of as an ancestral god, the spirit of Assaracus, who was the grandfather of Anchises. Ascanius invokes the spirits to witness his oath to the young men. **Vestae:** the goddess of fire was from ancient times associated with the lares and penates.

261–2 pono: the object of this verb is *quaecumque* in line 260. **conspectum:** supply *eius*. **nihil . . . triste:** supply *est* or *erit*.

Questions

1 Why do you think Virgil devotes two lines to describing other animals (lines 224–225)?

2 How does Virgil contrast the Trojan leaders with Nisus and Euryalus (lines 226–233)?

3 What impression do you get of Ascanius from his speech?

Euryalus asked Ascanius to take care of his mother if he failed to return. Ascanius promised to do so. Several of the leaders handed the two young men arms.

protinus armati incedunt; quos omnis euntes	308
primorum manus ad portas, iuvenumque senumque,	
prosequitur votis. nec non et pulcher Iulus,	310
ante annos animumque gerens curamque virilem,	
multa patri mandata dabat portanda; sed aurae	
omnia discerpunt et nubibus inrita donant.	
egressi superant fossas noctisque per umbram	
castra inimica petunt, multis tamen ante futuri	315
exitio. passim somno vinoque per herbam	
corpora fusa vident, arrectos litore currus,	
inter lora rotasque viros, simul arma iacere,	
vina simul. prior Hyrtacides sic ore locutus:	
'Euryale, audendum dextra: nunc ipsa vocat res.	320
hac iter est. tu, ne qua manus se attollere nobis	
a tergo possit, custodi et consule longe;	
haec ego vasta dabo et lato te limite ducam.'	

protinus	at once	*fundo, -ere, fudi, fusus*	I stretch out
incedo, -ere	I advance	*arrigo, -ere, -rexi, -rectus*	I set on end
primus, -i m.	leader	*litus, -oris* n.	shore
senex, -is m.	old man	*currus, -us* m.	chariot
prosequor, -i, -secutus sum	I escort	*inter* + acc.	between, among
votum, -i n.	310 prayer, vow	*lorum, -i* n.	strap
ante + acc.	before	*rota, -ae* f.	wheel
annus, -i m.	year	*simul*	at the same
gero, -ere	I wear, display		time
cura, -ae f.	care, concern	*iaceo, -ere*	I lie
virilis, -e	of a man	*prior, -us*	first
mandatum, -i n.	instruction	*loquor, -i, locutus sum*	I speak
discerpo, -ere	I scatter	*dextra, -ae* f.	320 right hand
nubes, -is f.	cloud	*voco, -are*	I call
inritus, -a, -um	useless	*hac*	this way
dono, -are	I give	*iter, itineris* n.	journey, way
egredior, -i, -gressus sum	I leave	*attollo, -ere*	I raise
supero, -are	I cross	*tergum, -i* n.	rear, back
fossa, -ae f.	ditch	*custodio, -ire*	I guard
umbra, -ae f.	shade, shelter	*consulo, -ere*	I keep watch
inimicus, -a, -um	315 hostile	*longe*	over a wide
peto, -ere	I seek, make for		area
exitium, -i n.	destruction	*vasta do, dare,*	I lay waste to
passim	everywhere	*latus, -a, -um*	broad
herba, -ae f.	grass	*limes, -itis* m.	path
corpus, -oris n.	body	*duco, -ere*	I lead, draw

308–10 **quos . . . euntes:** 'them as they went'. **iuvenumque senumque:** in apposition to
primorum, giving 'both younger and older (leaders)'; that is, both those still active in the
army and those who had retired from combat.

310–12 **nec non et:** 'and also'. **ante annos:** 'ahead of his years'. Note the <u>assonance</u>. **virilem:**
this repeats the idea of *ante annos*; note how the two phrases enclose the line. **patri . . .
portanda:** 'to be carried to his father'. Note that the <u>assonance</u> and <u>consonance</u> of *m, ma* and
an continue the theme of the previous line, indicating that the two lines together represent a
pivotal moment, full of pathos, as the next line shows.

312–13 **omnia, inrita:** supply *mandata*. The line indicates that Nisus failed to hear Ascanius'
instructions; at a deeper level it suggests that both Ascanius and Nisus were powerless in the
face of the inevitability of fate.

314–16 **fossas:** probably plural for singular; this would be the ditch dug outside the outer
wall of the camp, providing a first line of defence against attack; Virgil would have been
familiar with the military defences of his own day. **castra inimica:** perhaps simply 'the enemy
camp'. **tamen ante:** the thought behind these two words is very elliptical (compressed), being
in full 'however before (they were themselves killed), they would bring death to many'.
exitio: predicative dative, with *multis* a dative of disadvantage. Note the <u>enjambement</u>,
giving strong emphasis to *exitio*.

316–19 **somno vinoque:** dependent on *fusi*, these form a <u>hendiadys</u>, 'in drunken sleep', being
ablatives of manner or cause or instrument, depending on the reader's perspective. **arrectos:**
the chariots are tipped up so that they do not accidentally roll away. **litore:** local ablative.
simul . . . simul: the <u>anaphora</u> emphasises the disorder in the camp; note the <u>chiastic</u> word
order. **vina:** presumably '(jugs of) wine'.

319 **ore:** this word, which appears redundant to us, was frequently attached by Virgil to
verbs denoting speech; here it may be omitted. **locutus:** supply *est*.

320 **audendum dextra:** supply *est*; a very abbreviated phrase meaning 'we must be bold with
our right hands' (lit. 'it must be dared with the right hand'). The spondaic rhythm of the two
words and the <u>assonance</u> of *de* increase the urgency of Nisus' appeal. **res:** 'the situation'.
vocat: 'calls (for boldness)'.

321–2 **hac:** Nisus points out their route. **ne qua manus:** 'lest any group (of the enemy)'. **se
attollere:** 'rise up and attack'.

323 **haec:** Nisus points to the disorderly camp. **vasta dabo:** a Virgilian expression. **lato . . .
limite:** he will clear a wide path through the camp so that Euryalus will be safe.

Questions

1 In lines 308–310, how does Virgil indicate the importance of the expedition?

2 What picture of Ascanius does Virgil present?

3 Explain the pathos of lines 312–313.

4 How is the enemy camp described? What does this suggest about the Rutuli?

5 What is Nisus' plan?

6 What does Nisus intend Euryalus' role to be?

7 Pick out three examples of Virgil's use of word order, sound effects or rhythm from
these lines and discuss their effectiveness.

sic memorat vocemque premit, simul ense superbum
Rhamnetem adgreditur, qui forte tapetibus altis   325
exstructus toto proflabat pectore somnum,
rex idem et regi Turno gratissimus augur,
sed non augurio potuit depellere pestem.
tres iuxta famulos temere inter tela iacentes
armigerumque Remi premit aurigamque sub ipsis   330
nactus equis ferroque secat pendentia colla;
tum caput ipsi aufert domino truncumque relinquit
sanguine singultantem; atro tepefacta cruore
terra torique madent. nec non Lamyrumque Lamumque
et iuvenem Serranum, illa qui plurima nocte   335
luserat, insignis facie, multoque iacebat
membra deo victus; felix, si protinus illum
aequasset nocti ludum in lucemque tulisset:
impastus ceu plena leo per ovilia turbans
(suadet enim vesana fames) manditque trahitque   340
molle pecus mutumque metu; fremit ore cruento.

memoro, -are	I speak	*dominus, -i* m.	master
vox, vocis f.	voice	*truncus, -i* m.	torso
premo, -ere	I check, overpower	*relinquo, -ere*	I leave
		singulto, -are	I spout forth
ensis, -is m.	sword	*tepefacio, -ere, -feci, -factus*	I make warm
superbus, -a, -um	proud	*cruor, -oris* m.	spilt blood
Rhamnes, -etis m. 325	Rhamnes	*torus, -i* m.	bed
adgredior, -i, -gressus sum	I attack	*madeo, -ere*	I am wet
forte	by chance	*Lamyrus, -i* m.	Lamyrus
tapes, -etis m.	rug	*Lamus, -i* m.	Lamus
exstruo, -ere, -ruxi, -ructus	I raise up	*Serranus, -i* m. 335	Serranus
totus, -a, -um	the whole of	*ludo, -ere, lusi, lusus*	I play
proflo, -are	I breathe heavily	*insignis, -e*	distinguished
		facies, -ei f.	face
pectus, -oris n.	breast, chest	*membrum, -i* n.	limb
rex, regis m.	king	*vinco, -ere, vici, victus*	I conquer
idem, eadem, idem	the same	*felix, -icis*	happy, fortunate
gratus, -a, -um	pleasing	*protinus*	continuously
augur, -uris m.	augur	*aequo, -are, -avi, -atus*	I make equal
augurium, -i n.	augury	*ludus, -i* m.	game
depello, -ere	I drive away	*lux, lucis* f.	light, daylight
pestis, -is f.	danger	*impastus, -a, -um*	hungry
famulus, -i m.	servant	*leo, -onis* m.	lion
temere	by chance	*turbo, -are*	I cause havoc
armiger, -eri m. 330	armour-bearer	*suadeo, -ere* 340	I urge on
Remus, -i m.	Remus	*vesanus, -a, -um*	mad
auriga, -ae m.	charioteer	*fames, -is* f.	hunger
nanciscor, -i, nactus sum	I come upon	*mando, -ere*	I chew
seco, -are	I cut, cleave	*traho, -ere*	I drag
pendeo, -ere	I droop	*mollis, -e*	soft, weak
collum, -i n.	neck	*pecus, -oris* n.	flock, animal
caput, -itis n.	head	*metus, -us* m.	fear
aufero, -ferre	I remove	*cruentus, -a, -um*	blood-stained

324–5 superbum Rhamnetem: a character invented at this point by Virgil.

325–6 tapetibus: either local or instrumental ablative. **proflabat . . . somnum:** 'was breathing out sleep', a poetic image for snoring. **toto . . . pectore:** 'from' or 'with all his breast', indicating that his snoring was heavy, the result of a drunken stupor.

327 rex idem: 'himself too a king', perhaps not intended literally, but intended to indicate a high status, thereby making his killing a more noteworthy achievement for Nisus. **augur:** an augur foretold the future by observing the flight of birds. **regi Turno gratissimus:** 'most pleasing to king Turnus', and so 'a great favourite of king Turnus'. Note the polyptoton of *rex – regi*, pointing out the similarity of status of the two men.

328 non augurio potuit: 'he couldn't use his augury to . . .'. Note the heavy alliteration of *p*.

329–31 iuxta: i.e. near to Rhamnes. **tres . . . famulos:** the object of *premit*, as also *armigerum*; the servants belonged to Remus. Nisus killed first Remus' servants, then his armour-bearer, then his charioteer, and finally Remus himself. The sequence is not unlike an ascending tetracolon. **nactus:** supply *est*; the word is a euphemism for 'killed'. **sub ipsis . . . equis:** 'right alongside his horses'. **ferro:** 'with his sword'.

332–3 ipsi . . . domino: 'from his master himself' (dative of disadvantage). **sanguine singultantem:** lit. 'sobbing with blood', and so 'spouting forth blood'. Note the sibilance.

333–4 atro . . . cruore: 'by black blood', i.e. 'by dark blood'; in the near-darkness pooled blood would appear black. **madent:** also to be taken with *atro cruore*.

334–5 nec non: 'also'. **Lamyrumque Lamumque . . . Serranum:** all invented by Virgil for this episode; supply *premit* from line 330.

335–7 illa . . . nocte: ablative of time. **plurima . . . luserat:** 'had had a great deal of fun'; the verb covers a wide range of amusements. **facie:** ablative of respect. **multo . . . deo:** instrumental ablative: 'by a great deal of the god', referring either to the god of sleep or the god of wine. **membra . . . victus:** 'overcome in respect of his limbs', i.e. 'his limbs overcome'.

337–8 felix: supply *fuisset*, to provide the apodosis of a past unfulfilled condition. **aequasset:** = *aequavisset*; the idea is that if he had continued to play all night, he would not have been killed. **in lucemque tulisset:** 'and had continued it until dawn'.

339 The order is *ceu impastus leo turbans per plena ovilia. Ceu* is one of a number of words used by Virgil to introduce a simile. This simile has similarities with that in lines 59ff.

340–1 manditque trahitque: an example of polysyndeton. Note the alliteration and consonance of *m* and the assonance of *u*, giving a mournful tone to the simile. To complete the simile we have to supply some such idea as 'in the same way Nisus wreaked havoc'.

Questions

1 Why do you think Virgil gives names to the men killed by Nisus?

2 What picture of Rhamnes does Virgil present? How does this help the narrative?

3 What makes line 328 effective?

4 How does Virgil introduce variety into his account of the killing?

5 Are lines 331–334 too gory and explicit for modern tastes?

6 How effective is the simile?

7 Compare this simile with that of lines 59ff. Which do you think is the more effective?

nec minor Euryali caedes; incensus et ipse
perfurit ac multam in medio sine nomine plebem,
Fadumque Herbesumque subit Rhoetumque Abarimque
ignaros; Rhoetum vigilantem et cuncta videntem,   345
sed magnum metuens se post cratera tegebat.
pectore in adverso totum cui comminus ensem
condidit adsurgenti et multa morte recepit.
purpuream vomit ille animam et cum sanguine mixta
vina refert moriens, hic furto fervidus instat.   350
iamque ad Messapi socios tendebat; ibi ignem
deficere extremum et religatos rite videbat
carpere gramen equos, breviter cum talia Nisus
(sensit enim nimia caede atque cupidine ferri)
'absistamus' ait, 'nam lux inimica propinquat.   355
poenarum exhaustum satis est, via facta per hostes.'
multa virum solido argento perfecta relinquunt
armaque craterasque simul pulchrosque tapetas.

Euryalus seized trappings and a sword-belt from Rhamnes and put them over his shoulder.

tum galeam Messapi habilem cristisque decoram   365
induit. excedunt castris et tuta capessunt.

caedes, -is f.	slaughter	*Messapus, -i* m.	Messapus
incensus, -a, -um	inflamed	*tendo, -ere*	I proceed, offer
perfuro, -ere	I rage furiously	*ibi*	there
sine + abl.	without	*ignis, -is* m.	fire
nomen, -inis n.	name	*deficio, -ere*	I die down
plebs, plebis f.	ordinary men	*extremus, -a, -um*	last
Fadus, -i m.	Fadus	*religo, -are, -avi, -atus*	I tether
Herbesus, -i m.	Herbesus	*rite*	duly, properly
subeo, -ire	I creep up on	*carpo, -ere*	I crop
Rhoetus, -i m.	Rhoetus	*gramen, -inis* n.	grass
Abaris, -is m.	Abaris	*breviter*	briefly
ignarus, -a, -um 345	ignorant	*talis, -e*	such
vigilo, -are	I stay awake	*sentio, -ire, sensi, sensus*	I realise
cunctus, -a, -um	all	*nimius, -a, -um*	too much
metuo, -ere	I fear	*absisto, -ere* 355	I stop
post + acc.	behind	*propinquo, -are* + dat.	I approach
crater, -eris m. (acc. *-era*)	mixing bowl	*poena, -ae* f.	vengeance
comminus	hand to hand	*exhaurio, -ire, -ausi, -austus*	I drain
adsurgo, -ere	I rise up	*satis* + gen.	enough
mors, mortis f.	death	*solidus, -a, -um*	solid
purpureus, -a, -um	dark red	*argentum, -i* n.	silver
vomo, -ere	I pour forth	*perficio, -ere, -feci, -fectus*	I finish
anima, -ae f.	spirit	*cratera, -ae* f.	mixing bowl
misceo, -ere, miscui, mixtus	I mix	*habilis, -e* 365	well-fitting
refero, -ferre 350	I vomit up	*crista, -ae* f.	crest
morior, -i, mortuus sum	I die	*decorus, -a, -um*	adorned
furtum, -i n.	stealthy activity	*excedo, -ere*	I leave
insto, -are + dat.	I continue with	*capesso, -ere*	I make for

342–5 **caedes:** supply *erat*. **incensus:** i.e. 'inflamed with passion'. **multam . . . plebem:** 'many ordinary warriors', i.e. men of the lowest ranks; the verb governing these two words is *subit*. **in medio:** 'in the midst (of his killing)'. **sine nomine:** 'nameless', describing *plebem*; Virgil does not deem them worthy of being named. **Fadumque . . . Abarimque:** these men were presumably of more exalted status than the *plebem*, and so merited names, all invented for the occasion by Virgil; so too Rhoetus. **ignaros:** given prominence by the <u>enjambement</u>: the rest were all asleep, in contrast with Rhoetus.

345–6 **Rhoetum vigilantem:** this appears to contradict the previous line, which included Rhoetus among those asleep. Either a mistake was made by a copyist or Virgil deliberately corrects himself to make the narrative appear more natural. Supply *subit* again with *Rhoetum*. **magnum:** to be taken with *cratera* (a Greek accusative ending). **metuens:** we would have expected *metuentem*, following the construction of line 345, but Virgil has chosen instead to change to a new main clause. **magnum . . . cratera:** these bowls were used for mixing wine with water, as wine was generally drunk substantially diluted in classical times. They could be very big to cater for large numbers of men. The presence of such bowls in a military camp indicates the high priority given to wine as a staple drink, and also the use of ox-drawn carts to convey them.

347–8 **cui:** the connecting relative, with *pectore*: 'in his chest'. **adverso:** Rhoetus' chest was 'turned towards' him. **comminus:** to be taken with *adsurgenti* (agreeing with *cui*): 'rising up (to fight) hand to hand', and so more simply 'as he rose up to fight him'. **totum . . . ensem:** i.e. the whole length of the blade. **et multa morte recepit:** 'and withdrew it (the sword) with much death', i.e. 'steeped in death' (Whiteley); this whole phrase is unclear and the reading uncertain.

349–50 **purpuream . . . animam:** 'his blood-red life': blood poured from his mouth. **hic:** Euryalus, as opposed to *ille*. **furto:** the 'stealthy activity' is his stealthy movement from one sleeping enemy to another to kill them.

351 **Messapi:** Messapus was a cavalry leader, from Etruria, and the son of Neptune; he reappears in lines 523–4.

351–3 **ignem deficere extremum:** '(he saw) the last of the campfires dying down'. **rite:** to be taken with *religatos*. The horses would have been kept at the edge of the camp.

353–5 The order for the first clause is *cum Nisus breviter ait talia (verba)*. **ferri:** supply *eum* as its subject: '(he realised) that he (Euryalus) was being carried away (by the killing)'. **caede atque cupidine:** <u>hendiadys</u>: 'by lust for slaughter'. **lux inimica:** 'hostile light', i.e. 'the hostile light of dawn'.

356 **poenarum exhaustum satis est:** 'enough of vengeance has been drained', i.e. 'we have exacted enough vengeance'. **via facta:** supply *est*: 'we have made our way'.

357–8 **multa virum:** 'many things belonging to the men', as exemplified in line 358. **solido argento:** ablative of material. **armaque:** the first *-que* (an example of <u>polysyndeton</u>) can be ignored. **crateras:** see note on the alternative form of the word in line 346.

365–6 Euryalus could not resist despoiling the men he had killed; this act would cause disaster for the two men. It becomes clear later that he did not stop to kill Messapus. **tuta:** 'safety'.

Questions

1 What impression of Euryalus do you gain from these lines?

2 How does Virgil make his description of the slaughter varied and interesting?

3 How does Nisus show his sense of responsibility?

interea praemissi equites ex urbe Latina,
cetera dum legio campis instructa moratur,
ibant et Turno regi responsa ferebant,
ter centum, scutati omnes, Volcente magistro,   370
iamque propinquabant castris murosque subibant
cum procul hos laevo flectentes limite cernunt,
et galea Euryalum sublustri noctis in umbra
prodidit immemorem radiisque adversa refulsit.
haud temere est visum. conclamat ab agmine Volcens: 375
'state, viri. quae causa viae? quive estis in armis?
quove tenetis iter?' nihil illi tendere contra,
sed celerare fugam in silvas et fidere nocti.
obiciunt equites sese ad divortia nota
hinc atque hinc, omnemque abitum custode coronant.   380
silva fuit late dumis atque ilice nigra
horrida, quam densi complerant undique sentes;
rara per occultos lucebat semita calles.
Euryalum tenebrae ramorum onerosaque praeda
impediunt, fallitque timor regione viarum.   385
Nisus abit; iamque imprudens evaserat hostes,   386
ut stetit et frustra absentem respexit amicum: 389

praemitto, -ere, -misi, -missus	I send on ahead	*divortium, -i* n.	fork in the path
Latinus, -a, -um	Latin	*notus, -a, -um*	known, familiar
legio, -onis f.	legion, army	*hinc*	380 on this side
instruo, -ere, -uxi, -uctus	I draw up	*abitus, -us* m.	way out
moror, -ari, -atus sum	I wait, delay	*corono, -are*	I surround
responsum, -i n.	response	*dumus, -i* m.	thicket
ter	370 three times	*ilex, ilicis* f.	holm-oak
centum	one hundred	*horridus, -a, -um*	prickly
scutatus, -a, -um	bearing shields	*densus, -a, -um*	thick
Volcens, -entis m.	Volcens	*undique*	on/from all
magister, -tri m.	master, leader		sides
subeo, -ire	I come up to	*sentes, -ium* m.pl.	brambles
procul	from a distance	*occulo, -ere, -cului, -cultus*	I hide
laevus, -a, -um	on the left	*luceo, -ere*	I gleam
flecto, -ere	I turn, go	*semita, -ae* f.	path
sublustris, -e	dim	*callis, -is* m.	track, clearing
prodo, -ere, -didi, -ditus	I betray	*ramus, -i* m.	branch
immemor, -oris	forgetful	*onerosus, -a, -um*	heavy
radius, -i m.	ray	*praeda, -ae* f.	booty
refulgeo, -ere, -fulsi	I reflect	*impedio, -ire*	385 I hinder
temere	375 for nothing	*fallo, -ere*	I deceive
causa, -ae f.	reason	*timor, -oris* m.	fear
quo	to where	*regio, -onis* f.	direction, region
contra	in return	*abeo, -ire*	I depart
celero, -are	I speed up	*imprudens, -entis*	not realising
fuga, -ae f.	flight	*evado, -ere, evasi, evasus*	I escape from
silva, -ae f.	wood	*frustra*	in vain
fido, -ere + dat.	I trust in	*respicio, -ere, -spexi, -spectus*	I look back for
obicio, -ere	I position	*amicus, -i* m.	friend

367 praemissi: this force of 300 cavalrymen has been sent on ahead from Laurentum bringing the response to a message we must assume had previously been sent by Turnus to king Latinus.

368–9 cetera . . . legio: 'the rest of the army', reminding us that Turnus had rushed ahead to attack the Trojan camp, leaving the rest to catch up. **campis:** local ablative. **Turno regi:** since Latinus had refused to take responsibility for embarking upon hostilities against the Trojans (see Book VII.600), Turnus had become the supreme leader.

370 ter centum: 'three hundred'. **Volcente magistro:** 'under the leadership of Volcens'; he is not mentioned elsewhere.

371 castris, muros: these belong to the Rutulian camp.

372 hos: Nisus and Euryalus. **laevo flectentes limite:** 'turning along a path to the left' (ablative of route taken); while passing through the Latin camp they would have stayed close to the shore, heading SE; once clear of the camp, they would have had to turn to their left to head NE towards Pallanteum.

373–4 galea Euryalum . . . prodidit: 'the helmet betrayed Euryalus'; this is the helmet he had taken from Messapus (line 365). **sublustri noctis in umbra:** 'in the dim shadow of the night'; the darkness was relieved by starlight and, more importantly, moonlight. **immemorem:** Euryalus had forgotten Nisus' urgings in lines 355–6; perhaps also he had forgotten that he was wearing the helmet. **radiisque adversa refulsit:** 'and facing the rays (of the moon) reflected (them)'.

375 haud temere est visum: 'not for nothing was it seen', i.e. the Latins did not ignore the flash of light.

376–7 causa: supply *est*. **quove tenetis iter:** '(or) where are you going?' Virgil frequently separates a sequence of questions with *-ve*; in English this is not needed.

377–8 tendere, celerare, fidere: these are all historic infinitives. **nihil . . . contra:** 'nothing in reply'.

379–80 divortia: these would be secondary paths branching off the main path. **hinc atque hinc:** 'on both sides' (of the main path); the Italians, being familiar with the local network of paths, quickly took up positions to cut off any alternative routes the Trojans might take. **custode:** 'with guards' (singular for plural).

381–2 nigra, horrida: *nigra* qualifies *ilice*; *horrida* qualifies *silva*. **late:** 'over a wide area'. **compleverant:** = *compleverant*.

383 rara . . . semita: 'only rarely did the path . . .'. **per occultos . . . calles:** 'through the hidden clearings'; *calles* were clearings in woodland made by grazing cattle.

384–5 tenebrae ramorum: 'the darkness of branches', an inverted way of saying 'in the darkness branches . . .'. **praeda:** the weapons and armour he had stripped from the dead. **regione viarum:** 'in (respect of) the direction of the ways'; i.e. '(fear made him) lose his way'.

386 Nisus abit: Nisus was moving away from Euryalus. **imprudens:** 'not realising' (that he had left Euryalus behind).

389 ut: 'when', being used like the 'inverse *cum*' construction, with the indicative. Nisus suddenly realised he had lost his friend.

Questions

1 What impression do you get of Volcens' leadership qualities?

2 How does Volcens realised that the two men are hostile?

3 What evidence is there that the two Trojans were panicking?

'Euryale infelix, qua te regione reliqui?   390
quave sequar?' rursus perplexum iter omne revolvens
fallacis silvae simul et vestigia retro
observata legit dumisque silentibus errat.
audit equos, audit strepitus et signa sequentum.
nec longum in medio tempus, cum clamor ad aures   395
pervenit ac videt Euryalum, quem iam manus omnis
fraude loci et noctis, subito turbante tumultu,
oppressum rapit et conantem plurima frustra.

Nisus wondered what to do to save his friend. Praying to Luna, he hurled a spear and killed Sulmo. Emboldened by this success he hurled a second spear which killed Tagus.

saevit atrox Volcens nec teli conspicit usquam   420
auctorem nec quo se ardens immittere possit.
'tu tamen interea calido mihi sanguine poenas
persolves amborum' inquit; simul ense recluso
ibat in Euryalum. tum vero exterritus, amens,
conclamat Nisus nec se celare tenebris   425
amplius aut tantum potuit perferre dolorem:
'me, me, adsum qui feci, in me convertite ferrum,
o Rutuli! mea fraus omnis, nihil iste nec ausus
nec potuit; caelum hoc et conscia sidera testor;
tantum infelicem nimium dilexit amicum.'   430

infelix, -icis	390 unlucky	*auctor, -oris* m.	person responsible
rursus	back, again		
perplexus, -a, -um	tangled	*ardens, -entis*	fiery
revolvo, -ere	I go over again	*immitto, -ere*	I send (into)
fallax, -acis	treacherous	*calidus, -a, -um*	warm, hot
vestigium, -i n.	footstep	*poena, -ae* f.	penalty, punishment
retro	backwards		
observo, -are, -avi, -atus	I observe	*persolvo, -ere*	I pay in full
silens, -entis	silent	*ambo, -ae, -o*	both
erro, -are	I wander	*recludo, -ere, -usi, -usus*	I draw, unsheathe
strepitus, -us m.	din		
signum, -i n.	sign, token	*exterritus, -a, -um*	terrified
tempus, -oris n.	395 time, temple	*amens, -entis*	out of his mind
auris, -is f.	ear	*celo, -are*	425 I conceal, hide
pervenio, -ire	I reach	*amplius*	more, longer
fraus, fraudis f.	treachery	*perfero, -ferre*	I bear
turbo, -are	I bewilder, confuse	*converto, -ere*	I turn, direct
		iste, ista, istud	that (of yours)
tumultus, -us m.	commotion	*caelum, -i* n.	sky, heaven
opprimo, -ere, -ressi, -ressus	I overwhelm	*conscius, -a, -um*	aware
rapio, -ere	I seize	*sidus, -eris* n.	star
conor, -ari, -atus sum	I try	*testor, -ari, -atus sum*	I call to witness
atrox, -ocis	420 fierce	*tantum*	430 only, so greatly
conspicio, -ere	I see	*nimium*	too, too much
usquam	anywhere	*diligo, -ere, -lexi, -lectus*	I love

390–1 **qua . . . regione:** local ablative. **quave:** 'or by what (path) shall I follow (you)'.
392–3 **simul et:** 'at the same time also'. **vestigia retro observata legit:** 'he observed and picked his steps backwards'; i.e. he looked for his footprints and followed them backwards. **dumis:** local ablative. **signa sequentum:** probably the shouts of the pursuers.
395 **nec longum:** supply *erat*. **tempus in medio:** 'the intervening time'.
395–6 **cum . . . pervenit:** indicative because it is an 'inverted' *cum* clause.
396–8 **manus omnis:** 'the whole band'; the verb is *rapit*. **oppressum:** agrees with *quem* (as does *conantem*) and explained by *fraude . . . tumultu*: he was overwhelmed by the treachery of the place, etc. **subito turbante tumultu:** 'and by the sudden commotion that bewildered him'. **conantem plurima frustra:** 'and making very many attempts (to escape) in vain'.

420–1 **quo se . . . immitere possit:** 'where he could dash'.
422–4 The order is *interea tamen tu persolves mihi poenas amborum calido sanguine*. **interea:** i.e. until he found the killer. **tu:** he addresses Euryalus. **poenas . . . amborum:** 'the penalty (for the death) of both men'. Note the very fast rhythm of line 422, contrasting with line 421 and the first half of line 423. **ibat:** 'he began to move' (inceptive imperfect).
424–6 **exterritus, amens:** note the <u>asyndeton</u>, marking Nisus' panic. **tenebris:** local ablative.
427 **me, me:** the exclamatory accusatives show Nisus' desperation to divert Volcens' anger from Euryalus to himself. The disjointed structure of the line also shows his panic.
428–9 **mea fraus:** supply *est*. **iste:** indicating Euryalus. **ausus:** supply *est facere*. **hoc:** probably a second object of *testor* rather than simply indicating the sky: '(that) this is true'. **caelum . . . et conscia sidera:** both the sky and the stars were associated with deities, and so capable of witnessing what they 'saw'.
430 A few editors have ended the speech at *testor*, making line 430 a comment on Nisus' deep affection for his friend. Most however include the line in the speech, in which case the subject of *dilexit* is Euryalus and *amicus* is Nisus. **tantum:** if outside the speech, the meaning would be 'so greatly'; if inside, 'only' (the only reason he came along was because he loved his friend). The inclusion within the speech has been retained here, as this is by far the more common interpretation; there is much, however, to commend the exclusion of the line.

Questions

1 How effectively does Virgil describe Nisus' frantic search for his friend?

2 How is Euryalus' helplessness shown?

3 In lines 420–424, what impression do you gain of Volcens?

4 How does Virgil use rhythm, word order and sound effects to support his portrayal of Volcens?

5 How does Virgil make clear the panic and desperation of Nisus?

6 Do you think line 430 should be read as part of Nisus' speech or not? Give reasons for your answer.

talia dicta dabat, sed viribus ensis adactus
transabiit costas et candida pectora rumpit.
volvitur Euryalus leto, pulchrosque per artus
it cruor inque umeros cervix conlapsa recumbit:
purpureus veluti cum flos succisus aratro   435
languescit moriens, lassove papavera collo
demisere caput pluvia cum forte gravantur.
at Nisus ruit in medios solumque per omnes
Volcentem petit, in solo Volcente moratur.
quem circum glomerati hostes hinc comminus atque hinc   440
proturbant. instat non setius ac rotat ensem
fulmineum, donec Rutuli clamantis in ore
condidit adverso et moriens animam abstulit hosti.
tum super exanimum sese proiecit amicum
confossus, placidaque ibi demum morte quievit.   445
fortunati ambo! si quid mea carmina possunt,
nulla dies umquam memori vos eximet aevo,
dum domus Aeneae Capitoli immobile saxum
accolet imperiumque pater Romanus habebit.

*The Rutuli lamented the deaths of so many comrades and stuck the heads of Nisus and
Euryalus on pikes. The next morning they prepared to attack the Trojan camp again. When
the defenders saw the heads of the two dead men, they were stricken with grief, and chief
among the mourners was Euryalus' mother.*

dictum, -i n.	word	*insto, -are*	I persist
vires, virium f.pl.	strength	*setius*	less
adigo, -ere, -egi, -actus	I drive	*roto, -are*	I swing
transabeo, -ire, -ii	I pierce	*fulmineus, -a, -um*	lightning-fast
costa, -ae f.	rib	*donec*	until
candidus, -a, -um	white	*clamo, -are*	I shout
rumpo, -ere	I burst through	*super* + acc.	on top of
letum, -i n.	death	*exanimus, -a, -um*	dead
artus, -us m.	limb	*proicio, -ere, -ieci, -iectus*	I throw down
umerus, -i m.	shoulder	*confodio, -ere, -fodi, -fossus*	I stab through
cervix, -icis f.	neck	*demum* 445	at last
conlabor, -i, -lapsus sum	I fall, sink down	*quiesco, -ere, -evi, -etus*	I find rest
recumbo, -ere	I sink down	*fortunatus, -a, -um*	fortunate
flos, floris m. 435	flower	*carmen, -inis* n.	poem
succido, -ere, -idi, -isus	I cut down	*dies, -ei* f.	day
aratrum, -i n.	plough	*umquam*	ever
languesco, -ere	I droop, wilt	*memor, -oris*	remembering
lassus, -a, -um	drooping	*eximo, -ere*	I remove
papaver, -eris n.	poppy	*aevum, -i* n.	age, time
demitto, -ere, -misi, -missus	I drop	*Capitolium, -i* n.	Capitoline Hill
pluvia, -ae f.	rain	*immobilis, -e*	immovable
gravo, -are	I weigh down	*saxum, -i* n	rock
circum + acc. 440	around	*accolo, -ere*	I live near
proturbo, -are	I repel	*imperium, -i* n.	power

431–2 **ensis:** this is Volcens' sword. **viribus:** 'with strength' and so 'forcefully'. Note the chiasmus in line 432. **candida pectora:** the paleness suggests youthfulness and vulnerability.
433–4 **leto:** 'in death'. Note the strong alliteration of *c* in line 434.
435–7 Start with *veluti cum*, introducing a simile. **purpureus . . . flos:** Virgil does not name the species of flower; we are to imagine any purple or dark red flower that grows in meadows, such as an orchid. **pluvia . . . gravantur:** 'are weighed down by rain'. The simile is borrowed from Catullus, who in turn had borrowed it from Homer.
438–9 **solum . . . solo:** the polyptoton emphasises Nisus' single-mindedness.
440–1 **quem circum:** 'around him (i.e. Nisus)'. **hinc atque hinc:** 'from all sides'. **comminus:** 'fighting hand to hand'.
441–3 **instat:** contrasts with *proturbant*: the Rutuli drive him off but he keeps coming back. **non setius:** 'no less', and so 'just as forcefully'. **donec . . . condidit:** 'until he buried it'. **in ore . . . adverso:** 'full in the face'. **Rutuli clamantis:** 'of the screaming Rutulian'. **moriens:** he killed Volcens as he was himself dying from the wounds he had received. **hosti:** dative of disadvantage: 'from the enemy'.
444–5 **demum:** i.e. after all his struggles to keep Euryalus alive and then to avenge his death.
446–7 **fortunati ambo:** supply some such words as *quam estis*: 'how fortunate you two men are' (that is Nisus and Euryalus). Note the use of apostrophe. Virgil goes on to explain how they could be fortunate in death. **si quid . . . possunt:** 'if (my poems) have any power'. **memori . . . aevo:** 'from remembering time', i.e. 'from the memory of time'.
448–9 **dum:** 'as long as'. **domus Aeneae:** 'the house of Aeneas' – either just the *gens Iulia*, which Virgil claims is directly descended from Aeneas through Iulus; or alternatively (as most editors take it) the whole Roman people. **Capitoli:** the Capitoline Hill, on which was the citadel of Rome, and which symbolised Rome's imperial power. **pater Romanus:** probably generic, referring to all Roman fathers, rather than just to a single one, which would have to be Augustus.

Questions

1 How sensitively does Virgil describe the death of Euryalus?

2 Explain the simile in lines 435–437. How appropriate is it?

3 In the simile, why do you suppose Virgil chooses a single purple flower but more than one poppy?

4 Describe the deaths of Volcens and Nisus. How does Virgil bring out the pathos of the scene?

5 How does Virgil make clear the panic and desperation of Nisus?

6 Explain the meaning of lines 446–449. Why do you think Virgil wrote these lines?

7 Have you changed or developed your interpretation of the relationship between Nisus and Euryalus since their first appearance?

8 Do you think Nisus and Euryalus deserved their deaths? You may consider their youth and inexperience, their foolishness, their relationship and their responsibility to the Trojans.

The Rutuli charged the walls of the camp, trying to scale them, but the Trojans beat them off. Among the keenest attackers were Mezentius and Messapus, only outdone by Turnus himself. He set fire to a wooden tower, which collapsed, killing many within. The Rutuli rushed into the breach, and in the fighting that followed, many were killed on both sides. Then Remulus, a brother-in-law of Turnus, hurled insults at the Trojans and boasted of his people's prowess.

talia iactantem dictis ac dira canentem	621
non tulit Ascanius, nervoque obversus equino	
intendit telum diversaque bracchia ducens	
constitit, ante Iovem supplex per vota precatus:	
'Iuppiter omnipotens, audacibus adnue coeptis.	625
ipse tibi ad tua templa feram sollemnia dona,	
et statuam ante aras aurata fronte iuvencum	
candentem pariterque caput cum matre ferentem,	
iam cornu petat et pedibus qui spargat harenam.'	
audiit et caeli genitor de parte serena	630
intonuit laevum, sonat una fatifer arcus.	
effugit horrendum stridens adducta sagitta	
perque caput Remuli venit et cava tempora ferro	
traicit. 'i, verbis virtutem inlude superbis!	
bis capti Phryges haec Rutulis responsa remittunt.'	635

iacto, -are	I boast	*iuvencus, -i* m.		bullock	
cano, -ere	I sing, utter	*candens, -entis*		dazzling white	
nervus, -i m.	bowstring	*cornu, -us* n.		horn	
obversus, -a, -um	facing	*pes, pedis* m.		foot	
equinus, -a, -um	from a horse	*spargo, -ere*		I scatter	
intendo, -ere	I aim	*harena, -ae* f.		sand	
diversus, -a, -um	in different directions	*pars, partis* f.	630	part	
		serenus, -a, -um		clear	
bracchium, -i n.	arm	*intono, -are, -ui*		I thunder	
consisto, -ere, -stiti	I stop	*sono, -are*		I sound	
ante	before, first	*fatifer, -era, -erum*		deadly	
Iuppiter, Iovis m.	Jupiter	*arcus, -us* m.		bow	
supplex, -icis	as a suppliant	*effugio, -ere*		I escape	
precor, -ari, -atus sum	I pray to	*horrendus, -a, -um*		dreadful	
omnipotens, -entis	625 all-powerful	*strideo, -ere*		I hiss	
audax, -acis	bold, daring	*adduco, -ere, -xi, -ctus*		I draw to	
adnuo, -ere	I am favourable	*Remulus, -i* m.		Remulus	
coeptum, -i n.	undertaking	*traicio, -ere*		I pierce	
templum, -i n.	temple	*virtus, -utis* f.		valour	
sollemnis, -e	customary	*inludo, -ere*		I mock	
donum, -i n.	gift	*bis*	635	twice	
statuo, -ere	I place	*Phryges, -um* m.pl.		Trojans	
auratus, -a, -um	gilded	*remitto, -ere*		I send back	
frons, frontis f.	forehead				

621 **talia iactantem:** supply *Remulum*: '(Remulus) making such boasts'. **ac dira canentem:** 'and uttering dreadful words'.

622–4 **non tulit Ascanius:** 'Ascanius could not tolerate'. Note the word order: Virgil begins with the object, Remulus, and ends with the subject, Ascanius; this indicates a transfer of focus from the Rutulian to Ascanius, whose first battle success this will be. Much has been written about the probable age of Aeneas' son: in Books I and IV he was young enough to be fondled by Dido like a young child, and too young to take a full part in a hunting expedition; here however, he appears fairly mature. This is despite the fact that little time separates the two episodes. **obversus:** 'turning to face him'. **nervo . . . equino:** instrumental ablative: 'with the horse-gut bowstring'. **intendit telum:** probably 'he aimed the arrow', though some have taken these words to mean 'he stretched the bow'; however there is no evidence that *telum* was ever used to mean a bow. **diversaque bracchia ducens:** 'drawing his arms apart'; *diversa* is a <u>proleptic</u> usage (his arms would be apart only after the action was completed). **constitit:** 'he stood still' (in order to shoot). **ante:** 'before (he shot)', and so 'first'. **supplex:** 'as a suppliant', and so 'humbly'.

626 **ipse:** emphatic: 'personally'. **sollemnia:** in Virgil's day captured arms were taken as offerings to the Temple of Jupiter on the Capitoline Hill in Rome.

627–8 **aurata fronte:** ablative of description: 'with gilded forehead', meaning 'with gilded horns'; it was the practice in Virgil's day to gild the horns of cattle that were to be sacrificed. **iuvencum candentem:** again in Virgil's day cattle sacrificed to Jupiter were generally white. **pariter caput cum matre ferentem:** 'bearing its head on a level with its mother', i.e. it would be old enough to be considered suitable for sacrifice.

629 The order is *qui iam petat cornu et spargat harenam pedibus*. **petat cornu:** 'is (old enough) to attack with its horn(s)'; the subjunctive (like *spargat*) is generic. Virgil suggests that butting and pawing of sand were indications of maturity.

630–1 **genitor:** the father of the gods, i.e. Jupiter. **intonuit laevum:** 'thundered on the left'; Virgil several times has Jupiter sending a clap of thunder to show his response to a prayer; if on the left it was a sign of approval. Coming from a clear sky it could not be natural. **sonat . . . arcus:** 'the bow twanged'. **una:** 'at the same time'.

632 **horrendum:** adverbial accusative (like *laevum* in line 631): 'dreadfully'. **adducta:** 'having been pulled back' ready to shoot.

633–4 **ferro:** 'with its iron tip'. Note the fast rhythm of line 633. **traicit:** note the <u>enjambement</u>.

634 **i:** contemptuous. **verbis . . . superbis:** note the <u>enclosing word order</u>. Very noteworthy here are the sound effects, all designed to show Ascanius' contempt: *-icit i, verbis vir-, verbis superbis, -bis bis*. **virtutem:** supply *nostram*; much of Remulus' speech in lines 598–620 had been devoted to mockery of the Trojans' lack of courage. It could of course be argued that Ascanius, shooting from a distance, was not showing much bravery.

635 **bis capti Phryges:** Ascanius is throwing Remulus' mocking words back at him. Troy had been captured twice in Greek legend, firstly by Hercules, and then by the Greeks.

Questions

1 What can we learn from this passage of Roman religious beliefs and practices?

2 What is your impression of Ascanius after reading this passage?

3 How does Virgil make good use of sound effects in this passage?

The god Apollo saw Ascanius kill Remulus, and visited him in disguise. After congratulating him, he advised him not to continue fighting. Some of the Trojan elders recognised the god despite his disguise, and held back the triumphant Ascanius from taking further part in the action. The Rutuli renewed their attack, some getting inside the camp after Pandarus and his brother foolishly opened one of the gates.

hic Mars armipotens animum viresque Latinis	717
addidit et stimulos acres sub pectore vertit,	
immisitque Fugam Teucris atrumque Timorem.	
undique conveniunt, quoniam data copia pugnae,	720
bellatorque animo deus incidit.	
Pandarus, ut fuso germanum corpore cernit	
et quo sit fortuna loco, qui casus agat res,	
portam vi magna converso cardine torquet	
obnixus latis umeris, multosque suorum	725
moenibus exclusos duro in certamine linquit;	
ast alios secum includit recipitque ruentes,	
demens, qui Rutulum in medio non agmine regem	
viderit inrumpentem ultroque incluserit urbi,	
immanem veluti pecora inter inertia tigrim.	730
continuo nova lux oculis effulsit et arma	
horrendum sonuere, tremunt in vertice cristae	
sanguineae clipeoque micantia fulmina mittit.	
agnoscunt faciem invisam atque immania membra	
turbati subito Aeneadae. tum Pandarus ingens	735
emicat et mortis fraternae fervidus ira	
effatur:	

Mars, Martis m.	Mars	*demens, -entis*	mad
armipotens, -entis	powerful in arms	*inrumpo, -ere*	I burst in
Latini, -orum m.pl.	the Latins	*ultro*	spontaneously
stimulus, -i m.	goad, spur	*immanis, -e*	730 huge
verto, -ere, verti, versus	I apply	*iners, -ertis*	helpless
Fuga, -ae f.	Flight	*tigris, -is* (acc. *-im*) f.	tigress
convenio, -ire	720 I come together	*continuo*	at once
quoniam	since	*novus, -a, -um*	new
copia, -ae f.	opportunity	*oculus, -i* m.	eye
bellator, -oris m.	warrior	*effulgeo, -ere, -fulsi*	I blaze out
incido, -ere	I fall upon	*tremo, -ere*	I tremble
Pandarus, -i m.	Pandarus	*vertex, -icis* m.	head
germanus, -i m.	brother	*sanguineus, -a, -um*	blood-red
casus, -us m.	chance	*clipeus, -i* m.	shield
cardo, -inis m.	hinge	*fulmen, -inis* n.	lightning
torqueo, -ere	I twist, turn	*agnosco, -ere*	I recognise
obnitor, -i, -nixus sum	725 I push against	*invisus, -a, -um*	hated
excludo, -ere, -clusi, -clusus	I shut out	*subito*	735 suddenly
certamen, -inis n.	struggle	*emico, -are*	I dart out
linquo, -ere	I leave	*fraternus, -a, -um*	of a brother
ast	but	*effor, -fari, -fatus sum*	I speak out
includo, -ere, -clusi, -clusus	I shut in		

717–18 **hic:** 'at this point'. **Mars:** probably war personified, rather than the actual god of war, as in the myth he was a supporter of the Trojans during the Trojan War, and also was instrumental in establishing the royal line of Rome; thus it is unlikely that here he would be taking action against the Trojans. Virgil often personifies war, in order to account for particular acts of valour or sudden changes of fortune on the battlefield. **stimulos acres . . . vertit:** 'applied sharp spurs', a <u>metaphor</u> to explain the Rutulians' and Latins' sudden eagerness to fight.

719 **Fugam, Timorem:** two further personifications, as if these negative emotions were supernatural beings controlled by the god of war. Again Virgil is using these personifications to symbolise the loss of courage experienced by the Trojans. Fear is also personified in Homer. **atrum:** black was seen as a negative colour, associated with death and destruction.

720–1 **conveniunt:** supply *Latini* as the subject. **copia:** the 'opportunity' to fight was given them by the opening of the gate. **data:** supply *est*. **bellator . . . deus:** the war god, Mars; again Virgil attributes to the god the boost of courage in the hearts of the Latins and their allies. **animo . . . incidit:** '(had) fallen upon their heart(s)', i.e. 'had taken possession of their hearts'. Line 721 was left incomplete by Virgil, who died before he could fill in the gaps.

722 **fuso . . . corpore:** 'with his body laid low' (descriptive ablative).

723 **quo sit fortuna loco:** dependent on *cernit*: 'in what position fortune was', i.e. 'how lay the fortune of the battle'. **qui casus agat res:** 'what chance was driving the situation', i.e. 'what emergency was dictating the outcome of the battle'.

724 **portam . . . torquet:** 'swung the gate'. **converso cardine:** 'forcing the hinges to turn'. Note the slow rhythm, emphasising the amount of effort expended.

725–6 **moenibus:** 'outside the walls'.

727–9 **ruentes:** 'as they ran'. **qui . . . non . . . viderit:** the perfect subjunctive stands for the pluperfect in normal historic narrative, and gives the reason for describing him as 'mad': he failed to spot Turnus charging inside the walls. **in medio . . . agmine:** 'in the midst of the mass of his men'. **regem:** here 'prince'. **urbi:** here no more than 'settlement'. i.e. the camp.

730 **immanem:** generally transferred inside the <u>simile</u> to agree with *tigrim*: 'like a huge tigress'; it would work just as well to describe *regem*: 'huge like a tigress'.

731–3 **nova lux:** 'a new light', i.e. the fire in his eyes at the prospect of victory. **oculis:** 'from Turnus' eyes'. **horrendum:** adverbial (cf. line 632). **clipeo:** 'from his shield'. **mittit:** the subject is Turnus.

734–5 **agnoscunt:** the subject is *Aeneadae*. Note the <u>chiasmus</u> in line 734.

735–6 **mortis:** objective genitive. **ira:** causal ablative.

Questions

1 Many understand *Mars* (line 717) to refer to the god in person. What are the arguments for and against this view?

2 What happens to the Latins and the Trojans in lines 717–720?

3 *Demens* (line 727): what has Pandarus done to deserve this criticism?

4 How effective is the description of Turnus in lines 730–733)?

5 What causes Pandarus to dart out of the gateway?

6 Choose two examples of alliteration from this passage and discuss their effects.

'non haec dotalis regia Amatae,
nec muris cohibet patriis media Ardea Turnum.
castra inimica vides, nulla hinc exire potestas.'
olli subridens sedato pectore Turnus: 740
'incipe, si qua animo virtus, et consere dextram,
hic etiam inventum Priamo narrabis Achillem.'

*Pandarus hurled his spear, but Juno deflected it. Turnus clove Pandarus' head in two
with his sword. Filled with blood-lust, Turnus embarked on a killing spree, until the two
commanders, Mnestheus and Serestus, realised what was happening and rallied their men to
close ranks against Turnus, who became exhausted by the constant rain of missiles hurled at
him. He was soon covered in sweat and blood.*

tum demum praeceps saltu sese omnibus armis   815
in fluvium dedit. ille suo cum gurgite flavo
accepit venientem ac mollibus extulit undis
et laetum sociis abluta caede remisit.

dotalis, -e	given as a dowry	*invenio, -ire, -veni, -ventus*	I find
regia, -ae f.	palace	*Priamus, -i* m.	Priam
Amata, -ae f.	Amata	*narro, -are*	I relate
cohibeo, -ere	I confine	*Achilles, -is* m.	Achilles
patrius, -a, -um	native, ancestral	*praeceps, -cipitis*	815 headlong
Ardea, -ae f.	Ardea	*saltus, -us* m.	leap
hinc	from here	*fluvius, -i* m.	river
exeo, -ire	I leave, depart	*gurges, -itis* m.	swirling water
potestas, -atis f.	power	*flavus, -a, -um*	yellow
subrideo, -ere	740 I smile	*effero, -ferre, -tuli, -latus*	I lift, raise
sedatus, -a, -um	calm	*laetus, -a, -um*	happy
incipio, -ere	I begin	*abluo, -ere, -lui, -lutus*	I wash away
consero, -ere	I join		

737 **non haec:** in full this would be *haec non sunt*; *haec* refers to the camp. **dotalis regia Amatae:** 'Amata's palace, given (to you) as (your) dowry'; Amata was the queen of Laurentum and mother of Lavinia, to whom Turnus had been betrothed, until the arrival of Aeneas.

738 **media Ardea:** 'the middle of Ardea'; Ardea, an ancient town about 20 miles south of Rome, was traditionally the capital of the Rutuli and so the home of Turnus. **muris . . . patriis:** either local or instrumental ablative.

739 **nulla . . . potestas:** supply *est*.

740 **olli:** an archaic form of *illi*, often used by Virgil when he wants to introduce an element of dignity or formality. The slow rhythm adds to this effect and reflects Turnus' confidence in the face of Pandarus' verbal onslaught. **Turnus:** supply *dixit*.

741 **incipe:** i.e. begin the fight. **si qua . . . virtus:** supply *est*: 'if there is any courage'. **animo:** local ablative. **consere dextram:** this is a military phrase, meaning literally 'join (your) right hand', and so 'join battle'.

742 **hic etiam:** 'here also', i.e. as well as at Troy. **Priamo:** the late king of Troy. **inventum . . . Achillem:** supply *esse*: 'that an Achilles has been found'. Turnus compares himself to Achilles, as the main killer of Trojans. Priam is dead, and so Pandarus will deliver the message in the underworld.

815–16 **sese . . . dedit:** 'he gave himself', i.e. 'he leapt'.

816–18 **ille:** the Tiber. **gurgite flavo:** probably yellow-brown, from the sediment it carried. **extulit:** the river 'bore him up'. **abluta caede:** 'having washed off the blood'.

Questions

1 What is the tone of Pandarus' speech? How can you tell?

2 Explain the references to people and places in his speech.

3 How effective is Pandarus' speech?

4 How closely and effectively does Turnus' reply match Pandarus' speech?

5 Explain the references to Priam and Achilles.

6 How effective an ending to the book are lines 815–818?

7 Compile a diary of the events at the Trojan camp.

8 From your reading of Book IX, would you say that Virgil glorifies war? Give reasons for your answer.

Book 10

Aeneas has been away from the Trojan camp (at the mouth of the Tiber), seeking an alliance from king Evander of Pallanteum. Evander promised him the help of his son, Pallas, at the head of an army. During Aeneas' absence, Turnus has been leading the Latin attack on the Trojan camp. At the end of Book IX, he forced his way inside the camp and was repelled with great difficulty and loss of life.

panditur interea domus omnipotentis Olympi
conciliumque vocat divum pater atque hominum rex
sideream in sedem, terras unde arduus omnes
castraque Dardanidum aspectat populosque Latinos.
considunt tectis bipatentibus, incipit ipse: 5
'caelicolae magni, quianam sententia vobis
versa retro tantumque animis certatis iniquis?
abnueram bello Italiam concurrere Teucris.
quae contra vetitum discordia? quis metus aut hos
aut hos arma sequi ferrumque lacessere suasit?   10

pando, -ere	I open	*incipio, -ere*	I begin
interea	meanwhile	*caelicola, -ae* m.	god
domus, -us f.	house, home	*quianam*	why?
omnipotens, -entis	all-powerful	*sententia, -ae* f.	decision, purpose
Olympus, -i m.	Olympus	*verto, -ere, verti, versus*	I turn
concilium, -i n.	council	*retro*	backwards
voco, -are	I call	*tantum*	so much
divus, -i m.	god	*animus, -i* m.	mind, spirit
pater, patris m.	father	*certo, -are*	I compete, fight
homo, hominis m.	man(kind)	*iniquus, -a, -um*	unequal, hostile
rex, regis m.	king	*abnuo, -ere, -ui, -utus*	I refuse to allow
sidereus, -a, -um	starry	*bellum, -i* n.	war
sedes, sedis f.	seat, home	*Italia, -ae* f.	Italy
terra, -ae f.	land	*concurro, -ere* + dat.	I join battle with
unde	from where	*Teucri, -orum* m.pl.	Trojans
arduus, -a, -um	high up	*contra* + acc.	against
castra, -orum n.pl.	camp	*veto, -are, -ui, -itus*	I forbid
Dardanidae, -arum m.pl.	Trojans	*discordia, -ae* f.	discord
aspecto, -are	I observe	*metus, -us* m.	fear
populus, -i m.	people, race	*arma, -orum* n.pl. 10	weapons, arms
Latinus, -a, -um	Latin	*sequor, -i, secutus sum*	I follow
consido, -ere 5	I sit down	*ferrum, -i* n.	iron, sword
tectum, -i n.	roof, house	*lacesso, -ere*	I produce
bipatens, -entis	with double doors	*suadeo, -ere, -si, -sus* + dat.	I urge, persuade

1 **panditur:** historic present, Virgil's standard choice for narrative verbs. **interea:** i.e. while
all the fighting at the Trojan camp was taking place. **domus:** i.e. the palace of Jupiter on Mt
Olympus. **omnipotentis Olympi:** the adjective is transferred from Jupiter to the mountain on
which he lived (an example of hypallage). The palace is opened up either because a new day
has dawned or because Jupiter had summoned the other gods to enter.
2 **divum:** = *divorum*.
3–4 **sideream in sedem:** a Homeric expression. **unde:** to be taken before *terras*. **arduus:**
because Jupiter is on top of Olympus. **castra Dardanidum:** the Trojans had built their camp
as soon as they arrived at the mouth of the River Tiber, at the end of their epic journey from
Troy; *Dardanidum = Dardanidarum*. **aspectat:** the subject is Jupiter. **populosque Latinos:**
i.e. the Latins and their allies, principally the Rutulians, whose leader was Turnus. Note the
sibilance in line 3.
5 **considunt:** the subject is the gods. **tectis:** local ablative. **bipatentibus:** 'with doors at both
ends', facing the rising and setting sun. **ipse:** emphatic.
6–7 **quianam sententia vobis versa retro:** supply *est:* 'why has your decision been reversed?';
in Book I, Jupiter decreed that Juno should give up her hostility to the Trojans; this she has
not done, despite any promises she may have given him. The gods have taken sides, some
supporting Venus and the Trojans, others Juno and the Latins. Here Jupiter assumes that,
being aware of his will, the gods have decided to end their differences. **animis . . . iniquis:**
'with hostile minds' (ablative of manner).
8 **abnueram:** it is not made clear when he made this ban. All through the *Aeneid* there have
been prophecies of the war between Trojans and Latins, suggesting that Jupiter knew that
the war was predestined, even if he disapproved of it. **bello:** 'in war' (instrumental ablative).
Teucris: dative after the compound verb; *Teucri* is one of several names for the Trojans used
by Virgil and other ancient writers (cf. *Dardanidum*, lines 3–4 above); most are formed from
the names of founders or early kings of Troy.
9 **quae discordia:** supply *est haec:* 'what is this discord in the face of my prohibition?'
9–10 **quis metus:** 'what fear'; the precise meaning of this phrase depends on how *aut hos aut
hos* is interpreted. Some editors suppose that Jupiter is pointing down to the two opposing
sides in the human contest; in that case *metus* refers to the fear that the two opposing sides
have for their survival. The alternative view is that *hos . . . hos* signifies Jupiter pointing
to the two factions of gods; in this case *metus* refers to the fear that the gods have for the
humans that are dear to them. Both gods and humans could be described as 'pursuing armed
conflict'.

Questions

1 What has been happening in Latium before this book opens?

2 What picture do you receive of the home of the gods?

3 What is the tone of Jupiter's speech?

4 How does Jupiter make clear his attitude?

adveniet iustum pugnae, ne arcessite, tempus,
cum fera Karthago Romanis arcibus olim
exitium magnum atque Alpes immittet apertas:
tum certare odiis, tum res rapuisse licebit.
nunc sinite et placitum laeti componite foedus.'   15
Iuppiter haec paucis; at non Venus aurea contra
pauca refert:
'o pater, o hominum rerumque aeterna potestas
(namque aliud quid sit quod iam implorare queamus?),
cernis ut insultent Rutuli, Turnusque feratur   20
per medios insignis equis tumidusque secundo
Marte ruat? non clausa tegunt iam moenia Teucros;
quin intra portas atque ipsis proelia miscent
aggeribus murorum et inundant sanguine fossae.
Aeneas ignarus abest. numquamne levari   25
obsidione sines?'

advenio, -ire	I arrive, come	*cerno, -ere*	20	I see
iustus, -a, -um	just, right	*ut*		how
pugna, -ae f.	fight	*insulto, -are*		I triumph
arcesso, -ere	I summon	*Rutulus, -i* m.		Rutulian
tempus, -oris n.	time	*Turnus, -i* m.		Turnus
ferus, -a, -um	wild, cruel	*fero, ferre*		I carry
Karthago, -inis f.	Carthage	*medius, -a, -um*		the middle of
arx, arcis f.	citadel	*insignis, -e*		distinguished
olim	one day	*equus, -i* m.		horse
exitium, -i n.	destruction	*tumidus, -a, -um*		swollen
Alpes, -ium f.pl.	the Alps	*secundus, -a, -um*		favourable
immitto, -ere	I send against	*Mars, Martis* m.		Mars, war
aperio, -ire, -ui, apertus	I open	*ruo, -ere*		I rush
certo, -are	I compete	*claudo, -ere, -si, -sus*		I close
odium, -i n.	hatred	*tego, -ere*		I protect
res, rei f.	thing, matter	*moenia, -ium* n.pl.		walls
rapio, -ere, -ui, raptus	I seize	*quin*		indeed
licet, -ere	it is allowed	*intra* + acc.		inside
sino, -ere	15 I cease, give up	*porta, -ae* f.		gate
placitus, -a, -um	pleasing, agreed	*proelium, -i* n.		battle
laetus, -a, -um	glad	*misceo, -ere*		I join (battle)
compono, -ere	I put together	*agger, -eris* m.		rampart
foedus, -eris n.	treaty, agreement	*murus, -i* m.		wall
pauci, -ae, -a	few	*inundo, -are*		I overflow
Venus, -eris f.	Venus	*sanguis, -inis* m.		blood
aureus, -a, -um	golden	*fossa, -ae* f.		ditch
contra	against, in reply	*Aeneas, -ae* m.	25	Aeneas
refero, -ferre	I say in answer	*ignarus, -a, -um*		unawares
aeternus, -a, -um	eternal	*absum, -esse*		I am away
potestas, -atis f.	power	*numquam*		never
namque	for	*levo, -are*		I relieve
alius, -a, -ud	other	*obsidio, -onis* f.		siege
imploro, -are	I appeal to	*sino, -ere*		I allow
queo, -ire	I can			

11 iustum . . . tempus: 'the proper time'; Jupiter is referring to the 3rd century BC, when the first two Punic Wars took place between Rome and Carthage (both won by Rome). One of the reasons Juno has been trying so hard to prevent the Trojans from settling in Italy is her desire to protect Carthage from its eventual destruction by Aeneas' Roman descendants. Aeneas had also been responsible for the suicide of Dido, queen of Carthage, after he abandoned her to continue his destiny (Book IV). **ne arcessite:** 'don't summon (the time)', i.e. 'don't bring it forward'.

12–13 Romanis arcibus: either 'the hills of Rome' (of which one, the Capitol, was called the *Arx*), or 'Roman strongholds', i.e. cities throughout Italy that supported Rome in the Second Punic War. **immittet:** this verb is used with two meanings here, in a device known as a <u>zeugma</u>: Carthage 'will wreak great destruction' on the *arcibus* and will 'pitch the Alps' against them. **Alpes . . . apertas:** the Alps would be 'opened' in the sense of being breached by the Carthaginian general, Hannibal, who led his army from Spain across the Alps into Italy in 218 BC, effectively starting the Second Punic War. Hannibal defeated the Roman armies in three major battles, after which he won over many towns, leaving Rome short of allies in Italy.

14 odiis: 'with hatred' (plural because it applies to both sides). **res rapuisse:** 'to have seized plunder (from each other)'. Note the <u>anaphora</u> of *tum*, making it emphatic.

15 nunc: in clear contrast with *tum*. **sinite:** here unusually 'cease' (your opposition); in line 26 it has its far more usual meaning.

16–17 Iuppiter haec paucis: compressed: supply *verbis dixit*. **Venus aurea:** Aeneas' mother was called 'golden' by Homer. **non . . . pauca:** the position of *non* makes it emphatic, contrasting with *paucis*. Venus has no intention of abbreviating her arguments. The incompleteness of line 17 (one of many examples throughout the work) is evidence of the fact that Virgil died before he could complete the revision of the work.

18 hominum rerumque: equivalent to objective genitives. **potestas:** this abstraction is the opposite of personification.

19 aliud quid: = *quid aliud*. **sit:** 'might there be' (ie. if we were to search). **queamus:** subjunctive in a virtual result clause introduced by *quod*.

20–2 Turnus: Turnus was the leader of the Rutuli and of the Latin alliance against the Trojans. **feratur . . . equis:** 'is carried by horses', i.e. 'rides'. Turnus, spurred on by Juno's assistant Iris (goddess of the Rainbow), had led his cavalry ahead of the main infantry army to attack the Trojan camp. Venus' account in lines 20–5 provides a good summary of the events of Book IX. **tumidus:** 'swollen with pride'. **secundo Marte:** ablative absolute: 'with Mars favourable', i.e. 'favoured by Mars'. *Mars* is often a personification of war, and Venus may mean no more than that the war against the Trojans is going favourably for Turnus. **ruat:** 'charges ahead'. **non clausa . . . moenia:** the Latins had forced their way through the gates of the camp.

23–4 ipsis . . . aggeribus murorum: 'on the ramparts supporting the walls'; the ramparts, built up on the inside of the walls, allowed defenders to fight. **fossae:** these were the first line of defence, running parallel to the walls on the outside.

25–6 Aeneas abest: he has been in Pallanteum. **levari:** supply *Teucros* as subject. **obsidione:** 'from the siege' (ablative of separation).

Questions

1 How is Carthage connected to the story of the *Aeneid*?

2 Find out what happened in Book IX, so that you can understand the events in Book X.

3 How does Venus make her appeal to Jupiter effective?

Venus argues that it was surely wrong that the Trojans were threatened just as they were about to found their new city. If they had acted against Jupiter's will, let them atone for their sin. If however they acted according to the Fates, why should any god have the power to go against Jupiter's will? Juno has sent demons to stir up hostility.

'nil super imperio moveor; speravimus ista,	42
dum fortuna fuit; vincant, quos vincere mavis.	
si nulla est regio Teucris quam det tua coniunx	
dura, per eversae, genitor, fumantia Troiae	45
excidia obtestor: liceat dimittere ab armis	
incolumem Ascanium, liceat superesse nepotem.	
Aeneas sane ignotis iactetur in undis	
et quamcumque viam dederit Fortuna sequatur:	
hunc tegere et dirae valeam subducere pugnae.	50
est Amathus, est celsa mihi Paphus atque Cythera	
Idaliaeque domus: positis inglorius armis	
exigat hic aevum. magna dicione iubeto	
Karthago premat Ausoniam: nihil urbibus inde	
obstabit Tyriis.	55

nil, nihil n.	nothing	*ignotus, -a, -um*	unknown
super + abl.	about	*iacto, -are*	I toss about
imperium, -i n.	power	*unda, -ae* f.	wave, water
moveo, -ere	I move	*qui-, quae-, quodcumque*	whatever
spero, -are, -avi, -atus	I hope	*via, viae* f.	journey, way
iste, ista, istud	that (of yours)	*Fortuna, -ae* f.	Fortune, Fate
fortuna, -ae f.	fortune	*dirus, -a, -um* 50	dreadful
vinco, -ere	I win	*valeo, -ere*	I am able
malo, malle	I prefer	*subduco, -ere*	I remove
nullus, -a, -um	no	*Amathus, -untis* f.	Amathus
regio, -onis f.	region	*celsus, -a, -um*	lofty, high
do, dare	I give	*Paphus, -i* f.	Paphos
coniunx, -iugis f.	wife	*Cythera, -ae* f.	Cythera
durus, -a, -um 45	hard	*Idalia, -ae* f.	Idalia
everto, -ere, -ti, -sus	I overthrow	*pono, -ere, posui, positus*	I set down
genitor, -oris m.	father	*inglorius, -a, -um*	inglorious
fumo, -are	I smoke	*exigo, -ere*	I pass, thrust
Troia, -ae f.	Troy	*aevum, -i* n.	age, life-time
excidium, -i n.	destruction	*dicio, -onis* f.	power
obtestor, -ari, -atus sum	I beseech	*iubeo, -ere, iussi, iussus*	I order
dimitto, -ere	I send away	*premo, -ere, -pressi, -pressus*	I crush, press
incolumis, -e	safe	*Ausonia, -ae* f.	Ausonia, S. Italy
Ascanius, -i m.	Ascanius	*urbs, urbis* f.	city
supersum, -esse	I survive	*inde*	from there, then
nepos, -otis m.	grandson	*obsto, -are* + dat. 55	I obstruct
sane	of course	*Tyrius, -a, -um*	Carthaginian

42–3 **nil super imperio moveor:** there are two ways of construing *super*, as adverb or preposition; as the former it would mean 'I am not concerned any *more* by (thoughts of) empire'; as the latter it would mean 'I am not concerned at all *about* empire'. There is little difference between them. In Book I.279, Jupiter had promised Venus that Aeneas' descendants (i.e. the Romans) would have an 'empire without end'. Now she is being ironic. **ista:** i.e. the promises made to her in Book I. **dum fortuna fuit:** 'as long as there was good fortune' (*fortuna* may be good, bad or neutral).

44–6 **det:** potential subjunctive: 'could give'. **dura:** note the underlined enjambement. **obtestor:** supply *te*: 'I beseech you through . . .'. **per . . . fumantia . . . excidia:** 'through (i.e. 'in the name of') the smoking destruction'. **eversae . . . Troiae:** 'of overthrown Troy'; she is of course referring to the destruction of Troy by the Greeks at the end of the Trojan War.

46–7 **liceat:** 'may it be permitted', i.e. 'may I be allowed'. **Ascanium:** Aeneas' son by Creusa, and so Venus' grandson. Despite his youth, he has been taking an active part in the defence of the Trojan camp (Book IX). Note the underlined anaphora of *liceat*, making her appeal all the more poignant.

48–9 **sane:** used ironically. **ignotis in undis:** there are two interpretations of this: either she imagines Aeneas and the Trojans forced to leave Latium and embark on another journey across the sea; or she is exaggerating the dangers of his actual journey up the Tiber to Pallanteum (as Juno understood her to mean). **quamcumque viam . . . sequatur:** 'let him follow whatever route'. **dederit:** probably future perfect indicative.

50 **hunc:** Ascanius, in strong contrast with *Aeneas* two lines above. **dirae . . . pugnae:** 'from the dreadful battle' (a sort of dative of disadvantage, taken by most verbs of abstraction).

51–3 The places named were all centres of the worship of Venus. Cythera was off the south coast of Greece, the rest were in Cyprus. **Idaliaeque domus:** probably *domus* is nominative singular, parallel to the first three names: 'my home in Idalia'. **inglorius:** refers to Ascanius. **hic:** 'here', i.e. in one of the four named places.

53–5 **iubeto:** an old form of the imperative. **premat:** jussive subjunctive dependent on *iubeto*: 'give orders that Carthage crush Ausonia'. **magna dicione:** 'under its great power', probably an instrumental ablative. **Ausoniam:** this name is used regularly by Virgil to refer to the southern half of Italy. **nihil . . . obstabit Tyriis:** 'nothing will obstruct the Carthaginian cities'. **inde:** i.e. from Italy. **Tyriis:** Dido sailed from her native city of Tyre (in modern-day Lebanon) to found Carthage (on the North African coast). Carthage in historical times built up a great empire with many cities, comprising most of the Western Mediterranean. This empire was lost to the Romans in the 3rd century BC after the first two Punic Wars.

Questions

1 What are Venus' arguments in this speech?

2 To what extent do you think she meant what she said?

3 This speech is full of present subjunctives; what is their purpose?

4 How can we tell that this speech is entirely ironic?

5 Why do you think Venus chooses to use so much irony?

6 What do you think is Venus' priority in this speech?

               quid pestem evadere belli   55
iuvit et Argolicos medium fugisse per ignes
totque maris vastaeque exhausta pericula terrae,
dum Latium Teucri recidivaque Pergama quaerunt?
non satius cineres patriae insedisse supremos
atque solum quo Troia fuit? Xanthum et Simoenta   60
redde, oro, miseris iterumque revolvere casus
da, pater, Iliacos Teucris.' tum regia Iuno
acta furore gravi: 'quid me alta silentia cogis
rumpere et obductum verbis vulgare dolorem?
Aenean hominum quisquam divumque subegit   65
bella sequi aut hostem regi se inferre Latino?
Italiam petiit fatis auctoribus (esto)
Cassandrae impulsus furiis: num linquere castra
hortati sumus aut vitam committere ventis?'

pestis, -is f.	55 plague, ruin	*regius, -a, -um*	royal
evado, -ere	I escape from	*Iuno, -onis* f.	Juno
iuvo, -are, iuvi, iutus	I help	*ago, -ere, egi, actus*	I drive
Argolicus, -a, -um	Greek	*furor, -oris* m.	madness, rage
fugio, -ere, fugi, fugitus	I flee	*gravis, -e*	heavy, deep
ignis, -is m.	fire	*quid?*	why?
tot	so many	*altus, -a, -um*	high, deep
mare, -is n.	sea	*silentium, -i* n.	silence
vastus, -a, -um	vast	*cogo, -ere*	I force
exhaurio, -ire, -hausi, -stus	I endure	*rumpo, -ere*	I break, burst
periculum, -i n.	danger	*obduco, -ere, -duxi, -ductus*	I hide
Latium, -i n.	Latium	*verbum, -i* n.	word
recidivus, -a, -um	resurrected	*vulgo, -are*	I publish
Pergama, -orum n.pl.	Troy	*dolor, -oris* m.	pain, sorrow
quaero, -ere	I seek, ask	*quis-, quae-, quicquam* 65	anyone, any
satius	better, preferable	*subigo, -ere, -egi, -actus*	I compel
cinis, -eris m.	ash	*hostis, -is* m.	enemy
patria, -ae f.	native land	*infero, -ferre*	I carry forward
insido, -ere, -sedi, -sessus	I settle on	*peto, -ere*	I seek, make for
supremus, -a, -um	last	*fatum, -i* n.	fate
solum, -i n.	60 ground, soil	*auctor, -oris* m.	instigator
Xanthus, -i m.	river Xanthus	*Cassandra, -ae* f.	Cassandra
Simois, -entis (acc. *-enta*) m.	river Simois	*impello, -ere, -puli, -pulsus*	I impel, urge on
reddo, -ere	I give back	*furia, -ae* f.	fury, madness
oro, -are	I pray, beg	*num*	surely not
miser, -era, -erum	wretched	*linquo, -ere*	I leave
iterum	again	*hortor, -ari, -atus sum*	I urge
revolvo, -ere	I experience again	*vita, -ae* f.	life
casus, -us m.	misfortune	*committo, -ere*	I entrust
Iliacus, -a, -um	Trojan, of Troy	*ventus, -i* m.	wind

55–6 quid . . . iuvit: supply *Aenean*: 'how did it help him'. **belli:** i.e. the Trojan War, from which Aeneas escaped to lead the remnants of his people to a new home. **medium:** agrees with *Aenean* (inferred). **Argolicos . . . ignes:** the fires lit by the Greeks to destroy Troy.

57 totque . . . exhausta pericula: 'and (through) so many dangers that he endured'.

58 recidivaque Pergama: 'and Troy brought back to life', i.e. a new home in a new land; Pergama was the citadel of Troy, here used by <u>synecdoche</u> for the whole city.

59–60 non satius: supply *fuit*: 'would it not have been better' (Virgil often uses the indicative in this type of expression to present the idea almost as a fact). **solum quo Troia fuit:** 'the soil on which Troy stood'.

60–2 Xanthum et Simoenta: these two rivers flowed close to Troy. **miseris . . . Teucris:** dependent on both *redde* and *da*. **da:** 'grant', taking the infinitive. **casus . . . Iliacos:** 'the misfortunes of Troy', i.e. its destruction by the Greeks. Note the jumbled word order, which indicates Venus' agitation.

62–3 Iuno: supply *dixit*. **cogis:** is Juno addressing Jupiter or Venus?

63–4 alta silentia: Juno claims to have maintained a 'deep silence' over the warfare, a disingenuous claim, as recently she has been very active behind the scenes. **obductum . . . dolorem:** 'a pain I have kept hidden'; the 'pain' is her bitterness at how Aeneas has been allowed to progress so far.

65–6 quisquam . . . subegit: 'did anyone compel?' **divum:** = *divorum*. **bella sequi:** 'to follow wars', i.e. 'to choose to make war'. **hostem . . . se inferre:** 'carry himself an enemy to . . .', i.e. 'to go against (Latinus) as an enemy'.

67–8 Italiam petiit fatis auctoribus: Juno quotes Venus' strongest argument in support of Aeneas back at her, that he made for Italy by the authority of the fates. This is what did happen (see, for example, Mercury's delivery to Aeneas of Jupiter's orders in Book IV.265ff.). **esto:** 'let it be so' (a 3rd person imperative); she is being sarcastic: she can't deny the fact, but she can belittle it by adding *Cassandrae impulsus furiis*: 'impelled by the ravings of Cassandra'; Cassandra was a daughter of king Priam of Troy, who was a prophetess cursed by Apollo to predict the truth but never be believed by anyone.

68–9 linquere castra: i.e. leave the camp unprotected. **hortati sumus:** either a 'royal we' (using the masculine form as a convention), or intended to include other gods who support Juno against Venus. **ventis:** i.e. the winds that carried Aeneas' ships up-stream to Pallanteum.

Questions

1 What are Venus' arguments in lines 55–62?

2 What fundamental point is she making with these arguments?

3 What is the tone of Juno's response?

4 What arguments does she use to dismiss Venus' claims and complaints?

5 What makes Juno's speech a good example of oratory?

Juno continued to counter Venus' complaints, arguing that she was not responsible for making the Trojans declare war on the Latins. If Venus could get away with helping Aeneas, why should she, the queen of the gods, not help the Latins? After all, it was Venus' fault that the Trojan War broke out in the first place.

talibus orabat Iuno, cunctique fremebant	96
caelicolae adsensu vario, ceu flamina prima	
cum deprensa fremunt silvis et caeca volutant	
murmura venturos nautis prodentia ventos.	
tum pater omnipotens, rerum cui prima potestas,	100
infit (eo dicente deum domus alta silescit	
et tremefacta solo tellus, silet arduus aether,	
tum Zephyri posuere, premit placida aequora pontus):	
'accipite ergo animis atque haec mea figite dicta.	
quandoquidem Ausonios coniungi foedere Teucris	105
haud licitum, nec vestra capit discordia finem,	
quae cuique est fortuna hodie, quam quisque secat spem,	
Tros Rutulusne fuat, nullo discrimine habebo,	
seu fatis Italum castra obsidione tenentur	
sive errore malo Troiae monitisque sinistris.	110
nec Rutulos solvo. sua cuique exorsa laborem	
fortunamque ferent. rex Iuppiter omnibus idem.'	

talis, -e	such	*figo, -ere*		I fix, transfix
cunctus, -a, -um	all	*dictum, -i* n.		word
fremo, -ere	I murmur, roar	*quandoquidem*		since
adsensus, -us m.	agreement	*Ausonii, -orum* m.pl.	105	Italians
varius, -a, -um	various	*coniungo, -ere*		I join together
ceu	just like	*foedus, -eris* n.		treaty, pact
flamen, -inis n.	rustling of wind	*haud*		not
deprendo, -ere, -ndi, -nsus	I catch	*vester, -tra, -trum*		your
silva, -ae f.	wood	*capio, -ere*		I take
caecus, -a, -um	blind, unseen	*discordia, -ae* f.		discord
voluto, -are	I roll about, ponder	*finis, -is* m.		end
		quisque, quaeque, quidque		each (one)
murmur, -uris n.	murmur, rumbling	*hodie*		today
nauta, -ae m.	sailor	*seco, -are*		I cut, pursue
prodo, -ere	I reveal	*Tros, Trois* m.		Trojan
infit (defective verb)	101 he begins to speak	*discrimen, -inis* n.		distinction
silesco, -ere	I grow silent	*seu, sive*		whether, or
tremefacio, -ere, -feci, -factus	I shake	*Itali, -orum* m.pl.		Italians
solum, -i n.	foundation	*teneo, -ere*		I hold
tellus, -uris f.	earth	*error, -oris* m.	110	error
sileo, -ere	I am silent	*malus, -a, -um*		evil, bad
aether, -eris m. (acc. *-era*)	air	*monitum, -i* n.		warning
Zephyrus, -i m.	West Wind	*sinister, -tra, -trum*		improper, left
placidus, -a, -um	calm	*solvo, -ere*		I absolve, exempt
aequor, -oris n.	sea, water, plain	*exorsa, -orum* n.pl.		undertakings
pontus, -i m.	ocean	*labor, -oris* m.		work, toil
accipio, -ere	I receive, hear	*idem, eadem, idem*		the same
ergo	therefore			

96–7 **talibus:** supply *verbis*. **fremebant:** 'murmured' rather than 'roared', as shown by the simile that follows. **adsensu vario:** 'with varying agreement', i.e. some supported Venus and others Juno.

97–9 **ceu . . . cum:** introduces a simile. **flamina prima:** a *flamen* can be anything from a breath of wind to a full gale; here the emphatically-positioned *prima* indicates the former. **deprensa:** 'caught' by the trees. **silvis:** local ablative. **caeca volutant murmura:** 'roll unseen murmurs about (the forest)', i.e 'cause unseen murmurs to roll around'; the murmuring breeze is 'unseen' because it does not yet stir the trees. **prodentia:** here effectively 'presaging'.

100 **rerum:** objective genitive: 'over things', i.e. 'over (human) affairs'. **cui:** supply *est*: 'who has'. **prima:** 'first' in the sense of 'greatest'.

101 **eo dicente:** ablative absolute: 'while he spoke'. **deum:** = *deorum*.

102 **tremefacta . . . tellus:** supply *est*. **solo:** local ablative.

103 **posuere:** this is the shortened, mainly poetic, alternative to *posuerunt*; this form is commonly used by Virgil, and will not be commented on again. Here the verb is used as if intransitive, meaning 'dropped' or 'were stilled'. **premit:** 'pressed (the waters flat)', i.e. 'smoothed out (the waters)'. **placida:** proleptic, in that they became calm after his action.

104 **animis:** local ablative, to be taken with both *accipite* and *figite*.

105–6 **haud licitum:** supply *est*. **foedere:** instrumental ablative: 'by a treaty'. **vestra discordia:** i.e. the disagreement between Venus and Juno.

107 **quae cuique est:** 'whatever (fortune) each (side) has'. **quam quisque secat spem:** 'whatever hope each (side) pursues'.

108 **fuat:** an archaic form of *sit*: 'whether he be Trojan or Rutulian'. **habebo:** 'I shall treat'.

109 **fatis Italum:** causal ablative: 'because of the fates of the Italians', i.e. because the Italians are fated (to besiege the Trojan camp). **Italum:** = *Italorum*. **obsidione tenentur:** 'is held in siege', i.e. 'is being kept under siege'.

110 **errore malo Troiae:** 'by a bad error of Troy', i.e. 'because of a bad mistake by the Trojans'. **monitisque sinistris:** 'and because of improper advice', i.e. that given by prophets and deities to Aeneas at various times throughout the *Aeneid*.

111–12 **sua cuique exorsa:** 'to each man his own undertakings'. **laborem fortunamque:** opposites: 'trouble and good fortune'. Jupiter decrees that each human will be responsible for his own fortune, even though fate determines the overall shape of events and lives. **Iuppiter . . . idem:** supply *est*: he is the same for all, i.e. impartial.

Questions

1 What is the purpose of the simile in lines 97–99? How appropriate is it?

2 How does Virgil emphasise the power of Jupiter in lines 100–103?

3 What are the main points of Jupiter's speech?

4 How do his words show his power and authority?

5 What impression do you get from Jupiter's words of the relationship between gods and fate?

6 How does Jupiter show his impartiality?

Jupiter nodded, setting all Olympus quaking.

interea Rutuli portis circum omnibus instant	118
sternere caede viros et moenia cingere flammis.	
at legio Aeneadum vallis obsessa tenetur	120
nec spes ulla fugae. miseri stant turribus altis	
nequiquam et rara muros cinxere corona:	122
hi iaculis, illi certant defendere saxis	130
molirique ignem nervoque aptare sagittas.	
ipse inter medios, Veneris iustissima cura,	
Dardanius caput, ecce, puer detectus honestum,	
qualis gemma micat fulvum quae dividit aurum,	
aut collo decus aut capiti, vel quale per artem	135
inclusum buxo aut Oricia terebintho	
lucet ebur; fusos cervix cui lactea crines	
accipit et molli subnectens circulus auro.	

Also there were Ismarus, Mnestheus and Capys.

circum	around	*Dardanius, -a, -um*	Trojan
insto, -are	I press forward	*caput, -itis* n.	head
sterno, -ere	I strike down	*ecce*	look! see!
caedes, -is f.	slaughter	*detego, -ere, -texi, -tectus*	I uncover
cingo, -ere	I surround	*honestus, -a, -um*	handsome
flamma, -ae f.	flame	*qualis, -e*	just like
legio, -onis f.	120 army	*gemma, -ae* f.	jewel
Aeneades, -ae m.	follower of Aeneas	*mico, -are*	I shine, glitter
		fulvus, -a, -um	yellow, tawny
vallum, -i n.	rampart	*divido, -ere*	I divide
obsideo, -ere, -sedi, -sessus	I besiege	*aurum, -i* n.	gold
spes, spei f.	hope	*aut . . . aut*	135 either . . . or
ullus, -a, -um	any	*collum, -i* n.	neck
fuga, -ae f.	flight	*decus, -oris* n.	ornament
sto, stare	I stand	*vel*	or
turris, -is f.	tower	*ars, artis* f.	skill
nequiquam	in vain	*inclusus, -a, -um*	enclosed, inlaid
rarus, -a, -um	sparse	*buxus, -i* f.	boxwood
cingo, -ere, cinxi, cinctus	I ring, man	*Oricius, -a, -um*	of Oricum
corona, -ae f.	ring, cordon	*terebinthus, -i* f.	terebinth
iaculum, -i n.	130 javelin	*luceo, -ere*	I gleam
defendo, -ere	I defend	*ebur, eburis* n.	ivory
saxum, -i n.	rock	*fusus, -a, -um*	flowing
molior, -iri, -itus sum	I wield, force	*cervix, -icis* f.	neck
nervus, -i m.	bowstring	*lacteus, -a, -um*	milk-white
apto, -are	I fit	*crinis, -is* m.	hair
sagitta, -ae f.	arrow	*mollis, -e*	soft
inter + acc.	between, among	*subnecto, -ere*	I clasp
cura, -ae f.	care, anxiety	*circulus, -i* m.	circlet, ring

118–19 At this point the narrative resumes from the end of Book IX. **portis . . . omnibus:** local ablative; Virgil has in mind the standard Roman military camp with its four gates. **circum:** 'all round (the camp)'. **sternere:** here the infinitive expresses purpose.

120–1 **Aeneadum:** = *Aeneadarum*. **vallis:** local ablative: 'within their ramparts'. **obsessa tenetur:** 'is held under siege'. **spes ulla:** supply *est*.

121–2 **turribus:** local ablative. **nequiquam:** 'in vain', i.e. 'helpless'. **rara . . . corona:** ablative, as the scansion shows. **cinxere:** 'they ringed' the walls with defenders, insufficient (*rara*) to cover the whole length of the rampart.

123–9 These lines comprise a list of names of Trojan warriors manning the walls.

130–1 **hi . . . illi:** 'some . . . others'. **defendere:** supply *se* or *castra*. **molirique ignem:** 'and to wield fire', i.e. hurl blazing firebrands or shoot fire-arrows.

132 **ipse:** emphatic by position and because the person is not identified until the next line. **Veneris iustissima cura:** 'the most proper care of Venus', i.e. 'the most legitimate object of Venus' care and concern'. Because Ascanius was Venus' grandson and destined to continue the royal line that would lead to Augustus, it was perfectly reasonable for the goddess to wish to protect him. Virgil is thinking back to her plea to Jupiter in lines 46–7.

133 **Dardanius . . . puer:** i.e. Ascanius. **caput . . . detectus honestum:** 'uncovered with respect to his handsome head', and so 'his handsome head uncovered'; this is one of Virgil's favourite types of expression, modelled on the Greek middle verb. Ascanius is not wearing his helmet because he was warned by Apollo (towards the end of Book IX) not to continue fighting.

134 **qualis** (also *quale* in line 135): used frequently to introduce a simile. **quae:** to be taken before *fulvum*. **dividit:** the jewel 'divides' or 'splits' the gold, and so 'is set in'. The jewel is brighter than the gold that surrounds it, just as Ascanius is brighter than his fellows.

135–7 **per artem:** 'skilfully'. **inclusum . . . ebur:** 'ivory inlaid' in darker coloured woods. **buxo:** the box tree has yellowish wood. **terebintho:** the terebinth, or turpentine tree, has dark-coloured wood. **Oricia:** the terebinth tree was presumably known to grow in Oricum, a town in northern Greece.

137–8 **cui:** 'for whom' (i.e. for Ascanius), and so more simply 'whose'. **fusos . . . crines:** note how the 'flowing locks' surround the neck, as in real life (an example of enclosing word order). **accipit:** the neck 'receives' the hair; it is perhaps easier to turn the sentence round and translate as 'the flowing locks fall about his milk-white neck'. **circulus:** a band worn over the head to keep long hair in place. **molli . . . auro:** ablative of material: 'made of soft gold'; note again the enclosing word order. **subnectens:** supply *crines* as its object and *est* ('there is') as the verb of which *circulus* is the subject.

Questions

1 How are the Rutulians and Trojans contrasted in lines 118–131?

2 What defensive measures are the Trojans taking?

3 How does Virgil show that these measures are not entirely successful?

4 How is Ascanius depicted?

5 What is the simile and how is it appropriate?

6 What part do colours play in the description of Ascanius?

illi inter sese duri certamina belli   146
contulerant: media Aeneas freta nocte secabat.
namque ut ab Euandro castris ingressus Etruscis
regem adit et regi memorat nomenque genusque
quidve petat quidve ipse ferat, Mezentius arma   150
quae sibi conciliet, violentaque pectora Turni
edocet, humanis quae sit fiducia rebus
admonet immiscetque preces, haud fit mora, Tarchon
iungit opes foedusque ferit; tum libera fati
classem conscendit iussis gens Lydia divum   155
externo commissa duci. Aeneia puppis
prima tenet rostro Phrygios subiuncta leones,
imminet Ida super, profugis gratissima Teucris.
hic magnus sedet Aeneas secumque volutat
eventus belli varios, Pallasque sinistro   160
adfixus lateri iam quaerit sidera, opacae
noctis iter, iam quae passus terraque marique.

Many were the chieftains who sailed with their men in thirty ships to help the Trojans. The ships sped across the sea.

certamen, -inis n.	struggle	opes, opum f.pl.	resources
confero, -ferre, -tuli, -latus	I fight	ferio, -ire	I strike, conclude
fretum, -i n.	sea	liber, -era, -erum	free
nox, noctis f.	night	classis, -is f.	155 fleet
seco, -are	I cut, cleave	conscendo, -ere	I board
Euandrus, -i m.	Evander	iussum, -i n.	order
ingredior, -i, -gressus sum	I enter (+ dat.)	gens, gentis f.	race
Etruscus, -a, -um	Etruscan	Lydius, -a, -um	Lydian
adeo, -ire	I approach, go to	externus, -a, -um	foreign
memoro, -are	I relate	dux, ducis m.	leader
nomen, -inis n.	name	Aeneius, -a, -um	of Aeneas
genus, -eris n.	race	puppis, -is f.	stern, ship
Mezentius, -i m.	150 Mezentius	rostrum, -i n.	beak, prow
concilio, -are	I win over	Phrygius, -a, -um	Phrygian
violentus, -a, -um	violent	subiungo, -ere, -nxi, -nctus	I attach
pectus, -oris n.	breast, heart	leo, -onis m.	lion
edoceo, -ere	I inform	immineo, -ere	I loom above
humanus, -a, -um	human	Ida, -ae f.	Mt Ida
fiducia, -ae f.	confidence, reliance	super	above
		profugus, -a, -um	exiled
admoneo, -ere	I advise, point out	gratus, -a, -um	pleasing, dear
immisceo, -ere	I add	eventus, -us m.	160 outcome, fortune
prex, precis f.	prayer, entreaty	Pallas, -antis (acc. -a) m.	Pallas
fio, fieri	I am made, become	adfigo, -ere, -fixi, -fixus	I attach
		latus, -eris n.	side
mora, -ae f.	delay, mainstay, barrier	sidus, -eris n.	star
		opacus, -a, -um	dark
Tarchon, -onis m.	Tarchon	iter, itineris n.	course, route
iungo, -ere	I join	patior, -i, passus sum	I experience

146–7 **illi:** the two armies. **sese:** = *se*. **freta . . . secabat:** 'was cleaving (a path through) the sea'. Note the slow rhythm of line 146, appropriate to the context of a siege.

148–9 **ut:** 'when'. **ab Euandro:** 'after leaving Evander'; Evander was the king of Pallanteum, whose help Aeneas had been seeking. **castris . . . Etruscis:** dependent on *ingressus*, a rare use of the dative with this verb; it was Evander who told Aeneas (Book VIII) that the Etruscans, a nation living to the north of Pallanteum, were looking for someone to lead them in a war against the tyrant Mezentius, who had allied himself with Turnus after being driven out of Etruria. **regem adit:** '(when) he approaches the king'; the Etruscan king was Tarchon. The narrative resumes at this point from Book VIII.603, when Aeneas left Pallanteum. **nomenque genusque:** an example of <u>polysyndeton</u>; the first *-que* can be ignored in translation.

150 **quidve . . . quidve:** the disjunctive particles are parallel to the two conjunctive particles in the previous line, and are used for variety; they are commonly used in supplementary direct questions and can be retained when the questions are indirect, as here. **quidve ipse ferat:** 'or what (resources) he himself is bringing', i.e. the troops that Evander had given him.

150–2 The order is *quae arma Mezentius conciliet sibi*. **quae arma:** probably dependent on *memorat* rather than *edocet*; the *arma* are those of the Rutuli and Latins, whom Mezentius had persuaded to ally themselves to him. **edocet:** 'informs him of'.

152–3 The order is *admonet quae fiducia sit humanis rebus*: 'he points out what reliance there is in human affairs', i.e. 'what little reliance'; his argument is that without divine support, humans can achieve little. **preces:** either a plea to Tarchon, or a prayer to the gods.

153–4 **haud fit mora:** the first main verb in this long sentence, ironically brief after the protracted preamble; note the <u>asyndeton</u>, in contrast with the earlier <u>polysyndeton</u>.

154–6 The order is *tum, iussis divum, gens Lydia, libera fati, conscendit classem*. **gens Lydia:** the 'Lydian race' was the Etruscans, who were thought to have migrated to Etruria from Lydia in Asia Minor. **iussis divum:** = *iussis divorum*: 'by order of the gods': it had been the gods' will (as interpreted by a prophet) that the Etruscans should only march to war under a foreign leader; Aeneas now filled this role. **libera fati:** 'free of fate', i.e. 'freed from the demands of fate', now that they had a foreign leader.

156–8 **Aeneia puppis:** 'Aeneas' ship'; *puppis* is an example of <u>synecdoche</u>. **prima tenet:** 'holds first place'; *prima* is a neuter plural noun. **rostro:** 'on its beak', local ablative; the beak was the pointed front of the prow, often adorned with a figure-head. **Phrygios subiuncta leones:** 'attached in respect of Phrygian lions', i.e. 'with Phrygian lions attached (to its beak)'. Phrygia, in Asia Minor, was the seat of the worship of Cybele, called by the Romans *Magna Mater*; her cult was associated with lions. She was also associated with Mt Ida, a mountain close to Troy. **gratissima:** the Ida figure-head was dear to the Trojans because it reminded them of home.

159–61 **hic:** 'here', i.e. at the prow. **Pallas:** Pallas was the son of Evander. **adfixus:** 'attached', i.e. 'sitting close to'. **quaerit:** 'asks (Aeneas) about'. **iter:** in apposition to *sidera*, as the stars were the main nocturnal navigating aid. **passus:** supply *sit*: 'what experiences he has had'.

Questions

1 Summarise the meeting between Aeneas and Tarchon. How does Aeneas persuade Tarchon to join forces with him?

2 Why is Tarchon ready to join Aeneas? Give as many reasons as you can.

3 Why do you think Virgil gives details of the figure-head on Aeneas' ship?

4 Why does Pallas sit next to Aeneas?

iamque dies caelo concesserat almaque curru   215
noctivago Phoebe medium pulsabat Olympum:
Aeneas (neque enim membris dat cura quietem)
ipse sedens clavumque regit velisque ministrat.
atque illi medio in spatio chorus, ecce, suarum
occurrit comitum: nymphae, quas alma Cybebe   220
numen habere maris nymphasque e navibus esse
iusserat, innabant pariter fluctusque secabant,
quot prius aeratae steterant ad litora prorae.
agnoscunt longe regem lustrantque choreis.
quarum quae fandi doctissima Cymodocea   225
pone sequens dextra puppim tenet ipsaque dorso
eminet ac laeva tacitis subremigat undis.
tum sic ignarum adloquitur: 'vigilasne, deum gens,
Aenea? vigila et velis immitte rudentes.
nos sumus, Idaeae sacro de vertice pinus,   230
nunc pelagi nymphae, classis tua. perfidus ut nos
praecipites ferro Rutulus flammaque premebat,
rupimus invitae tua vincula teque per aequor
quaerimus.

dies, -ei m.	215 day	*prora, -ae* f.	prow
concedo, -ere, -cessi, -cessus	I withdraw	*agnosco, -ere*	I recognise
almus, -a, -um	kindly	*longe*	from afar
currus, -us m.	chariot	*lustro, -are*	I go round
noctivagus, -a, -um	night-wandering	*chorea, -ae* f.	dance
Phoebe, -es f.	Phoebe	*for, fari, fatus sum*	225 I speak
pulso, -are	I disturb	*doctus, -a, -um*	skilled
Olympus, -i m.	Olympus	*Cymodocea, -ae* f.	Cymodocea
membrum, -i n.	limb	*pone*	behind
quies, -etis f.	rest	*dextra, -ae* f.	right hand
clavus, -i m.	tiller, rudder	*dorsum, -i* n.	back
rego, -ere	I control	*emineo, -ere*	I project
velum, -i n.	sail	*laeva, -ae* f.	left hand
ministro, -are + dat.	I manage	*tacitus, -a, -um*	silent
spatium, -i n.	space, course	*subremigo, -are*	I paddle below
chorus, -i m.	band	*ignarus, -a, -um*	unaware
occurro, -ere + dat.	220 I meet	*adloquor, -i, -locutus sum*	I address
comes, -itis f.	companion	*vigilo, -are*	I am awake
nympha, -ae f.	nymph	*immitto, -ere*	I let go
Cybebe, -es f.	Cybele	*rudens, -entis* m.	rope
numen, -inis n.	divine power	*Idaeus, -a, -um*	230 of Mt Ida
navis, -is f.	ship	*sacer, -cra, -crum*	sacred
inno, -are	I swim in	*vertex, -icis* m.	summit, top
pariter	alongside	*pinus, -us* f.	pine tree
fluctus, -us m.	wave	*pelagus, -i* n.	open sea
quot	as many as	*perfidus, -a, -um*	treacherous
prius	previously	*praeceps, -cipitis*	headlong
aeratus, -a, -um	bronze-plated	*invitus, -a, -um*	unwilling
litus, -oris n.	shore	*vinculum, -i* n.	chain

215–16 **caelo:** 'from the sky' (ablative of separation). **almaque . . . Phoebe:** Phoebe was the goddess of the moon and sister of Phoebus Apollo, i.e. Diana. **curru noctivago:** local ablative; just as Apollo was believed to drive the sun chariot across the sky during the day, so Phoebe drove the moon chariot at night. **medium . . . Olympum:** Olympus was the mountain home of the gods, but poets use the word more generally to mean 'heaven', and so 'the sky'. Virgil is saying that it was the middle of the night.

217–18 **dat cura:** 'his anxiety allows'. **clavum:** the stearing rudder was shaped like a very large oar and extended from the stern rail down into the sea.

219–20 **medio in spatio:** i.e. half way back to the mouth of the Tiber. **illi:** dependent on *occurrit*.

220–2 **nymphae:** in Book IX.77ff., the goddess Cybele (often also called Cybebe) had saved the Trojan ships from being destroyed by fire by Turnus and his men. She turned each ship into a sea nymph. **numen habere maris:** 'to have divine power over the sea'; *maris* is akin to an objective genitive. **e navibus:** 'from (being) ships'. **pariter:** 'alongside (Aeneas' ship)'.

223 **quot:** there were as many nymphs as there had been prows. **ad litora:** 'drawn up on the shore'; ships were generally rowed prow-first onto a sandy beach.

224 **lustrantque choreis:** ablative of manner: 'they circle him in dance', i.e. 'they dance round him'. Note the slow rhythm.

225 **quarum quae:** 'of these the one who is . . .'. **fandi doctissima:** 'the most skilled at speaking'; *fandi* is genitive of respect of the gerund. The idea that most of the nymphs had not yet fully developed the faculty of speech calls to mind Ovid's *Metamorphoses*, as indeed does the whole episode.

226–7 **dextra, laeva:** instrumental ablatives. **dorso eminet:** 'projects (from the water) with her back', i.e. 'lifts her back out of the water'. **tacitis . . . undis:** 'in the silent waters': either she paddled silently, so that the waters remained undisturbed, or the waters were calm anyway.

228–9 **ignarum:** he had not yet noticed the nymphs. **deum gens:** = *deorum gens*: 'descendant of the gods'. **velis immitte rudentes:** 'let out the ropes to the sails'; probably *velis* is dative after the compound verb; the sails would have been furled on to a yard high up on the mast and held there by ropes fastened to the deck or rail; the sails would be lowered to catch the wind by untying the ropes.

230–1 The order is *nos sumus classis tua, Idaeae pinus de sacro vertice, nunc nymphae pelagi.* **Idae . . . pinus:** the ships were built from pine trees sacred to Cybele on Mt Ida near Troy.

231–2 The order is *ut perfidus Rutulus premebat nos praecipites ferro flammaque.* **perfidus . . . Rutulus:** Turnus. **premebat:** 'was driving'. **praecipites:** proleptic.

233–4 **tua vincula:** the chains that moored the ships to the shore, but also linked them to Aeneas. **rupimus, quaerimus:** note the change of tense: 'we broke your chains (in the past); (now) we seek you'. Note the alliteration of *p* in these lines.

Questions

1 How does Virgil describe the time? How is this better than simply saying *media nocte*?

2 How does Virgil make his description of the nymphs entertaining?

3 What does Cymodocea tell Aeneas to do? Why might she do this?

4 How do the nymph's words add force to her account?

5 Read a translation of the passage in Book IX that describes the attempt to burn the ships.

> hanc genetrix faciem miserata refecit
ed dedit esse deas aevumque agitare sub undis.   235
at puer Ascanius muro fossisque tenetur
tela inter media atque horrentes Marte Latinos.
iam loca iussa tenet forti permixtus Etrusco
Arcas eques; medias illis opponere turmas,
ne castris iungant, certa est sententia Turno.   240
surge age et Aurora socios veniente vocari
primus in arma iube, et clipeum cape quem dedit ipse
invictum Ignipotens atque oras ambiit auro.
crastina lux, mea si non inrita dicta putaris,
ingentes Rutulae spectabit caedis acervos.'   245
dixerat et dextra discedens impulit altam
haud ignara modi puppim: fugit illa per undas
ocior et iaculo et ventos aequante sagitta.
inde aliae celerant cursus. stupet inscius ipse
Tros Anchisiades, animos tamen omine tollit.   250

Offering a prayer to Cybele as day dawned, Aeneas ordered his men to get ready for action.

iamque in conspectu Teucros habet et sua castra   260
stans celsa in puppi, clipeum cum deinde sinistra
extulit ardentem.

genetrix, -icis f.	mother	Ignipotens, -entis m.	Vulcan
facies, -ei f.	shape	ora, -ae f.	edge, rim
miseror, -ari, -atus sum	I pity	ambio, -ire, -ii, -itus	I encircle
reficio, -ere, -feci, -fectus	I remake	crastinus, -a, -um	tomorrow's
dea, -ae f.	235 goddess	lux, lucis f.	light, dawn
aevum, -i n.	life-time	inritus, -a, -um	useless, invalid
agito, -are	I spend (time)	puto, -are	I think
puer, pueri m.	boy	ingens, -entis	245 huge
telum, -i n.	missile, weapon	specto, -are	I observe
horrens, -entis	bristling, rough	acervus, -i m.	heap
Latini, -orum m.pl.	the Latins	discedo, -ere	I depart
locus, -i m. (pl. loca)	place	modus, -i m.	method, means
fortis, -e	brave	ocior, -ius	swifter
permisceo, -ere, -ui, -mixtus	I mingle	iaculum, -i n.	javelin
Etruscus, -i m.	an Etruscan	aequo, -are	I equal
Arcas, -adis	Arcadian	celero, -are	I speed up
eques, -itis m.	cavalryman	cursus, -us m.	course
oppono, -ere	I set against	stupeo, -ere	I am astonished
turma, -ae f.	cavalry squadron	inscius, -a, -um	unawares
certus, -a, -um	140 certain	Anchisiades, -ae m.	250 son of Anchises
surgo, -ere	I rise	omen, -inis n.	omen
age, agite	come now	tollo, -ere, sustuli, sublatus	I raise, remove
Aurora, -ae f.	Dawn	conspectus, -us m.	sight
socius, -i m.	comrade, ally	effero, -ferre, extuli, elatus	I raise
clipeus, -i m.	shield	ardens, -entis	gleaming
invictus, -a, -um	invincible		

234–5 **genetrix:** i.e. Cybele. **hanc . . . faciem . . . refecit:** 'remade this shape', i.e. 'refashioned us into this shape' (Williams). **dedit esse:** 'granted to be', i.e. 'granted that we should be'. **sub undis:** i.e. they became sea-nymphs.

236–7 **muro fossisque tenetur:** 'is held (under siege) inside the wall and ditches' (of the camp). **horrentes Marte Latinos:** 'the Latins bristling with war', i.e. 'the Latins terrifying in war'; *Marte* is the personification of war, and is an ablative of respect.

238–9 **loca iussa:** i.e. the positions they have been ordered to take up. **Etrusco, Arcas Eques:** collective singular nouns standing for the plural; there has been no previous mention of cavalry from Etruria or Pallanteum being sent on ahead by land while Aeneas and the rest travelled by ship. The cavalry are called 'Arcadian' because king Evander came originally from Arcadia in Greece.

239–40 **medias:** 'between them and the camp'. **opponere:** the infinitive is dependent on *sententia*. **castris:** dative with the intransitive use of *iungant*. **Turno:** dative of person interested but to be translated as if genitive.

241–3 **primus iube:** 'first order', i.e. 'the first thing you must do is order'. **Ignipotens:** Vulcan is called 'powerful with fire' because he was the blacksmith god. **atque:** supply *cuius:* 'and the rim of which . . .'. **clipeum:** this is the shield Venus asked Vulcan to make for him; it is described in detail in Book VIII.

244–5 **si . . . putaris:** = *si putaveris:* future perfect for a future open condition. **ingentes . . . acervos:** note how the two words enclose the rest of the line, giving a neat <u>chiasmus</u>.

246–7 **dixerat:** Virgil often uses the pluperfect at the end of a speech; translate 'she finished speaking'. **dextra:** 'with her right hand'. Note the <u>alliteration</u>. **haud ignara modi:** 'not unaware of the method', i.e. 'knowing full well how to do so'; the <u>litotes</u> makes a strong assertion.

247–8 **et iaculo et . . . sagitta:** 'than both a javelin and an arrow'. **ventos aequante:** 'as swift as the winds'.

249–50 **aliae:** supply *nymphae*. **cursus:** 'the progress (of the ships)'; each nymph speeded up one ship. **inscius:** Aeneas did not understand what was happening. **animos . . . tollit:** 'he raised his spirits'. **omine:** causal ablative.

260–2 **habet:** the subject is Aeneas. **cum deinde:** 'when straightaway'; *cum* takes the indicative as it is an 'inverse *cum*' construction. **sinistra:** instrumental ablative.

Questions

1 *Miserata* (line 234): why did Cybele take pity on them?

2 What was happening at the Trojan camp?

3 What two things does Cymodocea tell Aeneas to do?

4 How do the nymphs help the Trojans and their allies?

5 What is the effect of the alliteration in line 246?

6 Why do you think Aeneas raises his shield?

                clamorem ad sidera tollunt
Dardanidae e muris, spes addita suscitat iras,
tela manu iaciunt, quales sub nubibus atris
Strymoniae dant signa grues atque aethera tranant   265
cum sonitu, fugiuntque Notos clamore secundo.
at Rutulo regi ducibusque ea mira videri
Ausoniis, donec versas ad litora puppes
respiciunt totumque adlabi classibus aequor.
ardet apex capiti cristisque a vertice flamma   270
funditur et vastos umbo vomit aureus ignes:
non secus ac liquida si quando nocte cometae
sanguinei lugubre rubent, aut Sirius ardor
ille sitim morbosque ferens mortalibus aegris
nascitur et laevo contristat lumine caelum.   275
haud tamen audaci Turno fiducia cessit
litora praecipere et venientes pellere terra.

Turnus addressed his men, urging them to fight valiantly to repel the Trojans. Meanwhile Aeneas began to lead his men ashore. All the ships ran safely on to the beach, except for that of Tarchon, which hit a reef and broke up, flinging the men into the sea. With difficulty they reached land. Aeneas was the first to engage the enemy, killing several. Soon a full-scale battle raged, with many casualties on both sides. Pallas observed that his men, not used to fighting pitched battles, were being driven back. He addressed them to boost their courage.

clamor, -oris m.	shout	*fundo, -ere*	I pour
addo, -ere, -didi, -ditus	I add	*umbo, -onis* m.	shield boss
suscito, -are	I rouse	*vomo, -ere*	I spew out
ira, -ae f.	anger	*secus*	otherwise
manus, -us f.	hand, group	*liquidus, -a, -um*	clear
iacio, -ere	I throw	*quando*	when, ever
nubes, -is f.	cloud	*cometes, -ae* m.	comet
Strymonius, -a, -um	265 of the Strymon	*sanguineus, -a, -um*	blood-red
signum, -i n.	sign, signal	*lugubris, -e*	ill-omened
grus, gruis f.	crane	*rubeo, -ere*	I am red
trano, -are	I fly through	*Sirius, -a, -um*	of Sirius
sonitus, -us m.	sound, noise	*ardor, -oris* m.	heat
Notus, -i m.	South Wind	*sitis, -is* f.	drought
secundus, -a, -um	following	*morbus, -i* m.	disease
mirus, -a, -um	amazing	*mortalis, -is* m.	mortal, human
videor, -eri, visus sum	I appear, seem	*aeger, -gra, -grum*	sick, sorrowful
Ausonius, -a, -um	Italian	*nascor, -i, natus sum*	275 I am born, rise
donec	until	*laevus, -a, -um*	left, inauspicious
respicio, -ere	I look round and see	*contristo, -are*	I sadden
		lumen, -inis n.	light, eye
totus, -a, -um	the whole (of)	*audax, -acis*	bold, daring
adlabor, -i, -lapsus sum	I roll towards	*cedo, -ere, cessi, cessus*	I give way
ardeo, -ere	270 I blaze	*praecipio, -ere*	I seize first
apex, -icis m.	top	*pello, -ere*	I drive
crista, -ae f.	crest		

262–3 **spes addita:** '(newly) added hope'.

264–6 **quales:** introduces a <u>simile</u>. **Strymoniae . . . grues:** the Strymon was a river in NE Greece, where cranes overwintered. **dant signa:** they signal to each other before setting off on their migration northward. **fugiuntque Notos:** 'and they flee the South Wind', i.e. they fly before the wind. **clamore secundo:** 'with joyful cries' makes better sense than 'with their cries following them'; they would be joyful because the winter is over and they are heading off to their breeding grounds.

267–9 **Rutulo regi ducibusque . . . Ausoniis:** note the <u>chiastic</u> word order. **ea:** the sudden shouting from the Trojan camp. **videri:** historic infinitive. **versas . . . puppes:** this time the ships are beached stern first. **totumque adlabi classibus aequor:** 'and the whole sea rolling towards (them) with fleets (of ships)'; this is a picturesque way of saying 'the sea was full of ships'.

270–1 **ardet . . . funditur:** note the extended <u>chiasmus</u>. **apex capiti:** 'the top of (Aeneas') helmet'; the dative is one of reference, akin to the more common dative of the person concerned. **cristisque a vertice:** 'and from the top of the crest'; *cristis* (plural for singular) is most easily taken as another dative of reference than an ablative of origin (the <u>chiasmus</u> would also point to a dative). **flamma:** probably a reflection of sunlight. **umbo . . . aureus:** the central boss of the shield would be hemispherical in shape, and so would catch and reflect the sun no matter at what angle the shield was held. **vastos . . . ignes:** <u>chiastic</u> again.

272–3 **non secus ac:** 'not otherwise than', i.e. 'in the same way as', introducing another <u>simile</u>. **liquida . . . nocte:** 'on a clear night' (ablative of time). **si quando:** 'when sometimes'. **cometae sanguinei:** comets do not normally appear red in colour, and so Virgil is using his imagination to emphasise the common belief that comets were portents of disaster. **lugubre:** adverbial.

273–5 **Sirius:** adjectival; Sirius was also known as the Dog Star; its rising heralded the hottest and most unpleasant season of the year; Sirius is also the brightest star in the night sky. **ille:** this makes the heat specific to Sirius, like a definite article. **aegris:** probably 'sorrowful' rather than 'sick', which would have to be <u>proleptic</u>, i.e. 'making them sick', which would be redundant. **laevo contristat lumine caelum:** 'saddens the sky with inauspicious light', a colourful image.

276–7 **audaci Turno:** dative of person interested. **praecipere, pellere:** infinitives dependent on *fiducia*: 'his confidence to seize . . . and drive'. **praecipere:** i.e. to stop the Trojans from landing. **venientes:** 'as they come (ashore)'. **terra:** ablative of separation.

Questions

1 Why do the Trojans shout?

2 Are the birds being compared with the javelins or the shouting?

3 Explain the use of the simile. How effective is it?

4 How does Aeneas stand out from the rest?

5 Explain the two similes (comets and Sirius).

6 Why do you think Virgil chose these two similes, which appear very negative?

7 How effective do you find these two similes?

'quo fugitis, socii? per vos et fortia facta,   369
per ducis Euandri nomen devictaque bella   370
spemque meam, patriae quae nunc subit aemula laudi,
fidite ne pedibus. ferro rumpenda per hostes
est via. qua globus ille virum densissimus urget,
hac vos et Pallanta ducem patria alta reposcit.
numina nulla premunt, mortali urgemur ab hoste   375
mortales; totidem nobis animaeque manusque.
ecce maris magna claudit nos obice pontus,
deest iam terra fugae: pelagus Troiamne petamus?'
haec ait, et medius densos prorumpit in hostes.
obvius huic primum fatis adductus iniquis   380
fit Lagus. hunc, vellit magno dum pondere saxum,
intorto figit telo, discrimina costis
per medium qua spina dabat, hastamque receptat
ossibus haerentem. quem non super occupat Hisbo,
ille quidem hoc sperans; nam Pallas ante ruentem,   385
dum furit, incautum crudeli morte sodalis
excipit atque ensem tumido in pulmone recondit.

Pallas continued his slaughter of the Italian foe. Seeing his success, his Arcadians took courage and turned back to face the enemy. Pallas killed Rhoeteus, who ran into the path of his spear, intended for Ilus.

quo	whither?	*Lagus, -i* m.	Lagus
devinco, -ere, -ici, -ictus	370 I win	*vello, -ere*	I pick up
subeo, -ire	I rise	*pondus, -eris* n.	weight
patrius, -a, -um	a father's	*intorqueo, -ere, -torsi, -tortus*	I hurl at
aemulus, -a, -um + dat.	rivalling, equalling	*discrimen, -inis* n.	separation
		costa, -ae f.	rib
laus, laudis f.	praise	*spina, -ae* f.	spine
fido, -ere + dat.	I trust	*hasta, -ae* f.	spear
pes, pedis m.	foot	*recepto, -are*	I tug hard at
qua	where	*os, ossis* n.	bone
globus, -i m.	mass, crowd	*haereo, -ere*	I stick to
densus, -a, -um	dense	*occupo, -are*	I catch
urgeo, -ere	I press	*Hisbo, -onis* m.	Hisbo
altus, -a, -um	glorious, high	*quidem*	385 indeed, however
reposco, -ere	I require	*ante*	before(hand)
totidem	376 the same number of	*furo, -ere*	I rage
		incautus, -a, -um	careless
anima, -ae f.	soul, life	*crudelis, -e*	cruel
obex, -icis f.	barrier	*mors, mortis* f.	death
desum, -esse	I am lacking	*sodalis, -is* m.	friend
aio (defective verb)	I say	*excipio, -ere*	I catch
prorumpo, -ere	I charge	*tumidus, -a, -um*	swelling
obvius, -a, -um + dat.	380 to meet	*pulmo, -onis* m.	lung
adduco, -ere, -duxi, -ductus	I induce	*recondo, -ere*	I bury

369–72 per . . . per: the anaphora of *per*, which also belongs with *bella* and *spem*, is formulaic, giving the justification for a strong entreaty (supply *oro* to complete the sense). **vos et fortia facta:** 'you and your brave deeds', both dependent on the first *per*. **devictaque bella:** 'and the wars he has won'. **spemque meam . . . quae . . . subit:** 'and my hope, which rises', i.e. 'grows in my mind'. **patriae . . . aemula laudi:** '(hope) rivalling my father's praise', i.e. 'of matching my father's renown'. **fidite ne pedibus:** 'do not trust feet', i.e. 'don't pin your hopes on running away'; the construction is poetic.

372–4 ferro: note the antithesis with *pedibus*. **globus ille:** Pallas pointed to the main body of enemy troops as he spoke. **virum:** = *virorum*. **hac:** 'here', answering *qua*.

375–6 numina nulla premunt: there are no gods fighting against them. **mortali . . . mortales:** the polyptoton and enjambement emphasise the point made by *numina nulla premunt*: their enemies, like themselves, are mortal. Pallas did not know of Juno's activities. **totidem nobis:** supply *sunt*; his argument is that they have just as many lives and hands as the enemy do.

377 The order is *ecce pontus claudit nos magna obice maris*. **pontus:** here distinct from *mare*: 'the deep' or 'the ocean'. **claudit nos:** 'bars our way'. Note the enclosing word order: *maris* and *pontus* (and also *magna* and *obice*) enclose *nos*, which is precisely Pallas' argument.

378 The land offered no way out, because of the Latin army. **pelagus Troiamne petamus:** 'are we to make for the open sea or Troy?' *petamus* is subjunctive for a deliberative question, here ironic. The particle *-ne* is used here instead of *an* ('or'), introducing the second of two alternatives; this is a rare usage. His argument is that he and his men have come to join forces with the Trojans; there is no way they can escape by land back to Pallanteum; therefore they must either head out to sea or fight their way into the Trojan camp (here called 'Troy').

379 medius: proleptic: he charged into the enemy so that he was 'in their midst'; translate as 'into the midst of the densely-packed enemy'.

380–1 fit Lagus: 'came Lagus'. Lagus, like Hisbo below, is not mentioned elsewhere.

381–2 hunc: object of *figit*. **magno . . . pondere:** ablative of description. **intorto . . . telo:** 'with the javelin he threw at him' (instrumental ablative). Note the slow rhythm of line 382.

382–3 The order is *per medium qua spina dabat discrimina costis*. **per medium:** 'through the middle (of his body)'. **discrimina . . . qua spina dedit:** 'where the spine gave separation to the ribs', i.e. 'where the spine separated his ribs'.

384–5 quem non super occupat Hisbo: there are various possible interpretations of this: 'Hisbo does not catch him (Pallas) (as he bends) over' (to pull out the spear); 'Hisbo does not catch him as he jumps on him'; 'Hisbo does not surprise him as he jumps on him'; 'moreover (*super*) Hisbo does not catch him'; simplest of all would be 'Hisbo does not fall upon him', where *super* duplicates and so clarifies the idea of *occupat*; there is, however, no parallel for this use of *super* with *occupat*. **ille:** i.e. Hisbo. **ille quidem:** Virgil uses this combination here and elsewhere to mean 'even though he'.

385–7: The order is *nam Pallas ante excepit (eum) ruentem, dum furit, incautum . . .* **ruentem:** 'as he rushed'. **incautum . . . morte:** 'made careless by the death'.

Questions

1 What arguments does Pallas use to persuade his warriors to fight?

2 How does Virgil make the two deaths varied and dramatic?

3 Which of the various interpretations of *quem . . . Hisbo* do you prefer? Give reasons.

at non caede viri tanta perterrita Lausus,   426
pars ingens belli, sinit agmina: primus Abantem
oppositum interimit, pugnae nodumque moramque.
sternitur Arcadiae proles, sternuntur Etrusci
et vos, o Grais imperdita corpora, Teucri.   430
agmina concurrunt ducibusque et viribus aequis;
extremi addensent acies nec turba moveri
tela manusque sinit. hinc Pallas instat et urget,
hinc contra Lausus, nec multum discrepat aetas,
egregii forma, sed quis Fortuna negarat   435
in patriam reditus. ipsos concurrere passus
haud tamen inter se magni regnator Olympi;
mox illos sua fata manent maiore sub hoste.
interea soror alma monet succedere Lauso
Turnum, qui volucri curru medium secat agmen.   440
ut vidit socios: 'tempus desistere pugnae;
solus ego in Pallanta feror, soli mihi Pallas
debetur; cuperem ipse parens spectator adesset.'
haec ait, et socii cesserunt aequore iusso.
at Rutulum abscessu iuvenis tum iussa superba   445
miratus stupet in Turno corpusque per ingens
lumina volvit obitque truci procul omnia visu,
talibus et dictis it contra dicta tyranni:

tantus, -a, -um	such great	*nego, -are, -avi, -atus*	I deny
perterritus, -a, -um	terrified	*reditus, -us* m.	return
Lausus, -i m.	Lausus	*patior, -i, passus sum*	I allow
pars, partis f.	part	*regnator, -oris* m.	ruler
agmen, -inis n.	army	*maneo, -ere*	I await
Abas, -ntis m.	Abas	*soror, -oris* f.	sister
oppono, -ere, -posui, -positus	I oppose	*moneo, -ere*	I warn, advise
interimo, -ere	I kill	*succedo, -ere* + dat.	I relieve
nodus, -i m.	knot	*volucer, -cris, -cre*	440 swift, flying
Arcadia, -ae f.	Arcadia	*desisto, -ere*	I stand down
proles, -is f.	offspring	*debeo, -ere*	I owe
Grai, -orum m.pl.	430 the Greeks	*cupio, -ere*	I desire, wish
imperditus, -a, -um	not slain	*parens, -entis* m/f.	parent
corpus, -oris n.	body	*spectator, -oris* m.	spectator
vires, -ium f.pl.	strength	*adsum, -esse*	I am here
aequus, -a, -um	equal	*abscessus, -us* m.	445 withdrawal
extremus, -a, -um	rearmost, last	*iuvenis, -is* m.	young man
addenseo, -ere	I close ranks	*superbus, -a, -um*	arrogant
acies, -ei f.	battle-line	*miror, -ari, -atus sum*	I am amazed at
turba, -ae f.	crowd, crush	*volvo, -ere*	I turn, roll
hinc	on one side	*obeo, -ire*	I survey, go round
discrepo, -are	I differ	*trux, trucis*	grim, fierce
aetas, -atis f.	age	*procul*	from a distance
egregius, -a, -um	435 outstanding	*visus, -us* m.	vision, stare
forma, -ae f.	appearance	*tyrannus, -i* m.	ruler

426–7 The order is *at Lausus, ingens pars belli, non sinit agmina (esse) perterrita tanta caede viri*. **caede viri tanta:** 'by so much killing of the man', and so 'by so much killing by the man', taking *viri* as subjective genitive referring to Pallas. **Lausus:** he was the young son of the tyrant Mezentius (see Book VIII.481ff.). **pars ingens:** 'a major participant'. He boosted the courage of his men by indulging in a killing spree himself.

427–8 **Abantem:** an Etruscan. **oppositum:** 'when he came against him'. **pugnae nodumque moramque:** 'a knot and delay of the war', i.e. 'a focal point and mainstay of the war'; in other words he was one of the toughest warriors.

429–30 **Arcadiae proles:** 'the offspring of Arcadia'; Evander had migrated to Italy from Arcadia in Greece; these 'offspring' are therefore the young warriors from Pallanteum. **sternitur . . . sternuntur:** the <u>polyptoton</u> emphasises the extent of the slaughter. **et vos:** the <u>apostrophe</u> indicates the special significance of the Trojans. **corpora:** in apposition to *Teucri*. **Grais imperdita:** the 'bodies not slain by the Greeks' are those who escaped from Troy; *Grais* is dative of the agent with the perfect passive participial form of *imperdita*.

431 **ducibus et viribus aequis:** ablative absolute. The leaders, here Pallas and Lausus, were of similar age and prowess.

432–3 **extremi:** the warriors at the back pressed forward. **turba:** the crush of men pressing forward.

433–4 **hinc . . . hinc:** 'on one side . . . on the other'. **instat et urget:** <u>tautological</u> for emphasis.

435–6 **quis:** = *quibus*. **negarat:** = *negaverat*. **reditus:** plural because there are two of them.

436–7 **ipsos:** Pallas and Lausus themselves. **passus haud:** = *haud passus erat*.

438 **illos sua fata manent:** 'his own fate awaits each of them'. **maiore sub hoste:** 'at the hands of a greater enemy': Aeneas would kill Lausus, Turnus would kill Pallas.

439–40 **soror alma:** Turnus' sister was the nymph Juturna, not mentioned by name until Book XII. She took a keen interest in the war and did her best to protect her brother. **succedere Lauso:** 'to relieve Lausus' by taking his place. **volucri curru:** local ablative. **secat:** 'cleared a path through'.

441 **tempus:** supply *est*. **pugnae:** 'from the battle' (probably dative of disadvantage).

442–3 **in Pallanta feror:** 'I'm going to fight Pallas'. **cuperem:** 'I would wish' (a potential or virtual conditional construction). **spectator:** 'as a spectator', i.e. 'to see it'.

444 **aequore iusso:** ablative of separation: 'from the ordered plain', i.e. 'from their ordered positions on the battle-ground'.

445–7 **iuvenis:** Pallas. **Rutulum** (= *Rutulorum*) **abscessu:** 'upon the withdrawal of the Rutuli' (ablative of time, as shown by *tum*). **stupet in Turno:** 'is astounded by (the sight of) Turnus'. **lumina volvit:** 'he casts his eyes'. **obitque . . . omnia:** 'and surveys all (aspects of him)'.

448 **et:** to be taken first. **it contra dicta:** 'counters the words'.

Questions

1 How does Virgil emphasise the achievements and valour of Lausus?

2 In what ways are Pallas and Lausus similar?

3 What impression do you get of Turnus from lines 440–443 (especially line 443)?

4 What effect does Turnus' sudden appearance have on Pallas?

'aut spoliis ego iam raptis laudabor opimis
aut leto insigni: sorti pater aequus utrique est.   450
tolle minas.' fatus medium procedit in aequor;
frigidus Arcadibus coit in praecordia sanguis.
desiluit Turnus biiugis, pedes apparat ire
comminus; utque leo, specula cum vidit ab alta
stare procul campis meditantem in proelia taurum,   455
advolat, haud alia est Turni venientis imago.

Pallas prepared to cast his javelin first, and prayed to Hercules, his patron deity, to help him.
Hercules heard but could not help. Jupiter consoled the sorrowful Hercules.

at Pallas magnis emittit viribus hastam   474
vaginaque cava fulgentem deripit ensem.   475
illa volans umeri surgunt qua tegmina summa
incidit, atque viam clipei molita per oras
tandem etiam magno strinxit de corpore Turni.
hic Turnus ferro praefixum robur acuto
in Pallanta diu librans iacit atque ita fatur: 480
'aspice num mage sit nostrum penetrabile telum.'
dixerat; at clipeum, tot ferri terga, tot aeris,
quem pellis totiens obeat circumdata tauri,
vibranti cuspis medium transverberat ictu
loricaeque moras et pectus perforat ingens.   485

spolia, -orum n.pl.	spoils	*volo, -are*	I fly
laudo, -are	I praise	*umerus, -i* m.	shoulder
opimus, -a, -um	rich	*tegmen, -inis* n.	covering
letum, -i n.	450 death	*summus, -a, -um*	topmost
sors, sortis f.	fate	*incido, -ere*	I fall upon
uterque, utraque, utrumque	both	*stringo, -ere, strinxi, strictus*	I graze, skim
mina, -ae f.	threat	*praefigo, -ere, -fixi, -fixus*	I tip
frigidus, -a, -um	cold, chill	*robur, -oris* n.	oak
coeo, -ire	I come together	*acutus, -a, -um*	sharp
praecordia, -orum n.pl.	heart	*diu*	for a long time
desilio, -ire, -ui, -sultus	I jump down	*libro, -are*	480 I balance, poise
biiugi, -orum m.pl.	two-horse chariot	*aspicio, -ere*	I look, look at
apparo, -are	I prepare	*mage*	more
comminus	hand to hand	*penetrabilis, -e*	able to penetrate
specula, -ae f.	view-point	*tergum, -i* n.	back, hide
meditor, -ari, -atus sum	455 I practise	*aes, aeris* n.	bronze
taurus, -i m.	bull	*pellis, -is* f.	hide, skin
advolo, -are	I rush towards	*totiens*	so often
imago, -inis f.	image	*circumdo, -dare, -dedi, -datus*	I surround
emitto, -ere	474 I throw	*vibro, -are*	I quiver
vagina, -ae f.	475 sheath	*cuspis, -idis* f.	point
cavus, -a, -um	hollow	*transverbero, -are*	I pierce
fulgeo, -ere	I gleam	*ictus, -us* m.	impact
deripio, -ere	I pull out	*lorica, -ae* f.	485 breastplate
ensis, -is m.	sword	*perforo, -are*	I pierce

449–50 **spoliis . . . raptis . . . opimis:** lit. 'rich spoils having been seized'; *spolia opima* is a special military term, meaning the spoils (i.e. armour and weapons) captured from an enemy commander killed in battle, a feat which (according to tradition) was achieved only three times in Roman history; translate '(I shall be praised) for having seized an enemy commander's spoils'. **leto insigni:** '(or I shall be praised) for a distinguished death' (causal ablative). **pater . . . aequus . . . est:** 'my father is equally prepared'.

451 **tolle minas:** 'enough of your threats'.

452 **Arcadibus:** dative of person interested; translate as if genitive.

453–4 **pedes:** not the plural of *pes*, 'a foot', but the singular noun *pedes*, 'one who goes on foot'; here it is in apposition to *Turnus*, and may be translated simply as 'on foot'.

454–6 **utque:** 'and just like', introducing a simile. **vidit:** the true perfect: 'has seen'. **in proelia:** 'for battles', i.e. against rival bulls. **venientis:** 'as he draws near'.

474–5 **vaginaque cava:** 'and from its hollow sheath', ablative of separation.

476–8 **illa:** the spear. **qua:** 'the point where', to be taken after *incidit* and before *umeri surgunt*. **umeri . . . tegmina summa:** 'the top part of the shoulder-guard', i.e. where the armour turns up at the neck. **viam . . . molita:** 'forcing its way'. **oras:** 'the rim'. **magno . . . de corpore:** 'past the great body'. Probably the spear actually grazed the shoulder of Turnus (thought the use of *de* here is highly unusual).

479–80 **hic:** 'thereupon'. **robur:** 'oak' and so anything made of oak, and so 'oak (shaft of his) javelin'. **ferro praefixum . . . acuto:** 'tipped with sharp iron'; although the Trojan War and its aftermath took place in the Bronze Age (if we accept the traditional chronology), they came late enough for iron to see occasional use. **diu librans:** i.e. he took careful aim before casting the javelin.

481 **mage:** an archaic form of *magis*. **penetrabile:** active rather than the more usual passive.

482–5 **clipeum:** the object of *transverberat*, the subject of which is *cuspis*; the word order is very complex. **tot ferri terga:** 'so many hides of iron', i.e. 'so many layers of iron', in apposition to *clipeum*; *terga* is used metaphorically. Virgil is saying that the javelin point pierced Pallas' shield, despite its many layers of iron and bronze and its covering of bull's hide. **quem . . . tauri:** '(the shield) which the hide of a bull surrounded and enclosed so many times'. One may wonder how heavy the shield must have been. **vibranti . . . ictu:** 'with quivering impact'. **medium:** agrees with *clipeum*. **loricaeque moras . . . perforat:** 'and pierced the barrier of his breastplate'. Note the sequence of the Latin: first the shield, then the breastplate and finally the chest.

Questions

1 What does Pallas say to Turnus? How far does he mean what he says? What is his purpose?

2 How do Pallas' men react to his words and actions? Why do they react in this way?

3 Summarise the simile. How appropriate is it?

4 Compare the two spear-casts. How does Virgil give more weight to that of Turnus?

ille rapit calidum frustra de vulnere telum:
una eademque via sanguis animusque sequuntur.
corruit in vulnus (sonitum super arma dedere)
et terram hostilem moriens petit ore cruento.
quem Turnus super adsistens: 490
'Arcades, haec' inquit 'memores mea dicta referte
Euandro: qualem meruit, Pallanta remitto.
quisquis honos tumuli, quidquid solamen humandi est,
largior. haud illi stabunt Aeneia parvo
hospitia.' et laevo pressit pede talia fatus   495
exanimem rapiens immania pondera baltei
impressumque nefas: una sub nocte iugali
caesa manus iuvenum foede thalamique cruenti,
quae Clonus Eurytides multo caelaverat auro;
quo nunc Turnus ovat spolio gaudetque potitus.   500
nescia mens hominum fati sortisque futurae
et servare modum rebus sublata secundis!
Turno tempus erit magno cum optaverit emptum
intactum Pallanta, et cum spolia ista diemque
oderit. at socii multo gemitu lacrimisque   505
impositum scuto referunt Pallanta frequentes.

calidus, -a, -um	warm, hot	*nefas* n. indecl.	wicked deed
frustra	in vain	*iugalis, -e*	of a wedding
vulnus, -eris n.	wound	*caedo, -ere, cecidi, caesus*	I slaughter
corruo, -ere	I collapse	*foedus, -a, -um*	foul
hostilis, -e	hostile	*thalamus, -i* m.	bedroom
morior, -i, mortuus sum	I die	*Clonus, -i* m.	Clonus
os, oris n.	mouth	*Eurytides, -ae* m.	son of Eurytus
cruentus, -a, -um	blood-stained	*caelo, -are, -avi, -atus*	I engrave
adsisto, -ere	490 I stand near	*ovo, -are*	500 I exult
memor, -oris	remembering	*spolium, -i* n.	booty
refero, -ferre	I take back	*gaudeo, -ere*	I rejoice
mereo, -ere, -ui, -itus	I deserve	*potior, -iri, -itus sum* + abl.	I acquire
remitto, -ere	I send back	*nescius, -a, -um*	unaware
quisquis, quidquid	whoever, whatever	*mens, mentis* f.	mind
		servo, -are	I keep, preserve
honos, -oris m.	honour	*modus, -i* m.	moderation
tumulus, -i m.	tomb	*opto, -are, -avi, -atus*	I wish, choose
solamen, -inis n.	consolation	*emo, -ere, emi, emptus*	I buy
humo, -are	I bury	*intactus, -a, -um*	untouched
largior, -iri, -itus sum	I give freely	*odi, -isse*	505 I hate
hospitium, -i n.	495 hospitality	*gemitus, -us* m.	lamentation
exanimis, -e	lifeless	*lacrima, -ae* f.	tear
immanis, -e	huge	*impono, -ere, -posui, -positus*	I place upon
balteus, -i m.	sword-belt	*scutum, -i* n.	shield
imprimo, -ere, -essi, -essus	I engrave	*frequens, -entis*	in a throng

486 **calidum . . . telum:** Virgil imagines the javelin tip to have been heated by the flesh around it. **frustra:** pulling the weapon out was 'in vain' because it hastened his death.
487 **una eademque via:** 'through one and the same route', i.e. the entry wound; *eadem* is scanned as two long syllables, rather than the normal short, long, long. **animus:** here 'life'.
488–9 **super:** 'on top of him'. **terram hostilem . . . petit:** 'he seeks the hostile ground', i.e. 'he bites the hostile earth', an image borrowed from Homer.
490 The line was left unfinished by Virgil.
491–2 **haec . . . mea dicta:** 'these words of mine'. **memores:** this has the force of a second imperative: 'remember . . . and take back'. **qualem meruit:** 'in the condition which he (Evander) deserved', i.e. dead. Turnus is saying contemptuously that the death of his son serves him right for having sent him to fight.
493–4 The argument is that he freely allowed the body to be returned for 'whatever honour . . . or consolation may be gained by burial'. The two genitives are partitive. **largior:** the enjambement places great emphasis on this word; he grants the return freely because it is of no consequence to him, as the next sentence makes clear.
494–5 **Aeneia hospitia:** 'the hospitality he gave to Aeneas'. **illi stabunt:** 'will cost him'. **haud . . . parvo:** 'not a little' (ablative of price). The litotes makes a strong affirmative: 'a great deal'.
495–7 Start with *talia fatus.* **exanimem:** 'the lifeless man'. **immania pondera baltei:** 'the huge weight of his sword-belt', i.e. 'his massively heavy sword-belt'. This was a crucial action by Turnus (though in Homeric warfare it was normal practice for the victor to strip the body of his slain foe of his armour); for at the end of the *Aeneid* it is the sight of Turnus wearing this very sword-belt that prompts Aeneas to kill rather than spare Turnus. **impressumque nefas:** 'and the wicked deed engraved upon it'; the deed in question was the myth of the marriage of the 50 sons of Aegyptus to the 50 daughters of Danaus; because of a prophecy that Danaus would be killed by a son-in-law, he ordered his daughters to murder their husbands on their wedding night; all but one obeyed.
497–9 **una sub nocte iugali:** 'on a single wedding night'. **manus:** i.e. the 49 sons of Aegyptus; nominative as if the start of a new sentence, even though the whole description is in apposition to the accusative *nefas.* **thalamique cruenti:** nominative plural, parallel to *manus.* **Clonus:** unknown.
500 **quo . . . spolio:** ablative dependent on *potitus.*
501–2 **nescia mens:** in full this would be *quam nescia est mens.* **fati sortisque:** objective genitives. **servare modum:** 'how to preserve moderation'. **sublata:** 'raised up', agreeing with *mens.*
503–5 Virgil steps outside the immediate narrative to look ahead to a later consequence of his action. **magno . . . emptum intactum Pallanta:** 'Pallas, bought at a great price, intact', i.e. he will have wished Pallas to have been left intact, bought at a high price, i.e. 'he would have given anything to have left Pallas untouched'.
505–6 **referunt:** 'take away from the battle'. **frequentes:** an adjective best taken as an adverb.

Questions

1 How does Virgil handle the death of Pallas? Does he display any emotion?

2 What impression of Turnus does Virgil give us?

3 Find three examples of Virgil's use of word order or sound and discuss their effects.

When Aeneas heard the news, he embarked on a frenzy of killing, sparing none. Jupiter granted Juno a wish to prolong the life of Turnus. Conjuring an image of Aeneas, she lured Turnus away from the battle and on to a boat, which she cast adrift. When he realised he had been tricked, Turnus was furious. In his absence, Mezentius was the most powerful of the warrior chiefs, killing many Trojans and their allies. Eventually Aeneas saw him and attacked him, wounding him in the groin with his spear. As Aeneas prepared to finish him with his sword, his son Lausus parried the blow and insisted on opposing Aeneas. Aeneas threatened Lausus.

'quo moriture ruis maioraque viribus audes?   811
fallit te incautum pietas tua.' nec minus ille
exsultat demens, saevae iamque altius irae
Dardanio surgunt ductori, extremaque Lauso
Parcae fila legunt: validum namque exigit ensem   815
per medium Aeneas iuvenem totumque recondit.
transiit et parmam mucro, levia arma minacis,
et tunicam molli mater quam neverat auro,
implevitque sinum sanguis; tum vita per auras
concessit maesta ad manes corpusque reliquit.   820
at vero ut vultum vidit morientis et ora,
ora modis Anchisiades pallentia miris,
ingemuit miserans graviter dextramque tetendit,
et mentem patriae subiit pietatis imago.

Aeneas allowed Lausus' companions to carry his body away, still clad in his armour. Mezentius, when he saw his son's body, was overcome with grief. Despite his grave wound, he charged back into the fray seeking revenge; there in single combat Aeneas slew him.

audeo, -ere	I dare	*minax, -acis*		threatening
fallo, -ere	I deceive	*tunica, -ae* f.		tunic
pietas, -atis f.	filial duty	*mater, -tris* f.		mother
minus	less	*neo, nere, nevi, netus*		I weave
exsulto, -are	I leap up	*impleo, -ere, -evi, -etus*		I fill
demens, -entis	mad	*sinus, -us* m.		lap, fold
saevus, -a, -um	cruel, fierce	*aura, -ae* f.		air, breeze
ductor, -oris m.	leader	*maestus, -a, -um*	820	sad
Parcae, -arum f.pl.	815 the Fates	*manes, -ium* m.pl.		souls of the dead
filum, -i n.	thread	*relinquo, -ere, -liqui, -lictus*		I leave
lego, -ere	I gather	*vero*		however
validus, -a, -um	strong	*vultus, -us* m.		face
transeo, -ire, -ii, -itus	I pass through	*modus, -i* m.		manner, way
parma, -ae f.	shield	*palleo, -ere*		I am pale
mucro, -onis m.	point	*ingemo, -ere, -ui*		I sigh for, mourn
levis, -e	light	*tendo, -ere, tetendi, tensus*		I extend

811 **quo:** 'to what purpose'. **moriture ruis:** 'are you rushing about to die', i.e. 'are you rushing to your death'. **maioraque viribus audes:** 'and are you daring greater things than strength', i.e. 'are you daring to do things beyond your strength'.

812 **pietas tua:** 'your duty to your father'; Aeneas, so frequently called *pius* by Virgil, ought not to criticise someone else for possessing the same quality; also, it is that very *pietas* that evokes pity in Aeneas after killing Lausus (line 824).

813–15 **nec minus:** 'none the less'. **ille:** Lausus. **iamque:** to be taken first. **Dardanio . . . ductori:** 'for the Trojan leader' (dative of the person interested), and so 'in the Trojan leader'. Note the position of *Dardanio*, at the opposite end of the line to *Lauso*, also a dative of the person interested. **Parcae:** the three sisters of Fate, named Clotho, Lachesis and Atropos; in Greek and Roman myth they spun out a thread for each mortal's life; when the thread ran out, the person died.

815–16 **namque:** to be taken first. **Aenean:** note the position of the name, inside *per medium iuvenem*, emphasising the central thrust of the sword, with Aeneas' full weight behind it; an example of <u>enclosing word order</u>.

817 **parmam:** a smaller shield than the *clipeus*. **levia arma minacis:** 'light arms of one threatening', and so 'arms too light for one making such threats'.

817–18 Note the predominance of *m* <u>alliteration</u> and <u>consonance</u>, indicative of high emotion.

818–19 **tunicam:** a second object of *transiit*. **molli . . . auro:** i.e. gold thread. **mater:** this reference gives a more personal dimension to the death. **sinum:** probably the folds of the tunic.

819–20 **vita:** 'life' in the sense of the 'life-force' or spirit. Note the *m* <u>alliteration</u> again.

821–2 **at vero:** these two words introduce a very strong contrast with the preceding event; here they mark a reversal of emotion in Aeneas. Note the strong <u>alliteration</u> of *v* and the slow rhythm of line 821. **vultum . . . et ora:** 'his face and countenance'. **ora, ora:** the repetition indicates the importance of his observing the young face that shocked Aeneas out of his blood-lust. **modis . . . miris:** 'in wondrous ways', i.e. 'amazingly', qualifying *pallentia*.

823–4 **dextramque tetendit:** a poignant action, showing sorrow for the death of one so young. **mentem . . . subiit:** 'there came into his mind'. **patriae . . . pietatis:** 'his duty towards his (own) father'.

Questions

1 Does Aeneas show any pity in his words to Lausus?

2 In lines 812–813, how far are the two men similar? Which words show this similarity?

3 Explain the reference to the *Parcae*.

4 How does Virgil make it clear that Aeneas does not hesitate to kill Lausus?

5 How does Virgil increase the pathos of the death scene?

6 Why does Aeneas abandon his anger?

7 What impression do you gain of Aeneas' character from this episode?

8 Compare the deaths of Pallas and Lausus: what similarities and what differences can you find?

9 Why are these two episodes important in the context of the *Aeneid* as a whole?

10 Does Virgil show compassion for Pallas in Book X?

Book 11

Battle has raged before the walls of the Trojan camp by the mouth of the river Tiber. The Latins and their allies, the Rutulians and the ousted Etruscan tyrant Mezentius, have been trying to capture the Trojan camp, which only survived because Aeneas returned from his mission to find allies in time to drive the Italians away. In the ensuing battle, Turnus killed Pallas, the son of king Evander of Pallanteum and principal ally of the Trojans. In revenge Aeneas killed the young Lausus and then his father Mezentius.

The next morning (as Book XI opens), both sides wanted to collect their dead and arrange funerals. First Aeneas set up a trophy consisting of a tree trunk adorned with the armour of Mezentius. Then, after telling his men to prepare to march on Laurentum, he gave orders for the last rites for the dead to be prepared.

'ite' ait, 'egregias animas, quae sanguine nobis	
hanc patriam peperere suo, decorate supremis	25
muneribus, maestamque Euandri primus ad urbem	
mittatur Pallas, quem non virtutis egentem	
abstulit atra dies et funere mersit acerbo.'	
sic ait inlacrimans, recipitque ad limina gressum	
corpus ubi exanimi positum Pallantis Acoetes	30
servabat senior, qui Parrhasio Euandro	
armiger ante fuit, sed non felicibus aeque	
tum comes auspiciis caro datus ibat alumno.	

eo, ire i(v)i, itus	I go	*acerbus, -a, -um*	bitter
aio (defective verb)	I say	*inlacrimo, -are*	I weep
egregius, -a, -um	splendid	*recipio, -ere*	I take back
anima, -ae f.	spirit	*limen, -inis* n.	threshold
sanguis, -inis m.	blood	*gressus, -us* m.	step
patria, -ae f. 25	homeland	*corpus, -oris* n. 30	body
pario, -ere, peperi, partus	I create	*exanimus, -a, -um*	dead
decoro, -are	I honour	*pono, -ere, posui, positus*	I place, set down
supremus, -a, -um	last		
munus, -eris n.	gift, tribute, rite	*Acoetes, -is* m.	Acoetes
maestus, -a, -um	sad, grieving	*servo, -are*	I watch over
Euandrus, -i m.	Evander	*senior, -oris*	elderly
primus, -a, -um	first	*Parrhasius, -a, -um*	Arcadian
urbs, urbis f.	city	*armiger, -eri* m.	armour-bearer
mitto, -ere	I send	*ante*	previously
Pallas, -antis m.	Pallas	*felix, -icis*	favourable, fortunate
virtus, -utis f.	courage		
egeo, -ere + gen.	I lack	*aequus, -a, -um*	equal, fair
aufero, -ferre, abstuli, ablatus	I steal, take away	*comes, -itis* m.	companion
ater, atra, atrum	black	*auspicium, -i* n.	omen
dies, diei m/f.	day	*carus, -a, -um*	dear
funus, -eris n.	death	*do, dare, dedi, datus*	I give, appoint
mergo, -ere, mersi, mersus	I bury, sink	*alumnus, -i* m.	pupil, ward

24–6 The order is *decorate egregias animas, quae peperere nobis hanc patriam suo sanguine, supremis muneribus*. decorate: imperative. sanguine . . . suo: ablative of instrument. hanc patriam peperere: *peperere = pepererunt* (a common alternative verse form of the 3rd person plural perfect; it will not be commented upon again): '(who) have created this (to be) our homeland'. supremis muneribus: 'with the last rites', i.e. the funerals.

26–7 The order is (and) *primus Pallas mittatur ad maestam urbem Euandri*. maestam: proleptic: Laurentum will be in mourning when it learns of Pallas' death. mittatur: 'let him be sent'. Note the heavy <u>alliteration</u> of *m* in these lines, indicating high emotion. quem: this is the object of both *abstulit* and *mersit*. non virtutis egentem: 'not lacking in courage'; the <u>litotes</u> makes a strong affirmative.

28 atra dies: *dies* may be masculine or feminine; in Roman calendars unlucky days were marked in black. funere acerbo: instrumental ablative. This line is a repeat of Book VI.429, giving it a slightly formulaic quality. Note the <u>assonance</u> of *a*, also showing high emotion.

29 recipitque . . . gressum: 'and retraced his step'; *recipit* is a historic present, regularly used by Virgil for his narrative. ad limina: 'to the entrance' (of his house or tent, depending on whether the Trojans had got as far as building individual houses inside their camp).

30–1 corpus ubi = *ubi corpus*: *ubi* here means 'where'. positum: 'laid out', ready for burial. Acoetes . . . senior: *senior* (the comparative of *senex*) does not usually bear its comparative meaning, simply meaning 'old' or 'elderly'; Acoetes had served as squire to Evander before they left Arcadia.

31–2 Parrhasio Euandro: Parrhasia was a town in Arcadia (in Greece), which had been Evander's homeland before moving to Italy. These two words 'break' the rules for the dactylic hexameter (see Introduction): the *-o* at the end of *Parrhăsĭo* gives a hiatus: it cannot elide (as that would leave too few syllables to complete the line); also *-o Euandro* gives a spondee in the 5th foot. This combination occurs only five times in the whole *Aeneid* (usually with Greek names), but is more common in Homer. armiger: this was a servant whose job it was to look after the armour and weapons of a leading warrior, like the medieval squire.

32–3 The order is *sed tum, datus comes caro alumno, ibat non aeque felicibus auspiciis*, i.e. the omens were not as favourable as when he had served Evander. comes: 'as companion'. caro . . . alumno: this suggests that Acoetes had taught the young Pallas the arts of war.

Questions

1 What orders does Aeneas give?

2 What emotions does Aeneas show in his speech?

3 How do his words show these emotions?

4 Find out all you can about Evander and Pallas.

5 How do lines 29–33 show Virgil's own attitude to death?

circum omnis famulumque manus Troianaque turba
et maestum Iliades crinem de more solutae.   35
ut vero Aeneas foribus sese intulit altis
ingentem gemitum tunsis ad sidera tollunt
pectoribus, maestoque immugit regia luctu.
ipse caput nivei fultum Pallantis et ora
ut vidit levique patens in pectore vulnus   40
cuspidis Ausoniae, lacrimis ita fatur obortis:
'tene' inquit, 'miserande puer, cum laeta veniret,
invidit Fortuna mihi, ne regna videres
nostra neque ad sedes victor veherere paternas?
non haec Euandro de te promissa parenti   45
discedens dederam, cum me complexus euntem
mitteret in magnum imperium metuensque moneret
acres esse viros, cum dura proelia gente.

circum	around	*pateo, -ere*	I gape open
omnis, -e	all	*vulnus, -eris* n.	wound
famulus, -i m.	servant, attendant	*cuspis, -idis* f.	spear-point
manus, -us f.	hand, group	*Ausonius, -a, -um*	Italian
Troianus, -a, -um	Trojan	*lacrima, -ae* f.	tear
turba, -ae f.	crowd	*ita*	so, as follows
Iliades, -um f.pl. 35	Trojan women	*for, fari, fatus sum*	I speak
crinis, -is m.	hair	*oborior, -iri, -ortus sum*	I well up, rise
mos, moris m.	custom	*inquam* (defective verb)	I say
solvo, -ere, solvi, solutus	I free, untie	*miserandus, -a, -um*	pitiable
ut + indic.	as, when	*puer, pueri* m.	boy
vero	however, indeed	*laetus, -a, -um*	glad, happy
Aeneas, -ae m.	Aeneas	*venio, -ire*	I come
foris, -is f.	door, entrance	*invideo, -ere, -vidi, -visus*	I begrudge
infero, -ferre, -tuli, -latus	I carry in	*Fortuna, -ae* f.	Fortune
altus, -a, -um	high	*regnum, -i* n.	kingdom, realm
ingens, -entis	huge	*sedes, -is* f.	seat, home
gemitus, -us m.	groan	*victor, -oris* m.	victor
tundo, -ere, tutudi, tunsus	I beat	*vehor, -i, vectus sum*	I am conveyed
sidus, -eris n.	star	*paternus, -a, -um*	native, ancestral
tollo, -ere	I raise	*promissum, -i* n. 45	promise
pectus, -oris n.	breast	*parens, -entis* m/f.	parent
immugio, -ire	I roar, resound	*discedo, -ere, -cessi, -cessus*	I depart, leave
regia, -ae f.	palace	*complector, -i, -plexus sum*	I embrace
luctus, -us m.	grief	*imperium, -i* n.	empire
ipse, ipsa, ipsum	-self	*metuo, -ere*	I fear
caput, -itis n.	head	*moneo, -ere*	I warn, advise
niveus, -a, -um	snow white	*acer, acris, acre*	keen, fierce
fulcio, fulcire, fulsi, fultus	I support, prop up	*vir, viri* m.	man
		durus, -a, -um	hard, harsh
os, oris n.	mouth, face	*proelium, -i* n.	battle
video, -ere, vidi, visus 40	I see	*gens, gentis* f.	race, people
lēvis, -e	smooth		

34–5 circum: supply *stabant*. **famulum:** archaic genitive plural. **-que . . . -que:** 'both . . . and', with the first one delayed to make *omnis* qualify both *manus* and *turba*. **maestum crinem solutae:** lit. 'loosened with respect to their sad hair', and so 'with their hair let down in mourning'. *Crinem* is perhaps best viewed as a borrowing from the Greek middle verb construction, in which *solutae* is treated as if active in meaning, like a deponent verb; *crinem* then becomes the direct object. This is one of Virgil's favourite constructions. **maestum:** an example of hypallage, as the adjective really describes the women rather than their hair. **de more:** 'according to custom': letting down their hair was a traditional symbol of mourning for Roman women.

36 foribus . . . altis: probably dative with the compound verb. This phrase may indicate that Aeneas' home was a house rather than a tent (cf. line 29), but a tent too may have a 'doorway'.

37–8 tollunt: the subject is the various people mentioned in lines 34–5. **tunsis . . . pectoribus:** the ablative absolute may be translated as if present active: 'beating their breasts'; this was a ritual expression of mourning for both men and women. **ad sidera:** an example of hyperbole. **maestoque immugit regia luctu:** *immugit* is a strong, onomatopoeic verb, suggesting the bellowing of cattle; it is translatable here as 'resounded'; note also the consonance of *m*, and the enclosing word-order. **regia:** simply the 'abode of the king', whether tent or something grander.

39–40 ipse . . . ut vidit: 'when he himself saw'. **nivei . . . Pallantis:** his skin has the pallor of death, following the loss of blood; the adjective may also suggest innocence and purity. **caput . . . fultum:** those looking after the body of Pallas had propped up his head with a cushion. **patens . . . vulnus:** 'the wound gaping open'. **levi . . . in pectore:** this is lēvi, not lĕvi (as the metre dictates), and so 'smooth', suggesting that Pallas was too young to have developed body hair.

41 cuspidis Ausoniae: '(the wound) caused by the Italian javelin'; the genitive is subjective, as the javelin caused the wound; Ausonia was a poetic name for South Italy. Note the fast rhythm of this line, indicating the immediacy of Aeneas' emotional response. **lacrimis . . . obortis:** ablative absolute; note the enclosing word-order.

42–4 tene: the position of *te* is emphatic at the start of the line and speech: 'was it you . . .?'; *te* is the object of *invidit*. **cum laeta veniret:** supply *Fortuna* as the subject of *veniret*, just as it is the subject of *invidit*; *laeta* has the idea of 'bringing joy'. Fortune (thought of as a deity) brought him good luck in that he won the battle, but bad luck in that he lost Pallas. **ne:** the negative purpose clause depends on *invidit*: Fortune begrudged Aeneas the life of Pallas, so that Pallas might not see the Trojan kingdom (*regna . . . nostra*) completed. **veherere** = *vehereris* (2nd singular imperfect subjunctive passive): a second negative purpose clause. **victor:** 'as victor', and so 'in victory'. **ad sedes . . . paternas:** i.e. Pallanteum.

45–6 non haec . . . promissa . . . dederam: i.e. 'this is not what I had promised'. He had promised Evander that he would look after Pallas. **me complexus euntem:** 'embracing me as I left'.

47–8 Note the very heavy alliteration of *m*-, added to that of *v*-, *p*- and then *d*- in the preceding lines, all underlining the powerful emotions of grief and bitterness. **in imperium:** 'to win an empire'. **viros:** i.e. the enemy. **proelia:** supply *esse* again. **dura . . . gente:** the metre makes *dura* agree with *gente*, not *proelia*.

Questions

1 How do the people standing round the body of Pallas show their grief?

2 How does Virgil's description of Pallas' body add poignancy to the scene?

3 How does Virgil use stylistic effects to intensify the grief of Aeneas?

et nunc ille quidem spe multum captus inani
fors et vota facit cumulatque altaria donis,   50
nos iuvenem exanimum et nil iam caelestibus ullis
debentem vano maesti comitamur honore.
infelix, nati funus crudele videbis!
hi nostri reditus exspectatique triumphi?
haec mea magna fides? at non, Euandre, pudendis   55
vulneribus pulsum aspicies, nec sospite dirum
optabis nato funus pater. hei mihi, quantum
praesidium, Ausonia, et quantum tu perdis, Iule!'

*Aeneas and his men prepared Pallas' body for the procession to Pallanteum, adorning it
with fine garments and piling all the trophies he had won in battle on to wagons. After
accompanying the procession for some distance, he turned back to take charge of the funeral
arrangements for all the other dead Trojans and their allies. He found ambassadors from
Laurentum waiting for him; they wanted a truce for the recovery of their dead.*

quos bonus Aeneas haud aspernanda precantes   106
prosequitur venia et verbis haec insuper addit:
'quaenam vos tanto fortuna indigna, Latini,
implicuit bello, qui nos fugiatis amicos?

quidem		indeed	
spes, spei f.		hope	
capio, -ere, cepi, captus		I take, capture	
inanis, -e		vain, empty	
fors	50	perhaps	
votum, -i n.		vow	
facio, -ere		I make, do	
cumulo, -are		I pile up	
altaria, -um n.pl.		altar(s)	
donum, -i n.		gift	
iuvenis, -is m.		young man, young	
nil		nothing	
caelestes, -ium m.pl.		heavenly gods	
ullus, -a, -um		any	
debeo, -ere		I owe	
vanus, -a, -um		empty	
comitor, -ari, -atus sum		I accompany	
honos, -oris m.		honour	
infelix, -icis		unlucky, unhappy	
natus, -i m.		son	
crudelis, -e		cruel	
reditus, -us m.		return	
exspecto, -are, -avi, -atus		I wait for, expect	
triumphus, -i m.		triumph	
fides, -ei f.	55	faith, pledge, reliability	
pudendus, -a, -um		shameful	
pello, -ere, pepuli, pulsus		I beat	
aspicio, -ere		I see, look upon	
sospes, -itis		safe, unhurt	
dirus, -a, -um		dreadful	
opto, -are		I wish	
pater, patris m.		father	
hei!		alas!	
quantus, -a, -um		how much	
praesidium, -i n.		protection	
Ausonia, -ae f.		Italy	
perdo, -ere		I lose	
Iulus, -i m.		Iulus, Ascanius	
bonus, -a, -um	106	good	
haud		not	
aspernor, -ari, -atus sum		I reject	
precor, -ari, -atus sum		I pray, plead	
prosequor, -i, -secutus sum		I honour with permission	
venia, -ae f.			
verbum, -i n.		word	
insuper		in addition	
addo, -ere		I add	
quinam, quaenam, quodnam		who, which	
indignus, -a, -um		unworthy	
Latini, -orum m.pl.		the Latins	
implico, -are, -ui, -itus		I involve	
bellum, -i n.		war	
fugio, -ere		I flee (from)	
amicus, -i m.		friend	

49 **ille quidem:** 'he certainly' (meaning Evander), contrasted with *nos* in line 51. **multum:** adverbial: 'completely'. **captus:** here 'taken in' or 'deceived'. **spe . . . inani:** 'by vain hope'.
50 Note the <u>chiasmus</u> in *vota facit cumulatque altaria*. **vota facit:** these would be vows to make offerings to the gods in return for his son's safe return; the next words make this clear.
51–2 **nos . . . maesti comitamur:** '(while) we sadly accompany'. **nil iam caelestibus ullis debentem:** 'now owing no debt to any of the heavenly gods'; in contrast with Evander, who is still making vows to the gods (*vota facit*), Pallas, being dead, has no such obligations. **vano . . . honore:** this phrase, enclosing *maesti comitamur*, must indicate how Aeneas and his people will accompany the body: 'with empty honour', i.e. the honour they have achieved in winning the overall battle is rendered nought by the death of Pallas.
53 **infelix:** Aeneas is addressing Evander as if he were present (an example of <u>apostrophe</u>). Note the heavily spondaic rhythm of this line.
54–5 These are <u>rhetorical questions</u>. Supply *sunt* with the first two clauses and *est* with the third. **nostri reditus:** 'our return' (plural for singular), i.e. the return of both the Trojans and Pallas to Pallanteum. **exspectatique triumphi:** they had hoped to return to Pallanteum in triumph after defeating the Latins and Rutulians. **magna fides:** the 'strong pledge' is the one made by Aeneas to Evander in Book VIII to look after Pallas.
55–6 **at:** introduces Aeneas' one consolation, that Pallas has not died a coward's death from *pudendis vulneribus* ('shameful wounds'), i.e. wounds in the back as he ran away. **aspicies:** supply *eum*. Note the heavy <u>alliteration</u> and <u>consonance</u> with *p*, marking Aeneas' bitterness.
56–7 'Nor will you wish for a dreadful death as a father when his son is safe'; a heroic death was considered far preferable to a cowardly death, which, according to heroic convention, would have heaped so much shame upon the dead man's father that he too would have wanted to die.
57–8 **quantum praesidium:** Aeneas suggests that, had Pallas lived, he would have become a champion protector of Southern Italy. **Ausonia:** supply *perdis*; in full this would be *quantum praesidium tu, Ausonia, perdis, et quantum praesidium tu, Iule, perdis* (suggesting that Iulus would have had a powerful supporter, had Pallas lived); it is possible, however, that the second *quantum* should be taken on its own: 'and how big your loss is, Iulus'. Iulus was Aeneas' son, also called Ascanius, whom Aeneas hoped would succeed him as ruler of the Trojans.

106–7 **haud aspernanda precantes:** '(since they are) requesting things that cannot be refused'; *precantes* agrees with *quos* (the ambassadors). **prosequitur venia:** 'he honours them with permission', and so 'he grants them permission'. **verbis . . . addit:** 'and to his words he adds . . .'. The *verbis* are the words with which he granted permission to collect the bodies. Note the <u>chiasmus</u> (*prosequitur venia . . . verbis addit*).
108–9 The order is *quaenam indigna fortuna, Latini, implicuit vos tanto bello*. **indigna:** here 'cruel'. **qui nos fugiatis amicos:** 'that you shun us as friends' (a result clause introduced by *tanto . . . qui* instead of *tanto . . . ut*).

Questions

1 In lines 49–52, what contrast does Aeneas draw between Evander and the Trojans?

2 How do Aeneas' words make this contrast poignant?

3 What emotions does Aeneas give voice to in lines 53–58? How does he show these?

4 In lines 106–109, how does Aeneas react to the request of the Latins?

pacem me exanimis et Martis sorte peremptis   110
oratis? equidem et vivis concedere vellem.
nec veni, nisi fata locum sedemque dedissent,
nec bellum cum gente gero; rex nostra reliquit
hospitia et Turni potius se credidit armis.
aequius huic Turnum fuerat se opponere morti.   115
si bellum finire manu, si pellere Teucros
apparat, his mecum decuit concurrere telis:
vixet cui vitam deus aut sua dextra dedisset.
nunc ite et miseris supponite civibus ignem.'
dixerat Aeneas. illi obstipuere silentes   120
conversique oculos inter se atque ora tenebant.
tum senior semperque odiis et crimine Drances
infensus iuveni Turno sic ore vicissim
orsa refert: 'o fama ingens, ingentior armis,
vir Troiane, quibus caelo te laudibus aequem?   125
iustitiaene prius mirer belline laborum?

pax, pacis f.	110 peace	*vita, -ae* f.	life
Mars, -tis m.	Mars, War	*deus, -i* m.	god
sors, sortis f.	lot, fate	*dext(e)ra, -ae* f.	right hand, hand
perimo, -ere, -emi, -emptus	to kill	*miser, -era, -erum*	poor, wretched
oro, -are	I beg	*suppono, -ere*	I place beneath
equidem	I for my part	*civis, -is* m.	citizen
vivus, -a, -um	alive, living	*ignis, -is* m.	fire
concedo, -ere	I grant	*dico, -ere, dixi, dictus*	120 I say
volo, velle	I wish, want	*obstipesco, -ere, -stipui*	I am astonished
nisi	if not, unless	*silens, -entis*	silent, in silence
fatum, -i n.	fate	*converto, -ere, -rti, -rsus*	I turn
locus, -i m.	place	*oculus, -i* m.	eye
gero, -ere	I wage, carry	*inter* + acc.	between, among
rex, regis m.	king	*teneo, -ere*	I hold, keep
relinquo, -ere, -liqui, -lictus	I leave, abandon	*semper*	always
hospitium, -i n.	friendship	*odium, -i* n.	hatred
Turnus, -i m.	Turnus	*crimen, -inis* n.	accusation
potius	rather	*Drances, -is* m.	Drances
credo, -ere	I entrust, trust	*infensus, -a, -um*	hostile
arma, -orum n.pl.	arms	*vicissim*	in turn
oppono, -ere	115 I expose	*orsa, -orum* n.pl.	words
mors, mortis f.	death	*refero, -ferre*	I give back
finio, -ire	I end	*fama, -ae* f.	glory, reputation
pello, -ere	I drive, defeat	*caelum, -i* n.	125 sky, heaven
Teucri, -orum m.pl.	Trojans	*laus, laudis* f.	praise
apparo, -are	I prepare	*aequo, -are*	I make equal
decet, -ere, -uit	it is right	*iustitia, -ae* f.	justice
concurro, -ere	I meet, join battle	*prius*	previously, first
telum, -i n.	weapon	*miror, -ari, -atus sum*	I admire
vivo, -ere, vixi, victus	I live	*labor, -oris* m.	work

110–11 **exanimis et . . . peremptis**: 'for the dead and those killed'. **oratis:** the <u>enjambement</u> adds heavy emphasis to this word; the tone is ironic. **et vivis concedere vellem:** 'I would have wished to grant (peace) also to the living'; *et = etiam*; *vellem* is a potential subjunctive.

112 **nec veni, nisi fata . . . dedissent:** 'I would not have come, had not fate granted . . .'; this combination of indicative and subjunctive in a conditional sentence is unusual (*venissem* would have been normal). **locum sedemque:** 'a place for a home' (<u>hendiadys</u>). **fata:** 'fate' (generally plural in the *Aeneid*), which is either an abstract concept of the fate that determines all human actions, or the personified Fates, three sisters in Greek mythology who spun out human lives.

113–14 **cum gente:** Aeneas has no quarrel with the Latin people as a whole: it was their king who renounced their friendship. **nostra . . . hospitia:** 'our ties of friendship'. **Turni . . . armis:** 'to the arms of Turnus'; Turnus was the leader of the Rutuli and had been betrothed to Latinus' daughter.

115 **aequius fuerat:** 'it would have been fairer'; the indicative is preferred, despite its being equivalent to a past unfulfilled condition. **se opponere:** 'to expose himself'. **huic . . . morti:** 'to this death'; Aeneas points to the corpses as he speaks.

116–17 **manu:** either 'by force of arms' or 'in hand-to-hand combat'. **decuit:** 'it was his duty', i.e. when the war broke out. **his . . . telis:** 'with these weapons'; again Aeneas points to the objects.

118 **vixet:** a contraction of *vixisset*; supply *is*: 'the one would have lived to whom . . .'. **deus aut sua dextra:** the gods or fate generally took a hand in heroic combat. **dedisset:** subjunctive because it is treated as part of a virtual conditional sentence, i.e. if Turnus had acted as he should.

119 **et miseris supponite civibus ignem:** 'and place the pyre beneath your poor citizens'; *civibus* is dative following the compound verb.

120 **dixerat:** Virgil regularly uses the pluperfect to show the end of a speech; translate as 'finished speaking'. The ambassadors (*illi*) are astonished because Aeneas has presented himself as fair-minded, and not at all as the ruthless enemy they had expected.

121 **conversique:** 'and turning round'. **inter se:** 'facing each other'. The idea is that the ambassadors are ashamed to meet Aeneas' gaze, as his words have set him morally above them.

122–4 **senior . . . Drances:** 'the elderly Drances', with *senior* contrasted with *iuveni* in the same position in the next line. Drances has not appeared previously in the *Aeneid*, but plays an important role in lines 336ff. **odiis et crimine . . . infensus:** 'showing his hostility [towards Turnus] with hatred and accusations'. Virgil compares the old Drances unfavourably with the young Turnus, despite the latter being the number one enemy of the Trojans; in heroic terms, Turnus is more open and honourable than Drances. **sic ore vicissim orsa refert:** lit. 'thus gives back words in turn with his mouth', i.e. 'speaks these words in response'.

124–5 **o fama ingens, ingentior armis:** *fama* is ablative, giving a <u>chiastic</u> order to these words: 'O (man) great in glory, greater in battle'. The ablatives are of respect. **quibus caelo te laudibus aequem:** lit. 'with what praises am I to make you equal to the sky?', i.e. 'what praises can I use to exalt you to the sky?' **aequem:** deliberative subjunctive, as is *mirer* below.

126 'Am I to marvel at you first for your justice or for your exertions in war?' **-ne . . . -ne:** an alternative to *utrum . . . an* introducing alternative questions. **iustitiae . . . laborum:** the genitives are very unusual, being modelled on Greek causal genitives. **mirer:** supply *te* as the object. **belli:** genitive of definition.

Questions

1 What are the main arguments of Aeneas' speech? How does he make these convincing?

2 What is the tone of Drances' reply? What shows this?

nos vero haec patriam grati referemus ad urbem
et te, si qua viam dederit fortuna, Latino
iungemus regi. quaerat sibi foedera Turnus.
quin et fatales murorum attollere moles 130
saxaque subvectare umeris Troiana iuvabit.'
dixerat haec unoque omnes eadem ore fremebant.
bis senos pepigere dies, et pace sequestra
per silvas Teucri mixtique impune Latini
erravere iugis. ferro sonat alta bipenni 135
fraxinus, evertunt actas ad sidera pinus,
robora nec cuneis et olentem scindere cedrum
nec plaustris cessant vectare gementibus ornos.
et iam Fama volans, tanti praenuntia luctus,
Euandrum Euandrique domos et moenia replet, 140
quae modo victorem Latio Pallanta ferebat.

gratus, -a, -um	grateful	*iugum, -i* n.	ridge
refero, -ferre	I take back, bring back	*ferrum, -i* n.	weapon, axe
		bipennis, -e	two-edged
via, -ae f.	way, road	*fraxinus, -i* f.	ash tree
Latinus, -i m.	Latinus	*everto, -ere*	I cast down
iungo, -ere	I join, unite	*ago, -ere, egi, actus*	I thrust, come on, drive
quaero, -ere	I seek		
foedus, -eris n.	treaty	*pinus, -us* f.	pine tree
quin	130 indeed	*robur, -oris* n.	oak tree
fatalis, -e	fated	*cuneus, -i* m.	wedge
murus, -i m.	wall	*olens, -entis*	fragrant
attollo, -ere	I raise up	*scindo, -ere*	I split
moles, -is f.	mass	*cedrus, -i* f.	cedar tree
saxum, -i n.	rock, stone	*plaustrum, -i* n.	cart, wagon
subvecto, -are	bring up, transport	*cesso, -are*	I stop, cease
		vecto, -are	I carry, convey
umerus, -i m.	shoulder	*gemo, -ere*	I groan
iuvat, -are	it pleases	*ornus, -i* f.	mountain-ash
idem, eadem, idem	the same	*Fama, -ae* f.	Rumour
fremo, -ere	I shout out, roar	*volo, -are*	I fly
bis	twice	*praenuntia, -ae* f.	foreteller
seni, -ae, -a	six, six each	*luctus, -us* m.	grief
pango, -ere, pepigi, pactus	I agree	*domus, -us* f.	140 house, home
sequestra, -ae f.	guarantor	*moenia, -ium* n.pl.	city, city walls
silva, -ae f.	wood	*repleo, -ere*	I fill
misceo, -ere, -ui, mixtus	I mix, mingle	*modo*	recently
impune	with impunity	*Latium, -i* n.	Latium
erro, -are, -avi, -atus	135 I wander	*fero, ferre*	I bring, carry

127–9 **nos vero:** 'we for our part', marking a transition from the lavish praise of Aeneas to how the ambassadors intend to respond. **haec:** supply *verba*. **patriam . . . ad urbem:** i.e. to Laurentum. **et te . . . Latino iungemus regi:** 'and we shall unite you with king Latinus', i.e. they will try to revive the original alliance agreed between the Latins and Trojans. **si qua viam dederit fortuna:** 'if any fortune provides a way'; *fortuna* here is good luck, which will be needed if the ambassadors are to succeed. **quaerat sibi foedera Turnus:** 'let Turnus seek treaties for himself', i.e. without our help.

130–1 **quin et:** short for *quin etiam*: 'indeed . . . even', introducing the climax to Drances' ornate and extravagant speech. **fatales murorum . . . moles:** lit. 'the fated masses of walls', and so 'the massive walls decreed by fate'; the walls are 'decreed by fate' because the Trojans had told Latinus as much when they first approached him for help. Note the slow rhythm of line 130. **attollere . . . subvectare:** both infinitives are dependent on the impersonal *iuvabit*. **saxa . . . Troiana:** 'Trojan stones', because the stones will be used to build a new city for the Trojans.

132 **omnes . . . fremebant:** 'all (the ambassadors) loudly spoke'; *fremebant* is a strong word in an emphatic position. **uno . . . ore:** 'with one voice'.

133 **bis senos pepigere dies:** 'they made an agreement for twelve days'. **pace sequestra:** 'with the peace as guarantor', i.e. 'under the protection of the truce'.

134 Note the slow rhythm. **impune:** each side has agreed not to attack the other.

135–6 **iugis:** local ablative; the woods are on the mountain ridges, presumably the Alban Hills, though apparently there were densely wooded marshes much closer to hand. They need timber for the funeral pyres. **alta . . . fraxinus:** the *fraxinus* was a remarkably slender, and so relatively tall, ash tree. **ferro . . . bipenni:** *bipennis* is most often used as a feminine noun; here it must have its basic adjectival force to agree with *ferro*: 'double-bladed'. **actas ad sidera:** 'soaring upwards to the stars'.

137–8 The order is *nec cessant scindere cuneis robora et olentem cedrum, nec (cessant) vectare ornos gementibus plaustris.* **cuneis:** wedges are hammered into logs to split them into planks. **plaustris . . . gementibus:** local or instrumental ablatives; the wagons are 'groaning' under the weight of the cut timber.

139–40 **Fama:** Rumour is frequently personified in the *Aeneid*; in Book IV.173ff, Virgil devotes sixteen lines to describing the deity, as a monstrous, ever-wakeful and multi-tongued creature that preys on mankind. **Euandrum . . . replet:** Rumour 'fills Evander', meaning either that she fills his ears with the news, or that she fills him with grief.

141 **quae:** the antecedent is *Fama*. **victorem:** best translated as an adjective: 'victorious'. **Latio:** local ablative. **ferebat:** 'brought the news of'. Rumour could spread both good news and bad.

Questions

1 Summarise the last five lines of Drances' speech. What is unusual about them?

2 Why do you think Virgil uses slow rhythm in lines 130 and 134?

3 Describe the activities in lines 134–138. How does Virgil make them interesting?

4 What is the sequence of the spread of Rumour? How does the order of line 140 show this? Is this the sequence you would expect? Why do you think Virgil chooses this sequence?

Arcades ad portas ruere et de more vetusto
funereas rapuere faces; lucet via longo
ordine flammarum et late discriminat agros.
contra turba Phrygum veniens plangentia iungit   145
agmina. quae postquam matres succedere tectis
viderunt, maestam incendunt clamoribus urbem.
at non Euandrum potis est vis ulla tenere,
sed venit in medios. feretro Pallanta reposto
procubuit super atque haeret lacrimansque gemensque,   150
et via vix tandem voci laxata dolore est:
'non haec, o Palla, dederas promissa petenti,
cautius ut saevo velles te credere Marti.
haud ignarus eram quantum nova gloria in armis
et praedulce decus primo certamine posset.   155
primitiae iuvenis miserae bellique propinqui
dura rudimenta, et nulli exaudita deorum
vota precesque meae! tuque, o sanctissima coniunx,
felix morte tua neque in hunc servata dolorem!

Arcades, -um m.pl.	Arcadians	*procumbo, -ere, -cubui, -itus*		I bend over
porta, -ae f.	gate	*super*	150	over, above
ruo, -ere, rui	I rush, fall down	*haereo, -ere*		I cling (to), stick
vetustus, -a, -um	old, ancient			
funereus, -a, -um	funereal	*lacrimo, -are*		I weep
rapio, -ere, -ui, raptus	I seize	*vix*		scarcely
fax, facis f.	torch	*tandem*		at last
luceo, -ere	I shine	*vox, vocis* f.		voice, word
longus, -a, -um	long	*laxo, -are, -avi, -atus*		I open
ordo, -inis m.	row, line	*dolor, -oris* m.		grief
flamma, -ae f.	flame	*peto, -ere*		I seek, ask
late	far and wide	*cautus, -a, -um*		cautious
discrimino, -are	I distinguish	*saevus, -a, -um*		cruel
ager, agri m.	field	*volo, velle*		I wish
contra	145 to meet them	*ignarus, -a, -um*		unaware
turba, -ae f.	crowd	*quantus, -a, -um*		how much
Phryges, -um m.pl.	Phrygians, Trojans	*novus, -a, -um*		new
		gloria, -ae f.		glory
plango, -ere	I mourn, lament	*praedulcis, -e*	155	very sweet
iungo, -ere	I join	*decus, -oris* n.		honour, glory
agmen, -inis n.	army, line of men	*primus, -a, -um*		first
postquam	after	*certamen, -inis* n.		contest
mater, -tris f.	mother	*possum, posse, potui*		I can, am able
succedo, -ere	I draw near (to)	*primitiae, -arum* f.pl.		first fruits
tectum, -i n.	roof, building	*propinquus, -a, -um*		neighbouring
incendo, -ere	I set on fire	*rudimentum, -i* n.		first attempt
clamor, -oris m.	shout, shouting	*exaudio, -ire, -ivi, -itus*		I listen to, hear
potis (indecl.)	able	*prex, precis* f.		prayer, entreaty
vis, vim, vi f.	force	*sanctus, -a, -um*		virtuous
medius, -a, -um	middle, middle of	*coniunx, -iugis* f.		wife
feretrum, -i n.	bier	*servo, -are, -avi, -atus*		I keep alive, protect
repono, -ere, -posui, -positus	I set down, restore			

142–3 ruĕre ... rapuēre: *ruĕre* is a historic infinitive, *rapuēre* perfect indicative. **de:** here 'in accordance with'. **funereas faces:** torches traditionally played an important role in Roman funerals, with four being placed at the corners of the bier, and many more being carried during the funeral procession through the streets.

143–4 lucet via ... discriminat agros: lit. 'the road shines and distinguishes the fields', i.e. the light cast by the torches moving along the road 'distinguishes' and so 'picks out' or 'lights up' the fields on either side; translate as 'the road is illuminated ... and this picks out the fields ...'.

145–6 contra ... veniens: the thousand men sent by Aeneas to accompany the body of Pallas come 'to meet them', though in reality it is Evander and his people who come to meet the Trojan procession. **plangentia ... agmina:** 'the throng of mourners'.

146–7 quae: a connecting relative, referring to *agmina*. **matres:** since the soldiers who had died were all young men, they were mourned by mothers rather than wives; it was not customary for fathers to show their grief in public. **maestam incendunt clamoribus urbem:** 'they set the sad city aflame with their cries'; the verb provides a powerful <u>metaphor</u>; *maestam* is an example of <u>hypallage</u>, more logically defining the cries.

148–9 potis est: archaic for *potest*. **tenere:** 'hold back'. **in medios:** supply *homines* or similar.

149–50 The order is *feretro reposto, (Euandrus) procubuit super Pallanta*. **feretro ... reposto:** 'when the bier has been set down'; *reposto* = *reposito*. **haeret:** 'clings to him' (a favourite word of Virgil).

151 via vix ... voci laxata ... est: 'a way was with difficulty opened up for his voice', i.e. he could barely speak because of his grief. Note the heavy <u>alliteration</u>.

152 non haec ... dederas promissa: 'this is not the promise you had given'; *non haec* is emphatic. **petenti:** the manuscripts all read *parenti* ('to your father'), but *petenti* (mentioned by Servius) gives better sense: 'to (me) pleading', and so 'to my plea that you should ...'.

153 ut: to be taken first; the word order emphasises *cautius* ('more cautiously' than he otherwise would). **saevo ... Marti:** 'to savage warfare'.

154–5 haud ignarus eram: 'I knew full well'. **quantum ... posset:** 'how much influence (new glory, etc.) could have'. **praedulce decus:** 'very sweet honour', a second subject of *posset*, parallel to *nova gloria*. **primo certamine:** 'in his first fight'. Evander's argument is that a young warrior's first victory in battle can too easily go to his head and lead him to recklessness.

156–7 primitiae ... miserae, dura rudimenta: these are vocatives, addressed in exclamation; *primitiae* are the 'first-fruits' and so the 'first victory' of war; *rudimenta* are 'first attempts' at warfare; they are 'hard' because they have led to an early death. **belli propinqui:** the fact that Pallas' first and fatal experience of war was so close to home makes it seem worse.

157–8 nulli exaudita deorum: '(vows and prayers) heeded by none of the gods'; *nulli* is dative of the agent dependent on the perfect passive participle. **vota precesque meae:** vocatives.

159 felix morte tua: 'fortunate in your death'; this is the only occasion that Virgil mentions Evander's dead wife. **neque in hunc servata dolorem:** 'nor kept alive to see this grief', giving the reason for her good fortune.

Questions

1 Summarise in your own words the sequence of events at Pallanteum (lines 142–147).

2 How does Virgil emphasise the pathos of these lines?

3 What makes Evander's actions and words particularly emotive?

contra ego vivendo vici mea fata, superstes   160
restarem ut genitor. Troum socia arma secutum
obruerent Rutuli telis! animam ipse dedissem
atque haec pompa domum me, non Pallanta, referret!'

'I don't blame you Trojans for his death, and Aeneas could not have provided a more
honourable funeral for him. But I must not let my grief keep the Trojans from the fight.'

'vadite et haec memores regi mandata referte: 176
quod vitam moror invisam Pallante perempto
dextera causa tua est, Turnum natoque patrique
quam debere vides. meritis vacat hic tibi solus
fortunaeque locus. non vitae gaudia quaero,   180
nec fas, sed nato manes perferre sub imos.'
Aurora interea miseris mortalibus almam
extulerat lucem referens opera atque labores:
iam pater Aeneas, iam curvo in litore Tarchon
constituere pyras. huc corpora quisque suorum   185
more tulere patrum, subiectisque ignibus atris
conditur in tenebras altum caligine caelum.
ter circum accensos cincti fulgentibus armis
decurrere rogos, ter maestum funeris ignem
lustravere in equis ululatusque ore dedere.   190

contra	160 on the other hand	*Aurora, -ae* f.	Dawn
vinco, -ere, vici, victus	I defeat	*interea*	meanwhile
superstes, -stitis	surviving	*mortales, -ium* m.pl.	mortals
resto, -are	I remain	*almus, -a, -um*	kindly
genitor, -oris m.	father	*effero, -ferre*	I bring out
Tros, Trois m.	Trojan	*lux, lucis* f.	light
socius, -a, -um	allied	*opus, -eris* n.	work
sequor, -i, secutus sum	I follow	*curvus, -a, -um*	curved
obruo, -ere	I overwhelm	*litus, -oris* n.	shore
Rutulus, -i m.	Rutulian	*Tarchon, -onis* m.	Tarchon
anima, -ae f.	soul, breath, life	*constituo, -ere, -ui, -utus*	185 I construct
pompa, -ae f.	procession	*pyra, -ae* f.	pyre
vado, -ere	176 I go	*quisque, quaeque, quidque*	each
memor, -oris	mindful, aware	*subicio, -ere, -ieci, -iectus*	I place under
mandatum, -i n.	command	*condo, -ere*	I plunge
moror, -ari, -atus sum	I delay, prolong	*tenebrae, -arum* f.pl.	darkness
invisus, -a, -um	hateful	*caligo, -inis* f.	gloom, mist
perimo, -ere, -emi, -emptus	I kill	*ter*	three times
causa, -ae f.	cause, reason	*circum* + acc.	around
meritum, -i n.	just desserts	*accendo, -ere, -cendi, -census*	I light
vaco, -are	I am left open	*cingo, -ere, cinxi, cinctus*	I surround
solus, -a, -um	only, alone	*fulgeo, -ere*	I gleam
gaudium, -i n.	180 joy	*decurro, -ere, -curri, -cursus*	I march
fas (indecl.) n.	right	*rogus, -i* m.	pyre
manes, -ium m.pl.	souls of the dead	*lustro, -are, -avi, -atus*	190 I go round
perfero, -ferre	I bear	*equus, -i* m.	horse
imus, -a, -um	deepest	*ululatus, -us* m.	wailing

160–1 vivendo vici mea fata: lit. 'I have conquered my destiny by living (on)', and so 'I have outlived my destined life-span'. **superstes restarem ut:** *ut* should be taken first: 'so that I was left surviving'. The argument is that fathers ought not to outlive their sons.

161–2 The order is *Rutuli obruerent telis (me) secutum socia arma Troum*. **obruerent:** supply *me*; the imperfect subjunctive is probably a more vivid alternative to the more usual pluperfect, meaning 'would that they had overwhelmed me'. **secutum:** '(me) after I had followed'.

162–3 dedissem . . . referret: each is the apodosis of an unfulfilled condition, the protasis to be inferred from the preceding wish: 'if the Rutuli had overwhelmed me, then I would have given . . . (and this procession) would be bringing me back'; the tenses are perfectly logical.

176 vadite: Evander turns to address the Trojans. **haec . . . mandata:** it is this commission that he sends to Aeneas that persuades Aeneas to kill Turnus at the end of Book XII. **memores:** 'not forgetting them'.

177–9 quod vitam moror invisam: 'why I prolong my life, hateful' (because of Pallas' death). **dextera causa tua est:** 'your right hand is the reason'; i.e. the killing of Turnus by Aeneas in retribution is the reason he prolongs his life. **Turnum natoque patrique quam debere vides:** difficult: '(your hand) which you see owes (the death of) Turnus to both father and son', i.e. to both Evander and Pallas.

179–80 vacat hic . . . solus . . . locus: 'this is the only course of action (lit. 'place') left open'. **meritis . . . fortunaeque:** 'to achieve just deserts and good fortune'; the argument is that Aeneas has no alternative but to kill Turnus if he wishes to act honourably and pay off his debt to Evander.

180–1 vitae: 'in (my) life'; now that his son is dead, there can be no more joys in his life. **nec fas:** supply *esset*: 'nor would it be right' (to seek such joys). **perferre:** depends on *quaero*: 'but (what I do seek) is to deliver (the joys to my son)'; *gaudia* are the joys emanating from the news of Turnus' death. **manes . . . sub imos:** 'deep down among the shades', i.e. in the underworld.

182–3 almam . . . lucem: 'kindly light' of day; there is a hint of irony in the word *almam*, because the reality was that the return of daylight revealed the huge number of dead bodies awaiting cremation, and so caused the lamentation to break out afresh. Note the heavy <u>alliteration</u> and <u>consonance</u> of *m*. **opera atque labores:** the tasks and toils of collecting and cremating the dead.

184–5 pater Aeneas: Virgil often calls Aeneas *pater* to remind us of his caring relationship with his people. **Tarchon:** the king of the Etruscans, who made an alliance with Aeneas in Book VIII.

185–6 The order is *quisque tulere (= tulerunt) huc corpora suorum more patrum*. **tulere:** plural following the sense. **more . . . patrum:** the 'custom of their ancestors' is the collection by each man of the bodies of relatives or friends.

186–7 subiectis ignibus: torches are applied to the bases of the pyres. **atris:** both 'black' (from the smoke) and 'funereal'. **altum caligine:** the word order and Virgilian usage suggest that *caligine* is dependent upon *altum*: the sky is 'filled to a great height with smoke (lit. 'gloom')'.

188–90 The <u>anaphora</u> of *ter*, one of Virgil's favourite expressions, emphasises the ritual nature of the military honours. **circum accensos . . . rogos:** 'round the pyres they had lit'. Note the slow rhythm of line 188 and the <u>alliteration</u> of *c*. **decurrēre:** a military word to describe troops marching round a pyre in ritual procession; *lustravere* has a similar meaning, but is less technical. **ululatus:** an <u>onomatopoeic</u> word reflecting the sound of the lamentation. **ore:** ablative of origin.

Questions

1 How does Evander show the depth of his grief in his speech?

2 How does Virgil bring out the pathos of the funeral scene?

spargitur et tellus lacrimis, sparguntur et arma,
it caelo clamorque virum clangorque tubarum.
hic alii spolia occisis derepta Latinis
coniciunt igni, galeas ensesque decoros
frenaque ferventesque rotas; pars munera nota,   195
ipsorum clipeos et non felicia tela.
multa boum circa mactantur corpora Morti,
saetigerosque sues raptasque ex omnibus agris
in flammam iugulant pecudes. tum litore toto
ardentes spectant socios semustaque servant   200
busta, neque avelli possunt, nox umida donec
invertit caelum stellis ardentibus aptum.
nec minus et miseri diversa in parte Latini
innumeras struxere pyras, et corpora partim
multa virum terrae infodiunt, avectaque partim   205
finitimos tollunt in agros urbique remittunt.
cetera confusaeque ingentem caedis acervum
nec numero nec honore cremant; tunc undique vasti
certatim crebris conlucent ignibus agri.

spargo, -ere	I scatter	*avello, -ere*	I tear away
tellus, -uris f.	ground	*nox, noctis* f.	night
clangor, -oris m.	strident sound	*umidus, -a, -um*	damp, dewy
tuba, -ae f.	trumpet	*donec*	until
spolia, -orum n.pl.	spoils	*inverto, -ere*	I invert
occido, -ere, -cidi, -cisus	I kill	*stella, -ae* f.	star
deripio, -ere, -ripui, -reptus	I strip, pull off	*aptus, -a, -um*	studded (with)
conicio, -ere	I throw	*minus*	less
galea, -ae f.	helmet	*diversus, -a, -um*	different
ensis, -is m.	sword	*innumerus, -a, -um*	countless
decorus, -a, -um	decorated	*struo, -ere, struxi, structus*	I build
frena, -orum n.pl. 195	bridles	*partim*	partly
fervens, -entis	red-hot	*terra, -ae* f. 205	ground, earth
rota, -ae f.	wheel	*infodio, -ere*	I bury
pars, partis f.	part, some	*aveho, -ere, avexi, avectus*	I carry away
notus, -a, -um	known, familiar	*finitimus, -a, -um*	neighbouring
clipeus, -i m.	shield	*tollo, -ere*	I remove
bos, bovis m.	ox	*remitto, -ere*	I send back
circa	round about	*ceteri, -ae, -a*	the rest (of)
macto, -are	I sacrifice	*confundo, -ere, -fudi, -fusus*	I jumble together
Mors, Mortis f.	Death	*caedes, -is* f.	slaughter
saetiger, -era, -erum	bristly	*acervus, -i* m.	pile, heap
sus, suis m.	pig, boar	*numerus, -i* m.	number
iugulo, -are	I slaughter	*cremo, -are*	I cremate
pecus, -udis f.	cow, sheep	*tunc*	then
totus, -a, -um	all, the whole	*undique*	on all sides
ardeo, -ere 200	I burn	*vastus, -a, -um*	extensive
specto, -are	I watch over	*certatim*	eagerly
socius, -i m.	comrade	*creber, crebra, crebrum*	numerous
semustus, -a, -um	half-burnt	*conluceo, -ere*	I shine brightly
bustum, -i n.	lit pyre		

191 spargitur . . . sparguntur: <u>anaphora</u> combined with <u>polyptoton</u>.

192 caelo: poetic for *in caelum.* **-que . . . -que:** 'both . . . and'. Note the heavy <u>alliteration</u> of *c-* and the <u>assonance</u> of *clamor* and *clangor*, reflecting the sounds. **virum:** = *virorum.*

193–6 hic: 'at this point'. **alii:** 'some', followed in line 195 by *pars* ('others'). **occisis . . . Latinis:** 'from the killed Latins': either ablative of separation or (more probably) dative of disadvantage. **igni:** 'onto the fire'. The burning of enemy arms on funeral pyres was a Roman custom. **galeas ensesque . . . frenaque . . . rotas:** all are in apposition to, and explanatory of, *spolia.* **ferventesque rotas:** the chariot wheels are described as 'red-hot' because in use they turn so fast; here the adjective is less appropriate. **pars:** supply *conicit igni* from line 195. **munera nota:** either 'well-known offerings' or 'traditional offerings' (editorial opinion is divided). **clipeos . . . tela:** in apposition to *munera* (cf. *spolia* above). **ipsorum:** these shields and spears had belonged to the men whose bodies were being cremated, rather than being captured armour; this may explain *nota*, indicating that this armour was well-known to the men. **non felicia tela:** the weapons are 'not fortunate' because they did not save their owners' lives.

197 Morti: Death is personified as a god who had to be appeased with sacrifices.

198–9 raptasque . . . pecudes: probably 'flocks' rather than 'herds' as oxen have already been mentioned. **in flammam:** 'into the flames'; *iugulare* involves cutting the animals' throats, so that the blood would spurt into the flames.

199–201 litore toto: local ablative. **semustaque servant busta:** 'and they keep watch over the half-burnt pyres'; *busta* are pyres that have been set on fire.

201–2 donec: to be taken first. **invertit caelum:** night is thought of as 'turning the sky round', because it was widely believed that there were two hemispheres of sky, one bright for the daytime and one dark for night-time.

203 et: 'also'. **nec minus . . . miseri:** an example of <u>litotes</u>, with <u>alliteration</u> and <u>assonance</u>. **diversa in parte:** 'in a different part (of the battlefield)'.

205–6 virum: = *virorum.* **terrae infodiunt:** 'they bury in the ground'; inhumation was more common than cremation in early Rome. By Virgil's day cremation was almost universal, but public records survived from the 5th century BC listing both cremation and inhumation. In Homer's world cremation was the norm; here perhaps Virgil wishes to emphasize the diversity of cultures that he imagined must have existed in this early period. **avectaque partim . . . tollunt:** 'and other (bodies) they carry away and remove'. **finitimos . . . in agros:** 'into neighbouring territories': i.e. the Latin allies who had come from beyond the territory of Laurentum were taken home for burial, if they were not cremated on the spot. **urbique remittunt:** 'and (others) they send back to the city', i.e. to Laurentum.

207–8 cetera: supply *corpora.* **confusaeque ingentem caedis acervum:** 'a huge pile of dead all jumbled together'; the *-que* simply explains or amplifies *cetera.* Note the heavy <u>alliteration</u> of *c-* here and in line 209. **nec numero nec honore:** lit. 'with neither number nor honour'; *nec numero* probably means 'without counting them'. These bodies are presumably those of rank and file soldiers, who did not merit special treatment.

208–9 vasti . . . agri: 'fields far and wide'. **certatim:** 'eagerly', in the sense that fire eagerly took hold of the timber of the pyres. Note the slow rhythm and heavy <u>alliteration</u> of line 209.

Questions

1 Make a list of the various stages in the funeral rites.

2 How does Virgil make clear his horror of war in this passage?

3 What makes this description of the funerals an effective piece of writing?

The funeral rites lasted for three days. Meanwhile the people of Laurentum, who had lost so many husbands and sons, argued that Turnus should face Aeneas in single combat to decide the war. During the heated debate that followed, messengers arrived from Diomede, a neighbouring king whose alliance they had sought. Diomede had rejected their request. This prompted king Latinus to recommend making peace with the Trojans. Turnus responded angrily, arguing that they had many other allies to call upon. As the leaders squabbled, news arrived that the Trojans had moved their camp close to the city and were poised to attack. The young men called for their arms, and immediately Turnus issued orders to his allied leaders to prepare for battle.

cingitur ipse furens certatim in proelia Turnus.	486
iamque adeo rutilum thoraca indutus aënis	
horrebat squamis surasque incluserat auro,	
tempora nudus adhuc, laterique accinxerat ensem,	
fulgebatque alta decurrens aureus arce.	490
exsultatque animis et spe iam praecipit hostem:	
qualis ubi abruptis fugit praesepia vinclis	
tandem liber equus, campoque potitus aperto	
aut ille in pastus armentaque tendit equarum	
aut adsuetus aquae perfundi flumine noto	495
emicat, arrectisque fremit cervicibus alte	
luxurians luduntque iubae per colla, per armos.	

furens, -entis	raging	*abrumpo, -ere, -rupi, -ruptus*	I break
certatim	eagerly	*praesepe, -is* n.	stable, pen
adeo	so much	*vinclum, -i* n.	chain, bond
rutilus, -a, -um	red	*liber, -era, -erum*	free
thorax, -acis m.	breast-plate	*campus, -i* m.	plain
induo, -ere, -ui, -utus	I put on	*potior, -iri, -itus sum* + abl.	I gain, reach
aënus, -a, -um	bronze	*apertus, -a, -um*	open
horreo, -ere	I am stiff	*aut . . . aut*	either . . . or
squama, -ae f.	scale	*pastus, -us* m.	pasture
sura, -ae f.	calf (of the leg)	*armentum, -i* n.	herd
includo, -ere, -clusi, -clusus	I enclose	*tendo, -ere*	I proceed, extend
aurum, -i n.	gold	*equa, -ae* f.	mare
tempus, -oris n.	temple	*adsuesco, -ere, -evi, -etus* 495	I accustom
nudus, -a, -um	bare	*aqua, -ae* f.	water
adhuc	still	*perfundo, -ere*	I pour over
latus, -eris n.	side	*flumen, -inis* n.	river
accingo, -ere, -nxi, -nctus	I fix in place	*emico, -are*	I dart out, rush
aureus, -a, -um 490	golden	*arrigo, -ere, -rexi, -rectus*	I raise
arx, arcis f.	citadel	*cervix, -icis* f.	neck
exsulto, -are	I exult	*luxurio, -are*	I am exuberant
animus, -i m.	spirit, courage	*ludo, -ere*	I play, frolic
praecipio, -ere	I anticipate	*iuba, -ae* f.	mane
hostis, -is m.	enemy	*collum, -i* n.	neck
qualis, -e	just like	*armus, -i* m.	shoulder

486 **cingitur:** 'is girded (by his armour)', and so 'puts on his armour'. **in proelia:** 'ready for battle'. Note the postponement of *Turnus* to the end of the line for dramatic effect.

487–8 **iamque adeo:** *adeo* is used to emphasise *iam*: 'and indeed already'. **indutus:** the participle is used as if active in meaning, a favourite usage of Virgil modelled on the Greek middle voice: 'having put on'. **aënis horrebat squamis:** note the enclosing word order, reflecting the reality: he wore scale-armour. **incluserat:** the pluperfect is used instead of the historic present (like *cingitur*) to indicate that he had put on the greaves before the breastplate (similarly *accinxerat* below). **auro:** i.e. with golden greaves.

489 **tempora nudus:** '(he is) bare in relation to his temples', i.e. 'his temples are bare' or more simply 'he is bare-headed'; *tempora* is an accusative of respect. **laterique:** 'and at his side'; *lateri* is dative with the compound verb.

490 **alta . . . arce:** 'from the high citadel' (ablative of separation). Lines 487–90 exemplify the words *cingitur furens certatim* in line 486.

491 **animis:** 'in his high spirits' (ablative of respect or possibly cause). **spe:** 'in his hopes' (local ablative). **praecipit hostem:** 'he anticipates his enemy', in the sense that he imagines he is already face-to-face with Aeneas in combat.

492–7 This is a long simile, introduced as so often by *qualis ubi*; *qualis* agrees with *equus*, the subject of the simile.

492–3 **abruptis . . . vinclis:** ablative absolute. **tandem liber:** i.e. free after a long struggle. **equus:** here 'a stallion'.

494 **ille:** i.e. the stallion.

495–6 **adsuetus aquae:** 'accustomed to the water'. **perfundi:** 'to be poured over' and so 'to bathe'; infinitive of purpose, instead of *ut* and subjunctive of prose. **flumine noto:** 'in the familiar river', i.e. the one he frequented before he was captured. The above interpretation of the Latin is not the only one possible; another is 'or, accustomed to bathe in the familiar river of water, he darts out'. In this second version, *aquae* is weak.

496–7 **cervicibus, iubae, colla:** regularly used in the plural in preference to the singular. **alte:** probably to be taken with both *arrectis* and *luxurians*. **per colla:** 'over its neck'.

Questions

1 In what order does Turnus put on his armour?

2 What shows that he is 'raging and eager' (*furens certatim*)?

3 What use does Virgil make of colour in lines 486–490?

4 What is the purpose of the simile in lines 491–497?

5 Explain the stallion's behaviour and actions.

6 How appropriate is this simile?

7 From lines 486–497, what picture emerges of Turnus? Is it a consistent picture?

obvia cui Volscorum acie comitante Camilla
occurrit portisque ab equo regina sub ipsis
desiluit, quam tota cohors imitata relictis   500
ad terram defluxit equis; tum talia fatur:
'Turne, sui merito si qua est fiducia forti,
audeo et Aeneadum promitto occurrere turmae
solaque Tyrrhenos equites ire obvia contra.
me sine prima manu temptare pericula belli,   505
tu pedes ad muros subsiste et moenia serva.'
Turnus ad haec oculos horrenda in virgine fixus:
'o decus Italiae virgo, quas dicere grates
quasve referre parem? sed nunc, est omnia quando
iste animus supra, mecum partire laborem.   510
Aeneas, ut fama fidem missique reportant
exploratores, equitum levia improbus arma
praemisit, quaterent campos; ipse ardua montis
per deserta iugo superans adventat ad urbem.
furta paro belli convexo in tramite silvae,   515
ut bivias armato obsidam milite fauces.

obvius, -a, -um + dat.	to meet	*decus, -oris* n.	glory, honour
Volsci, -orum m.pl.	the Volsci	*Italia, -ae* f.	Italy
acies, -ei f.	battle line	*grates* f.pl.	thanks
comitor, -ari, -atus sum	I accompany	*paro, -are*	I prepare
Camilla, -ae f.	Camilla	*quando*	since
occurro, -ere, -curri, -cursus	I run to meet, face	*iste, ista, istud*	510 that (of yours)
regina, -ae f.	queen, princess	*supra* + acc.	beyond
sub + abl.	under	*partior, -iri, -itus sum*	I share
desilio, -ire, -ui, -sultus	500 I jump down	*fama, -ae* f.	rumour
cohors, -ortis f.	cohort, squadron	*reporto, -are*	I report
imitor, -ari, -atus sum	I imitate, copy	*explorator, -oris* m.	scout
defluo, -ere, -fluxi, -fluxus	I sweep down	*levis, -e*	light
talis -e	such	*improbus, -a, -um*	shameless
merito	deservedly	*praemitto, -ere, -misi, -missus*	I send ahead
fiducia, -ae f.	confidence	*quatio, -ere*	I shake, trample,
fortis, -e	brave		brandish
audeo, -ere	I dare	*arduus, -a, -um*	high
Aeneades, -ae m.	follower of	*mons, montis* m.	mountain
	Aeneas	*deserta, -orum* n.pl.	deserted areas
promitto, -ere	I promise	*supero, -are*	I cross over
turma, -ae f.	squadron	*advento, -are*	I approach
Tyrrhenus, -a, -um	Etruscan		quickly
equites, -um m.pl.	cavalry	*furtum, -i* n.	515 trick, stratagem
sino, -ere	505 I allow	*convexus, -a, -um*	arched
tempto, -are	I try, test	*trames, -itis* m.	path
periculum, -i n.	danger	*bivius, -a, -um*	forking
pedes, -itis m.	foot-soldier	*armo. -are, -avi, -atus*	I arm
subsisto, -ere	I stop, halt	*obsido, -ere*	I occupy, block
horrendus, -a, -um	awe-inspiring	*miles, -itis* m.	soldier
virgo, -inis f.	maiden	*fauces, -ium* f.pl.	pass, defile
figo, -ere, fixi, fixus	I fix		

498–9 The order is *Camilla occurrit obvia cui, acie Volscorum comitante*. **cui:** Turnus.
Camilla: the daughter of the king of the Volsci, a tribe living near the southern borders
of Latium; raised as a warrior, she served the cult of Diana, the goddess of hunting. Virgil
models her on the Amazons, a race of warrior-maidens whom legend placed on the fringes
of the Greek world. The heavy <u>alliteration</u> of *c-* draws attention to this first appearance of
Camilla in the war.
499–501 regina: 'princess'; Virgil points out Camilla's high status, which makes her
deference to Turnus (dismounting from her horse) all the more respectful. The same
deference is shown by all her cavalrymen (*tota cohors*), who 'swept down' from their horses
in imitation of her (*quam . . . imitata*). **relictis . . . equis:** ablative absolute: 'leaving their
horses' (as they dismounted). **talia:** 'these words'.
502 The order is *si merito est forti qua fiducia sui*: 'if there is deservedly for a brave person
any confidence in himself/herself', i.e. 'if a brave person deservedly has any confidence in
himself/herself'. **sui:** objective genitive with *fiducia*. **est:** the use of *esse* + dative expresses
possession.
503 audeo: supply *occurrere*. **promitto occurrere:** poetic for *promitto me occursuram esse*.
turmae: dative dependent on the compound verb; a *turma* was a squadron of cavalry, and
Camilla intends to use her own cavalry to attack that of the Trojans.
504 sola: 'alone' because she wants to leave Turnus and the rest of his allies free to make
other arrangements to defend the city. **obvia contra:** the same idea repeated; *contra* follows
its dependent noun (*equites*). This line largely repeats the promise made in the previous line.
505 me sine: 'allow me': Camilla defers to Turnus. **prima:** agrees with *pericula*, not *manu*;
prima tells us this will be her first foray into the war. **manu:** 'with my hand', i.e. 'in combat'.
506 pedes: nom.: 'as a foot-soldier'. **ad muros:** 'at the walls'.
507 oculos . . . fixus: 'with his eyes fixed'; see note on line 35 for the construction.
508–9 quas . . . parem: in full this would be *quas grates parem dicere, quasve grates parem
referre*. **parem:** subjunctive in a deliberative question. **referre:** 'repay' (i.e. with deeds).
509–10 nunc: 'as it is'. **quando:** to be taken first. **est supra omnia:** 'is beyond all thanks'.
partire: 'share' (imperative).
511–13 fidem . . . reportant: lit. 'bring back reliability', and so 'report reliably'. **improbus:**
best here as an adverb: 'shamelessly'; this is not objective criticism of Aeneas for sending
forward troops, but a generic description. **equitum levia . . . arma:** 'light arms of cavalry',
and so 'lightly-armed cavalry'. **quaterent:** jussive subjunctive, in an implied indirect
command: 'with orders to . . .'; the verb has been variously interpreted as 'harass', 'scour', or
'reconnoitre', but 'trample' is a reasonable compromise.
513–14 ipse: supply *Aeneas*. **ardua montis:** 'the heights of the mountain'. **iugo:** 'by the ridge'.
515 furta . . . belli: lit. 'tricks of war', and so 'an ambush'. **convexo in tramite silvae:** either
'on the path arched-over by woodland' or 'on the path sloping down through the wood'.
516 bivias . . . fauces: either 'both ends of the pass' or 'the pass where it forks'. **milite:**
collective singular: 'with soldiers'.

Questions

1 What impression are we given of the relationship between Camilla and Turnus?

2 What are their separate plans of campaign for the coming battle?

3 How does Virgil make Turnus' words more than a simple statement of plans?

tu Tyrrhenum equitem conlatis excipe signis;
tecum acer Messapus erit turmaeque Latinae
Tiburtique manus, ducis et tu concipe curam.'
sic ait, et paribus Messapum in proelia dictis   520
hortatur sociosque duces et pergit in hostem.

Turnus set up an ambush at the head of a valley that the Trojans must pass through on their way to Laurentum.

velocem interea superis in sedibus Opim,   532
unam ex virginibus sociis sacraque caterva,
compellabat et has tristes Latonia voces
ore dabat: 'graditur bellum ad crudele Camilla,   535
o virgo, et nostris nequiquam cingitur armis,
cara mihi ante alias. neque enim novus iste Dianae
venit amor subitaque animum dulcedine movit.'

'Her father, Metabus, dedicated her to me when she was still a baby. She learned to cast a javelin and whirl a sling from a very young age. When she grew up she rejected all suitors, being content to serve as a hand-maid to me.'

        'vellem haud correpta fuisset   584
militia tali conata lacessere Teucros: 585
cara mihi comitumque foret nunc una mearum.
verum age, quandoquidem fatis urgetur acerbis,
labere, nympha, polo finesque invise Latinos,
tristis ubi infausto committitur omine pugna.

eques, -itis m.	cavalry(man)	*ante* + acc.	before
confero, -ferre, -tuli, -latus	I bring together	*alius, -a, -ud*	other
excipio, -ere	I intercept	*amor, -oris* m.	love
signum, -i n.	sign, standard	*subitus, -a, -um*	sudden
Messapus, -i m.	Messapus	*dulcedo, -inis* f.	sweetness
Tiburtus, -i m.	Tiburtus	*moveo, -ere, movi, motus*	I move
dux, ducis m.	leader	*corripio, -ere, -ripui, -reptus*	I seize
concipio, -ere	I take on	*militia, -ae* f. 585	warfare
cura, -ae f.	duty, anxiety	*conor, -ari, -atus sum*	I try
par, paris 520	equal, similar	*lacesso, -ere*	I challenge
dictum, -i n.	word	*verum*	but
hortor, -ari, -atus sum	I urge, encourage	*quandoquidem*	since
pergo, -ere	I proceed	*urgeo, -ere*	I attack, press
velox, -ocis 532	swift	*acerbus, -a, -um*	bitter
superus, -a, -um	above, of heaven	*labor, -i, lapsus sum*	I glide down, fall
Opis, -is (acc. *-im*) f.	Opis	*nympha, -ae* f.	nymph
sacer, sacra, sacrum	sacred, holy	*polum, -i* n.	sky
caterva, -ae f.	crowd, band	*fines, -ium* m.pl.	territory
compello, -are	I address	*inviso, -ere*	I visit
tristis, -e	sad	*infaustus, -a, -um*	unfavourable
Latonia, -ae f.	Diana	*committo, -ere*	I join (battle)
gradior, -i, -gressus sum 535	I go	*omen, -inis* n.	omen
nequiquam	in vain	*pugna, -ae* f.	fight, battle

517 Tyrrhenum equitem: singular for plural; the Etruscans were allied to the Trojans.
conlatis signis: a military phrase meaning literally 'having brought the standards together',
i.e. 'having taken up position'. **excipe:** another military word.
518–19 Messapus: a Latin cavalry commander often mentioned in this half of the *Aeneid*.
turmaeque Latinae: supply *erunt tecum*. **Tiburti manus:** 'and the contingent of Tiburtus
(will be with you)'; Tiburtus was the son of the founder of the city of Tibur near Rome and
brother of two Latin commanders. **ducis et tu concipe curam:** 'you also must take on the
duty of (being) leader', i.e. along with Messapus and Tiburtus.
520–1 paribus . . . dictis: 'with similar words', i.e. he gives the same orders to Messapus,
Tiburtus and the other leaders of the Latin cavalry. This suggests they share the command with
Camilla, rather than being under her command. **in proelium:** he encourages them 'to fight'.

532–5 interea: this marks a change of scene. **superis in sedibus:** 'in the dwellings of heaven'.
velocem . . . Opim: a nymph and attendant of Diana; she is described as 'swift' as she too was
a huntress. The subject is *Latonia* and the verb *compellabat*. **virginibus sociis sacraque caterva:**
'her sacred band of companion maidens' (an example of <u>hendiadys</u>); just as Diana remained a
virgin, so did her companions. **ore dabat:** 'gave from her mouth' and so 'began to utter'.
536 nostris . . . armis: i.e. javelin, bow and arrows, as used in hunting. **nequiquam:** 'in vain'
because she is fated to die. **cingitur:** 'puts on'. Note the <u>enclosing word-order</u>.
537–8 novus iste Dianae venit amor: 'that love of Diana has (not) come new', and so 'that
love which Diana has for her is no new phenomenon'. The force of *iste* has been variously
interpreted, as 'which I have', 'that you know', 'that I have just mentioned'; it is better to
suppose that Diana imagines herself addressing Camilla ('the love I have for you'); this may
explain why Diana refers to herself in the 3rd person. **subita:** conveys the same idea as *novus*.

584–5 vellem: 'I could have wished': imperfect subjunctive to express a wish in past time;
the speaker is Diana, picking up from line 537. **haud correpta fuisset:** 'that she had not
become caught up in'; the 'double' pluperfect passive is best treated as equivalent to *correpta
esset* (subjunctive in a past unfulfilled wish). **tali:** 'such as this', i.e. between the Trojans and
Latins. **conata:** in full this would be *neve conata fuisset*: 'and that she had not tried'.
586 foret (= *esset*): most editors take this to be a further wish: 'and that she were . . .';
however the <u>asyndeton</u> suggests an alternative: '(if only she had not got caught up in the war),
she would now be . . .'. **cara mihi:** 'dear to me' would be illogical, as clearly Camilla is still
dear to Diana; elsewhere (e.g. line 215) Virgil uses the adjective with an active meaning; if it
is used in this way here, the dative would be one of advantage and the meaning 'affectionate
towards me' or 'loving of me'; the logic would be that, in turning from hunting to warfare,
Camilla has abandoned Diana (and so she is no longer one of the goddess's companions).
587 verum age: marks a change from digression to command. **urgetur:** the subject is Camilla.
588 labere: 'glide down' (imperative). **polo:** ablative of separation.
589 The order is *ubi tristis pugna committitur infausto omine*. Note the <u>chiastic</u> order.
infausto . . . omine: Diana knows that Camilla is fated to die, a fate she cannot change.

Questions

1 List the command structure of the Latin forces.

2 Give examples from lines 535–538 of *has tristes voces*.

3 How does Diana show her feelings towards Camilla in lines 584–589?

haec cape et ultricem pharetra deprome sagittam: 590
hac, quicumque sacrum violarit vulnere corpus,
Tros Italusque, mihi pariter det sanguine poenas.
post ego nube cava miserandae corpus et arma
inspoliata feram tumulo patriaeque reponam.'
dixit, at illa leves caeli delapsa per auras   595
insonuit nigro circumdata turbine corpus.

The cavalry of the Trojans and their allies approached Laurentum. The Latins and their allies rode to meet them. After some skirmishing, the two sides became locked together in combat, with neither side giving way.

at medias inter caedes exsultat Amazon
unum exserta latus pugnae, pharetrata Camilla,
et nunc lenta manu spargens hastilia denset,   650
nunc validam dextra rapit indefessa bipennem;
aureus ex umero sonat arcus et arma Dianae.
illa etiam, si quando in tergum pulsa recessit,
spicula converso fugientia derigit arcu.
at circum lectae comites, Larinaque virgo   655
Tullaque et aeratam quatiens Tarpeia securim,
Italides, quas ipsa decus sibi dia Camilla
delegit pacisque bonas bellique ministras.

Her attendants were like the Amazonsof Thrace.

ultrix, -icis f.	590	avenging	*pharetratus, -a, -um*		bearing a quiver
pharetra, -ae f.		quiver	*lentus, -a, -um*	650	tough, flexible
depromo, -ere		I draw out	*hastile, -is* n.		javelin
sagitta, -ae f.		arrow	*denseo, -ere*		I make thick
qui-, quae-, quodcumque		whoever, whatever	*validus, -a, -um*		strong
			indefessus, -a, -um		tireless
violo, -are, -avi, -atus		I violate, harm	*bipennis, -is* f.		two-edged axe
Italus, -i m.		an Italian	*sono, -are*		I sound
pariter		equally	*arcus, -us* m.		bow
poena, -ae f.		penalty	*tergum, -i* n.		back, rear
post		afterwards	*recedo, -ere, -cessi, -cessus*		I retreat
nubes, -is f.		cloud	*spiculum, -i* n.		arrow
cavus, -a, -um		hollow	*derigo, -ere*		I aim
miseror, -ari, -atus sum		I pity	*lego, -ere, legi, lectus*	655	I choose
inspoliatus, -a, -um		not despoiled	*Larina, -ae* f.		Larina
tumulus, -i m.		tomb	*Tulla, -ae* f.		Tulla
delabor, -i, -lapsus sum	595	I glide down	*aeratus -a, -um*		bronze-plated
aura, -ae f.		air, breeze	*Tarpeia, -ae* f.		Tarpeia
insono, -are, -ui		I resound	*securis, -is* (acc. *-im*) f.		axe
niger, nigra, nigrum		black	*Italis, -idis* f.		an Italian woman
circumdo, -dare, -dedi, -datus		I surround			
turbo, -inis m.		whirlwind	*dius, -a, -um*		godlike
Amazon, -onis f.	648	Amazon	*deligo, -ere, -legi, -lectus*		I choose
exsertus, -a, -um		bared, uncovered	*ministra, -ae* f.		attendant

590 **haec:** her own bow and arrows. **ultricem . . . sagittam:** 'an arrow to avenge her'.
pharetra: ablative of separation.
591–2 **hac:** supply *sagittā*. **violarit:** = *violaverit* (future perfect indicative). **sacrum . . . corpus:**
Camilla's body is sacred because vowed to Diana. **Italusque:** 'or Italian'; *-que* is used to
indicate that these are the Italian allies of the Trojans. **det:** 'let him pay'.
593–4 **nube cava:** 'in a hollow cloud'; in Greek mythology deities often wrapped themselves
or others in a cloud or mist to conceal them. **inspoliata:** best taken with both *corpus* and
arma. **tumulo:** dative of goal of motion (= *ad tumulum*; sim. *patriae*). **patriaeque reponam:**
'and restore (them) to her native land'.
595–6 **illa:** Opis. **delapsa:** 'as she sped down'. **insonuit:** either she herself made a noise as she
flew, or her weapons clashed against each other. **circumdata . . . corpus:** 'her body wrapped':
Greek middle construction (see note on line 35).

648–9 **exsultat Amazon:** 'the Amazon runs amok'; most editors translate *Amazon* as 'like
an Amazon', but surely the word carries more force as a <u>metaphor</u> than as a <u>simile</u>? Then
Camilla, deferred till the end of the second line, becomes a climax. Amazons supposedly cut
off one breast so as not to hinder bowshots. **unum exserta latus:** 'with one side (i.e. breast)
bared'; Greek middle construction – see note on line 35. **pugnae:** dative of purpose.
650–1 **lenta . . . hastilia:** either 'tough' or 'flexible' javelins. **spargens . . . denset:** 'she hurls
thick and fast'; this is <u>hyperbole</u>, as there must have been a limit to the number of spears
she could carry. **dextra:** ablative. Camilla's *aristeia* is introduced with the mention of three
distinct weapons, indicating her versatility as a warrior.
652 **aureus . . . arcus:** the bow is 'golden' either because it is gilded or because it is made of
gold-coloured wood; the adjective should be taken with both *arcus* and *arma*. **sonat:** Virgil
is fond of referring to the sound effects of weapons, whether javelins or arrows, as they fly
through the air.
653–4 **in tergum:** 'backwards'. **spicula . . . fugientia:** 'fleeing arrows', i.e. 'arrows as she flees'
(an example of <u>hypallage</u>). **converso . . . arcu:** 'with her bow turned back'. In Virgil's day, the
cavalry of Parthia (close to the traditional home of the Amazons) were famous for shooting
backwards from their horses.
655–6 **Larina . . . Tulla . . . Tarpeia:** supply *erant*; these are all invented by Virgil, but they
are given names that readers would associate with well-known places or people.
657–8 **Italides:** a word coined by Virgil. **decus sibi:** 'as a guard of honour for herself'.
bonas . . . ministras: like *decus*, *ministras* is predicative: 'and to be her good attendants'.

Questions

1 What does Diana order Opis to do?

2 What will Diana herself do?

3 How does Diana show her feelings towards Camilla in lines 590–596?

4 Why is Camilla described as an 'Amazon'?

5 How does Camilla show her prowess as a warrior?

6 How does Virgil make his account of Camilla's actions vivid and dynamic?

quem telo primum, quem postremum, aspera virgo,
deicis? aut quot humi morientia corpora fundis?   665
Eunaeum Clytio primum patre, cuius apertum
adversi longa transverberat abiete pectus.
sanguinis ille vomens rivos cadit atque cruentam
mandit humum moriensque suo se in vulnere versat.
tum Lirim Pagasumque super, quorum alter habenas   670
suffuso revolutus equo dum colligit, alter
dum subit ac dextram labenti tendit inermem,
praecipites pariterque ruunt. his addit Amastrum
Hippotaden, sequiturque incumbens eminus hasta
Tereaque Harpalycumque et Demophoonta Chromimque;   675
quotque emissa manu contorsit spicula virgo,
tot Phrygii cecidere viri. procul Ornytus armis
ignotis et equo venator Iapyge fertur,
cui pellis latos umeros erepta iuvenco
pugnatori operit, caput ingens oris hiatus   680
et malae texere lupi cum dentibus albis,
agrestisque manus armat sparus;

postremus, -a, -um	last	*incumbo, -ere*	I fall upon, attack
asper, -era, -erum	harsh, violent		
deicio, -ere	665 I cast down	*eminus*	from a distance
quot	how many	*hasta, -ae* f.	spear, javelin
humus, -i f.	ground, earth	*Tereus, -eos* (acc. *-ea*) 675	Tereus
morior, -i, mortuus sum	I die	*Harpalycus, -i* m.	Harpalycus
fundo, -ere	I lay low	*Demophoon, -ntis* (acc. *-nta*)	Demophoon
Eunaeus, -i m.	Eunaeus	*Chromis, -is* (acc. *-im*)	Chromis
Clytius, -i m.	Clytius	*emitto, -ere, -misi, -missus*	I throw
adversus, -a, -um	facing, opposite	*contorqueo, -ere, -torsi, -rtus*	I brandish, throw
transverbero, -are	I pierce		
abies, -etis f.	fir, pine	*tot*	so many
pectus, -oris n.	breast	*Phrygius, -a, -um*	Trojan
vomo, -ere	I spew out	*procul*	far off
rivus, -i m.	stream	*Ornytus, -i* m.	Ornytus
cado, -ere	I fall	*ignotus, -a, -um*	unfamiliar
cruentus, -a, -um	blood-stained	*venator, -oris* m.	hunter
mando, -ere	I chew	*Iapyx, -igis*	South Italian
verso, -are	I twist, writhe	*pellis, -is* f.	skin
Liris, -is (acc. *-im*) m. 670	Liris	*latus, -a, -um*	broad
Pagasus, -i m.	Pagasus	*eripio, -ere, -ripui, -reptus*	I strip, pull off
alter, -era, -erum	the one, the other	*iuvencus, -i* m.	bullock
habena, -ae f.	rein	*pugnator, -oris* m. 680	fighter
suffundo, -ere, -fudi, -fusus	I stumble	*operio, -ire*	I cover
revolvo, -ere, -volvi, -volutus	I roll backwards	*hiatus, -us* m.	gape
colligo, -ere	I gather	*mala, -ae* f.	jaw
subeo, -ire	I approach	*tego, -ere, texi, tectus*	I cover, protect
inermis, -e	unarmed	*lupus, -i* m.	wolf
praeceps, -cipitis	headlong	*dens, dentis* m.	tooth
Amastrus, -i m.	Amastrus	*albus, -a, -um*	white
Hippotades, -ae (acc. *-en*) m.	descendant of Hippotes	*agrestis, -e*	rustic
		sparus, -i m.	hunting-spear

664–5 quem . . . quem . . . quot: <u>rhetorical questions</u> addressed in <u>apostrophe</u> to Camilla; they serve as a way of introducing Camilla's *aristeia* (an account of her heroic success in battle; in Homer's *Iliad*, each of the main heroes had a book dedicated to his *aristeia*). This follows the completion of her description. **deicis . . . fundis:** the historic present tenses present Camilla's combats as if being acted out on the stage in front of the reader's eyes. **humi . . . fundis:** 'you strew on the ground'; *humi* is locative case.

666–7 None of the characters killed by Camilla has appeared previously; several have Greek names, and so their accusative endings are Greek forms. **Clytio . . . patre:** 'whose father was Clytius' (ablative absolute). **cuius apertum . . . pectus:** 'whose exposed breast'. **adversi:** 'as he faced her' (agreeing with *cuius*). **longa . . . abiete:** 'with her long pine spear'.

668–9 mandit humum: like our 'bites the dust'. **suo se in vulnere versat:** 'twists himself in his wound', and so 'writhes around his wound'.

670–1 Lirim Pagasumque: supply *transverberat* or similar. **super:** 'on top of him'. **quorum . . . colligit:** the order is *quorum alter, revolutus suffuso equo dum colligit habenas.* **revolutus equo:** 'having rolled backwards off his horse'. **suffuso:** 'which had stumbled': an unusual use of the verb.

671–2 dextram . . . inermem: because he had to let go of his weapons to help his friend. **labenti:** 'to the falling man' (to be taken with both *subit* and *tendit*).

673 praecipites pariterque ruunt: *-que* needs to be taken first: 'and they fall headlong together'.

673–4 Amastrum Hippotaden: it is impossible to say which Hippotes Virgil meant.

676–7 quot . . . tot: 'as many (fell) as (the javelins she threw)'. **emissa** 'after releasing them'.

677–8 armis ignotis: 'with unfamiliar arms' (because he was a hunter rather than a warrior). **et:** joins two strange features of the man: he is riding (*fertur*) with unfamiliar arms and on an Iapygian horse.

679–80 cui: 'whose (shoulders)'. **iuvenco pugnatori:** '(stripped) from a fighting (i.e. wild) bullock' (dative of disadvantage); some editors take *pugnatori* with *cui*, lit. 'to him as a fighter', i.e. 'when he became a fighter'; the word order allows both interpretations.

680–1 ingens oris hiatus et malae: 'the huge gape of the mouth and jaws (of a wolf)'; he had made the wolf's head into a helmet. **caput . . . texere:** 'covered his head'.

682 agrestis . . . sparus: 'a rustic hunting-spear'.

Questions

1 What do you think is the effect of Virgil's interrupting the narrative to insert lines 664–665?

2 Describe the deaths of each of the men listed in lines 666–676.

3 How does Virgil make this more than a repetitive list? How many different ways can you identify?

4 What details are we given about Ornytus?

5 What makes him different from the average warrior?

ipse catervis
vertitur in mediis et toto vertice supra est.
hunc illa exceptum (neque enim labor agmine verso)
traicit et super haec inimico pectore fatur: 685
'silvis te, Tyrrhene, feras agitare putasti?
advenit qui vestra dies muliebribus armis
verba redargueret. nomen tamen haud leve patrum
manibus hoc referes, telo cecidisse Camillae.'

While Camilla continued her killing spree, Jupiter inspired the Etruscan leader, Tarchon, to rally his troops, who charged the enemy.

tum fatis debitus Arruns
velocem iaculo et multa prior arte Camillam   760
circuit, et quae sit fortuna facillima temptat.
qua se cumque furens medio tulit agmine virgo,
hac Arruns subit et tacitus vestigia lustrat;
qua victrix redit illa pedemque ex hoste reportat,
hac iuvenis furtim celeres detorquet habenas.   765
hos aditus iamque hos aditus omnemque pererrat
undique circuitum et certam quatit improbus hastam.

Camilla spied a warrior handsomely dressed and riding an expensively armoured horse. She determined to kill him, as she coveted the gold that adorned the man and his horse. Arruns chose this moment to attack her, and prayed to Apollo as he cast his javelin. Apollo heard his prayer.

ergo ut missa manu sonitum dedit hasta per auras,
converterq animos acres oculosque tulere   800
cuncti ad reginam Volsci.

$$- \bar{\cup} \mid / \; - \cup \cup \mid / - - \mid / - \cdot \cup \mid / - \; \cup \cup \mid / - \; -$$

verto, -ere	I turn	*circueo, -ire*	I circle round
vertex, -icis m.	top, head	*facilis, -e*	easy
supra	above	*quacumque*	wherever
agmen, -inis n.	army	*hac*	here
traicio, -ere	685 I pierce	*tacitus, -a, -um*	silent
inimicus, -a, -um	hostile	*vestigium, -i* n.	footstep
fera, -ae f.	wild beast	*qua*	where
agito, -are	I chase	*victrix, -icis*	victorious
puto, -are, -avi, -atus	I think	*redeo, -ire*	I return
advenio, -ire	I arrive, come	*reporto, -are*	I take back
vester, -tra, -trum	your	*furtim*	765 furtively
muliebris, -e	of a woman	*celer, -eris, -ere*	swift
redarguo, -ere	I refute	*detorqueo, -ere*	I turn aside
nomen, -inis n.	name	*aditus, -us* m.	approach
manes, -ium m.pl.	shades, souls	*pererro, -are*	I try
Arruns, -ntis m.	759 Arruns	*circuitus, -us* m.	way round
iaculum, -i n.	760 javelin	*sonitus, -us* m.	799 sound, noise
prior, prius	first		

did you think you bear/carry to

682–3 vertitur: 'he turns' (in retreat). **toto vertice supra est:** lit. 'is above with his whole head', i.e. 'he is a whole head taller than the rest'. His height and strange garb make him conspicuous.

684–5 hunc illa exceptum ... traicit: 'this man she intercepts and transfixes'. **labor:** supply *erat:* 'there was no toil', and so 'it was not difficult'. **agmine verso:** 'with the army in retreat'. **super:** '(standing) over him'. **haec:** supply *verba.* **inimico pectore:** 'from her hostile heart'.

686 silvis: 'in the woods' (local ablative). **putasti** = *putavisti:* 'did you think'.

687–8 The order is ~~dies advenit qui redargueret~~ *vestra verba muliebribus armis.* **qui ... redargueret:** lit. 'which might refute', i.e. 'to refute'. **vestra ... verba:** *vestra* refers to the boasts and taunts of the Etruscans generally. **muliebribus armis:** 'by means of a woman's arms' (instrumental ablative).

688–9 nomen ... haud leve ... hoc: most editors take *nomen* to mean 'glory', i.e. the glory of having been killed by someone as famous as Camilla; an alternative interpretation is to take it literally: 'this is no insignificant name you will report: that you fell to the weapon of Camilla'. **patrum manibus:** 'to the shades of your forefathers', in the Underworld. Note the climactic position of *Camillae.*

759–61 fatis debitus Arruns 'Arruns owed to fate', i.e. 'destined to die'; he will kill Camilla and so be killed in turn by Opis, as Diana had decreed (lines 591–2); Arruns has not appeared elsewhere. The order is *tum Arruns, debitus fatis, prior circuit velocem Camillam iaculo et multa arte.* **prior:** variously interpreted as 'first', 'superior in cunning', 'anticipating her movements', 'keeping one step ahead'. **fortuna:** 'opportunity' (to strike). **temptat:** 'tries to determine'.

762 qua ... cumque: the single word *quacumque* has been split in two (a feature called *tmesis*). **se ... tulit:** 'bore herself' and so 'dashed'.

763 hac: neatly counterbalances *qua:* 'here'. **vestigia lustrat:** 'observes her footsteps'.

764–5 qua ... hac: 'where ... here', repeating the balanced phrase. **pedem reportat:** 'retires'. **celeres detorquet habenas:** to turn the horse round; the reins are 'swift' because Arruns is using them to make the horse move quickly (an example of hypallage).

766–7 hos aditus iamque hos aditus ... pererrat: 'he tries (now) one approach and now another'. **omnemque pererrat undique circuitum:** 'and circles all round her'. **pererrat:** a difficult word, used with two objects (*aditus* and *circuitum*), requiring a different meaning for each phrase (zeugma); its basic meaning is 'wander through', which fits neither context literally. **improbus:** 'wicked' because he is going to kill a leader in a sly manner (cf. line 512).

799 sonitum dedit: cf. line 652 note.

800–801 convertere: = *converterunt*; the subject is *Volsci.* **animos acres:** 'their attention keenly'. Note the chiasmus in line 800. **Volsci:** deferred until the end to raise suspense: the irony is that every Voscian was aware of the javelin cast except for its target.

Questions

1 Summarise what Camilla says to the dying Ornytus. What is the tone of these words?

2 Which of the two interpretations of *nomen* (line 688) do you prefer, and why?

3 How does Arruns stalk Camilla?

4 How does Virgil make his account of Arruns' preparations to attack Camilla interesting?

           nihil ipsa nec aurae
nec sonitus memor aut venientis ab aethere teli,
hasta sub exsertam donec perlata papillam
haesit virgineumque alte bibit acta cruorem.
concurrunt trepidae comites dominamque ruentem   805
suscipiunt. fugit ante omnes exterritus Arruns
laetitia mixtoque metu, nec iam amplius hastae
credere nec telis occurrere virginis audet.   808
illa manu moriens telum trahit, ossa sed inter   816
ferreus ad costas alto stat vulnere mucro.
labitur exsanguis, labuntur frigida leto
lumina, purpureus quondam color ora reliquit.
tum sic exspirans Accam ex aequalibus unam   820
adloquitur, fida ante alias quae sola Camillae
quicum partiri curas, atque haec ita fatur:
'hactenus, Acca soror, potui: nunc vulnus acerbum
conficit, et tenebris nigrescunt omnia circum.
effuge et haec Turno mandata novissima perfer: 825
succedat pugnae Troianosque arceat urbe.
iamque vale.' simul his dictis linquebat habenas
ad terram non sponte fluens. tum frigida toto
paulatim exsolvit se corpore, lentaque colla
et captum leto posuit caput, arma relinquens,   830
vitaque cum gemitu fugit indignata sub umbras.

Opis immediately took her revenge by shooting a deadly arrow at Arruns.

ādlŏquĭtur, fĭdă āntĕ ălĭās quāe sōlă Cāmīllăe

aether, -eris (acc. *-era*) m.	air	*purpureus, -a, -um*	red
perfero, -ferre, -tuli, -latus	I carry through	*quondam*	once
papilla, -ae f.	breast	*color, -oris* m.	colour
virgineus, -a, -um	of a maiden	*exspiro, -are*	820 I expire
bibo, -ere, bibi	I drink	*Acca, -ae* f.	Acca
cruor, -oris m.	spilt blood	*aequalis, -e*	of the same age
concurro, -ere	805 I rush together	*adloquor, -i, -locutus sum*	I speak to
trepidus, -a, -um	anxious	*fidus, -a, -um*	faithful
domina, -ae f.	mistress	*hactenus*	until now
suscipio, -ere	I take up, catch	*soror, -oris* f.	sister
exterritus, -a, -um	terrified	*conficio, -ere*	I destroy
laetitia, -ae f.	joy	*nigresco, -ere*	I grow dark
amplius	more, longer	*effugio, -ere*	825 I escape
traho, -ere	816 I draw, pull	*arceo, -ere*	I keep . . . away
os, ossis n.	bone	*vale*	farewell
ferreus, -a, -um	made of iron	*simul*	at the same time
costa, -ae f.	rib	*linquo, -ere*	I leave
sto, stare	I stand	*sponte*	by (her) will
mucro, -onis m.	point	*fluo, -ere*	I flow, fall
exsanguis, -e	bloodless, pale	*paulatim*	gradually
frigidus, -a, -um	cold	*exsolvo, -ere*	829 I release
letum, -i n.	death	*indignor, -ari, -atus sum*	I complain
lumen, -inis n.	light, eye	*umbra, -ae* f.	shade, darkness

801–2 **ipsa:** in contrast with the rest of the Volsci. **aurae:** 'of the movement through the air'. **memor:** supply *fuit*. **aut:** used as a variation for *nec*.

803–4 **donec:** to be taken first. **perlata:** 'reaching all the way'. **haesit:** the <u>enjambement</u> heavily emphasises the fact the the javelin stayed fixed under the breast. **alte . . . acta:** 'driven deep'. **bibit cruorem:** a strong <u>metaphor</u>.

805 **ruentem:** 'as she fell'.

806–8 **exterritus:** as this governs both *laetitia* and *metu*, it must mean 'dazed' rather than the literal 'terrified'. **nec iam amplius:** 'and no longer'. **telis occurrere virginis:** since Camilla was dying, it was highly unlikely that she would be able to retaliate; the point is that Arruns did not stop to see whether he had inflicted a mortal wound; Camilla's awesome reputation was enough to make him flee.

816–17 **trahit:** 'tugs at'. **ossa . . . mucro:** the order is *sed ferreus mucro stat inter ossa ad costas alto vulnere* (*sed* and *inter* are postponed). Note the double <u>alliteration</u>. **stat:** this verb is qualified by three adverbial phrases, all giving the spearhead's location: *inter ossa* ('between the (rib) bones'); *ad costas* ('by her ribs'); *alto vulnere* ('in a deep wound').

818–19 Note the <u>alliteration</u> again, and the <u>polyptoton</u> of *labitur / labuntur* (here 'drooping'). **frigida leto lumina:** 'her eyes, cold in death' (causal ablative).

820–2 **sic:** to be taken with *adloquitur*. **Accam . . . unam:** 'Acca alone'; she is not mentioned elsewhere. **fida . . . Camillae:** the order is *quae (erat) sola ante alias fida Camillae*. **ante alias . . . sola:** this does not mean that Acca was the only one faithful to Camilla, but that she was loyal far above the rest. **quicum:** this is an archaic form of *quacum*: 'with whom'. **partiri:** 'she (Camilla) used to share' (a sort of historic infinitive).

823–4 **hactenus . . . potui:** 'until now I have been able' (to keep the Trojans at bay). **Acca soror:** not meant literally. **conficit:** supply *me*. **tenebris:** 'in darkness'.

825 **novissima:** poignant: her 'last' instructions.

826 **succedat pugnae:** 'let him take over command of the battle'. At the time Turnus is lying in ambush to catch the main infantry body of the Trojan army as it marches to Laurentum; now he is needed to save the city from the more immediate threat of the Trojan cavalry, which it has been Camilla's job to keep at bay.

827–8 **simul his dictis:** 'as soon as she had spoken these words'. **non sponte:** 'against her will'.

828–31 **toto paulatim exsolvit se corpore:** 'slowly she withdrew (herself) from the whole of her body'; the idea is that on death the soul has to disentangle itself from the whole body, throughout which it has been diffused. **captum leto:** 'overcome by death'. **indignata:** 'complaining', because her death was untimely. **sub umbras:** 'down to the Shades' (of the Underworld).

Questions

1 How exactly does Camilla die?

2 Is Virgil entirely objective in the way he describes her death?

3 How does Arruns' behaviour contrast with that of Camilla?

4 How does Virgil make Camilla's death scene vivid and compelling?

5 Why do you think Virgil devotes half of Book XI to the exploits and death of a woman?

6 Which half of Book XI do you prefer, and why?

Book 12

The Trojans and the Latins have been locked in battle before the walls of Laurentum. Many warriors on both sides have lost their lives, including several heroes. The last of these to die was Camilla, a warrior princess allied to the Latins.

At the beginning of Book XII, Turnus longed for battle and determined to face Aeneas in single combat to end the war one way or another. King Latinus and his wife Amata tried unsuccessfully to dissuade him. He sent a messenger to Aeneas bearing a challenge to combat at dawn the next day. While he waited for a response, he restlessly checked his horses and his armour.

his agitur furiis, totoque ardentis ab ore
scintillae absistunt, oculis micat acribus ignis,
mugitus veluti cum prima in proelia taurus
terrificos ciet atque irasci in cornua temptat
arboris obnixus trunco, ventosque lacessit   105
ictibus aut sparsa ad pugnam proludit harena.
nec minus interea maternis saevus in armis
Aeneas acuit Martem et se suscitat ira,
oblato gaudens componi foedere bellum.

ago, -ere	I drive, act	*truncus, -i* m.	trunk
furia, -ae f.	frenzy, madness	*ventus, -i* m.	wind
totus, -a, -um	all, the whole	*lacesso, -ere*	I challenge
ardeo, -ere	I burn, am on fire	*ictus, -us* m.	blow
os, oris n.	mouth, face	*spargo, -ere, -rsi, -rsus*	I scatter
scintilla, -ae f.	spark	*pugna, -ae* f.	fight
absisto, -ere	I fly off, cease	*proludo, -ere*	I practise before
oculus, -i m.	eye	*harena, -ae* f.	sand
mico, -are	I flash	*minus*	less
acer, acris, acre	keen, fierce	*interea*	meanwhile
ignis, -is m.	fire	*maternus, -a, -um*	a mother's
mugitus, -us m.	bellow	*saevus, -a, -um*	fierce, cruel
veluti	just like	*arma, -orum* n.pl.	arms
primus, -a, -um	first	*Aeneas, -ae* m.	Aeneas
proelium, -i n.	battle, fight	*acuo, -ere*	I sharpen
taurus, -i m.	bull	*Mars, Martis* m.	Mars, war
terrificus, -a, -um	frightening	*suscito, -are*	I rouse
cieo, -ere	I produce, stir up	*ira, -ae* f.	anger
irascor, -i, -iratus sum	I am angry	*offero, offerre, obtuli, oblatus*	I offer
cornu, -us n.	horn	*gaudeo, -ere*	I rejoice
tempto, -are	I try	*compono, -ere*	I settle, agree
arbos, -oris f. 105	tree	*foedus, -eris* n.	agreement
obnitor, -i, -nixus sum + dat.	I push against	*bellum, -i* n.	war

101–2 **agitur:** the subject is Turnus; the tense is historic present, which Virgil uses as standard for his past narrative; it is usual to translate these as past tenses. **his . . . furiis:** 'by these frenzied actions'. **totoque . . . ab ore:** 'from (his) whole face'. **ardentis:** 'of the burning man', i.e. 'of the man as he burned (with passion)'. **scintillae absistunt:** 'sparks fly off'; this is a strong <u>metaphor</u>, and an example of <u>hyperbole</u>, intended to emphasise the strength of Turnus' raging emotions. **oculis . . . acribus:** ablative of separation, and another <u>metaphor</u>.

103–4 **veluti cum:** one of Virgil's standard ways of introducing an extended <u>simile</u>, which serves a similar purpose to the <u>metaphors</u> above. The order is *veluti cum taurus in prima proelia ciet terrificos mugitus*. **mugitus:** placed first for emphasis. **prima in proelia:** '(as he goes) into the start of a fight'. **terrificos:** note the position of this adjective, which parallels that of its noun. **irasci in cornua temptat:** 'and tries to be angry at his horns', i.e. 'tries to fuel anger into his horns'.

105–6 **ventos lacessit ictibus:** 'challenges the winds with blows'; the bull tosses its head in the air, goring an imaginary opponent. **ad pugnam proludit:** 'rehearses the fight'. **sparsa . . . harena:** 'on the scattered sand'; *sparsa* is <u>proleptic</u>, as it is the bull's hooves that scatter the sand.

107–8 **nec minus:** an example of <u>litotes</u> (making a strong affirmative). **maternis . . . in armis:** 'in his mother's arms'; in Book VIII, Aeneas' mother, the goddess Venus, persuaded Vulcan (the blacksmith god) to make a set of armour for him. **saevus:** note the position of this word, inside the phrase *maternis in armis*; this is an example of <u>enclosing word order</u>. **acuit Martem:** Aeneas 'sharpens war', i.e. 'whets his appetite for battle'; this is a <u>metaphor</u> from the sharpening of weapons before battle. **se suscitat ira:** 'he rouses himself with anger', meaning that he uses his anger as a spur to increase his determination.

109 **oblato . . . foedere:** 'by the offer of an agreement', i.e. the offer by Turnus to settle the war by single combat. **componi . . . bellum:** indirect statement.

Questions

1 Read the first hundred lines in translation.

2 How does Virgil bring out the emotional state of Turnus?

3 How effective are the metaphors in line 102?

4 What does Virgil compare Turnus to?

5 How effective is the simile (lines 103–106)?

6 Find out all you can about the armour Vulcan made for Aeneas.

7 What are we told about Aeneas in lines 107–109?

8 As described by Virgil, how does Aeneas differ from Turnus?

tum socios maestique metum solatus Iuli   110
fata docens, regique iubet responsa Latino
certa referre viros et pacis dicere leges.
postera vix summos spargebat lumine montes
orta dies, cum primum alto se gurgite tollunt
Solis equi lucemque elatis naribus efflant: 115
campum ad certamen magnae sub moenibus urbis
dimensi Rutulique viri Teucrique parabant
in mediosque focos et dis communibus aras
gramineas. alii fontemque ignemque ferebant
velati limo et verbena tempora vincti.   120
procedit legio Ausonidum, pilataque plenis
agmina se fundunt portis.

socius, -i m.	110 ally	*naris, -is* f.	nostril
maestus, -a, -um	sad	*efflo, -are*	I breathe out
metus, -us m.	fear	*campus, -i* m.	plain
solor, -ari, -atus sum	I console	*certamen, -inis* n.	contest
Iulus, -i m.	Iulus, Ascanius	*moenia, -ium* n.pl.	city walls, city
fatum, -i n.	fate	*urbs, urbis* f.	city
doceo, -ere	I teach, tell of	*dimetior, -iri, -mensus sum*	I measure out
rex, regis m.	king	*Rutuli, -orum* m.pl.	Rutulians
iubeo, -ere	I order	*Teucri, -orum* m.pl.	Trojans
responsum, -i n.	answer	*paro, -are*	I prepare
Latinus, -i m.	Latinus	*medius, -a, -um*	the middle of
certus, -a, -um	certain, definite	*focus, -i* m.	hearth, brazier
refero, -ferre	I take back, bear again	*deus, -i* m.	god
		communis, -e	shared
vir, viri m.	man	*ara, -ae* f.	altar
pax, pacis f.	peace	*gramineus, -a, -um*	grassy, of turf
dico, -ere	I say, tell	*alius, -a, -ud*	other
lex, legis f.	law, rule	*fons, fontis* m.	fountain, spring
posterus, - a, -um	next	*fero, ferre*	I carry, bring
vix	scarcely	*velo, -are, -avi, -atus*	120 I veil, cover
summus, -a, -um	the top of, highest	*limus, -i* m.	ceremonial apron
		verbena, -ae f.	sacred foliage
lumen, -inis n.	light, life	*tempus, -oris* n.	temple, time
mons, montis m.	mountain	*vincio, -ire, -nxi, -nctus*	I bind
orior, -iri, ortus sum	I arise	*procedo, -ere*	I procede
dies, diei m/f.	day, daylight	*legio, -onis* f.	legion, army
altus, -a, -um	high, deep	*Ausonidae, -arum* m.pl.	peoples of Italy
gurges, -itis m.	deep water	*pilatus, -a, -um*	armed with javelins, dense
tollo, -ere, sustuli, sublatus	I raise		
Sol, Solis m.	115 the Sun God, sun	*plenus, -a, -um*	full
equus, -i m.	horse	*agmen, -inis* n.	army
lux, lucis f.	light	*fundo, -ere, fudi, fusus*	I pour, sprout
effero, -ferre, extuli, elatus	I raise up	*porta, -ae* f.	gate

110–11 **maestique metum . . . Iuli:** 'the fear of the sorrowful Iulus'; Aeneas' son Iulus, also known as Ascanius, is downcast because he is anxious about the outcome of the combat. **fata docens:** 'telling them of what is fated'; throughout the *Aeneid* various prophets and deities have made clear the destiny of the Trojans, to settle successfully in Italy. This should reassure his people and his son.

111–12 The order is *iubetque viros referre certa responsa regi Latino et dicere leges pacis.* **leges pacis:** 'the laws of peace', i.e. 'the conditions for a settlement'.

113–15 The order is *postera dies orta vix spargebat summos montes lumine, cum primum equi Solis tollunt se alto gurgite.* **postera dies orta:** 'the next day having risen', i.e. 'the next day having dawned'. **vix spargebat:** inceptive imperfect: 'was scarcely beginning to scatter (i.e. bathe)'. **cum:** 'at the moment when'. **equi Solis:** according to Greek mythology, the sun god carried the sun across the sky in a chariot pulled by winged horses. **alto . . . gurgite:** 'from the depths of the ocean'. **lucemque . . . efflant:** 'and breathe out light'; the horses were believed to breathe out fire.

116–19 **dimensi:** the subject is *Rutulique viri Teucrique*: 'both Rutulian men and the Trojans'; they first measured out the ground for the combat, and then prepared for the religious solemnification of the action. **parabant:** inceptive imperfect again: 'began to prepare'. **-que . . . et:** 'both . . . and'. **in medios:** 'in the midst (of the people)' rather than the apparent 'into the middle of the braziers', which gives no sense. **focos . . . aras:** both are the objects of *parabant*; the braziers are for the burning of the sacrificial animals, after they have been slaughtered on the altars. **gramineas:** because the Trojans have not yet had time or opportunity to build permanent altars to their gods, these are made of turf.

119–20 **fontem:** here simply 'water'. **velati limo:** 'wearing a ceremonial apron'; like the following phrase, this is symbolic of their status as priests or their assistants. **tempora vincti:** 'their temples bound'; the construction is modelled on the Greek middle voice, the participles of which are active in meaning; alternately *tempora* could be viewed as an accusative of respect, lit. 'bound with respect to their temples'. In Roman times priests always wore headbands of one sort or another when participating in religious rites. Note the chiasmus in line 120.

121–2 **procedit:** i.e. out of the city. **Ausonidum:** = *Ausonidarum* (an archaic form); Ausonia was an ancient name for Southern Italy. **pilata . . . agmina:** either 'columns of men armed with javelins', or 'densely-packed columns of men'; *pilata* is a very rare word, which ought to mean 'armed with javelins', but Servius (an ancient commentator on Virgil) insists the word meant 'dense'. **plenis . . . portis:** 'through the crowded gates'.

Questions

1 In lines 110–111, what are the *fata*? Why does Aeneas refer to them?

2 In lines 113–115, what is being described?

3 Find out all you can about ancient beliefs about the sun and its travels.

4 Why do you think Virgil devotes three lines to this image?

5 What are the preparations for the combat?

6 What makes line 120 an impressive piece of poetry? Find as many points as you can.

7 How does Virgil give an aura of solemnity to lines 121–122?

                    hinc Troius omnis
Tyrrhenusque ruit variis exercitus armis,
haud secus instructi ferro quam si aspera Martis
pugna vocet. nec non mediis in milibus ipsi   125
ductores auro volitant ostroque superbi,
et genus Assaraci Mnestheus et fortis Asilas
et Messapus equum domitor, Neptunia proles;
utque dato signo spatia in sua quisque recessit,
defigunt tellure hastas et scuta reclinant.   130
tum studio effusae matres et vulgus inermum
invalidique senes turres ac tecta domorum
obsedere, alii portis sublimibus astant.

But from the summit of a nearby mountain the goddess Juno was observing the two sides gathering together for combat.

hinc	on this side, from here	*domitor, -oris* m.	tamer
Troius, -a, -um	Trojan	*Neptunius, -a, -um*	of Neptune
omnis, -e	all	*proles, -is* f.	offspring
Tyrrhenus, -a, -um	Etruscan	*ut* + indic.	as, when
ruo, -ere	I rush	*do, dare, dedi, datus*	I give
varius, -a, -um	various	*signum, -i* n.	signal
exercitus, -us m.	army	*spatium, -i* n.	space, place
haud	not	*quisque, quaeque, quidque*	each
secus	otherwise	*recedo, -ere, -cessi, -cessus*	I withdraw
instruo, -ere, -struxi -structus	I equip	*defigo, -ere* 130	I plant, fix
ferrum, -i n.	iron, weapon	*tellus, -uris* f.	earth, ground
quam	than	*hasta, -ae* f.	spear
asper, -era, -erum	savage	*scutum, -i* n.	shield
voco, -are 125	I call	*reclino, -are*	I lean
mille, pl. *milia*	thousand	*studium, -i* n.	enthusiasm
ipse, ipsa, ipsum	-self	*effundo, -ere, -fudi, -fusus*	I pour out
ductor, -oris m.	leader	*mater, -tris* f.	mother
aurum, -i n.	gold	*vulgus, -i* n.	mass, multitude
volito, -are	I fly about	*inermus, -a, -um*	unarmed
ostrum, -i n.	purple	*invalidus, -a, -um*	weak, feeble
superbus, -a, -um	magnificent	*senex, -is* m.	old man
genus, -eris n.	descendant	*turris, -is* f.	tower
Assaracus, -i m.	Assaracus	*tectum, -i* n.	roof
Mnestheus, -i m.	Mnestheus	*domus, -us* f.	house
fortis, -e	brave	*obsideo, -ere, -sedi, -sessus*	I settle upon
Asilas, -ae m.	Asilas	*sublimis, -e*	high, tall
Messapus, -i m.	Messapus	*asto, -are*	I stand on

123 **Tyrrhenus:** the Etruscans, who lived to the north of Rome, had allied themselves to the Trojans under their king, Tarchon. **variis armis:** each nationality had its own array of weapons.

124–5 **instructi ferro:** 'equipped with weapons'. **Martis pugna:** 'the fighting of warfare'; as often in verse, war is personified as the god. **vocet:** 'were summoning them'; present subjunctive in an unfulfilled present conditional clause; Virgil's continuing use of the historic present demands the present subjunctive rather than the normal imperfect.

125–6 **nec non:** the <u>litotes</u> makes a strong affirmative: 'also'. **volitant:** the verb suggests continual rapid movement, presumably as they impose order on their troops. **auro . . . ostroque superbi:** 'resplendent in gold and purple'; these colours were generally reserved for royalty: there were kings and princes from allied tribes fighting on both sides.

127–8 **et . . . et:** 'both . . . and'. **Mnestheus, Asilas:** prominent leaders on the Trojan side. **Messapus:** a prominent leader on the Latin side. The three names are in apposition to *ductores*.

129 **spatia in sua:** 'to his allocated place'.

130 **scuta reclinant:** 'they lean their shields against them (the spears)'.

131–3 **studio:** 'enthusiastically' (ablative of manner). **effusae:** 'pouring out' (of the city). **vulgus:** all the non-combatants of the city. **obsedere:** = *obsederunt*; this alternative form of the 3rd person plural, perfect indicative is very common in verse, and will not be commented on again. **portis:** either dative dependent on the compound verb, or local ablative.

Questions

1 What is the force of *hinc* (line 122) and what is it contrasted with?

2 Can you discover why the Etruscans chose to ally themselves with the Trojans?

3 Why do you think Virgil adds the comparison *haud secus . . . quam si . . . pugna vocet*?

4 Why do you think the leaders are decked out in gold and purple?

5 What can you find out about the three characters named in lines 127–128?

6 How does Virgil make lines 127–128 more than just a list of names?

7 Why do you think Virgil singles out *matres* and *senes* for particular mention?

8 Sometimes poetry is defined as using words to paint a picture. What makes this passage (lines 122–133) a particularly good example of this?

extemplo Turni sic est adfata sororem   138
diva deam, stagnis quae fluminibusque sonoris
praesidet (hunc illi rex aetheris altus honorem   140
Iuppiter erepta pro virginitate sacravit):
'nympha, decus fluviorum, animo gratissima nostro,
scis ut te cunctis unam, quaecumque Latinae
magnanimi Iovis ingratum ascendere cubile,
praetulerim caelique libens in parte locarim: 145
disce tuum, ne me incuses, Iuturna, dolorem.
qua visa est Fortuna pati Parcaeque sinebant
cedere res Latio Turnum et tua moenia texi:
nunc iuvenem imparibus video concurrere fatis,
Parcarumque dies et vis inimica propinquat.   150
non pugnam aspicere hanc oculis, non foedera possum.
tu pro germano si quid praesentius audes,
perge; decet. forsan miseros meliora sequentur.'

extemplo	immediately	*pars, partis* f.	part, place
adfor, -fari, -fatus sum	I address	*loco, -are, -avi, -atus*	I place
soror, -oris f.	sister	*disco, -ere*	I learn
diva, -ae f.	goddess	*incuso, -are*	I accuse
dea, -ae f.	goddess	*Iuturna, -ae* f.	Juturna
stagnum, -i n.	pool	*dolor, -oris* m.	pain, grief
flumen, -inis n.	river	*qua*	where
sonorus, -a, -um	roaring, clashing	*videor, -eri, visus sum*	I seem
praesideo, -ere + dat.	140 I preside over	*Fortuna, -ae* f.	Fate, Fortune
aether, -eris (acc. *-era*) m.	air	*patior, -i, passus sum*	I allow, suffer
honos, -oris m.	honour	*Parcae, -arum* f.pl.	the Fates
Iuppiter, Iovis m.	Jupiter	*sino, -ere*	I allow
eripio, -ere, -ui, -reptus	I steal, snatch, tear out	*cedo, -ere*	I turn out well, accrue to, withdraw
pro + abl.	for, in return for		
virginitas, -atis f.	virginity	*res, rei* f.	thing, matter
sacro, -are, -avi, -atus	I dedicate, give	*Latium, -i* n.	Latium
nympha, -ae f.	nymph	*tego, -ere, texi, tectus*	I cover, protect
decus, -oris n.	glory	*iuvenis, -is* m.	young man
fluvius, -i m.	river	*impar, imparis*	unequal
animus, -i m.	mind, heart	*concurro, -ere*	I join battle
gratus, -a, -um	pleasing, dear	*vis, vim, vi* f.	150 force, violence
scio, -ire	I know	*inimicus, -a, -um*	hostile
cuncti, -ae, -a	all	*propinquo, -are*	I approach
unus, -a, -um	one, alone	*aspicio, -ere*	I watch, behold
qui-, quae-, quodcumque	whoever, whatever	*possum, posse*	I can
		germanus, -i m.	brother
Latinus, -a, -um	Latin	*praesens, -entis*	effective
magnanimus, -a, -um	great-hearted	*audeo, -ere*	I dare
ingratus, -a, -um	ungrateful	*pergo, -ere*	I go ahead
ascendo, -ere, -endi, -ensus	I climb into	*decet, -ere*	it is proper, right
cubile, -is n.	bed	*forsan*	perhaps
praefero, -re, -tuli, -latus 145	I prefer	*miser, -era, -erum*	wretched
caelum, -i n.	heaven, sky	*meliora, -um* n.pl.	better things
libens, -entis	willing, glad	*sequor, -i, secutus sum*	I follow

138–9 **Turni . . . sororem:** Turnus' sister was Juturna, who was made a nymph (a minor nature deity) and so immortal by Jupiter in recompense for his having raped her. **diva deam:** 'goddess to goddess'.

139–40 **quae:** to be translated first; the antecedent is *deam / sororem*.

140–1 The order is *altus Iuppiter rex aetheris sacravit hunc honorem illi pro erepta virginitate*. **hunc honorem:** i.e. responsibility for pools and rivers.

142 **decus:** vocative, in apposition to *nympha*.

143–5 **scis ut te . . . praetulerim:** 'you know how I have preferred you'. **cunctis:** 'out of all'; supply *Latinis* from the next clause, into which it has been attracted. The combination means '(you alone) out of all the Latin women who(ever)'. **magnanimi:** ironic. **ingratum . . . cubile:** Jupiter's bed is 'ungrateful' because in most cases the unfortunate women suffered wretched fates. **caelique . . . in parte locarim:** 'I have placed you in a part of heaven', i.e. 'I have given you your own place in heaven', meaning that she did not oppose Juturna's deification. **locarim:** = *locaverim*.

146 **disce tuum . . . dolorem:** 'learn your grief', i.e. 'learn the grief that will be yours'. **ne me incuses:** 'so that you may not (later) blame me (for it)'. Her argument is that by warning Juturna now, she absolves herself of responsibility for what will happpen.

147–8 **Fortuna, Parcae:** personifications viewed as female deities. Even the gods were generally subject to their predestination. **cedere res Latio:** 'affairs to turn out well for Latium'. Note the strong <u>alliteration</u> of *t*.

149–50 **nunc:** i.e. the fates have now turned against Latium. **iuvenem:** i.e. Turnus. **imparibus . . . fatis:** 'with unequal fates', i.e. fate unequal to that of Aeneas. **Parcarum dies:** in effect 'the day of doom', when Turnus is fated to die. **vis inimica:** the 'hostile force' is that threatened by Aeneas.

151 **non foedera:** 'nor the truce' agreed earlier to allow the single combat to go ahead.

152–3 **si quid:** 'if anything'. **praesentius:** 'more immediate', and so 'more effective'. **miseros meliora sequentur:** 'better times will follow for the wretched ones'; *miseros* is probably meant to include Turnus and Juturna; Juno knows this will not happen, but tries to give Juturna hope.

Questions

1 What can you find out about nymphs in Greco-Roman mythology?

2 Can you explain why line 138 has a very slow rhythm?

3 What can we learn from lines 140–144 about Jupiter's character and behaviour?

4 What is the tone of Juno's speech?

5 How would you describe the relationship between Juno and Juturna?

6 Why has Juno been hostile to the Trojans?

7 Find out all you can about the relationship between the gods and Fate.

8 How does Juno make her speech persuasive?

vix ea, cum lacrimas oculis Iuturna profudit
terque quaterque manu pectus percussit honestum.   155
'non lacrimis hoc tempus' ait Saturnia Iuno;
'accelera et fratrem, si quis modus, eripe morti;
aut tu bella cie conceptumque excute foedus.
auctor ego audendi.' sic exhortata reliquit
incertam et tristi turbatam vulnere mentis.   160

Meanwhile Latinus, Turnus and Aeneas came forth, followed by Ascanius. As animals were prepared for sacrifice, Aeneas prayed openly to the principal gods.

'cesserit Ausonio si fors victoria Turno,   183
convenit Euandri victos discedere ad urbem,
cedet Iulus agris, nec post arma ulla rebelles   185
Aeneadae referent ferrove haec regna lacessent.
sin nostrum adnuerit nobis Victoria Martem
(ut potius reor et potius di numine firment),
non ego nec Teucris Italos parere iubebo
nec mihi regna peto: paribus se legibus ambae   190
invictae gentes aeterna in foedera mittant.
sacra deosque dabo; socer arma Latinus habeto,
imperium sollemne socer; mihi moenia Teucri
constituent urbique dabit Lavinia nomen.'

lacrima, -ae f.	tear	*vinco, -ere, vici, victus*	I defeat, win
profundo, -ere, -fudi, -fusus	I pour forth	*discedo, -ere*	I depart
ter	155 three times	*ager, agri* m.	185 field, land
quater	four times	*post*	afterwards
percutio, -ere, -cussi, -cussus	I strike, beat	*ullus, -a, -um*	any
honestus, -a, -um	beautiful	*rebellis, -e*	rebellious
aio (defective verb)	I say	*Aeneades, -ae* m.	Trojan
Saturnius, -a, -um	of Saturn	*regnum, -i* n.	kingdom, realm
accelero, -are	I hurry	*adnuo, -ere, -ui, -utus*	I grant
frater, -tris m.	brother	*potius*	rather
modus, -i m.	way	*reor, reri, ratus sum*	I think
mors, mortis f.	death	*numen, -inis* n.	divine power
concipio, -ere, -cepi, -ceptus	I draw up	*firmo, -are*	I confirm
excutio, -ere	I strike down	*Itali, -orum* m.pl.	Italians
auctor, -oris m/f.	proposer, master	*pareo, -ere* + dat.	I obey
exhortor, -ari, -atus sum	I urge, encourage	*peto, -ere*	190 I seek, ask for
relinquo, -ere, -liqui, -lictus	I leave	*par, paris*	equal, similar
incertus, -a, -um	160 uncertain	*ambo, ambae, ambo*	both
tristis, -e	sad, bitter	*invictus, -a, -um*	unconquered
turbo, -are, -avi, -atus	I trouble	*gens, gentis* f.	race, nation
vulnus, -eris n.	wound	*aeternus, -a, -um*	everlasting
mens, mentis f.	mind, heart	*mitto, -ere*	I send
Ausonius, -a, -um	183 Italian	*sacra, -orum* n.pl.	sacred objects
fors	by chance	*imperium, -i* n.	power
victoria, -ae f.	victory	*sollemnis, -e*	customary
convenit, -ire	it is agreed	*constituo, -ere*	I establish
Euandrus, -i m.	Evander	*nomen, -inis* n.	name

155–6 vix ea: supply *dixerat*: 'scarcely had she spoken these words'. **oculis:** 'from her eyes'. **profudit:** indicative in an 'inverse *cum*' clause. **terque quaterque:** an example of polysyndeton. Note the percussive alliteration of *p*.

156 non . . . hoc tempus: supply *est*. **Saturnia Iuno:** Juno was the daughter of Saturn.

157 si quis modus: supply *est*. **morti:** 'from death'; verbs that mean to abstract or take something away generally take a dative (of disadvantage).

158 aut tu bella cie: if Juturna cannot save her brother by snatching him away to safety, she should stir up open war again so that the two leaders may not meet in single combat. Juno knows that either action would only defer the inevitable death of Turnus, but she wants to make victory as difficult as possible for the Trojans.

159–60 auctor ego audendi: supply *sum*: 'I am the proposer of your daring', i.e. 'I take responsibility for your daring (to do this)'. **exhortata reliquit:** supply *eam*. **tristi . . . vulnere mentis:** 'by the bitter wound to her heart'; *mentis* is an objective genitive.

183 The order is *si fors victoria cesserit Ausonio Turno*.

184 convenit: followed by an indirect statement, with the accusative *nos (Troianos)* to be supplied. **victos:** i.e. the Trojans. **Euandri . . . ad urbem:** i.e. Pallanteum, the settlement on the site of the future Rome, that Aeneas visited in Book VIII when in search of allies.

185–6 cedet Iulus agris: 'Iulus will withdraw from these lands'; in the event of Aeneas' death at the hands of Turnus, Iulus will become the Trojan leader. **arma . . . referent:** 'will take up arms again'. **ferro:** 'with arms'.

187 sin: 'but if', introducing the opposite possibility. **Victoria:** personified as a goddess. **nostrum . . . Martem:** 'that the (outcome of) the war be our (victory)'.

188 potius . . . potius: the anaphora expresses strongly Aeneas' belief and hope. **firment:** subjunctive to express a wish. **di:** = *dei*. **numine:** 'with their divine will'.

189–90 non . . . nec . . . nec: the first negative simply serves to emphasise the other two. **nec mihi regna peto:** Aeneas is saying that he does not want to be king at the head of a kingdom, but merely the leader of the new Troy.

190–1 invictae: i.e. neither conquered by the other. **se . . . mittant:** another wish: 'may they send themselves', i.e. 'may they enter into'.

192 sacra deosque dabo: 'I shall give (to the united cities) the sacred objects and gods' that Aeneas brought with him away from Troy, at the behest of the ghost of his dead distant cousin, Hector (see Book II).

192–3 soter . . . Latinus: On arrival in Latium, Latinus had promised Aeneas the hand of his daughter, Lavinia; unfortunately she was already betrothed to Turnus, who initiated the war (spurred on by Juno) rather than surrender his bride-to-be. **habeto:** a rare 3rd person imperative. **soter . . . soter:** the repetition, forming a chiasmus, adds force to his pledge.

193–4 mihi: placed next to *soter* for maximum contrast. **nomen:** the Trojans' first settlement by the Tiber would be named Lavinium.

Questions

1 What alternative courses of action does Juno offer Juturna? How would they have differed?

2 List and evaluate the terms offered by Aeneas. Are they reasonable?

3 If you had been Latinus, how would you have responded to these terms?

4 How does Virgil make Aeneas' speech measured and emphatic?

Latinus then swore an oath to the gods.

'nulla dies pacem hanc Italis nec foedera rumpet,   202
quo res cumque cadent; nec me vis ulla volentem
avertet, non si tellurem effundat in undas
diluvio miscens caelumque in Tartara solvat,   205
ut sceptrum hoc' – dextra sceptrum nam forte gerebat –
'numquam fronde levi fundet virgulta nec umbras,
cum semel in silvis imo de stirpe recisum
matre caret posuitque comas et bracchia ferro
olim arbos, nunc artificis manus aere decoro   210
inclusit patribusque dedit gestare Latinis.'
talibus inter se firmabant foedera dictis
conspectu in medio procerum. tum rite sacratas
in flammam iugulant pecudes et viscera vivis
eripiunt, cumulantque oneratis lancibus aras.   215
at vero Rutulis impar ea pugna videri
iamdudum et vario misceri pectora motu,
tum magis ut propius cernunt non viribus aequis.

nullus, -a, -um	no	*bracchium, -i* n.	arm, limb
rumpo, -ere	I break, break through	*olim*	210 once, formerly
		artifex, -icis m.	craftsman
quocumque	however	*aes, aeris* n.	bronze
cado, -ere	I fall, turn out	*decorus, -a, -um*	ornate
volo, velle	I want, wish	*includo, -ere, -usi, -usus*	I enclose, sheathe
averto, -ere	I turn aside	*pater, patris* m.	father, elder
unda, -ae f.	wave, water	*gesto, -are*	I bear
diluvium, -i n.	205 flood	*talis, -e*	such
misceo, -ere, -ui, mixtus	I mix, mingle	*inter* + acc.	between, among
Tartara, -orum n.pl.	Tartarus	*dictum, -i* n.	word
solvo, -ere	I let loose, relax	*conspectus, -us* m.	sight
sceptrum, -i n.	sceptre	*procer, -eris* m.	noble, prince
dextra, -ae f.	right hand, hand	*rite*	duly
forte	by chance	*flamma, -ae* f.	flame, fire
gero, -ere	I wage, carry, wear	*iugulo, -are*	I slaughter
		pecus, -udis f.	beast
numquam	never	*viscera, -um* n.pl.	innards, entrails
frons, -ndis f.	foliage, leaves	*vivus, -a, -um*	alive
levis, -e	light	*cumulo, -are*	215 I pile, heap up
virgulta, -orum n.pl.	shoots	*onero, -are, -avi, -atus*	I load
umbra, -ae f.	shade, shadow	*lanx, lancis* f.	dish, platter
semel	once	*vero*	however
imus, -a, -um	the bottom of	*iamdudum*	for long now
stirps, -is m.	stem, trunk	*motus, -us* m.	emotion
recido, -ere, -cidi, -cisus	I cut off	*magis*	more
careo, -ere + abl.	I lack	*prope*	near
pono, -ere, posui, positus	I place, set down	*cerno, -ere*	I see
coma, -ae f.	hair, foliage	*vires, -ium* f.pl.	strength

202–3 **pacem . . . foedera:** *pax* is the absence of hostilities, *foedera* the agreement that has brought this about. **quo . . . cumque:** this compound word is split by a device called *tmesis*.
203–4 **me . . . volentem avertet:** 'shall divert me (from this oath) willingly'.
204–5 **effundat:** the subject is *vis*; the present subjunctive is for a future remote condition: 'if it were to cast out'. **diluvio miscens:** 'confusing them (land and sea) in a flood'. **caelumque in Tartara solvat:** 'and set heaven loose in the underworld'.
206–7 **ut:** 'just as'. **fronde levi . . . virgulta:** 'shoots of light foliage' (ablative of description). **nec umbras:** 'nor shade', i.e. that would be provided by foliage. Note the slow rhythm of 206.
208–9 **cum semel:** 'since once', i.e. 'ever since'. **imo de stirpe:** 'from the base of the trunk'. **matre caret:** 'it lacks its mother-tree'. **posuitque:** 'and has shed'. **comas et bracchia:** a common metaphor in respect of trees. **ferro:** may be taken with *recisum*: 'by an axe'.
210–11 **olim arbos:** 'once (it was) a tree'. **patribus . . . Latinis:** probably here 'to Latin rulers' rather than more generally 'elders'. **gestare:** 'to bear' (an epexegetic or explanatory infinitive).
212–13 **talibus . . . dictis:** 'with such words'. **conspectu in medio:** 'in full view'.
213–15 **sacratas . . . pecudes:** 'the beasts that have been consecrated', i.e. 'prepared for sacrifice'. **in flammam iugulant:** 'they slit (their) throats onto the flame'. **vivis:** 'from them while still alive' (dative of disadvantage after a verb of abstraction (cf. line 157)). The entrails were removed so that the *haruspex* could examine them to determine whether the omens were good or bad. **oneratis lancibus:** local ablative. The dishes contained the entrails and other parts of the sacrificed animals as offerings to the gods. Note the chiastic order of lines 214–15.
216–18 **at vero:** introducing a strong contrast. **videri, misceri:** historic infinitives. **vario misceri pectora motu:** 'their hearts have been troubled by a mixture of emotions'. **tum magis:** opposed to *iamdudum*: 'even more so then, when . . .'. **propius:** 'at closer quarters', because Aeneas and Turnus approach one another and may be compared directly. **non viribus aequis:** supply *eos esse* (indirect statement dependent on *cernunt*: 'that they are of unequal strength' (ablative of description).

Questions

1 What oaths does Latinus swear?

2 How does Latinus make his oaths more dramatic and powerful?

3 What does Latinus say about his sceptre? What is the purpose of this detail?

4 What happens during the sacrifice?

5 How does Virgil make lines 213–215 dramatic and effective?

6 What causes anxiety among the Rutulians?

When Juturna realised how the Rutulians were feeling, she adopted the form of Camers, a high-born warrior, and went amongst the ranks rousing their pity for Turnus and shame that they were leaving the fighting to a single man. She then caused an omen to appear in the sky, when an eagle, having pounced on a swan, was forced by other swans to drop its prey and fly off. A prophet immediately interpreted this as a sign from heaven than the Rutulians and Latins should save Turnus from Aeneas and drive the Trojan invader away. Young men called for their arms as the prophet cast the first spear, which killed an Etruscan youth. The dead man's brothers immediately retaliated, and in moments a full-scale battle had erupted. Latinus fled back into his city as the slaughter intensified on both sides.

at pius Aeneas dextram tendebat inermem	311
nudato capite atque suos clamore vocabat:	
'quo ruitis? quaeve ista repens discordia surgit?	
o cohibete iras! ictum iam foedus et omnes	
compositae leges, mihi ius concurrere soli,	315
me sinite atque auferte metus; ego foedera faxo	
firma manu, Turnum debent haec iam mihi sacra.'	
has inter voces, media inter talia verba	
ecce viro stridens alis adlapsa sagitta est,	
incertum qua pulsa manu, quo turbine adacta,	320
quis tantam Rutulis laudem, casusne deusne,	
attulerit; pressa est insignis gloria facti,	
nec sese Aeneae iactavit vulnere quisquam.	
Turnus ut Aenean cedentem ex agmine vidit	
turbatosque duces, subita spe fervidus ardet;	325

pius, -a, -um	dutiful	*strideo, -ere*	I hiss
tendo, -ere	I hold out,	*ala, -ae* f.	wing
	proceed	*adlabor, -i, -lapsus sum*	I fly towards
inermis, -e	unarmed	*sagitta, -ae* f.	arrow
nudo, -are, -avi, -atus	I bare	*pello, -ere, pepuli, pulsus* 320	I drive, impel
caput, -itis n.	head	*turbo, -inis* m.	twisting force
clamor, -oris m.	shout	*adigo, -ere, -egi, -actus*	I drive, impel
quo	whither?	*tantus, -a, -um*	such great
iste, ista, istud	that of yours	*laus, laudis* f.	praise
repens, -entis	sudden	*casus, -us* m.	chance
discordia, -ae f.	strife	*adfero, -ferre, attuli, adlatus*	I bring to
surgo, -ere	I rise	*premo, -ere, pressi, pressus*	I suppress
cohibeo, -ere	I restrain	*insignis, -e*	distinguished
ico, -ere, ici, ictus	I strike, ratify	*gloria, -ae* f.	glory
ius, iuris n. 315	right	*factum, -i* n.	deed
solus, -a, -um	alone	*iacto, -are, -avi, -atus*	I toss, boast
aufero, -ferre	I set aside	*quis-, quae-, quicquam*	anyone, anything
firmus, -a, -um	firm	*dux, ducis* m. 325	leader
debeo, -ere	I owe	*subitus, -a, -um*	sudden
vox, vocis f.	voice, word	*spes, spei* f.	hope
ecce	see, behold	*fervidus, -a, -um*	fiery, eager

311–12 at pius Aeneas: this is Virgil's favourite description of Aeneas, especially at significant moments. *Pius* signifies dutifulness to one's gods, one's country, one's people and one's family; also to be added here is dutifulness to the treaty that has just been agreed and solemnised. **inermem nudato:** juxtaposed for maximum emphasis: while everyone else is armed and fighting, Aeneas alone is unarmed and exposed, as he did not wear his armour during the religious rites. **clamore:** ablative of manner, meaning little more than 'loudly'.

313 quo ruitis: to be taken <u>metaphorically</u>: his real intent is to wonder, 'where is this all going to lead?' There are echoes here of the breakdown of agreements that led to civil war in Virgil's own day at the end of the Republic. **quaeve ista . . . discordia surgit:** *-ve* regularly introduces a follow-up question and may be omitted in translation: 'what is this strife that is breaking out among you?'

314–15 iras: plural because it applies to so many people. **ictum . . . foedus:** supply *est*: 'the treaty has been ratified'. **compositae:** supply *sunt*. **leges:** the terms of the treaty, as before. **ius:** supply *est*: 'it is right'.

316–17 me sinite: supply *concurrere solum* from the previous line. **auferte metus:** 'dispel your fears'; he assumes that his men have started to fight because they are afraid for him. **faxo:** an archaic form of *faciam*, the future indicative. **firma:** scansion shows that this qualifies *foedera*, not *manu*. **manu:** i.e. using his hand to kill Turnus. **haec . . . sacra:** 'these sacred rites' that have just been performed. **mihi:** 'to me' (and no one else). Note the heavy <u>alliteration</u> of *f*, showing strength of feeling.

318 media inter talia verba: <u>tautologous</u> to spell out the circumstances in which the following critical action occurred.

319 ecce: this word is used to seize the attention of the reader for what follows. **viro:** 'against the man' (i.e.Aeneas); dative of disadvantage, or goal of motion. **stridens:** arrows make a whistling or hissing sound as they fly. **alis:** 'flying with wings towards (the man)', i.e. 'in winged flight'. **sagitta:** left until near the end of the line, after its effects have been described; this is Virgil's way of raising anticipation.

320 incertum: supply *est*. **pulsa:** supply *sit* for the indirect question. **quo turbine adacta:** supply *sit* again: 'by what force it was impelled'; **turbo** means 'whirlwind' and by extension anything that turns or twists, as an arrow does as it flies.

321–2 quis . . . attulerit: also dependent on *incertum*. **tantam Rutulis laudem:** whoever shot Aeneas would deserve the praise of his fellows. **casusne deusne:** Virgil gives only two of the three possibilities for the shooting: chance and a god; the possibility of a deliberate human action is ignored, as the epic tradition required humans to be the tools of fate or the gods. **pressa est . . . gloria:** 'the glory was suppressed', i.e. no one claimed the glory, as the next line makes clear. **insignis:** genitive.

323 nec sese iactavit . . . quisquam: 'and no one boasted'. **sese:** = *se*. **vulnere:** this is the first indication that the arrow wounded Aeneas, but as yet we are not told where or how seriously.

324–5 fervidus ardet: 'is eagerly inflamed'.

Questions

1 *At pius Aeneas:* how far do you think Aeneas deserves this epithet?

2 What are Aeneas' main thoughts and emotions in his speech?

3 How does Aeneas make clear his feelings?

4 How does Virgil build up suspense in lines 318–323?

5 How does Turnus change?

poscit equos atque arma simul, saltuque superbus
emicat in currum et manibus molitur habenas.
multa virum volitans dat fortia corpora leto,
seminecis volvit multos aut agmina curru
proterit aut raptas fugientibus ingerit hastas.   330

Turnus was like Mars when dashing off to herald war.

talis equos alacer media inter proelia Turnus   337
fumantes sudore quatit, miserabile caesis
hostibus insultans; spargit rapida ungula rores
sanguineos mixtaque cruor calcatur harena.   340

Many were the warriors brought low by Turnus, who fought both from his chariot and on foot.

atque ea dum campis victor dat funera Turnus,   383
interea Aenean Mnestheus et fidus Achates
Ascaniusque comes castris statuere cruentum   385
alternos longa nitentem cuspide gressus.
saevit et infracta luctatur harundine telum
eripere auxilioque viam, quae proxima, poscit:

posco, -ere	I demand, ask for	*ros, roris* m.	dew, moisture
simul	at the same time	*sanguineus, -a, -um*	340 bloody
saltus, -us m.	leap, bound	*cruor, -oris* m.	spilt blood
emico, -are	I dart out	*calco, -are*	I trample
currus, -us m.	chariot	*victor, -oris* m.	383 victor
molior, -iri, -itus sum	heave on, tug at	*funus, -eris* n.	death
habena, -ae f.	rein	*fidus, -a, -um*	faithful
corpus, -oris n.	body	*Achates, -ae* m.	Achates
letum, -i n.	death	*Ascanius, -i* m.	385 Ascanius, Iulus
seminecis, -is	half-dead	*comes, -itis* m.	companion
volvo, -ere	I roll, throw down	*castra, -orum* n.pl.	camp
		statuo, -ere, -ui, -utus	I place
protero, -ere	330 I trample	*cruentus, -a, -um*	blood-stained
rapio, -ere, rapui, raptus	I seize	*alternus, -a, -um*	every other
fugio, -ere	I flee	*longus, -a, -um*	long
ingero, -ere	I throw	*nitor, -i, nixus sum* + abl.	I lean on
alacer, -cris, -cre	337 keen	*cuspis, -idis* f.	spear
fumo, -are	I smoke, steam	*gressus, -us* m.	step
sudor, -oris m.	sweat	*saevio, -ire*	I rage
quatio, -ere	I spur on	*infractus, -a, -um*	broken
miserabilis, -e	wretched	*luctor, -ari, -atus sum*	I struggle
caedo, -ere, cecidi, caesus	I slaughter	*harundo, -inis* f.	shaft, arrow
hostis, -is m.	enemy	*telum, -i* n.	missile, dart
insulto, -are	I leap upon	*auxilium, -i* n.	help
rapidus, -a, -um	rapid	*proximus, -a, -um*	nearest
ungula, -ae f.	hoof		

326–7 **saltu:** ablative of manner. **superbus:** best translated as an adverb. **molitur:** this verb always implies exertion or working hard to achieve something; the idea here is that Turnus is striving to set the horses galloping into battle. Note the <u>alliteration</u> and <u>consonance</u> of *s* and then *m*, indicative of his charged emotions.

328 **virum:** = *virorum*. **volitans:** 'as he dashes around'. **multa virum . . . dat fortia corpora leto:** 'he gives many brave bodies of men to death', a poetic way of saying that he kills many brave men. Note the fast rhythm of the line, reinforcing the image of speed given by the verbs *emicat* and *volitans*.

329–30 **volvit:** when struck by Turnus' javelins, the men tumble over as they die. **agmina:** 'groups of men'. **curru:** i.e. by driving his chariot over them if they stand their ground. **raptas . . . hastas:** he snatches spears from the dead as he drives past them. **fugientibus:** dative of goal of motion, or simply dependent on the compound verb.

337–9 **talis:** 'like Mars'. **inter:** 'through'. **quatit:** the verb generally implies shaking; here Turnus shakes the reins to spur on the horses. **miserabile:** adverbial accusative, to be translated as an adverb qualifying *caesis*. **hostibus:** dative after the compound verb.

339–40 **rapida ungula:** singular for plural. **rores sanguineos:** 'bloody dew': a poetic <u>metaphor</u>. **mixtaque cruor calcatur harena:** 'and spilt blood, with sand mixed, is trampled', i.e. 'and spilt blood mixed with sand is trampled on'.

383 **ea . . . dat funera:** 'causes these deaths', i.e. those listed in the preceding lines. **campis:** local ablative. **victor:** 'victoriously'. Note how Virgil likes to keep the subject's name back until the end of the line; cf. line 337.

384–6 **Aenean:** the object of *statuere*. **Mnestheus:** see line 128. **fidus Achates:** Achates has been presented as Aeneas' closest friend throughout the *Aeneid*; he is always called *fidus*. **Ascanius:** Aeneas' son, also called *Iulus*. **comes:** 'as companion', i.e. 'who is accompanying him'. **castris:** local ablative. **alternos . . . gressus:** 'every other step'; note the <u>chiastic</u> word order. Note also the slow rhythm of line 386.

387–8 **infracta . . . harundine:** ablative absolute: 'the shaft having broken off'. **telum:** i.e. 'the arrow-head', which was embedded in the wound. **auxilioque viam . . . poscit:** 'and demands the means of helping him'. **quae proxima:** supply *est*: 'which is nearest'; all together this means 'demands the quickest possible means of assistance'. Note the fast rhythm of line 388.

Questions

1 In lines 326–330, how does Virgil use sound effects and word order to emphasise the haste and fiery temper of Turnus?

2 In lines 337–340, how does Virgil increase the pathos of the scene?

3 Why does Aeneas 'rage' (*saevit*, line 387)?

4 Why are the rhythms of lines 386 and 388 effective?

ense secent lato vulnus telique latebram
rescindant penitus, seseque in bella remittant.   390
iamque aderat Phoebo ante alios dilectus Iapyx
Iasides, acri quondam cui captus amore
ipse suas artes, sua munera, laetus Apollo
augurium citharamque dabat celeresque sagittas.
ille, ut depositi proferret fata parentis,   395
scire potestates herbarum usumque medendi
maluit et mutas agitare inglorius artes.
stabat acerba fremens ingentem nixus in hastam
Aeneas magno iuvenum et maerentis Iuli
concursu, lacrimis immobilis. ille retorto   400
Paeonium in morem senior succinctus amictu
multa manu medica Phoebique potentibus herbis
nequiquam trepidat, nequiquam spicula dextra
sollicitat prensatque tenaci forcipe ferrum.
nulla viam fortuna regit, nihil auctor Apollo   405
subvenit, et saevus campis magis ac magis horror
crebrescit propiusque malum est.

ensis, -is m.	sword	*mutus, -a, -um*	silent
seco, -are	I cut	*agito, -are*	I practise
latus, -a, -um	broad	*inglorius, -a, -um*	lacking glory
latebra, -ae f.	hiding-place	*acerbus, -a, -um*	bitter
rescindo, -ere	390 I cut open	*fremo, -ere*	I shout out, roar
penitus	deep within		
remitto, -ere	I send back	*ingens, -entis*	huge
adsum, -esse	I am present	*maereo, -ere*	I lament
Phoebus, -i m.	Phoebus (Apollo)	*concursus, -us* m.	400 gathering
ante + acc.	before	*immobilis, -e*	unmoved
diligo, -ere, -legi, -lectus	I love	*retorqueo, -ere, -torsi, -tortus*	I fold over
Iapyx, -ygis m.	Iapyx	*Paeonius, -a, -um*	of Paeon, medicinal
Iasides, -ae m.	descendant of Iasius	*mos, moris* m.	custom
quondam	once	*senior, -ioris*	elderly
amor, -oris m.	love	*succingo, -ere, -cinxi, -cinctus*	I tuck up
ars, artis f.	art, skill	*amictus, -us* m.	garment
munus, -eris n.	gift	*medicus, -a, -um*	healing
laetus, -a, -um	glad, happy	*potens, -entis*	powerful
Apollo, -inis m.	Apollo	*nequiquam*	in vain
augurium, -i n.	prophecy	*trepido, -are*	I bustle about
cithara, -ae f.	cithara, lute	*spiculum, -i* n.	arrow
celer, -eris, -ere	swift	*sollicito, -are*	I disturb
depono, -ere, -posui, -positus	I despair of	*prenso, -are*	I clutch at
profero, -ferre	395 I postpone	*tenax, -acis*	gripping
parens, -entis m.	parent, father	*forceps, -ipis* m.	forceps, tongs
potestas, -atis f.	power	*rego, -ere*	405 I direct
herba, -ae f.	herb	*subvenio, -ire*	I help
usus, -us m.	use	*horror, -oris* m.	horror
medeor, -eri	I heal, remedy	*crebresco, -ere*	I increase
malo, malle	I prefer	*malum, -i* n.	evil, disaster

389–90 **secent, rescindant, mittant:** jussive subjunctives: '(he begs them) to cut . . . and open up . . . and send him'. **teli latebram:** 'the hiding-place of the missile', i.e. the flesh where the arrowhead is buried.

391–2 **Iapyx Iasides:** the healer Iapyx is known from other sources, but Virgil appears to have invented the name of his father (both names suggest the Greek verb meaning 'to heal'). **Phoebo:** dative of the agent; the god Apollo is often referred to as Phoebus.

392–4 The order is *cui Apollo ipse, quondam captus acri amore, laetus dabat suas artes, sua munera, augurium citharamque, celeresque sagittas.* **acri amore:** Apollo appears to have been viewed in mythology as bisexual. **artes, munera:** perhaps tautological; in Greek mythology Apollo was invested with many skills and responsibilities, including the sun, music, archery, prophecy and healing. **dabat:** conative imperfect: 'tried to give'. Note the fast rhythm of line 394, showing Apollo's keenness to reward his lover.

395 **ille:** Iapyx; subject of *maluit*. **proferret fata:** 'postpone the death'. **depositi . . . parentis:** lit. 'of his set-down father'; according to the ancient commentator Servius, people who were desperately ill were at one time put outside their homes; thus *depositi* may be translated as 'despaired of', 'desperately ill' or 'dying'.

396–7 **mutas . . . artes:** 'silent arts'; medicine did not 'speak' to the poets in the same way the other skills of Apollo did; thus a man who practised medicine was *inglorius*. Note the heavy <u>alliteration</u> of *m*.

398–400 **acerba fremens:** 'calling out bitterly'. **magno . . . concursu:** 'in the midst of a large gathering' (ablative of attendant circumstances). **et maerentis Iuli:** 'including the lamenting Iulus'. **lacrimis immobilis:** not 'motionless in tears' but 'unmoved by (their) tears'.

400–403 **ille:** Iapyx, subject of *trepidat*. **retorto . . . succinctus amictu:** 'tucked up with his robe folded over', i.e. 'with his robe hitched up and folded over; it was the custom to pull the robe up over the belt at the waist to free the legs for action. **Paeonium in morem:** 'in the manner of Paeon'; *Paeon* was an epithet of Apollo as healer-god. **multa . . . trepidat:** 'bustles about trying many remedies'. **manu medica:** 'with his healing hand'. **nequiquam:** repeated for emphasis.

403–4 **spicula:** plural for singular. Note the extended <u>chiasmus</u> in these two lines.

405–7 **nulla viam fortuna regit:** 'no good fortune directs his course'; *fortuna* may be good, bad or neutral. **nihil . . . subvenit:** 'gives him no help'. **saevus . . . horror:** either 'the fierce horror of battle' or ' the cruel horror (of panic among the Trojans)'. **campis:** local ablative. **malum:** the disaster of defeat for the Trojans in the absence of their leader.

Questions

1 In lines 389–390, how does Aeneas show his anxiety?

2 Why do you think Virgil gives us the back story of Iapyx?

3 Why did Iapyx choose medicine rather than any of the other gifts?

4 Why is Iapyx described as *inglorius*?

5 Why is Aeneas 'unmoved by the tears' of his fellows?

6 In what two ways does Iapyx try to remove the arrowhead? How does Virgil use word-order and sound to make lines 400–404 particularly effective?

7 In lines 405–407, how does Virgil bring out a sense of failure and doom?

iam pulvere caelum
stare vident: subeunt equites et spicula castris
densa cadunt mediis. it tristis ad aethera clamor
bellantum iuvenum et duro sub Marte cadentum.   410
hic Venus indigno nati concussa dolore
dictamnum genetrix Cretaea carpit ab Ida,
puberibus caulem foliis et flore comantem
purpureo; non illa feris incognita capris
gramina, cum tergo volucres haesere sagittae.   415
hoc Venus obscuro faciem circumdata nimbo
detulit, hoc fusum labris splendentibus amnem
inficit occulte medicans, spargitque salubres
ambrosiae sucos et odoriferam panaceam.
fovit ea vulnus lympha longaevus Iapyx   420
ignorans, subitoque omnis de corpore fugit
quippe dolor, omnis stetit imo vulnere sanguis.
iamque secuta manum nullo cogente sagitta
excidit, atque novae rediere in pristina vires.
'arma citi properate viro! quid statis?' Iapyx   425
conclamat primusque animos accendit in hostem.

pulvis, -eris m.	dust	*circumdo, -dare, -dedi, -datus*	I enclose
subeo, -ire	I approach	*nimbus, -i* m.	cloud
equites, -um m.pl.	cavalry	*defero, -ferre*	I bring down
densus, -a, -um	thick, dense	*labrum, -i* n.	tub
bello, -are	410 I fight	*splendens, -entis*	gleaming
durus, -a, -um	hard, harsh	*amnis, -is* m.	stream, liquid
Venus, -eris f.	Venus	*inficio, -ere*	I mix with
indignus, -a, -um	undeserved	*occultus, -a, -um*	secret
natus, -i m.	son	*medico, -are*	I treat
concutio, -ere, -cussi, -cussus	I shake	*salubris, -e*	health-giving
dictamnum, -i n.	dittany	*ambrosia, -ae* f.	ambrosia
genetrix, -icis f.	mother	*sucus, -i* m.	juice
Cretaeus, -a, -um	Cretan	*odoriferus, -a, -um*	fragrant
carpo, -ere	I pluck	*panacea, -ae* f.	all-heal
Ida, -ae f.	Mt Ida	*foveo, -ere, fovi, fotus*	420 I foment
pubes, -eris	downy	*lympha, -ae* f.	water
caulis, -is m.	stem, stalk	*longaevus, -a, -um*	old
folium, -i n.	leaf	*ignoro, -are*	I do not know
flos, floris m.	flower	*subito*	suddenly
comans, -ntis	hairy	*quippe*	of course
purpureus, -a, -um	purple, red	*sanguis, -inis* m.	blood
ferus, -a, -um	wild	*cogo, -ere*	I force
incognitus, -a, -um	unknown	*excido, -ere*	I fall out
caper, -ri m.	goat	*novus, -a, -um*	new
gramen, -inis n.	415 grass, herb	*redeo, -ire*	I return
tergum, -i n.	back	*pristinus, -a, -um*	former
volucer, -cris, -cre	swift, flying	*citus, -a, -um*	425 quick
haereo, -ere, haesi, haesus	I cling, stick	*propero, -are*	I hasten
obscurus, -a, -um	dark	*conclamo, -are*	I shout
facies, -ei f.	face, form	*accendo, -ere, -ndi, -nsus*	I incite

407–8 pulvere . . . stare: 'standing thick with dust' – an unusual use of *stare*.

408–9 castris . . . mediis: local ablative; note the <u>enclosing word-order</u>.

409–10 bellantum . . . cadentum: the <u>assonance</u> neatly encloses the line.

411–12 hic: 'at this point'. **dictamnum:** the Cretan dittany (*origanum dictamnus*) is a herb that today grows only on the island of Crete; it has long been used as a medicinal herb to cure internal disorders and skin lesions. Virgil invests it with magical properties, as befits its use by a goddess. **genetrix:** added to emphasise the closeness of their relationship and so the depth of her care. **Cretaea . . . ab Ida:** 'from Cretan Ida', as opposed to the Mt Ida near Troy.

413–14 puberibus . . . foliis: the plant has silvery-white leaves covered in fine hairs; note the <u>enclosing word-order</u>. **caulem:** in apposition to *dictamnum*, but may be translated as 'with a stem' or 'its stem'. **puberibus . . . purpureo:** a neat <u>chiasmus</u>.

414–15 incognita: supply *sunt*. **feris . . . capris:** there was a tradition that dittany could dislodge arrows from goats' bodies. **tergo:** *haereo* can take a dative or ablative.

416–17 hoc: the dittany, object of *detulit*. **faciem circumdata:** 'surrounded with respect to her form', and so 'her form enclosed'; for the construction, see note on line 120.

417–18 hoc: 'with this', dependent on *inficit*. **fusum . . . amnem:** 'the stream of liquid they had poured'. **labris:** dative of goal of motion. **medicans:** the idea of this participle is 'giving (the liquid) medicinal potency'.

418–19 ambrosiae: ambrosia was the food of the gods, with special health-giving properties. **panaceam:** probably another mythical plant associated with the gods; it is a Greek word, meaning 'all-heal', and may be thought of as another herb.

420–2 fovit: i.e. Iapyx applied a warm lotion, made up of the mixture, to the wound. **ea . . . lympha:** instrumental ablative. **ignorans:** he did not know the lotion had been added to; note the <u>enjambement</u>, which gives the word extra force. **quippe:** the idea behind this word is 'yes: this really did happen'. **stetit:** 'stood still', i.e. 'stopped flowing'.

423–4 secuta manum: 'having followed (Iapyx's) hand', i.e. 'coming away with his hand'. **nullo cogente:** 'with nothing forcing it', i.e. 'without the need for any force'. **in pristina:** 'to its former level'.

425–6 arma . . . properate: 'bring arms quickly'. **quid statis:** 'why are you standing still?' Note the staccato nature of line 425, showing Iapyx's excitement. **animos:** the minds of the warriors present. **in hostem:** 'against the enemy'.

Questions

1 In lines 407–410, how does Virgil indicate the quickly-growing danger?

2 What three elements does Venus add to the lotion?

3 Why do you think Venus disguises herself?

4 How does Virgil show the effectiveness of the lotion?

5 What is Iapyx's reaction to the sudden cure, and how does he show it?

'non haec humanis opibus, non arte magistra
proveniunt, neque te, Aenea, mea dextera servat:
maior agit deus atque opera ad maiora remittit.'
ille avidus pugnae suras incluserat auro   430
hinc atque hinc oditque moras hastamque coruscat.
postquam habilis lateri clipeus loricaque tergo est,
Ascanium fusis circum complectitur armis
summaque per galeam delibans oscula fatur:
'disce, puer, virtutem ex me verumque laborem,   435
fortunam ex aliis. nunc te mea dextera bello
defensum dabit et magna inter praemia ducet.
tu facito, mox cum matura adoleverit aetas,
sis memor et te animo repetentem exempla tuorum
et pater Aeneas et avunculus excitet Hector.'   440

*Aeneas marshalled his troops and led them out to battle. The Latins and their allies retreated
before their onslaught. Aeneas focused his attention on Turnus alone. Juturna, fearing
for her brother, took the place of his charioteer and drove Turnus all over the battlefield.
Aeneas went in pursuit, but Juturna always kept her brother away from his reach. When a
Latin threw a spear at Aeneas and sliced the crest off his helmet, Aeneas gave up his pursuit
of Turnus and turned his anger upon the rest of the enemy. There followed a mass killing
perpetrated by both Turnus and Aeneas. Aeneas was then prompted to attack the city of
Laurentum directly; he thought razing it to the ground would surely end the war at once.
The Latins were terrified at the sight of their enemies marching to the attack. Queen Amata,
convinced that Turnus must be dead, hanged herself in the palace. Latinus and Lavinia were
grief-stricken. Turnus, who by now had recognised his sister masquerading as his charioteer,
heard from afar the sounds of grief and insisted on rushing to defend the city, despite her
protestations.*

humanus, -a, -um	human	*summus, -a, -um*	the tip of
ops, opis f.	help	*galea, -ae* f.	helmet
magistra, -ae f.	instructress	*delibo, -are*	I taste
provenio, -ire	I arise, happen	*osculum, -i* n.	little mouth
dextera, -ae f.	hand, right	*for, fari, fatus sum*	I speak
	hand	*puer, pueri* m. 435	boy
servo, -are	I save, heal	*virtus, -utis* f.	courage
opus, -eris n.	work, task	*verus, -a, -um*	true
avidus, -a, -um 430	eager	*labor, -oris* m.	work
sura, -ae f.	calf (of the leg)	*defendo, -ere, -fendi, -fensus*	I defend
odi, -isse	I hate	*praemium, -i* n.	prize, reward
mora, -ae f.	delay	*duco, -ere*	I lead
corusco, -are	I brandish	*maturus, -a, -um*	mature
postquam	after	*adolesco, -ere, -evi*	I grow up
habilis, -e	handy	*aetas, -atis* f.	age
latus, -eris n.	side	*memor, -oris*	mindful
clipeus, -i m.	shield	*repeto, -ere*	I recall
lorica, -ae f.	cuirass	*exemplum, -i* n.	example
fundo, -ere, fudi, fusus	I pour	*avunculus, -i* m. 440	uncle
circum	around	*excito, -are*	I rouse, inspire
complector, -i, -plexus sum	I embrace	*Hector, -oris* m.	Hector

427–8 haec: the cure. **humanis opibus, arte magistra:** ablatives of cause or origin. **arte magistra:** 'from the instructress, skill', a Virgilian way of saying 'from any guidance given by my skill'.

429 maior agit deus: not 'a greater god is acting', but 'a greater power, a god, is acting'. **remittit:** supply *te*. **opera ad maiora:** 'to do greater deeds', i.e. fight and win.

430–1 ille: Aeneas. **incluserat:** the pluperfect indicates the speed with which he had armed himself. **auro:** i.e. in golden greaves; these, along with the rest of his armour, had been made for him by the god Vulcan, at the behest of his mother. **hinc atque hinc:** 'on this side and on that', i.e. 'both right and left'. **odit, coruscat:** a return to the historic present to show his impatience; note the <u>chiasmus</u>.

432 habilis . . . clipeus: 'a comfortably-fitting shield'. **lateri, tergo:** a sort of dative of possession; translate as 'when a . . . shield has been made comfortable for his side and a cuirass for his back'; the idea is that the pieces of armour were adjusted until they were comfortable to wear. **lorica:** a cuirass was a combination of breast- and back-plate, fastened together with thongs.

433 fusis circum . . . armis: 'with his armour poured around (him)', i.e. 'throwing his armoured arms around (him)'; *arma* cannot mean 'arms' in the sense of limbs.

434 summaque . . . delibans oscula: a difficult phrase, literally 'tasting the tops of his small lips'; since *oscula* frequently carried a connotation of kissing, the phrase is generally paraphrased as 'lightly kissing his lips'. Whether the diminutive is intended to indicate that Ascanius was still a child is open to question. Clearly the helmet would prevent Aeneas from kissing his son properly.

435–6 verumque laborem: 'true hardship' – the struggle necessary to achieve difficult targets. **fortunam ex aliis:** 'good fortune from others', because Aeneas feels he has been dogged by bad fortune ever since the day of the Greek capture of Troy.

436–7 bello defensum dabit: 'will defend you in war'; Virgil likes to use the perfect participle with *dare* in place of a simple verb.

438–40 tu facito: the emphatic form of the imperative: 'you see to it that . . .', followed by the jussive subjunctive *sis*. **cum matura adoleverit aetas:** 'when your age will have reached maturity'; *matura* is <u>proleptic</u>. **sis memor:** 'be mindful (of what I say)'. **te . . . repetentem:** 'you when you recall'. **tuorum:** 'of your kindred'. **excitet:** to be taken with both subjects: 'let (them) inspire you'. **avunculus . . . Hector:** Ascanius' mother, Creusa, was a sister of Hector, a son of king Priam of Troy and the leader of the Trojan army at Troy; he was killed by Achilles.

Questions

1 What conclusion does Iapyx draw about the cure?

2 How does Aeneas show his impatience to get back to the battle?

3 How does Aeneas show his love for his son?

4 List all the advice given by Aeneas to his son.

5 Why do you think Aeneas gives this advice to his son at this point?

6 Why do you think Aeneas mentions himself and Hector at the end of his speech?

'iam iam fata, soror, superant, absiste morari;   676
quo deus et quo dura vocat Fortuna sequamur.
stat conferre manum Aeneae, stat, quidquid acerbi est,
morte pati, neque me indecorem, germana, videbis
amplius. hunc, oro, sine me furere ante furorem.'   680
dixit et e curru saltum dedit ocius arvis
perque hostes, per tela ruit maestamque sororem
deserit ac rapido cursu media agmina rumpit.
ac veluti montis saxum de vertice praeceps
cum ruit avulsum vento, seu turbidus imber   685
proluit aut annis solvit sublapsa vetustas;
fertur in abruptum magno mons improbus actu
exsultatque solo, silvas armenta virosque
involvens secum: disiecta per agmina Turnus
sic urbis ruit ad muros, ubi plurima fuso   690
sanguine terra madet striduntque hastilibus aurae,
significatque manu et magno simul incipit ore:
'parcite iam, Rutuli, et vos tela inhibite, Latini;
quaecumque est fortuna, mea est; me verius unum
pro vobis foedus luere et decernere ferro.'   695
discessere omnes medii spatiumque dedere.

*As soon as Aeneas heard men shouting Turnus' name, he broke off his attack on the city and
strode in search of his foe. All the warriors set down their arms and sought the best view.*

supero, -are	I prevail	*sublabor, -i, -lapsus sum*	I undermine
moror, -ari, -atus sum	I delay	*vetustas, -atis* f.	old age
confero, -ferre	I meet	*abruptum, -i* n.	headlong fall
quisquis, quidquid	whoever, whatever	*improbus, -a, -um*	enormous
		actus, -us m.	impulse
indecor, -oris	dishonourable	*exsulto, -are*	I bound over
germana, -ae f.	sister	*solum, -i* n.	ground
amplius	680 more, longer	*silva, -ae* f.	wood
oro, -are	I beg	*armentum, -i* n.	herd
furo, -ere	I rage	*involvo, -ere*	I envelop
furor, -oris m.	madness, rage	*disicio, -ere, -ieci, -iectus*	I scatter
ocior, -ius	swifter, swiftly	*murus, -i* m.	690 wall
arvum, -i n.	field	*madeo, -ere*	I am wet
desero, -ere	I abandon, leave	*strido, -ere*	I hiss, whirr
cursus, -us m.	course, run	*hastile, -is* n.	javelin
saxum, -i n.	rock	*aura, -ae* f.	air
vertex, -icis m.	top, summit	*significo, -are*	I signal
praeceps, -cipitis	headlong	*incipio, -ere*	I begin
avello, -ere, -velli, -vulsus	685 I tear off	*parco, -ere*	I spare, stop
seu	whether	*inhibeo, -ere*	I check
turbidus, -a, -um	wild	*meus, -a, -um*	my, mine
imber, -bris m.	rain storm	*luo, -ere*	695 I atone for
proluo, -ere, -lui, -lutus	I wash away	*decerno, -ere*	I decide
annus, -i m.	year		

676 **iam iam:** the doubling reinforces the idea of immediacy. **fata . . . superant:** 'the fates prevail', i.e. they cannot continue to try to put off the fate that awaits him.

677 **sequamur:** 'let us follow', a first person command.

678–80 **stat:** 'it stands fixed', i.e. 'it is my resolve'; the <u>anaphora</u> shows his determination. **quidquid acerbi est:** partitive genitive: 'whatever there is of bitterness (in death)', i.e. 'all the bitterness there is'. **amplius:** the <u>enjambement</u> gives his resolve a finality that cannot be questioned.

680 **hunc . . . furere . . . furorem:** 'to rage this rage', i.e. 'to give vent to this madness'; the cognate accusative gives great force to the idea. Virgil has portrayed Turnus as *furens* and possessed of *furor* throughout the second half of the *Aeneid*. **ante:** adverbial: 'before (I die)'.

681–3 **ocius:** this comparative adverbial form, which lacks a positive, is sometimes used as a positive, as here. **arvis:** dative of goal of motion (= *ad arva*). **rapido cursu:** 'running swiftly' (ablative of manner).

684–9 An extended <u>simile</u> compares Turnus' charge to a falling rock.

684–5 **veluti:** a standard word for introducing a simile, to be taken with *cum*. **montis:** to be taken with *de vertice*.

685–6 **seu . . . aut:** 'whether . . . or if', giving two alternative explanations for the dislodging of the rock. **turbidus imber:** 'torrential rain'. **annis . . . sublapsa vetustas:** 'the long passage of years has undermined it', lit. 'age having undermined (it) with the years'.

687–9 **fertur in abruptum:** 'it is carried into a headlong fall', i.e. 'it is carried down headlong'. **mons:** an example of <u>hyperbole</u>, as it is only a small part of the mountain. **exsultatque solo:** local ablative: 'over the ground'. **silvas armenta:** <u>asyndeton</u>.

689–90 **disiecta . . . agmina:** both armies are 'scattered' because they did not fight in formation. **urbis . . . ad muros:** he runs there because that was where he assumes Aeneas would be.

690–1 **ubi plurima . . . terra madet:** 'where the ground is most wet.' **aurae:** plural for singular.

692 **magno . . . ore:** 'with a mighty shout'. Note the <u>chiasmus</u>.

693 **parcite:** 'spare (the fighting)', and so 'cease fighting'.

694 **quaecumque est fortuna, mea est:** 'whatever the outcome (of the battle) may be, it is mine', i.e. it is solely for him to take responsibility for it.

694–5 The order is *(est) verius me unum luere foedus et decernere ferro pro vobis*. **verius:** 'truer' and so 'fairer', followed by accusative and infinitive. **me unum:** '(for) me alone'. **foedus luere:** 'to atone for the treaty'; whether he means 'to atone for the broken treaty' or 'to atone for having made a treaty' is open to question.

696 **medii:** here 'from the middle'.

Questions

1 What picture of Turnus emerges from his words to his sister?

2 Why do you think he ends his speech (line 680) with *furere furorem*?

3 How does Virgil show Turnus' swiftness of action in lines 681–683?

4 How appropriate is the simile in lines 684–689?

5 How does Virgil add extra detail and force to the simile?

6 What are the main points of Turnus' speech to his men?

7 Which of the two interpretations of *foedus luere* do you prefer, and why?

atque illi, ut vacuo patuerunt aequore campi,   710
procursu rapido coniectis eminus hastis
invadunt Martem clipeis atque aere sonoro.
dat gemitum tellus; tum crebros ensibus ictus
congeminant, fors et virtus miscentur in unum.
ac velut ingenti Sila summove Taburno   715
cum duo conversis inimica in proelia tauri
frontibus incurrunt, pavidi cessere magistri,
stat pecus omne metu mutum, mussantque iuvencae
quis nemori imperitet, quem tota armenta sequantur;
illi inter sese multa vi vulnera miscent   720
cornuaque obnixi infigunt et sanguine largo
colla armosque lavant, gemitu nemus omne remugit:
non aliter Tros Aeneas et Daunius heros
concurrunt clipeis, ingens fragor aethera complet.
Iuppiter ipse duas aequato examine lances   725
sustinet et fata imponit diversa duorum,
quem damnet labor et quo vergat pondere letum.
emicat hic impune putans et corpore toto
alte sublatum consurgit Turnus in ensem
et ferit; exclamant Troes trepidique Latini,   730
arrectaeque amborum acies.

vacuus, -a, -um	710 empty	*armus, -i* m.		shoulder
pateo, -ere, -ui	I lie open	*lavo, -are*		I bathe, drench
aequor, -oris n.	plain	*remugio, -ire*		I resound
procursus, -us m.	charge	*aliter*		differently
conicio, -ere, -ieci, -iectus	I throw	*Tros, Trois* m.		Trojan
eminus	from a distance	*Daunius, -a, -um*		Daunian
invado, -ere	I attack, attempt	*heros, -ois* m.		hero
gemitus, -us m.	groan	*fragor, -oris* m.		crash, din
creber, -bra, -brum	frequent	*compleo, -ere*		I fill
congemino, -are	I double	*aequo, -are*	725 I make equal
fors, fortis f.	chance	*examen, -inis* n.		balance, tongue
velut	715 just like	*lanx, lancis* f.		scale
Sila, -ae f.	Mt Sila	*sustineo, -ere*		I hold up
Taburnus, -i m.	Mt Taburnus	*impono, -ere*		I place on
converto, -ere, -verti, -versus	I turn	*diversus, -a, -um*		different
frons, -ntis f.	forehead	*duo, duae, duo*		two
incurro, -ere	I attack	*damno, -are*		I condemn
pavidus, -a, -um	frightened	*vergo, -ere*		I sink down
magister, -tri m.	herdsman	*pondus, -eris* n.		weight
pecus, -oris n.	herd	*impune*		with impunity
musso, -are	I am uncertain	*puto, -are*		I think, calculate
iuvenca, -ae f.	heifer	*consurgo, -ere*		I rise up
nemus, -oris n.	grove	*ferio, -ire*	730 I strike
imperito, -are + dat.	I rule, command	*exclamo, -are*		I shout out
infigo, -ere	721 I thrust, drive in	*trepidus, -a, -um*		anxious
largus, -a, -um	copious	*arrigo, -ere, -rexi, -rectus*		I rouse
collum, -i n.	neck	*acies, -ei* f.		battle line, army

710 **illi:** Aeneas and Turnus. **ut:** 'when'. **vacuo . . . aequore:** 'with empty level ground'.

711–12 **procursu rapido:** ablative of manner. **coniectis eminus hastis:** in epic single combat, the two opponents first threw their javelins whilst still apart; they then drew their swords and closed for hand-to-hand combat. **invadunt Martem:** 'hasten to make war'. **clipeis atque aere sonoro:** <u>hendiadys</u>: 'with shields and clashing bronze', i.e. 'with the clashing of bronze shields'.

713–14 **dat gemitum tellus:** Virgil personifies the Earth, imagining it reflecting the sounds of the battle. **congeminant:** the <u>enjambement</u> intensifies the image of the sword-blows becoming ever more frequent. **fors et virtus miscentur in unum:** a furious close combat inevitably combines chance and skill and blurs the distinction between them.

715–22 **ac velut . . . cum:** this phrase introduces one of Virgil's longest extended <u>similes</u>.

715 **Sila, Taburno:** local ablatives; these two mountain ranges are in Southern Italy.

716–17 **conversis . . . frontibus:** 'their brows turned to face one another' (ablative absolute). **duo . . . tauri:** earlier in the book Turnus was compared to a bull; here both adversaries are so compared. In epic poetry bulls, like lions, often provide comparisons for heroes. **cessere:** perfect to show that the herdsman have run off before the bulls start fighting.

718–19 **metu mutum, mussant:** an effective combination of <u>alliteration</u> and <u>assonance</u>; there is probably also an element of <u>onomatopoeia</u>. **quis imperitet, quem . . . sequantur:** indirect deliberative questions dependent on *mussant*.

720 **vulnera miscent:** 'trade blows'. Note the combination of slow rhythm and <u>chiastic alliteration</u>, emphasising the duration of the contest.

721–2 **obnixi:** 'thrusting against each other'. **nemus omne:** the mountains are covered in groves of trees, through which the cattle move; here the cattle fill the woodland with their lowing.

723–4 **Daunius heros:** Turnus was the son of Daunus. **fragor:** the clash of shield on shield.

725–6 The image is of weighing the fates of the two men in the pans of a balance; the one whose pan proves heavier is doomed to die. This was a common image in Greek literature. **aequato examine:** the scales, or balance, had two pans suspended from each end of a horizontal beam; a centrally-placed 'tongue' (*examen*) showed when the two pans were exactly in balance. **duas . . . duorum:** note the <u>polyptoton</u> neatly enclosing the image.

727 **quem damnet labor:** indirect question dependent loosely on the previous line: supply 'to see'; *labor* is the struggle of battle. **quo vergat pondere letum:** probably 'on which side death would sink down with its weight' (Williams); some take *quo* with *pondere*: 'with which weight death would sink', where the sense is inferior; whatever the translation, the underlying idea is the same: the sinking of one pan signifies death.

728–31 **hic:** 'at this point'. **emicat:** the subject, *Turnus*, as frequently is delayed to raise suspense. **impune putans:** 'thinking he would be safe'. **consurgit Turnus:** 'Turnus rises'; as he raises his sword high above his head (*alte sublatum . . . ensem*), he throws himself upwards to put his weight behind the downward thrust. Note the slow rhythm of line 729. **et ferit:** the <u>enjambement</u>, combined with the fast dactyl after the previous spondees, and then the sharp pause, gives a dramatic effect. **arrectaeque amborum acies:** supply *sunt: acies* could mean either 'the eyes' or 'the armies'; both would give good sense.

Questions

1 In lines 710–714, how does Virgil make the contest dramatic and exciting?

2 Explain the significance and appropriateness of the simile.

3 How does Virgil show his narrative genius in lines 725–731?

                    at perfidus ensis
frangitur in medioque ardentem deserit ictu,
ni fuga subsidio subeat. fugit ocior Euro
ut capulum ignotum dextramque aspexit inermem.   734

In his haste for battle, Turnus had seized his charioteer's sword instead of his father's
superior weapon. This sword was effective until it came up against armour forged by Vulcan.
Turnus fled, seeking a way out on to the plain, but the Trojans hemmed him in. Aeneas
pursued him and would have caught him if it had not been for his knee injury, which slowed
him down. Aeneas saw the javelin he had thrown stuck in an old tree stump. He tried in vain
to pull it out. While he was doing this, Juturna, disguised again as the charioteer, brought
Turnus his father's sword. When Venus saw this, she angrily plucked Aeneas' javelin from the
stump and gave it to him. The two men faced one another again. Meanwhile Jupiter ordered
his wife to stop hindering the Trojans. He reminded her that it was Aeneas' destiny to be
raised to heaven as a god of Italy. Juno agreed, on the condition that Jupiter promised that,
after peace was declared, the Latins would keep their name and language, and not become
Trojans. Jupiter so promised. Next Jupiter sent a demon disguised as a bird to frighten
Juturna away from her brother. Juturna recognised the demon and understood its purpose.
Sobbing, she said farewell to Turnus and disappeared. The two heroes taunted each other,
before Turnus tried to hurl a mighty boulder at his foe; the demon, however, cast a spell over
his limbs and weakened him.

cunctanti telum Aeneas fatale coruscat,   919
sortitus fortunam oculis. et corpore toto   920
eminus intorquet. murali concita numquam
tormento sic saxa fremunt nec fulmine tanti
dissultant crepitus. volat atri turbinis instar
exitium dirum hasta ferens orasque recludit
loricae et clipei extremos septemplicis orbes;   925
per medium stridens transit femur. incidit ictus
ingens ad terram duplicato poplite Turnus.

perfidus, -a, -um	treacherous	volo, -are	I fly
frango, -ere	I break	ater, atra, atrum	black, dark
fuga, -ae f.	flight	turbo, -inis m.	tornado
subsidium, -i n.	aid, relief	instar + gen.	the size of, like
Eurus, -i m.	East Wind	exitium, -i n.	death
capulus, -i m.	hilt	dirus, -a, -um	dreadful
ignotus, -a, -um	unfamiliar	ora, -ae f.	edge, rim
cunctor, -ari, -atus sum	919 I delay	recludo, -ere	I break apart
fatalis, -e	deadly	extremus, -a, -um	925 the edge of
sortior, -iri, -itus sum	920 I seek	septemplex, -icis	sevenfold
intorqueo, -ere	I hurl	orbis, -is m.	circle, disc
muralis, -e	attacking walls	transeo, -ire	I pass through
concieo, -iere, -ivi, -itus	I hurl	femur, -oris n.	thigh
tormentum, -i n.	siege-weapon	incido, -ere	I fall
fulmen, -inis n.	lightning	ico, -ere, ici, ictus	I strike
dissulto, -are	I burst apart	duplico, -are, -avi, -atus	I double, bend
crepitus, -us m.	crash, crack	poples, -itis m.	knee

731–3 **in medioque:** = *inque medio.* **ardentem:** 'the hot-headed man'. **ni:** = *nisi.* **ni fuga subsidio subeat:** 'if flight had not rendered him assistance'; the present is a vivid alternative to the more normal past; there is a considerable ellipse here, requiring us to insert something along the lines of *periisset,* 'he would have perished'.

733–4 **ut:** 'when'. **capulum ignotum:** because it was not the sword he thought he had.

919–20 **cunctanti:** 'at him as he hesitated' (dative of disadvantage). **telum . . . fatale:** *fatale* means not only 'deadly' but also 'fated', in the sense that the weapon was fated to inflict the fatal wound. Note the slow rhythm, reflecting Turnus' hesitation. **sortitus:** may be translated as present. **fortunam:** 'a lucky opening' for his spear.

920–1 **corpore toto:** 'putting his whole body behind it'.

921–3 The order is *saxa concita murali tormento numquam sic fremunt nec tanti crepitus dissultant fulmine.* This comparison takes the place of the more usual extended <u>similes</u>. **murali . . . tormento:** 'a siege-weapon for attacking (city) walls'; such a weapon would be a *ballista,* which hurled rocks. **dissultant:** a vivid word, suggesting that the sound of a thunderclap bursts outward as if shattered. It is the noise made by the flight of the missile that is being compared with that of the hurled rock and the thunderclap.

923–5 **volat:** the subject is *hasta.* **atri turbinis instar:** 'as mighty as a black tornado'. **orasque recludit loricae:** 'and broke apart the hem of his cuirass', i.e. 'forced its way past the (bottom) edge of his cuirass'. **extremos . . . orbes:** 'the edge of the seven-layered shield'; Virgil has inverted the sequence of the strikes. **clipei . . . septemplicis:** the shield was composed of seven layers of material, the outermost one being of bronze.

926 Note the <u>enclosing word order</u>: *medium . . . femur* encloses the spear.

926–7 **incidit ictus ingens:** note the heavy <u>assonance</u> of *i*; the subject is Turnus. **duplicato poplite:** 'with his knee bent under him'. Note how once again the subject is relegated to the end for maximum impact.

Questions

1 In lines 731–734, what impression are we given of Turnus?

2 From your reading of the passage in English, how far would you say the gods were responsible for the outcome of the combat?

3 How does Virgil make lines 919–921 effective?

4 What comparison does Virgil make in lines 921–923?

5 How effective is this comparison?

6 How does Virgil make lines 923–927 particularly striking?

[Handwritten annotations:]

ABL/DAT

verb   → ABL

NOM → saxa concita [murali tormento]
PREP
numquam sic fremunt] nec tanti → ofsuch
crepitus dissultant fulmine.
↳ABL
clattering   stone shot from the siege-weapon
for attacking city-walls

consurgunt gemitu Rutuli totusque remugit
mons circum et vocem late nemora alta remittunt.
ille humilis supplexque oculos dextramque precantem   930
protendens 'equidem merui nec deprecor' inquit;
'utere sorte tua, miseri te si qua parentis
tangere cura potest, oro (fuit et tibi talis
Anchises genitor) Dauni miserere senectae
et me, seu corpus spoliatum lumine mavis,   935
redde meis, vicisti et victum tendere palmas
Ausonii videre; tua est Lavinia coniunx,
ulterius ne tende odiis.' stetit acer in armis
Aeneas volvens oculos dextramque repressit;
et iam iamque magis cunctantem flectere sermo   940
coeperat, infelix umero cum apparuit alto
balteus et notis fulserunt cingula bullis
Pallantis pueri, victum quem vulnere Turnus
straverat atque umeris inimicum insigne gerebat.
ille, oculis postquam saevi monimenta doloris   945
exuviasque hausit, furiis accensus et ira
terribilis: 'tune hinc spoliis indute meorum
eripiare mihi? Pallas te hoc vulnere, Pallas
immolat et poenam scelerato ex sanguine sumit.'

exitium dirum hasta ferens orasque recludit
Ioicae et clipei extremos septemplicis orbes.

late		far and wide	*flecto, -ere*	940 I persuade
humilis, -e	930	brought low	*sermo, -onis* m.	speech
supplex, -icis		suppliant	*coepi, -isse*	I began
precor, -ari, -atus sum		I pray, beg	*infelix, -icis*	ill-starred
protendo, -ere		I extend	*umerus, -i* m.	shoulder
equidem		I for my part	*appareo, -ere, -ui, -itus*	I appear
mereo, -ere, -ui, -itus		I deserve, earn	*balteus, -i* m.	sword-belt
deprecor, -ari, -atus sum		I plead in excuse	*notus, -a, -um*	familiar
inquam (defective verb)		I say	*fulgeo, -ere*	I gleam
utor, uti, usus sum + abl.		I use, enjoy	*cingulum, -i* n.	belt
sors, sortis f.		lot, fate	*bulla, -ae* f.	stud
tango, -ere		I touch, move	*Pallas, -antis* m.	Pallas
cura, -ae f.		care, sorrow	*sterno, -ere, stravi, stratus*	I strike down
Anchises, -ae m.		Anchises	*insigne, -is* n.	badge
genitor, -oris m.		father	*monimentum, -i* n.	945 reminder
Daunus, -i m.		Daunus	*exuviae, -arum* f.pl.	spoils
misereor, -eri, -itus sum + gen.		I pity	*haurio, -ire, hausi, haustus*	I drink in
senecta, -ae f.		old age	*furia, -ae* f.	madness, fury
spolio, -are, -avi, -atus	935	I despoil	*terribilis, -e*	terrible
malo, malle		I prefer	*spolia, -orum* n.pl.	spoils
reddo, -ere		I give back	*indutus, -a, -um*	dressed
palma, -ae f.		hand	*immolo, -are*	I sacrifice
coniunx, -iugis f.		wife	*poena, -ae* f.	punishment
ulterius		further	*sceleratus, -a, -um*	accursed
odium, -i n.		hatred	*sumo, -ere*	I take, exact
reprimo, -ere, -essi, -essus		I check		

928–9 Note the heavy <u>assonance</u> of *u*, reinforced by the <u>onomatopoeic</u> *remugit*. Even the woods and mountains take note of and respond to the human tragedy. **vocem:** sound.

930–1 **ille:** Turnus. **humilis supplexque:** the mighty Turnus has been brought as low as could be. **oculos . . . protendens:** 'extending his eyes', i.e. 'raising his eyes'; this use of a verb with two objects and a slightly different meaning with each is an example of <u>zeugma</u>. **precantem:** 'in entreaty'. **merui:** 'I have earned (this fate)'; he acknowledges that it was his choice to fight, and so accepts the outcome. **nec deprecor:** 'nor do I make any excuses'.

932 **utere sorte tua:** 'enjoy your (good) fortune'.

932–3 **si qua . . . parentis . . . cura:** 'if any sorrow of a parent'. **miseri:** promoted for emphasis.

933–4 **et:** 'also'. **talis:** 'of such a kind', i.e. old and sorrowful. **Anchises:** Aeneas' father played a significant role in the first half of the *Aeneid*, but died when in Sicily (end of Book III).

934–6 **Dauni:** Turnus' father, who is still alive. **et me, seu corpus:** 'and (return) me, or my body if (you prefer)'. **spoliatum lumine:** 'despoiled of life'. **meis:** 'to my people'.

936–7 **victum tendere palmas:** 'the defeated one hold out his hands (in acknowledgement of his defeat)'. Thus no one can question the outcome of the fight or Turnus' complete loss of status. **videre:** = *viderunt*.

937–8 **Lavinia:** see lines 192–3n. **ulterius ne tende odiis:** 'do not proceed further with your hatreds'.

938–9 **stetit acer in armis Aeneas:** note the huge contrast with *ille humilis supplexque* (line 930). **volvens oculos:** 'rolling his eyes', i.e. 'shifting his gaze around', indicating his hesitation.

940–1 **iam iamque:** the repetition indicates just how close Aeneas came to reaching a decision. **magis:** to be taken with *cunctantem*: 'as he hesitated more and more'.

941–3 **cum:** to be taken first; the following indicative shows this is an 'inverse *cum*' construction. **infelix . . . balteus:** 'the ill-starred sword-belt'; this was the sword-belt that Turnus had stripped from the body of the young Pallas after killing him (Book X.495–6). **umero . . . alto:** local ablative. **apparuit:** 'appeared', i.e. 'met his gaze'. **cingula:** i.e. the *balteus*. **notis . . . bullis:** in Book X.497–8, Virgil described the decoration on the belt, which would have been very familiar to Aeneas. **pueri:** probably no more than 'young', as Pallas had commanded his father's forces; it is added her to increase the pathos.

943–4 **quem:** i.e. Pallas. **atque:** supply 'which' (the sword-belt); this clause is not properly attached to the preceding clause. **inimicum insigne:** 'as a badge taken from his enemy'.

945–7 **ille:** Aeneas. **oculis postquam . . . hausit:** 'after he had drunk in with his eyes', i.e. 'after he had feasted his eyes upon'. **monimenta doloris:** 'a reminder of his grief'. **furiis, ira:** instrumental ablatives. **terribilis:** supply *dixit*.

947–8 **tune . . . eripiare** (= *eripiaris*): 'are you to be snatched from me'; the subjunctive is for a deliberative question. **mihi:** verbs meaning to remove or take away generally take a dative (of disadvantage). **spoliis indute meorum:** 'dressed in the spoils of my friends'; *indute* is vocative.

948–9 **Pallas . . . Pallas:** as he says the name he transfixes Turnus with his sword. **immolat:** a religious word, indicating that killing Turnus was a religious duty. **poenam . . . sumit:** Aeneas' words indicate that he is killing Turnus for revenge.

Questions

1 How does Turnus try to persuade Aeneas? How well-chosen are his arguments?

2 How nearly does Turnus succeed?

3 Why does the sight of the sword-belt have such a profound effect upon Aeneas?

4 What impression do you have of Aeneas from lines 945–949?

hoc dicens ferrum adverso sub pectore condit   950
fervidus. ast illi solvuntur frigore membra
vitaque cum gemitu fugit indignata sub umbras.

adversus, -a, -um	950 turned towards	*membrum, -i* n.	limb
condo, -ere	I plunge	*vita, -ae* f.	life
ast	but	*indignor, -ari, -atus sum*	I complain
frigus, -oris n.	cold		

950–1 **fervidus:** note the enjambement; Aeneas was 'boiling' with anger. Note also the slow rhythm.
951–2 **illi:** Turnus; dative of disadvantage but translatable as possessive with *membra*.
frigore: note the strong contrast with *fervidus*, introduced by *ast illi*. **vita:** 'life', i.e. 'soul'. **sub umbras:** i.e. down into the underworld. The rhythm of line 952 is fast, apart from *indignata*.

Questions

1 How does Virgil use contrast in these three lines? How effective is it?

2 How does Virgil make good use of rhythm in these lines?

3 Do you think Turnus deserves to die?

4 Is Aeneas justified in killing Turnus?

5 Did you change your opinion of Aeneas at the end?

6 How satisfying do you find this conclusion to the *Aeneid*?

General questions (covering the whole Aeneid)

1 Aeneas is frequently described as *pius*. What qualities does this word imply? Do you think Aeneas possessed these qualities?

2 How would you assess the character of Aeneas? Does he change during the course of the *Aeneid*?

3 How important are female characters in the *Aeneid*?

4 'It is the gods who determine the events of the *Aeneid*.' Do you agree?

5 How important is prophecy in the *Aeneid*?

6 Do you think Virgil liked and glorified warfare?

7 How different are Virgil's heroes from those of Homer?

8 Virgil wanted to glorify Rome, its history and its rulers. How did he do this? Was he successful?

9 Is Virgil a mere shadow of Homer, or does he add depth to him?

10 Would you agree that the *Aeneid* is one of the world's greatest poems in any language?

11 What have you enjoyed most in the *Aeneid*? What have you not enjoyed?

12 What do you think the *Aeneid* has to offer a 21st-century reader?

Word list

Abaris, -is m. — Abaris
Abas, -antis m. — Abas
abdo, -ere — I hide
abeo, -ire — I depart
abies, -etis f. — fir, pine, fir-wood
abitus, -us m. — departure, way out
abiuro, -are, -avi, -atus — I deny on oath
abluo, -ere, -lui, -lutus — I wash away
abnego, -are — I deny, refuse
abnuo, -ere, -nui, -nutus — I refuse to allow
abolesco, -ere — I decay, vanish
abrumpo, -ere, -rupi, -ruptus — I break
abruptum, -i n. — headlong fall
abscessus, -us m. — withdrawal
absens, -entis — absent
absisto, -ere — I depart, give up, stop, fly off, cease
abstraho, -ere, -traxi, -tractus — I drag out
absum, -esse — I am absent, I am away
abunde — in abundance
Acca, -ae f. — Acca
accelero, -are — I hurry
accendo, -ere, -cendi, -census — I set on fire, inflame, light, incite
accessus, -us m. — approach
accido, -ere, -cidi, -cisus — I use up
accingo, -ere — I arm
accingo, -ere, -cinxi, -cinctus — I fix in place
accio, -ire — I summon
accipio, -ere, -cepi, -ceptus — I welcome, receive, hear
accolo, -ere — I live near
acer, acris, acre — sharp, bitter, fierce, valiant, keen
acerbus, -a, -um — bitter
acervus, -i m. — pile, heap
Achates, -ae m. — Achates
Acheron, -ontis m. (acc. -a) — river Acheron
Achilles, -is m. — Achilles
acies, -ei f. — battle, army, battle line
Acoetes, -is m. — Acoetes
Actius, -a, -um — of Actium
actus, -us m. — impulse
acuo, -ere — I sharpen
acutus, -a, -um — sharp
addenseo, -ere — I close ranks
addo, -ere, -didi, -ditus — I add

adduco, -ere, -duxi, -ductus — I induce, draw to
adeo — indeed, so much
adeo, -ire — I approach, go to
adfero, -ferre, attuli, adlatus — I bring to
adfigo, -ere, -fixi, -fixus — I attach, fix, nail (to)
adfor, -fari, -fatus sum — I address
adgredior, -i, -gressus sum — I attack
adhibeo, -ere — I add
adhuc — still
adigo, -ere, -egi, -actus — I drive, impel
aditus, -us m. — entrance, approach
adiungo, -ere, -iunxi, -iunctus — I join to, join, attach, unite
adlabor, -i, -lapsus sum — I glide, roll towards, fly towards
adloquor, -i, -locutus sum — I speak to, address
adludo, -ere — I jest
admisceo, -ere — I mingle, mix
admitto, -ere — I admit
admoneo, -ere — I advise, point out
adnitor, -i, -nixus sum — I lean upon
adnuo, -ere — I am favourable, grant
adoleo, -ere — I sacrifice at
adolesco, -ere, -evi — I grow up
adoreus, -a, -um — made of spelt
adorior, -iri, -ortus sum — I venture upon
adsensus, -us m. — agreement
adsiduus, -a, -um — constant
adsisto, -ere — I stand near
adsuesco, -ere, -suevi, -suetus — I accustom, become used
adsum, adesse — I am present, here
adsurgo, -ere — I rise up
advena, -ae m/f. — foreign
advenio, -ire — I arrive, come
advento, -are — I arrive, approach
adventus, -us m. — arrival
adversus, -a, -um — facing, opposite, against, turned towards
adverto, -ere — I pay attention, direct
advoco, -are — I call upon
advolo, -are — I rush towards
adytum, -i n. — shrine, sanctuary
aeger, aegra, aegrum — sick, sorrowful
aemulus, -a, -um + dat. — rivalling, equalling

Aeneades, -ae m.	follower of Aeneas, Trojan	*Amazon, -onis* f.	Amazon
Aeneas, -ae m. (acc. *-an*)	Aeneas	*ambio, -ire, -ii, -itus*	I encircle
Aeneius, -a, -um	of Aeneas	*ambo, ambae, ambo*	both
aënus, -a, -um	bronze	*ambrosia, -ae* f.	ambrosia
aequalis, -e	of the same age	*amens, -entis*	out of his mind, mad
aequo, -are	I equal, make equal, make level	*amicitia, -ae* f.	friendship
aequor, -oris n.	sea, water, plain, flat expanse	*amictus, -us* m.	garment
		amicus, -a, -um	friendly
aequus, -a, -um	equal, fair, level, just	*amicus, -i* m.	friend
		amnis, -is m.	river, tributary, stream, liquid
aeratus -a, -um	bronze-plated, bronze-clad	*amor, -oris* m.	love
		Amphytrionides, -ae m.	Hercules
aërius, -a, -um	lofty	*amplector, -i, -plexus sum*	I embrace
aes, aeris n.	bronze	*amplius*	more, longer
aestuo, -are	I seethe	*an*	or
aetas, aetatis f.	age, time	*Anchises, -ae* m.	Anchises
aeternus, -a, -um	eternal, everlasting	*Anchisiades, -ae* m.	son of Anchises
aether, -eris (acc. *-era*) m.	air	*ango, -ere*	I strangle
aetherius, -a, -um	of the upper world	*anguis, -is* m.	snake
Aetnaeus, -a, -um	of Mt Etna	*anima, -ae* f.	spirit, life, soul, breath
aevum, -i n.	age, time, life-time		
age, agite	come now	*animal, -alis* n.	animal
ager, agri m.	field, land	*animus, -i* m.	mind, spirit, fury, courage, heart
agger, -eris m.	rampart		
agito, -are	I urge, spend (time), chase, practise	*annus, -i* m.	year
		ante	ahead, forwards, before, first, beforehand, previously
agmen, -inis n.	army, column, line of men		
agnosco, -ere	I recognise	*ante* + acc.	before
agnus, -i m.	lamb	*antiquus, -a, -um*	ancient
ago, agere, egi, actus	I thrust, come on, drive, act, harass	*antrum, -i* n.	cave
		aperio, -ire, aperui, apertus	I open, reveal
agrestis, -e	wild, rustic	*apertus, -a, -um*	open
Agyllinus, -a, -um	of Agylla	*apex, -icis* m.	top, crown
aio (defective verb)	I say	*apis, -is* f.	bee
ala, -ae f.	wing	*Apollo, -inis* m.	Apollo
alacer, alacris, alacre	eager, keen	*appareo, -ere, -ui*	I appear
Alba, -ae f.	Alba Longa	*apparo, -are*	I prepare
albus, -a, -um	white	*appello, -ere, -puli, -pulsus*	I bring (to)
Alcides, -ae m.	Hercules	*apto, -are*	I hang, fit
aliquando	at last	*aptus, -a, -um*	studded (with)
aliquis, -quid	someone, something	*aqua, -ae* f.	water
		ara, arae f.	altar
aliter	differently	*aratrum, -i* n.	plough
alius, -a, -ud	other	*arbos, -oris* f.	tree
Allecto (acc. *-o*) f.	Allecto	*Arcades, -um* m.pl.	Arcadians
almus, -a, -um	kindly	*Arcadia, -ae* f.	Arcadia
Alpes, -ium f.pl.	the Alps	*arcanus, -a, -um*	secret
altaria, -ium n.pl.	altar(s)	*Arcas, -adis*	Arcadian
alter, -era, -erum	a second, other, the one, the other	*arceo, -ere*	I keep ... away
		arcesso, -ere	I summon
alternus, -a, -um	each in turn, every other	*arcus, -us* m.	bow
		Ardea, -ae f.	Ardea
altus, -a, -um	high, deep, glorious	*ardens, -entis*	fiery, gleaming
		ardeo, -ere	I burn, blaze, am on fire
alumnus, -i m.	pupil, ward		
alveus, -i m.	river bed	*ardor, -oris* m.	keenness, heat
Amastrus, -i m.	Amastrus	*arduus, -a, -um*	steep, towering, high, high up
Amata, -ae f.	Amata		
Amathus, -untis f.	Amathus	*argentum, -i* n.	silver

Argi, -orum m.pl.	Argos	*Ausonius, -a, -um*	Italian
Argolicus, -a, -um	Greek	*auspicium, -i* n.	omen
arma, -orum n.pl.	arms, weapons, war	*aut*	or
		aut . . . aut	either . . . or
armentum, -i n.	herd, cattle	*auxilium, -i* n.	help
armiger, -eri m.	armour-bearer	*aveho, -ere, avexi, avectus*	I carry away
armipotens, -entis	powerful in arms	*avello, -ere, avelli, avulsus*	I tear off, tear away
armo, -are, -avi, -atus	I arm		
armus, -i m.	shoulder	*Aventinus, -i* m.	the Aventine Hill
arrigo, -ere, -rexi, -rectus	I set on end, raise, rouse	*averto, -ere, averti, aversus*	I lead away, turn aside
Arruns, -ntis m.	Arruns	*avidus, -a, -um*	eager
ars, artis f.	art, skill	*avius, -a, -um*	pathless
artifex, -icis m.	craftsman	*avunculus, -i* m.	uncle
artus, -us m.	limb	*avus, -i* m.	grandfather
arvum, -i n.	field, land	*Bacchus, -i* m.	Bacchus
arx, arcis f.	citadel	*balatus, -us* m.	bleating
Ascanius, -i m.	Ascanius, Iulus	*balteus, -i* m.	sword-belt
ascendo, -ere, -cendi, -census	I climb into, onto	*barathrum, -i* n.	abyss
Asilas, -ae m.	Asilas	*bellator, -oris* m.	warrior
aspecto, -are	I observe	*bello, -are*	I fight
asper, -era, -erum	cruel, harsh, violent, savage	*Bellona, -ae* f.	Bellona
		bellum, -i n.	war
aspernor, -ari, -atus sum	I reject	*bibo, -ere, bibi*	I drink
aspicio, -ere	I observe, see, look at, look upon, watch, behold	*biiugi, -orum* m.pl.	two-horse chariot
		bipatens, -entis	with double doors
aspiro, -are	I breathe into	*bipennis, -e*	two-edged
Assaracus, -i m.	Assaracus	*bipennis, -is* f.	two-edged axe
ast	but	*bis*	twice
asto, -are	I stand, stand on	*bivius, -a, -um*	forking
astrum, -i n.	star	*bonus, -a, -um*	good
atavus, -i m.	ancestor	*bos, bovis* m/f.	bull, cow, ox
ater, atra, atrum	black, dark	*bracchium, -i* n.	arm, limb
atrium, -i n.	hall	*breviter*	briefly
atrox, -ocis	fierce	*bulla, -ae* f.	stud
attactus, -us m.	touch	*bustum, -i* n.	lit pyre
attollo, -ere	I lift up, raise, raise up	*buxum, -i* n.	boxwood
		buxus, -i f.	boxwood
attonitus, -a, -um	astonished	*Cacus, -i* m.	Cacus
attorqueo, -ere	I tilt upwards	*cadaver, -eris* n.	corpse
auctor, -oris m/f.	person responsible, instigator, master, proposer	*cado, -ere, cecidi, casus*	I fall, set, turn out
		caecus, -a, -um	blind, unseen, dark
		caedes, -is f.	slaughter
audax, -acis	rash, bold, daring	*caedo, -ere, cecidi, caesus*	I slaughter
audeo, -ere	I dare	*caelestis, -is* m.	god, heavenly god
aufero, -ferre, abstuli, ablatus	I set aside, remove, steal, take away	*caelicola, -ae* m.	god
		caelo, -are, -avi, -atus	I engrave
augeo, -ere	I increase, pile up	*caelum, -i* n.	sky, heaven
augur, -uris m.	augur	*caeruleus, -a, -um*	dark blue
augurium, -i n.	augury, prophecy	*caerulus, -a, -um*	dark blue
auguro, -are	I prophesy	*Caesar, -aris* m.	Caesar
Augustus, -i m.	Augustus	*Caicus, -i* m.	Caicus
aura, -ae f.	air, breeze	*calco, -are*	I trample
auratus, -a, -um	gilded	*calidus, -a, -um*	warm, hot
aureus, -a, -um	golden	*caligo, -inis* f.	fog, murk, gloom, mist
auriga, -ae m.	charioteer		
auris, -is f.	ear	*callis, -is* m.	track, clearing
Aurora, -ae f.	Dawn	*Camilla, -ae* f.	Camilla
aurum, -i n.	gold	*campus, -i* m.	plain, open ground
Ausonia, -ae f.	Ausonia, S. Italy	*candens, -entis*	dazzling, dazzling white
Ausonidae, -arum m.pl.	peoples of Italy		
Ausonii, -orum m.pl.	Italians	*candidus, -a, -um*	white

cano, -ere	I sing, prophesy, utter	*circuitus, -us* m.	way round
canus, -a, -um	ancient	*circulus, -i* m.	circlet, ring
caper, -ri m.	goat	*circum*	around
capesso, -ere	I take over, make for	*circum* + acc.	around
		circumdo, -dare, -dedi, -datus	I surround, enclose
capio, -ere, cepi, captus	I take, capture	*circumsisto, -ere*	I surround
Capitolium, -i n.	Capitoline Hill	*Cisseis, -idis* f.	Hecuba
capulus, -i m.	hilt	*cithara, -ae* f.	cithara, lute
caput, -itis n.	head	*citus, -a, -um*	quick
cardo, -inis m.	hinge	*civis, -is* m.	citizen
careo, -ere + abl.	I lack	*clamo, -are*	I shout
carina, -ae f.	hull, ship	*clamor, -oris* m.	shout, shouting, lowing
carmen, -inis n.	poem		
carpo, -ere	I crop, pluck	*clangor, -oris* m.	strident sound
carus, -a, -um	dear	*clarus, -a, -um*	famous
Cassandra, -ae f.	Cassandra	*classis, -is* f.	fleet
castra, -orum n.pl.	camp	*claudo, -ere, clausi, clausus*	I shut in, close
castus, -a, -um	unblemished	*clavus, -i* m.	tiller, rudder
casus, -us m.	chance, misfortune	*clipeus, -i* m.	shield
catena, -ae f.	chain	*Clonus, -i* m.	Clonus
caterva, -ae f.	crowd, band	*Clytius, -i* m.	Clytius
cauda, -ae f.	tail	*coeo, -ire*	I come together
caulae, -arum f.pl.	enclosure	*coepi, -isse*	I began
caulis, -is m.	stem, stalk	*coeptum, -i* n.	undertaking
causa, -ae f.	cause, reason	*coerceo, -ere*	I enclose, command
cautus, -a, -um	cautious	*cognomen, -inis* n.	name
caverna, -ae f.	cave, cavern	*cogo, -ere, coegi, coactus*	I gather, force
cavus, -a, -um	hollow	*cohibeo, -ere*	I confine, restrain
cedo, -ere, cessi, cessus	I turn out well, accrue to, withdraw, give way	*cohors, -ortis* f.	cohort, squadron
		colligo, -ere, -legi, -lectus	I gather
		collis, -is m.	hill
		collum, -i n.	neck
cedrus, -i f.	cedar tree	*colonus, -i* m.	settler
celer, -eris, -ere	swift	*color, -oris* m.	colour
celero, -are	I speed up	*coma, -ae* f.	foliage, hair
celo, -are	I conceal, hide	*comans, -ntis*	hairy
celsus, -a, -um	high, lofty	*comes, -itis* m/f.	companion
centum	one hundred	*cometes, -ae* m.	comet
Cerealis, -e	of Ceres, corn	*comito, -are, -avi, -atus*	I accompany
Ceres, Cereris f.	Ceres, corn	*comitor, -ari, -atus sum*	I accompany
cerno, -ere	I see, watch	*comminus*	hand to hand
certamen, -inis n.	struggle, contest	*commisceo, -ere, -miscui, -mixtus*	I mix together
certatim	eagerly		
certo, -are	I compete, fight	*committo, -ere*	I join (battle), entrust
certus, -a, -um	certain, definite, sure	*communis, -e*	shared
cervix, -icis f.	neck	*compello, -are*	I address
cesso, -are	I stop, cease	*complector, -i, -plexus sum*	I embrace
ceteri, -ae, -a	the rest (of)	*compleo, -ere*	I fill
ceu	just like	*complexus, -us* m.	embrace
chalybs, -ibis m.	steel	*compono, -ere*	I fix together, put together, settle, agree
chorea, -ae f.	dance		
chorus, -i m.	band		
Chromis, -is (acc. *-im*)	Chromis	*comprendo, -ere*	I catch
cieo, -ere	I produce, stir up, summon	*concedo, -ere, -cessi, -cessus*	I withdraw, subside, grant
cingo, -ere, cinxi, cinctus	I surround, ring, man	*concieo, -iere, -ivi, -itus*	I hurl
		concilio, -are	I win over
cingulum, -i n.	belt	*concilium, -i* n.	council
cinis, -eris m.	ash	*concipio, -ere, -cepi, -ceptus*	I draw up, take on
circa	round about	*conclamo, -are*	I shout
circueo, -ire	I circle round	*concolor, -oris*	of the same colour

concurro, -ere	I meet, join battle (with), rush together	*corpus, -oris* n.	body
concursus, -us m.	gathering	*corripio, -ere, -ripui, -reptus*	I seize
concutio, -ere, -cussi, -cussus	I shake	*corruo, -ere*	I collapse
condensus, -a, -um	packed together	*corusco, -are*	I brandish
condo, -ere	I found, hide, bury, enclose, plunge	*costa, -ae* f.	rib
confero, -ferre, -tuli, -latus	I join together, meet, fight, bring together	*crastinus, -a, -um*	tomorrow's
		crater, -eris m. (acc. *-era*)	mixing bowl
		cratera, -ae f.	mixing bowl
		creber, -bra, -brum	numerous, frequent
confestim	hastily	*crebresco, -ere*	I increase
conficio, -ere	I destroy	*credo, -ere* + dat.	I trust, entrust
confodio, -ere, -fodi, -fossus	I stab through	*cremo, -are*	I consume by fire, cremate
confugio, -ere	I seek refuge	*crepito, -are*	I crackle
confundo, -ere, -fudi, -fusus	I jumble together	*crepitus, -us* m.	crash, crack
congemino, -are	I double	*Cretaeus, -a, -um*	Cretan
conicio, -ere, -ieci, -iectus	I throw	*crimen, -inis* n.	crime, charge, accusation
coniugium, -i n.	marriage	*crinis, -is* m.	hair
coniungo, -ere	I join together	*crista, -ae* f.	crest
coniunx, -iugis m/f.	husband, wife	*crudelis, -e*	cruel
conlabor, -i, -lapsus sum	I fall, sink down	*cruentus, -a, -um*	blood-stained
conluceo, -ere	I shine brightly	*cruor, -oris* m.	spilt blood
conor, -ari, -atus sum	I try	*crustum, -i* n.	pastry
conscendo, -ere, -scendi, -scensus	I ascend to, board	*cubile, -is* n.	bed
		cultum, -i n.	farmland
conscius, -a, -um	aware	*cum* + abl.	with
consero, -ere	I join	*cumulo, -are*	I pile up, heap up
consido, -ere, -sedi, -sessus	I settle, sit down	*cuncti, -ae, -a*	all
consilium, -i n.	consultation, plan	*cunctor, -ari, -atus sum*	I hesitate, delay
consisto, -ere, -stiti	I stop, halt	*cunctus, -a, -um*	all
conspectus, -us m.	sight	*cuneus, -i* m.	wedge
conspicio, -ere	I see	*cupido, -inis* f.	desire
constituo, -ere, -ui, -utus	I construct, establish	*cupio, -ere*	I desire, wish
consulo, -ere	I keep watch	*cura, -ae* f.	anxiety, care, duty, sorrow, concern
consumo, -ere, -sumpsi, -sumptus	I consume		
consurgo, -ere	I rise up, rise together	*currus, -us* m.	chariot
		cursus, -us m.	course, running, run
contentus, -a, -um	content		
continuo	at once	*curvatus, -a, -um*	curved
contorqueo, -ere, -torsi, -tortus	I brandish, throw	*curvus, -a, -um*	curved
contra	on the other hand, opposed, in reply, in return, against, to meet them, on the other hand	*cuspis, -idis* f.	point, spear, spear-point
		custodio, -ire, -ivi, -itus	I guard
		custos, -odis m.	guard, sentry
	against	*Cybebe, -es* f.	Cybele
contra + acc.	against	*Cyclops, -opis* m.	Cyclops
contristo, -are	I sadden	*Cymodocea, -ae* f.	Cymodocea
conubium, -i n.	marriage	*Cythera, -ae* f.	Cythera
convenio, -ire	I come together	*damno, -are*	I condemn
convenit, -ire	it is agreed	*daps, dapis* f.	meal
converto, -ere, -verti, -versus	I turn, direct	*Dardania, -ae* f.	Troy
convexus, -a, -um	arched	*Dardanidae, -arum* m.pl.	Trojans
copia, -ae f.	opportunity	*Dardanius, -a, -um*	Trojan
coquo, -ere	I torment	*Dardanus, -a, -um*	Trojan
cor, cordis n.	heart, pleasure	*Daunius, -a, -um*	Daunian
coram	face to face	*Daunus, -i* m.	Daunus
cornu, -us n.	horn	*dea, -ae* f.	goddess
corona, -ae f.	garland, crown, ring, cordon	*debeo, -ere, -ui, -itus*	I owe
		decerno, -ere	I decide
corono, -are	I surround	*decet, -ere, -uit*	it is proper, right

decoro, -are	I honour	*discessus, -us* m	departure
decorus, -a, -um	adorned, decorated, ornate	*disco, -ere*	I learn
		discordia, -ae f.	discord, strife
decurro, -ere, -curri, -cursus	I march	*discrepo, -are*	I differ
decus, -oris n.	ornament, honour, glory	*discrimen, -inis* n.	distinction, separation
defendo, -ere, -fendi, -fensus	I defend	*discrimino, -are*	I distinguish
defero, -re	I bring down	*disicio, -ere, -ieci, -iectus*	I scatter
defessus, -a, -um	weary	*disiectus, -a, -um*	split off
deficio, -ere	I die down	*dissulto, -are*	I burst apart, leap apart
defigo, -ere	I plant, fix		
defluo, -ere, -fluxi, -fluxus	I sweep down	*diu*	for a long time
dehisco, -ere	I gape wide	*dius, -a, -um*	godlike
deicio, -ere, -ieci, -iectus	I let fall, cast down	*diva, -ae* f.	goddess
delabor, -i, -lapsus sum	I glide down	*diversus, -a, -um*	different, in different directions
delibo, -are	I taste		
deligo, -ere, -legi, -lectus	I choose		
delubrum, -i n.	shrine	*dives, -itis*	rich
demens, -entis	mad	*divido, -ere*	I divide
demitto, -ere, -misi, -missus	I drop	*divinus, -a, -um*	divine
Demophoon, -ntis (acc. *-nta*)	Demophoon	*divortium, -i* n.	fork in the path
demum	at last	*divus, -i* m.	god
dens, dentis m.	tooth	*do, dare, dedi, datus*	I give, appoint
denseo, -ere	I make thick	*doceo, -ere*	I teach, tell of
densus, -a, -um	dense, thick	*doctus, -a, -um*	skilled
denus, -a, -um	ten	*dolor, -oris* m.	pain, grief, anger, rage, sorrow
depello, -ere	I drive away		
depono, -ere, -posui, -positus	I despair of, lay down	*dolus, -i* m.	trickery
		domina, -ae f.	mistress
deprecor, -ari, -atus sum	I plead in excuse	*dominor, -ari, -atus sum*	I reign, rule
deprendo, -ere, -ndi, -nsus	I catch, catch unawares	*dominus, -i* m.	master
		domitor, -oris m.	tamer
depromo, -ere	I draw out	*domus, -us* f.	house, home
derigesco, -ere, -rigui	I become fixed	*donec*	until
derigo, -ere	I aim	*dono, -are*	I give
deripio, -ere, -ripui, -reptus	I strip, pull off, pull out	*donum, -i* n.	gift
		dorsum, -i n.	back, ridge, rock
desero, -ere, -serui, -sertus	I abandon, leave	*dos, dotis* f.	dowry
deserta, -orum n.pl.	deserted areas	*dotalis, -e*	given as a dowry
desertus, -a, -um	abandoned	*doto, -are*	I give as dowry
desilio, -ire, -silui, -sultus	I jump down	*Drances, -is* m.	Drances
desisto, -ere	I stand down	*dubito, -are*	I consider
desum, -esse	I am lacking	*duco, -ere*	I lead, draw
desuper	from above	*ductor, -oris* m.	leader
detego, -ere, -texi, -tectus	I reveal, uncover	*dulcedo, -inis* f.	sweetness
detorqueo, -ere	I turn aside	*dumus, -i* m.	thicket
deus, -i m.	god	*duo, duae, duo*	two
devinco, -ere, -vici, -victus	I win	*duplico, -are, -avi, -atus*	I double, bend
dext(e)ra, -ae f.	right hand, hand on the right	*durus, -a, -um*	hard, harsh
dexter, -tra, -trum		*dux, ducis* m.	leader
dicio, -onis f.	power	*ebur, eburis* n.	ivory
dico, -ere, dixi, dictus	I say, tell (of)	*ecce*	look! see! behold!
dictamnum, -i n.	dittany	*ecquis, -quae, -quid*	any one?
dictum, -i n.	word	*edo, -ere*	I eat
dies, diei m/f.	day, daylight	*edoceo, -ere*	I inform
diligo, -ere, -legi, -lectus	I love	*effero, efferre, extuli, elatus*	I raise, raise up, lift, bring out
diluvium, -i n.	flood		
dimetior, -iri, -mensus sum	I measure out	*efferus, -a, -um*	savage
dimitto, -ere	I send away	*effetus, -a, -um*	worn out
diripio, -ere, -ripui, -reptus	I plunder	*effigies, -ei* f.	statue
dirus, -a, -um	dreadful	*efflo, -are*	I breathe out
discedo, -ere, -cessi, -cessus	I depart, leave	*effor, -fari, -fatus sum*	I speak out
discerpo, -ere	I scatter	*effugio, -ere*	I escape

effulgeo, -ere, -fulsi	I blaze out, shine	*excio, -ire, -ivi, -itus*	I rouse
effundo, -ere, -fudi, -fusus	I pour out, pour forth	*excipio, -ere, -cepi, -ceptus*	I welcome, catch, follow on, intercept
egeo, -ere + gen.	I lack, need		
egredior, -i, egressus sum	I leave	*excito, -are*	I rouse, inspire
egregius, -a, -um	outstanding, splendid	*exclamo, -are*	I shout out
		excludo, -ere, -clusi, -clusus	I shut out
elabor, -i, elapsus sum	I slip away	*excutio, -ere*	I drive out, strike down
electrum, -i n.	electrum		
elido, -ere, -isi, -isus	I prise out	*exemplum, -i* n.	example
emico, -are	I dart out, rush	*exeo, -ire*	I leave, depart
emineo, -ere	I project	*exerceo, -ere*	I keep spinning, employ, carry on
eminus	from a distance		
emitto, -ere, emisi, emissus	I throw	*exercitus, -us* m.	army
emo, -ere, emi, emptus	I buy	*exhaurio, -ire, -hausi, -haustus*	I endure, drain
emunio, -ire, -ii, -itus	I fortify	*exhorresco, -ere*	I am frightened of
en	see!	*exhortor, -ari, -atus sum*	I urge, encourage
enarrabilis, -e	describable	*exigo, -ere*	I pass, thrust
enitor, -i, enixus sum	I give birth to	*exiguus, -a, -um*	thin, small
ensis, -is m.	sword	*exim*	then
eo, ire i(v)i, itus	I go	*eximo, -ere*	I remove
epulae, -arum f.pl.	feast, meal	*exitium, -i* n.	destruction, death
equa, -ae f.	mare	*exordium, -i* n.	beginning
eques, -itis m.	cavalry(man)	*exorsa, -orum* n.pl.	undertakings
equidem	I for my part	*expedio, -ire*	I relate, settle
equinus, -a, -um	from a horse	*experior, -iri, -pertus sum*	I try to move, test
equites, -um m.pl.	cavalry	*expleo, -ere*	I satisfy
equus, -i m.	horse	*explorator, -oris* m.	scout
Erato (nom. only) f.	Erato	*exposco, -ere*	I beg
ergo	therefore	*exsanguis, -e*	bloodless, pale
erigo, -ere, erexi, erectus	I raise	*exscindo, -ere*	I destroy
Erinys, -os f.	a Fury	*exsertus, -a, -um*	bared, uncovered
eripio, -ere, eripui, ereptus	I snatch away, strip, pull off, steal, snatch, tear	*exsilium, -i* n.	exile
		exsolvo, -ere	I release
		exspecto, -are, -avi, -atus	I wait for, expect, await
erro, -are, -avi, -atus	I wander	*exspiro, -are*	I expire
error, -oris m.	mistake, error	*exstinguo, -ere, -stinxi, -stinctus*	I extinguish
esto	let it be so	*exstruo, -ere, -struxi, -structus*	I raise up
Etruria, -ae f.	Etruria	*exsulto, -are*	I leap up, exult, bound over
Etruscus, -a, -um	Etruscan		
Etruscus, -i m.	an Etruscan	*exsupero, -are*	I overpower
etsi	although	*extemplo*	straightaway, immediately
Euandrus, -i m.	Evander		
Eunaeus, -i m.	Eunaeus	*externus, -a, -um*	foreign
Eurus, -i m.	East Wind	*exterritus, -a, -um*	terrified
Euryalus, -i m.	Euryalus	*extremus, -a, -um*	rearmost, last, furthest, the edge of
Eurytides, -ae m.	son of Eurytus		
evado, -ere, evasi, evasus	I escape from		
eventus, -us m.	outcome, fortune	*exuro, -ere*	I burn down
everto, -ere, everti, eversus	I overthrow, cast down	*exuviae, -arum* f.pl.	spoils
		facesso, -ere	I carry out
evolo, -are	I dash forth	*facies, -ei* f.	form, shape, face
evomo, -ere	I belch forth	*facilis, -e*	easy
examen, -inis n.	balance, tongue, swarm	*facio, -ere*	I make, do
		factum, -i n.	deed
exanimis, -e	lifeless	*Fadus, -i* m.	Fadus
exanimus, -a, -um	dead	*fallax, -acis*	treacherous
exardesco, -ere, exarsi, exarsus	I am roused	*fallo, -ere, fefelli, falsus*	I deceive
exaudio, -ire, -ivi, -itus	I listen to, hear	*falsus, -a, -um*	false
excedo, -ere	I leave	*fama, -ae* f.	repute, renown, fame, reputation, glory, rumour
excidium, -i n.	destruction		
excido, -ere	I fall out		

Fama, -ae f.	Rumour
fames, -is f.	hunger
famulus, -i m.	servant, attendant
fas (indecl.) n.	right, law
fastigium, -i n.	roof-top
fatalis, -e	fated, deadly, fateful
fateor, -eri, fassus sum	I admit
fatifer, -era, -erum	deadly
fatigo, -are	I weary, tire, torment
fatum, -i n.	fate
fauces, -ium f.pl.	pass, defile, throat, jaws
Faunus, -i m.	Faunus
favilla, -ae f.	embers, ashes
fax, facis f.	torch
fel, fellis n.	bile, gall
felix, -icis	happy, fortunate, favourable
femineus, -a, -um	womanly
femur, -oris n.	thigh
fera, -ae f.	wild beast
feretrum, -i n.	bier
ferio, -ire	I strike, conclude, speak of
fero, ferre	I speak of, bring, carry
ferox, -ocis	fierce
ferreus, -a, -um	made of iron
ferrum, -i n.	iron, sword, weapon, axe
ferus, -a, -um	wild, cruel
fervens, -entis	red-hot
fervidus, -a, -um	burning, seething, fiery, violent, eager
fervo, -ere	I stir, am roused
fessus, -a, -um	weary
fetus, -a, -um	newly delivered
fetus, -us m.	litter
fides, -ei f.	faith, pledge, trust, reliability
fido, -ere + dat.	I trust in, trust
fiducia, -ae f.	confidence, reliance
fidus, -a, -um	faithful, loyal
figo, -ere, fixi, fixus	I fix, pierce, transfix
filia, -ae f.	daughter
filius, -i m.	son
filum, -i n.	thread
fines, -ium m.pl.	territory
fingo, -ere	I invent, make, shape
finio, -ire	I end
finis, -is m.	end
finitimus, -a, -um	neighbouring
fio, fieri, factus sum	I become, am made
firmo, -are	I confirm
firmus, -a, -um	firm
flagro, -are	I blaze
flamen, -inis n.	rustling of wind
flamma, -ae f.	flame, fire
flammeus, -a, -um	flaming
flavus, -a, -um	yellow
flecto, -ere	I turn, go, change, persuade
fleo, -ere, -evi, -etus	I weep (for)
flexus, -us m.	bend
floreo, -ere	I flourish
flos, floris m.	flower
fluctus, -us m.	wave
flumen, -inis n.	river
fluo, -ere	I flow, run, fall
fluvialis, -e	of a river
fluvius, -i m.	river
focus, -i m.	hearth, brazier
foedus, -a, -um	foul
foedus, -eris n.	treaty, peace treaty, pact, agreement
folium, -i n.	leaf
follis, -is m.	bellows
fons, fontis m.	fountain, spring
for, fari, fatus sum	I say, speak
forceps, -ipis m/f.	forceps, tongs
foris, -is f.	door, entrance
forma, -ae f.	beauty, appearance
formido, -inis f.	dread
fornax, -acis f.	furnace
fors	by chance, perhaps
fors, fortis f.	chance
forsan	perhaps
forte	by chance
fortis, -e	brave
fortuna, -ae f.	chance, fortune, emergency, fate
Fortuna, -ae f.	Fortune, Fate
fortunatus, -a, -um	fortunate
fossa, -ae f.	ditch
foveo, -ere, fovi, fotus	I foment, keep to
fragor, -oris m.	crash, din
frango, -ere	I break
frater, -tris m.	brother
fraternus, -a, -um	of a brother
fraus, fraudis f.	treachery
fraxinus, -i f.	ash tree
fremitus, -us m.	roar
fremo, -ere	I shout for, shout out, grumble, howl, roar, murmur
frena, -orum n.pl.	bridles
frequens, -entis	in a throng
fretum, -i n.	sea
frigidus, -a, -um	cold, chill
frigus, -oris n.	cold
frondens, -entis	leafy
frondosus, -a, -um	leafy
frons, frontis f.	forehead
frons, -ndis f.	foliage, leaves
frustra	in vain
fuga, -ae f.	flight
Fuga, -ae f.	Flight
fugio, -ere, fugi, fugitus	I flee (from)
fulcio, fulcire, fulsi, fultus	I support, prop up, secure
fulgeo, -ere	I gleam

fulmen, -inis n.	lightning	*gremium, -i* n.	bosom, lap
fulmineus, -a, -um	lightning-fast	*gressus, -us* m.	step
fulvus, -a, -um	yellow, tawny, deep yellow	*grex, gregis* m.	litter
		grus, gruis f.	crane
fumidus, -a, -um	smoking, smoky	*gurges, -itis* m.	swirling water, deep water
fumifer, -era, -erum	smoke-filled		
fumo, -are	I smoke, steam, reek	*guttur, -uris* n.	throat
		gyrus, -i m.	circle
fumus, -i m.	smoke	*habena, -ae* f.	whip, rein
fundo, -are, -avi, -atus	I found	*habilis, -e*	well-fitting, handy
fundo, -ere, fudi, fusus	I pour, sprout, lay low, stretch out	*habitus, -us* m.	style
		hac	this way, here
funereus, -a, -um	funereal	*hactenus*	until now
funestus, -a, -um	deadly	*haereo, -ere, haesi, haesus*	I cling (to), stick (to)
funus, -eris n.	death		
furens, -entis	mad, raging	*harena, -ae* f.	sand
furia, -ae f.	fury, madness, frenzy	*Harpalycus, -i* m.	Harpalycus
		harundo, -inis f.	shaft, arrow
furialis, -e	fearful	*haruspex, -icis* m.	soothsayer
furibundus, -a, -um	mad	*hasta, -ae* f.	spear, javelin
furo, -ere	I rave, rage	*hastile, -is* n.	javelin
furor, -oris m.	madness, rage	*haud*	not
furtim	furtively	*haurio, -ire, hausi, haustus*	I drink in
furtum, -i n.	stealthy activity, trick, stratagem	*Hector, -oris* m.	Hector
		hei!	alas!
fusus, -a, -um	flowing	*heia!*	come on!
galea, -ae f.	helmet	*herba, -ae* f.	grass, herb
Ganges, -is m.	river Ganges	*Herbesus, -i* m.	Herbesus
gaudeo, -ere	I rejoice	*heres, heredis* m.	heir
gaudium, -i n.	joy	*heros, -ois* m.	hero
gelu, -us n.	cold	*Hesperia, -ae* f.	Hesperia
geminus, -a, -um	twin, two	*heu!*	alas!
gemitus, -us m.	groan, lamentation	*heus!*	hey!
gemma, -ae f.	jewel	*hiatus, -us* m.	gape
gemo, -ere	I groan	*hic*	here
gener, -eri m.	son-in-law	*hiems, hiemis* f.	storm
genetrix, -icis f.	mother	*hinc*	on this side, on one side, from here
genitor, -oris m.	father		
gens, gentis f.	people, race, nation	*Hippotades, -ae* (acc. *-en*)	descendant of Hippotes
genus, -eris n.	race, people, type, kind, descendant	*Hisbo, -onis* m.	Hisbo
		hodie	today
germana, -ae f.	sister	*homo, hominis* m.	man(kind), person
germanus, -i m.	brother	*honestus, -a, -um*	handsome, beautiful
gero, -ere	I wear, display, wage, carry		
		honos, -oris m.	honour
Geryones, -ae m.	Geryon	*horrendus, -a, -um*	dreadful, awe-inspiring
gesto, -are	I bear		
globus, -i m.	mass, crowd	*horrens, -entis*	bristling, rough
glomero, -are, -avi, -atus	I mass, gather into a mass	*horreo, -ere*	I am stiff
		horridus, -a, -um	dreadful, prickly
gloria, -ae f.	glory	*horrisonus, -a, -um*	dreadful-sounding
Gorgoneus, -a, -um	of the Gorgons	*horror, -oris* m.	horror
gradior, -i, -gressus sum	I go	*hortor, -ari, -atus sum*	I urge, encourage
Grai, -orum m.pl.	the Greeks	*hospes, -itis* m.	guest, host
gramen, -inis n.	grass, herb	*hospitium, -i* n.	hospitality, friendship
gramineus, -a, -um	grassy, of turf		
grates f.pl.	thanks	*hostilis, -e*	hostile
gratia, -ae f.	gratitude	*hostis, -is* m.	enemy
gratus, -a, -um	pleasing, dear, grateful	*huc*	to here
		huc atque huc	this way and that
gravis, -e	heavy, severe, deep	*humanus, -a, -um*	human
gravo, -are	I weigh down	*humilis, -e*	brought low
gravo, -are, -avi, -atus	I make heavy	*humo, -are*	I bury

humus, -i f.	ground, earth	*impello, -ere, -puli, -pulsus*	I thrust impel, urge on
hydrus, -i m.	serpent		
hymenaeus, -i m.	marriage	*imperditus, -a, -um*	not slain
Hyrtacides, -ae m.	son of Hyrtacus	*imperito, -are* + dat.	I rule, command
iaceo, -ere	I lie	*imperium, -i* n.	command, power, empire
iacio, -ere, ieci, iactus	I throw, hurl		
iacto, -are	I toss about, boast	*impleo, -ere, -evi, -etus*	I fill
iaculum, -i n.	javelin	*implico, -are, -ui, -itus*	I involve, entangle
iam	now	*imploro, -are*	I appeal to
iamdudum	for long now	*impono, -ere, -posui, -positus*	I place upon
Iapyx, -igis	South Italian	*imprimo, -ere, -pressi, -pressus*	I engrave
Iapyx, -ygis m.	Iapyx	*improbus, -a, -um*	reckless, shameless, enormous
Iasides, -ae m.	descendant of Iasius		
ibi	there	*improvisus, -a, -um*	unexpected
ico, -ere, ici, ictus	I strike, ratify	*imprudens, -entis*	not realising
ictus, -us m.	impact, blow	*impubes, -is*	youthful
Ida, -ae f.	Mt Ida	*impulsus, -us* m.	pressure, shock
Idaeus, -a, -um	of Mt Ida	*impune*	with impunity
Idalia, -ae f.	Idalia	*imus, -a, -um*	lowest, deepest, the bottom of
idem, eadem, idem	the same		
ignarus, -a, -um	ignorant, unaware, unawares	*inaccessus, -a, -um*	not reached
		Inachius, -a, -um	of Inachus
ignesco, -ere	I ignite	*inanis, -e*	empty, useless, vain
igneus, -a, -um	fiery		
Ignipotens, -entis	Mighty with fire	*inausus, -a, -um*	undared
Ignipotens, -entis m.	Vulcan	*incassum*	in vain
ignis, -is m.	fire, flame	*incautus, -a, -um*	careless
ignoro, -are	I do not know	*incedo, -ere*	I advance, move
ignotus, -a, -um	unfamiliar, unknown	*incendium, -i* n.	fire
		incendo, -ere	I set on fire
ilex, ilicis f.	holm-oak tree	*incensus, -a, -um*	inflamed
Iliacus, -a, -um	Trojan, of Troy	*inceptum, -i* n.	undertaking
Iliades, -um f.pl.	Trojan women	*incertus, -a, -um*	uncertain
ilicet	straightaway, at once	*incido, -ere*	I fall, fall upon
		incipio, -ere, -cepi, -ceptus	I begin
Ilioneus, -i m.	Ilioneus	*includo, -ere, -clusi, -clusus*	I enclose, shut in, sheathe
illic	there		
illuc	to there	*inclusus, -a, -um*	enclosed, inlaid
imago, -inis f.	image, representation	*incognitus, -a, -um*	unknown
		incolo, -ere	I inhabit
imber, -bris m.	rain, rain storm	*incolumis, -e*	safe
imbuo, -ere	I stain	*incumbo, -ere* + dat.	I fall upon, attack, set to work, lean on, lean
imitor, -ari, -atus sum	I imitate, copy		
immanis, -e	huge		
immemor, -oris	forgetful	*incurro, -ere*	I attack
immensus, -a, -um	vast, huge	*incus, -udis* f.	anvil
immineo, -ere	I loom above	*incuso, -are*	I accuse
immisceo, -ere	I add	*inde*	from there, then
immitto, -ere	I send (into), send against, let go	*indecor, -oris*	dishonourable
		indecoris, -e	shameful
immo	yes indeed	*indefessus, -a, -um*	tireless
immobilis, -e	immovable, unmoved	*indicium, -i* n.	sign, trace
		indignor, -ari, -atus sum	I complain
immolo, -are	I sacrifice	*indignus, -a, -um*	unworthy, undeserved
immortalis, -e	immortal		
immotus, -a, -um	unmoved	*indulgeo, -ere* + dat.	I am kind to
immugio, -ire	I roar, resound	*induo, -ere, -dui, -dutus*	I put on
impar, -paris	unequal	*indutus, -a, -um*	dressed
impastus, -a, -um	hungry	*inermis, -e*	unarmed
impavidus, -a, -um	fearless	*inermus, -a, -um*	unarmed
impedio, -ire	I encircle, hinder	*iners, -rtis*	cowardly, helpless

infandus, -a, -um	unspeakable	*insto, -are*	I threaten, persist, press forward, continue with
infaustus, -a, -um	unfavourable		
infelix, -icis	unlucky, unhappy, ill-starred		
infensus, -a, -um	hostile	*instruo, -ere, -struxi, -structus*	I equip, draw up
infernus, -a, -um	of the underworld	*insuetus, -a, -um*	unaccustomed
infero, -ferre, -tuli, -latus	I carry in, carry forward	*insulto, -are*	I leap upon, triumph
inficio, -ere, -feci, -fectus	I infect, taint, mix with	*insuper*	in addition
		insurgo, -ere	I rise, rise up
infigo, -ere	I thrust, drive in	*intactus, -a, -um*	untouched
infit (defective verb)	he begins to speak	*intendo, -ere*	I aim
		intentus, -a, -um + dat.	intent upon
infodio, -ere	I bury	*inter* + acc.	between, among
informis, -e	shapeless	*interea*	meanwhile
informo, -are	I shape	*interimo, -ere*	I kill
infractus, -a, -um	broken	*intimus, -a, -um*	innermost
infrendo, -ere	I gnash the teeth	*intono, -are, -ui*	I thunder
ingemino, -are	I redouble	*intonsus, -a, -um*	unshaven
ingemo, -ere, -ui	I sigh for, mourn	*intorqueo, -ere, -torsi, -tortus*	I hurl, hurl at
ingens, -entis	huge	*intra* + acc.	inside
ingero, -ere	I throw	*intractatus, -a, -um*	untried
inglorius, -a, -um	inglorious, lacking glory	*intro, -are, -avi, -atus*	I enter
		inundo, -are	I overflow
ingratus, -a, -um	ungrateful	*invado, -ere*	I attack, attempt
ingredior, -i, -gressus sum	I embark upon, enter (+ dat.)	*invalidus, -a, -um*	weak, feeble
		inveho, -ere, -vexi, -vectus	I carry into
inhaereo, -ere, -haesi, -haesum	I cling to	*invehor, -i, -vectus sum*	I ride, go into
inhibeo, -ere	I check	*invenio, -ire, -veni, -ventus*	I find
inimicus, -a, -um	hostile	*inverto, -ere*	I invert
iniquus, -a, -um	unequal, hostile	*invictus, -a, -um*	invincible, unconquered
inlacrimo, -are	I weep		
inludo, -ere	I mock	*invideo, -ere, -vidi, -visus*	I begrudge
inlustris, -e	illustrious	*inviso, -ere*	I visit
innecto, -ere	I mingle with	*invisus, -a, -um*	hated, hateful
inno, -are	I sail upon, swim in	*invitus, -a, -um*	unwilling
		involvo, -ere	I envelop
innocuus, -a, -um	harmless	*ipse, ipsa, ipsum*	-self
innumerus, -a, -um	countless	*ira, irae* f.	anger
inops, -opis	poor, meagre	*irascor, -i, -iratus sum*	I am angry
inquam (defective verb)	I say	*iste, ista, istud*	that (of yours)
inrideo, -ere, -risi, -risus	I ridicule	*ita*	so, as follows
inritus, -a, -um	useless, invalid	*Itali, -orum* m.pl.	Italians
inrumpo, -ere	I burst in	*Italia, -ae* f.	Italy
insania, -ae f.	insanity	*Italis, -idis* f.	an Italian woman
insanus, -a, -um	insane, mad	*Italus, -a, -um*	Italian
inscius, -a, -um	unaware, unawares	*Italus, -i* m.	an Italian
		iter, itineris n.	course, route, way, journey
insidiae, -arum f.pl.	treachery		
insidior, -ari, -atus sum + dat.	I plot against	*iterum*	again
insido, -ere, -sedi, -sessus	I settle, settle on	*iuba, -ae* f.	mane
		iubeo, -ere, iussi, iussus	I order
insigne, -is n.	badge	*iugalis, -e*	nuptial, of a wedding
insignia, -ium n.pl.	regalia, insignia		
insignis, -e	distinguished	*iugulo, -are*	I slaughter
insono, -are, -ui	I resound, make to sound	*iugum, -i* n.	ridge
		Iulus, -i m.	Iulus, Ascanius
insperatus, -a, -um	unexpected	*iungo, -ere*	I join, unite, make
inspiro, -are	I breathe into	*Iuno, Iunonis* f.	Juno
inspoliatus, -a, -um	not despoiled	*Iuppiter, Iovis* m.	Jupiter
instar + gen.	the size of, like	*ius, iuris* n.	right
instituo, -ere	I make ready	*iussum, -i* n.	order
		iustitia, -ae f.	justice

iustus, -a, -um	just, right	*lenio, -ire, -ii, -itus*	I calm
Iuturna, -ae f.	Juturna	*lentus, -a, -um*	tough, flexible
iuvat, -are	it pleases	*leo, -onis* m.	lion
iuvenca, -ae f.	heifer	*letum, -i* n.	death
iuvencus, -i m.	bullock	*Leucate, -es* m. (acc. *-en*)	Leucate
iuvenis, -is	young, young man	*levis, -e*	light
iuvenis, -is m.	young man	*lēvis, -e*	smooth
iuventa, -ae f.	youth	*levo, -are*	I relieve
iuventus, -utis f.	young men	*lex, legis* f.	law, rule
iuvo, -are, iuvi, iutus	I help	*libens, -entis*	willing, glad
iuxta	alongside	*liber, -era, -erum*	free
iuxta + acc.	next to	*libo, -are*	I offer, pour
Karthago, -inis f.	Carthage	*libro, -are*	I balance, poise
labor, -i, lapsus sum	I glide, glide down, fall	*libum, -i* n.	pancake
		licenter	freely
labor, -oris m.	work, labour, toil	*licet, -ere*	it is allowed
labrum, -i n.	tub	*limen, -inis* n.	threshold
lacesso, -ere	I produce, challenge	*limes, -itis* m.	path
		limus, -i m.	ceremonial apron
lacrima, -ae f.	tear	*lingua, -ae* f.	tongue, language
lacrimo, -are	I cry, weep	*linquo, -ere*	I leave
lacteus, -a, -um	milk-white	*liquesco, -ere*	I melt
lacus, -us m.	lake, tank	*liquidus, -a, -um*	clear
laetitia, -ae f.	happiness, joy	*Liris, -is* (acc. *-im*) m.	Liris
laetus, -a, -um	glad, happy, joyful	*litoreus, -a, -um*	on the shore
laeva, -ae f.	left hand	*litus, -oris* n.	shore
laevus, -a, -um	left, on the left, inauspicious	*loco, -are, -avi, -atus*	I place
		locus, -i m. (pl. *loca*)	place
Lagus, -i m.	Lagus	*longaevus, -a, -um*	long-lived, old
lambo, -ere	I lick	*longe*	over a wide area, from afar
Lamus, -i m.	Lamus		
Lamyrus, -i m.	Lamyrus	*longus, -a, -um*	long
languesco, -ere	I droop, wilt	*loquor, -i, locutus sum*	I speak
lanx, lancis f.	dish, platter, scale	*lorica, -ae* f.	cuirass, breastplate
lar, -is m.	lar	*lorum, -i* n.	strap
largior, -iri, -itus sum	I give freely	*lubricus, -a, -um*	slippery
largus, -a, -um	copious	*luceo, -ere*	I gleam, shine
Larina, -ae f.	Larina	*luctamen, -inis* n.	struggle
lassus, -a, -um	drooping	*luctificus, -a, -um*	causing grief
late	far and wide	*luctor, -ari, -atus sum*	I struggle
latebra, -ae f.	hiding-place	*luctus, -us* m.	grief
lateo, -ere	I lie hidden	*lucus, -i* m.	grove
Latini, -orum m.pl.	the Latins	*ludo, -ere, lusi, lusus*	I play, frolic, delude
Latinus, -a, -um	Latin		
Latinus, -i m.	Latinus	*ludus, -i* m.	game
Latium, -i n.	Latium	*lues, -is* f.	pest, blight
Latonia, -ae f.	Diana	*lugubris, -e*	ill-omened
latus, -a, -um	broad	*lumen, -inis* n.	light, eye, life
latus, -eris n.	side	*luo, -ere*	I atone for
laudo, -are	I praise	*lupa, -ae* f.	female wolf
Laurens, -entis	of Laurentum	*lupus, -i* m.	wolf
Laurens, -entis m.	a Laurentian	*lustro, -are, -avi, -atus*	I go round, scan
Laurentum, -i n.	Laurentum	*lux, lucis* f.	light, daylight, dawn
laurus, -i f.	laurel tree		
laus, laudis f.	praise	*luxurio, -are*	I am exuberant
Lausus, -i m.	Lausus	*Lydius, -a, -um*	Lydian
Lavinia, -ae f.	Lavinia	*lympha, -ae* f.	water
lavo, -are	I bathe, drench	*lympho, -are, -avi, -atus*	I drive mad
laxo, -are, -avi, -atus	I open, release, relax	*macto, -are*	I sacrifice
		macula, -ae f.	spot
legio, -onis f.	legion, army	*madeo, -ere*	I am wet
lego, -ere	I gather	*Maeonia, -ae* f.	Maeonia, Lydia
lego, -ere, legi, lectus	I choose	*maereo, -ere*	I lament

maestus, -a, -um	sad, grieving	*minus*	less
mage	more	*mirabilis, -e*	amazing,
magis	more		wonderful
magister, -tri m.	teacher, master,	*miror, -ari, -atus sum*	I am amazed at,
	leader, herdsman		admire, marvel at
magistra, -ae f.	instructress	*mirus, -a, -um*	wondrous,
magistra, -ae f. adj.	of a master		amazing
magnanimus, -a, -um	great-hearted	*misceo, -ere, miscui, mixtus*	I mix, mingle, join
mala, -ae f.	jaw		(battle)
malo, malle	I prefer	*miser, -era, -erum*	wretched, poor
malum, -i n.	evil, disaster	*miserandus, -a, -um*	pitiable
malus, -a, -um	evil, bad	*misereor, -eri, -itus sum* + gen.	I pity
mandatum, -i n.	instruction,	*miseror, -ari, -atus sum*	I pity
	command	*mitis, -e*	gentle
mando, -are	I entrust	*mitto, -ere, misi, missus*	I send
mando, -ere	I chew	*Mnestheus, -i* m.	Mnestheus
maneo, -ere	I await	*modo*	only, recently
manes, -ium m.pl.	souls of the dead	*modus, -i* m.	method, means,
manus, -us f.	hand, band of		end, manner,
	men, group		moderation, way
mare, -is n.	sea	*moenia, -ium* n.pl.	city walls, city
Mars, Martis m.	Mars, war	*molaris, -is* m.	mill-stone
Marvors, -ortis m.	Mars	*moles, -is* f.	mass, boulder,
massa, -ae f.	mass		embankment
mater, matris f.	mother	*molior, -iri, -itus sum*	I wield, force,
maternus, -a, -um	a mother's		heave on, tug at,
maturus, -a, -um	ripe, ready, mature		build
medeor, -eri	I heal, remedy	*mollis, -e*	soft, weak
medico, -are	I treat	*moneo, -ere*	I warn, advise
medicus, -a, -um	healing	*monimentum, -i* n.	reminder
meditor, -ari, -atus sum	I practise	*monitum, -i* n.	warning
medium, -i n.	middle	*mons, montis* m.	mountain
medius, -a, -um	middle, middle of	*monstro, -are*	I indicate, show
meliora, -um n.pl.	better things	*monstrum, -i* n.	portent, monster
membrum, -i n.	limb	*mora, -ae* f.	delay, mainstay,
memini, -isse	I remember		barrier
memor, -oris	remembering,	*morbus, -i* m.	disease
	mindful, aware	*morior, -i, mortuus sum*	I die
memoro, -are	I relate, speak	*moror, -ari, -atus sum*	I wait, delay,
mens, mentis f.	mind, heart		prolong
mensa, -ae f.	table	*mors, mortis* f.	death
merces, -edis f.	payment, price	*morsus, -us* m.	bite, tooth
mereo, -ere, -ui, -itus	I deserve, earn	*mortales, -ium* m.pl.	mortals
mergo, -ere, mersi, mersus	I bury, sink	*mortalis, -is* m.	mortal, human
merito	deservedly	*mortuus, -a, -um*	dead
meritum, -i n.	just desserts	*mos, moris* m.	custom, manner,
meritus, -a, -um	righteous		habit
Messapus, -i m.	Messapus	*motus, -us* m.	emotion
metallum, -i n.	ore, metal	*moveo, -ere, movi, motus*	I move, begin
metuo, -ere	I fear	*mucro, -onis* m.	point
metus, -us m.	fear, awe	*mugio, -ire*	I low, moo
meus, -a, -um	my, mine	*mugitus, -us* m.	bellow
Mezentius, -i m.	Mezentius	*mulceo, -ere*	I caress
mico, -are	I shine, glitter,	*muliebris, -e*	of a woman
	flash	*munus, -eris* n.	gift, tribute, rite
miles, -itis m.	soldier	*muralis, -e*	attacking walls
militia, -ae f.	military service,	*murmur, -uris* n.	murmur, rumbling
	warfare	*murus, -i* m.	wall
mille, pl. *milia*	thousand	*musso, -are*	I am uncertain
mina, -ae f.	threat	*mutus, -a, -um*	silent
minax, -acis	threatening	*namque*	for
ministra, -ae f.	attendant	*nanciscor, -i, nactus sum*	I come upon
ministro, -are + dat.	I manage	*naris, -is* f.	nostril

narro, -are	I relate
nascor, -i, natus sum	I am born, rise
nata, -ae f.	daughter
natus, -i m.	son, offspring
nauta, -ae m.	sailor
navis, -is f.	ship
nebula, -ae f.	mist, pall
necdum	and not yet
neco, -are	I kill
necto, -ere, nexui, nexus	I join together
nefas n. indecl.	monstrous thing, wicked deed
nego, -are, -avi, -atus	I deny
nemus, -oris n.	grove
neo, nere, nevi, netus	I weave
nepos, -otis m.	descendant, grandson
Neptunius, -a, -um	of Neptune
nequeo, -ire	I cannot
nequiquam	in vain
nervus, -i m.	bowstring
nescio, -ire	I do not know
nescius, -a, -um	unaware
neu	and do not
neu . . . neu	neither . . . nor
nex, necis f.	slaughter
ni	unless
nidus, -i m.	nest
niger, -gra, -grum	black
nigresco, -ere	I grow dark
nihil, nil n. (indecl.)	nothing
Nilus, -i m.	river Nile
nimbus, -i m.	cloud
nimium	too, too much
nimius, -a, -um	too much
nisi	if not, unless
Nisus, -i m.	Nisus
nitor, -i, nixus sum + abl.	I lean on, press (upon)
niveus, -a, -um	snow white
noctivagus, -a, -um	night-wandering
nodus, -i m.	knot
nomen, -inis n.	name
notus, -a, -um	known, familiar
Notus, -i m.	South Wind
novus, -a, -um	new
nox, noctis f.	night
noxius, -a, -um	harmful
nubes,-is f.	cloud
nubilis, -e	ready for marriage
nudo, -are, -avi, -atus	I bare
nudus, -a, -um	bare
nullus, -a, -um	no
num	surely not
numen, -inis n.	divine will, divine power, god
numerus, -i m.	rhythm, time, number
numquam	never
nuntius, -i m.	message, news
nutus, -us m.	nod, will
nympha, -ae f.	nymph
obduco, -ere, -duxi, -ductus	I hide
obeo, -ire	I survey, go round
obex, obicis m/f.	barrier
obicio, -ere	I position, close
obliviscor, -i, oblitus sum	I forget
obnitor, -i, -nixus sum + dat.	I push against
oborior, -iri, -ortus sum	I well up, rise
obruo, -ere	I overwhelm
obscurus, -a, -um	dark
observo, -are, -avi, -atus	I observe
obsideo, -ere, -sedi, -sessus	I occupy, besiege, settle upon
obsidio, -onis f.	siege
obsido, -ere	I occupy, block
obstipesco, -ere, -stipui	I am amazed
obsto, -are + dat.	I block the way, obstruct
obtestor, -ari, -atus sum	I beseech, appeal to
obtrunco, -are	I cut to pieces
obversus, -a, -um	facing
obvius, -a, -um + dat.	to meet
occido, -ere, -cidi, -cisus	I kill
occulo, -ere, -cului, -cultus	I hide
occulto, -are	I hide
occultus, -a, -um	secret
occupo, -are	I seize, catch
occurro, -ere, -curri, -cursus	I meet, run to meet, face
Oceanus, -i m.	Ocean
ocior, ocius	swifter, swiftly
ocrea, -ae f.	greave
oculus, -i m.	eye
odi, -isse	I hate
odium, -i n.	hatred
odoriferus, -a, -um	fragrant
offero, offerre, obtuli, oblatus	I offer, expose
olens, -entis	fragrant
olim	one day, once, formerly
oliva, -ae f.	olive
Olympus, -i m.	Olympus
omen, -inis n.	omen
omnipotens, -entis	all-powerful
omnis, -e	all
onero, -are, -avi, -atus	I load
onerosus, -a, -um	heavy
opacus, -a, -um	shady, dark
operio, -ire	I cover
opes, opum f.pl.	resources
opimus, -a, -um	rich
Opis, -is (acc. *-im*) f.	Opis
oppono, -ere, -posui, -positus	I set against, expose, oppose
opportunus, -a, -um	suitable
opprimo, -ere, -pressi, -pressus	I overwhelm
ops, opis f.	help, power
opto, -are, -avi, -atus	I wish, choose
opulentia, -ae f.	wealth
opus, -eris n.	work, task
ora, -ae f.	shore, edge, rim
orator, -oris m.	envoy
orbis, -is m.	circle, disc, orbit
ordior, -iri, orsus sum	I begin

ordo, -inis m. — sequence, line, row
Oricius, -a, -um — of Oricum
orior, -iri, ortus sum — I arise, rise
ornatus, -us m. — apparel
ornus, -i f. — mountain-ash
Ornytus, -i m. — Ornytus
oro, -are — I beg, pray
orsa, -orum n.pl. — beginnings, words
os, oris n. — mouth, face
os, ossis n. — bone
osculum, -i n. — little mouth
ostendo, -ere — I show
ostrum, -i n. — purple
ovile, -is n. — sheep-fold
ovo, -are — I rejoice, exult
Pachynus, -i m. — Pachynus
pacifer, -fera, -ferum — peace-bearing
Paeonius, -a, -um — of Paeon, medicinal
Pagasus, -i m. — Pagasus
palam — openly
Pallanteum, -i n. — Pallanteum
Pallanteus, -a, -um — of Pallanteum
Pallas, -antis (acc. -a) m. — Pallas
palleo, -ere — I am pale
pallidus, -a, -um — pale
palma, -ae f. — hand
palus, -udis f. — marsh
panacea, -ae f. — all-heal
Pandarus, -i m. — Pandarus
pando, -ere — I open, throw open
pango, -ere, pepigi, pactus — I agree
papaver, -eris n. — poppy
Paphus, -i f. — Paphos
papilla, -ae f. — breast
par, paris — equal, similar
Parcae, -arum f.pl. — the Fates
parco, -ere + dat. — I spare, stop
parens, -entis m/f. — parent, father, mother
pareo, -ere + dat. — I obey, consent
pario, -ere, peperi, partus — I accomplish, win, establish
Paris, -idis m. — Paris
pariter — equally, alongside
parma, -ae f. — shield
paro, -are, -avi, -atus — I prepare
Parrhasius, -a, -um — Arcadian
pars, partis f. — part, direction, some, place
partim — partly
partior, -iri, -itus sum — I share
partus, -us m. — child, offspring
passim — everywhere
pastus, -us m. — pasture
patens, -entis — open, available
pateo, -ere, -ui — I lie open, gape open
pater, patris m. — father, elder, senator
patera, -ae f. — bowl
paternus, -a, -um — of a father, native, ancestral

patior, -i, passus sum — I allow, suffer, experience
patria, -ae f. — homeland, native land
patrius, -a, -um — native, a father's, ancestral
patulus, -a, -um — spreading, broad
pauci, -ae, -a — few
paulatim — gradually
pauper, -eris — poor
pavidus, -a, -um — frightened
pavor, -oris m. — terror
pax, pacis f. — peace
pectus, -oris n. — breast, chest, heart
pecus, -oris n. — flock, herd, animal
pecus, -udis f. — cow, sheep, beast
pedes, -itis m. — foot-soldier
pelagus, -i n. — open sea
pellis, -is f. — hide, skin
pello, -ere, pepuli, pulsus — I drive, defeat, beat, impel
penates, -ium m.pl. — penates
pendeo, -ere, pependi — I hang, droop
pendo, -ere — I pay
penetrabilis, -e — able to penetrate
penetralia, -ium n.pl. — shrine, innermost part
penitus — deep inside, deep within
penuria, -ae f. — need, lack
per mutua — together
percipio, -ere, -cepi, -ceptus — I perceive, learn, note
percutio, -ere, -cussi, -cussus — I strike, beat
perdo, -ere — I lose
pererro, -are — I wander through, try
perfero, ferre, -tuli, -latus — I carry through, bear
perficio, -ere, -feci, -fectus — I complete, finish
perfidus, -a, -um — treacherous
perforo, -are — I pierce
perfundo, -ere — I drench, pour over
perfuro, -ere — I rage furiously
Pergama, -orum n.pl. — Pergama, Troy
pergo, -ere — I proceed, go ahead
periclum, -i n. — danger
periculum, -i n. — danger
perimo, -ere, -emi, -emptus — I kill
permisceo, -ere, -miscui, -mixtus — I mingle, confuse
perpetior, -i, -pessus sum — I endure
perplexus, -a, -um — tangled
persolvo, -ere — I pay, pay in full, offer
pertempto, -are — I pervade
perterritus, -a, -um — terrified
pervenio, -ire — I reach
perversus, -a, -um — perverse
pes, pedis m. — foot

pestis, -is f.	plague, ruin, danger
peto, - ere	I seek, ask, ask for, make for
pharetra, -ae f.	quiver
pharetratus, -a, -um	bearing a quiver
Phoebe, -es f.	Phoebe
Phoebus, -i m.	Phoebus (Apollo)
Phryges, -um m.pl.	Phrygians, Trojans
Phrygius, -a, -um	Phrygian, Trojan
piceus, -a, -um	(of) pitch
pietas, -atis f.	filial duty
piget, -ere	it causes regret
pilatus, -a, -um	armed with javelins, dense
pingo, -ere, pinxi, pictus	I paint, embroider
pinguis, -e	rich, fertile
pinus, -us f.	pine tree, pine-torch
pius, -a, -um	dutiful
placidus, -a, -um	peaceful, calm
placitus, -a, -um	pleasing, agreed
plaga, -ae f	blow
plango, -ere	I mourn, lament
plaustrum, -i n.	cart, wagon
plausus, -us m.	applause
plebs, plebis f.	ordinary men
plenus, -a, -um	full
pluvia, -ae f.	rain
poena, -ae f.	penalty, punishment, vengeance
polum, -i n.	sky
pompa, -ae f.	procession
pomum, -i n.	fruit
pondus, -eris n.	weight
pone	behind
pono, -ere, posui, positus	I place, set down
pontus, -i m.	ocean
poples, -itis m.	knee
populus, -i m.	people, race
porro	besides
porta, -ae f.	gate
portendo, -ere	I portend
portentum, -i n.	portent, omen
porto, -are	I carry
portus, -us m.	harbour
posco, -ere	I demand, call upon, ask, ask for
possum, posse, potui	I can, am able
post	afterwards
post + acc.	behind
posterus, - a, -um	next
postis, -is m.	door-post
postquam	after
postremus, -a, -um	last
potens, -entis	powerful
potentia, -ae f.	power
potestas, -atis f.	power
potior, -iri, -itus sum + abl.	I acquire, gain, reach
potis (indecl.)	able
potius	rather

praecedo, -ere, -cessi, -cessus	I precede
praeceps, -cipitis	headlong
praeceptum, -i n.	command
praecipio, -ere, -cepi, -ceptus	I instruct, anticipate, seize first
praecipito, -are	I cast aside
praecisus, -a, -um	steep, sheer
praeclarus, -a, -um	illustrious
praecordia, -orum n.pl.	heart
praeda, -ae f.	booty
praedulcis, -e	very sweet
praefero, -ferre, -tuli, -latus	I prefer
praefigo, -ere, -fixi, -fixus	I tip
praegnas, -atis	pregnant
praemitto, -ere, -misi, -missus	I send ahead, send on ahead
praemium, -i n.	prize, reward
praenuntia, -ae f.	foreteller
praesens, -entis	present, effective
praesentia, -ae f.	presence
praesepe, -is n.	stable, pen
praesideo, -ere + dat.	I preside over
praesidium, -i n.	protection
praestans, -ntis	outstanding
praetendo, -ere	I hold out
praeterea	furthermore
precor, -ari, -atus sum	I pray, beg, plead, pray to
premo, -ere, pressi, pressus	I suppress, press, attack, check, crush, overpower, stop
prenso, -are	I clutch at
pretium, -i n.	price
prex, precis f.	prayer, entreaty
Priamus, -i m.	Priam
primitiae, -arum f.pl.	first fruits
primum	first
primus, -a, -um	first
primus, -i m.	leader
principium, -i n.	beginning
prior, prius	first
pristinus, -a, -um	former
prius	previously, first
pro + abl.	for, in return for
proavus, -i m.	great-grandfather
procedo, -ere	I procede
procella, -ae f.	storm, violence
procer, -eris m.	noble, prince
procul	far away, far off, from a distance
procumbo, -ere, -cubui, -cubitus	I lie down, sink down, bend over
procursus, -us m.	charge
prodo, -ere, -didi, -ditus	I betray, reveal
proelium, -i n.	battle, fight
profero, -re	I postpone
proficiscor, -i, -fectus sum	I set out, originate
proflo, -are	I breathe heavily
profugus, -a, -um	exiled
profundo, -ere, -fudi, -fusus	I pour forth
progenies, -ei f.	child

progredior, -i, -gressus sum	I proceed	*qui-, quae-, quodcumque*	whoever, whatever
prohibeo, -ere	I ban	*quianam*	why?
proicio, -ere, -ieci, -iectus	I throw down	*quid*	why?
proles, -is f.	child, offspring	*quidem*	indeed, however
proludo, -ere	I practise before	*quies, -etis* f,	rest
proluo, -ere, -lui, -lutus	I wash away	*quiesco, -ere, -evi, -etus*	I find rest
promissum, -i n.	promise	*quin*	no, indeed, yes
promitto, -ere	I promise		indeed
pronuba, -ae f.	brideswoman	*quinam, quaenam, quodnam*	who, which
pronus, -a, -um	leaning forward	*quippe*	of course
prope	near	*quis-, quae-, quicquam*	anyone, anything,
propero, -are	I hasten		any
propinquo, -are + dat.	I approach	*quisque, quaeque, quidque*	each (one)
propinquus, -a, -um	neighbouring	*quisquis, quidquid*	whoever, whatever
prora, -ae f.	prow	*quo*	to where, whither?
prorumpo, -ere, -rupi, -ruptus	I break out, charge	*quocumque*	however
prosequor, -i, -secutus sum	I escort, honour	*quondam*	once, sometimes
	with	*quoniam*	since
prospectus, -us m.	sight, view	*quot*	as many as, how
prospicio, -ere, -spexi, -spectus	I look out, observe		many
protendo, -ere	I extend		
protero, -ere	I trample	*rabidus, -a, -um*	raving
protinus	at once,	*rabies, -ei* f.	rage, fury
	continuously	*radius, -i* m.	ray
protraho, -ere	I drag forth	*radix, -icis* f.	root
proturbo, -are	I repel	*ramus, -i* m.	branch
provenio, -ire	I arise, happen	*rapidus, -a, -um*	rapid
proximus, -a, -um	nearest	*rapina, -ae* f.	theft
pubes, -eris	downy	*rapio, -ere, rapui, raptus*	I seize
pubes, -is f.	adult, people, men	*rarus, -a, -um*	scattered, sparse
pudendus, -a, -um	shameful	*ratio, -ionis* f.	means
pudor, -oris m.	shame	*ratis, -is* f.	boat
puer, pueri m.	boy	*rebellis, -e*	rebellious
pugna, -ae f.	fight, battle	*recedo, -ere, -cessi, -cessus*	I retreat, withdraw
pugnator, -oris m.	fighter	*recens, -entis*	fresh
pugno, -are, -avi, -atus	I fight	*recepto, -are*	I tug hard at
pulcher, -ra, -rum	beautiful,	*recessus, -us* m.	recess
	handsome	*recidivus, -a, -um*	returning,
pulmo, -onis m.	lung		resurrected
pulso, -are	I disturb	*recido, -ere, -cidi, -cisus*	I cut off
pulvis, -eris m.	dust	*recipio, -ere, -cepi, -ceptus*	I recover, take
puppis, -is f.	stern, ship		back
purpureus, -a, -um	purple, red, dark	*reclino, -are*	I lean
	red	*recludo, -ere, -clusi, -clusus*	I draw, unsheathe,
puto, -are, -avi, -atus	I think, calculate		open, break apart
pyra, -ae f.	pyre	*recoctus, -a, -um*	refined
qua	where	*recognosco, -ere*	I review
quacumque	wherever	*recondo, -ere*	I bury
quadra, -ae f.	square, table	*rectus, -a, -um*	straight, right
quaero, -ere, -sivi, -situs	I seek, ask, search,	*recubo, -are*	I lie
	win	*recumbo, -ere*	I sink down
qualis, -e	such as, just like	*recurro, -ere*	I run back
quam	than	*redarguo, -ere*	I refute
quamvis	although	*reddo, -ere, reddidi, -ditus*	I return, give back,
quando	when, since, ever		restore
quandoquidem	since	*redeo, -ire*	I return, go back
quantus, -a, -um	how much	*reditus, -us* m.	return
quare	and so, therefore	*reduco, -ere, -duxi, -ductus*	I bring back
quater	four times	*refero, -ferre*	I take back, reply,
quatio, -ere	I shake, trample,		give back, bring
	brandish, spur on		back, bear again,
queo, -ire	I can		say in answer,
querela, -ae f.	complaint		vomit up
		reficio, -ere, -feci, -fectus	I remake

reflecto, -ere, -flexi, -flexus	I bend back	*robur, -oris* n.	oak, oak tree, oak club, strength
refluo, -ere	I flow back, recoil		
refulgeo, -ere, -fulsi	I reflect	*rogo, -are*	I ask for
regalis, -e	regal, royal	*rogus, -i* m.	pyre
regia, -ae f.	palace	*Romanus, -a, -um*	Roman
regina, -ae f.	queen, princess	*ros, roris* m.	dew, moisture
regio, -onis f.	region, direction	*rostrum, -i* n.	beak, prow
regius, -a, -um	royal	*rota, -ae* f.	wheel
regnator, -oris m.	ruler	*roto, -are*	I swing
regnum, -i n.	kingdom, realm	*rubeo, -ere*	I am red
rego, -ere	I rule, deal, direct, control	*ruber, -bra, -brum*	red
		rudens, -entis m.	rope
religo, -are, -avi, -atus	I tether	*rudimentum, -i* n.	first attempt
relinquo, -ere, -liqui, -lictus	I leave, abandon	*rudo, -ere*	I roar
remigium, -i n.	rowing	*ruina, -ae* f.	ruin, destruction
remitto, -ere	I send back	*rumor, -oris* m.	rumour, approval
remugio, -ire	I resound	*rumpo, -ere*	I break, burst, break through, break off, burst through
Remulus, -i m.	Remulus		
remus, -i m.	oar		
Remus, -i m.	Remus		
reor, reri, ratus sum	I think	*ruo, -ere, rui*	I rush, fall down
repello, -ere, reppuli, repulsus	I thrust back	*rupes, -is* f.	crag, cliff
repens, -entis	sudden	*rursus*	back, again
repente	suddenly	*rutilus, -a, -um*	red
reperio, -ire	I find	*Rutuli, -orum* m.pl.	Rutulians
repeto, -ere	I recall	*Rutulus, -a, -um*	Rutulian
repleo, -ere	I fill	*Rutulus, -i* m.	Rutulian
repono, -ere, -posui, -positus	I set down, restore, put back	*Sabellus, -a, -um*	Sabine
		sacer, sacra, sacrum	sacred, holy
reporto, -are	I report, take back	*sacra, -orum* n.pl.	sacred objects
		sacrilegus, -a, -um	sacrilegious
reposco, -ere	I demand back, require	*sacro, -are, -avi, -atus*	I dedicate, give, consecrate
reprimo, -ere, -pressi, -pressus	I check	*sacrum, -i* n.	sacred object, rite
requiro, -ere	I look for		
res, rei f.	thing, matter, affair, realm	*saeclum, -i* n.	years, age
		saepio, -ire, saepsi, saeptus	I enclose, fence, shut
rescindo, -ere	I cut open		
resero, -are	I unlock, reveal	*saeta, -ae* f.	bristle
reservo, -are	I reserve	*saetiger, -era, -erum*	bristly
resido, -ere, -sedi	I settle back	*saevio, -ire*	I rage, rave
respergo, -ere, -spersi, -spersus	I spatter	*saevus, -a, -um*	fierce, cruel
respicio, -ere, -spexi, -spectus	I look back for, take notice of, look round and see	*sagitta, -ae* f.	arrow
		saltus, -us m.	leap, bound
		salubris, -e	health-giving
		salus, -utis f.	safety
responsum, -i n.	response, answer	*salve, salvete*	hail
resto, -are	I remain	*sanctus, -a, -um*	sacred, virtuous
retineo, -ere	I hold back	*sane*	of course
retorqueo, -ere, -torsi, -tortus	I fold over backwards	*sanguineus, -a, -um*	blood-red, bloody
retro		*sanguis, -inis* m.	blood
reveho, -ere	I bring back	*sanies, abl. sanie* f.	gore
revello, -ere, -velli, -vulsus	I tear off	*sat* (indecl.)	enough
revoco, -are	I recall	*satis* + gen.	enough
revolvo, -ere, -volvi, -volutus	I roll backwards, go over again, experience again	*satius*	better, preferable
		Saturnia, -ae f.	Juno
		Saturnius, -a, -um	of Saturn
rex, regis m.	king	*Saturnus, -i* m.	Saturn
Rhamnes, -etis m.	Rhamnes	*saturo, -are, -avi, -atus*	I fill
Rhoetus, -i m.	Rhoetus	*satus, -a, -um*	sown, sprung
ripa, -ae f.	bank	*saxeus, -a, -um*	rocky
rite	duly, properly	*saxum, -i* n	rock, stone
rivus, -i m.	stream	*sceleratus, -a, -um*	vicious, accursed

scelus, -eris n.	crime	*Sila, -ae* f.	Mt Sila
sceptrum, -i n.	sceptre	*silens, -entis*	silent, in silence
scindo, -ere	I split	*silentium, -i* n.	silence
scintilla, -ae f.	spark	*sileo, -ere*	I am silent
scio, -ire	I know	*silesco, -ere*	I grow silent
scopulus, -i m.	rock, crag	*silex, -icis* f.	crag
scutatus, -a, -um	bearing shields	*silva, -ae* f.	wood
scutum, -i n.	shield	*Simois, -entis* (acc. *-enta*) m.	river Simois
seco, -are	I cut, cleave, pursue	*simul*	at the same time
		simulo, -are, -avi, -atus	I pretend
secundo, -are	I favour	*sine* + abl.	without
secundus, -a, -um	favourable, following	*singulto, -are*	I spout forth
		sinister, -tra, -trum	improper, left
securis, -is (acc. *-im*) f.	axe	*sino, -ere*	I allow, cease, give up
secus	otherwise		
sedatus, -a, -um	calm, tranquil	*sinus, -us* m.	bosom, lap, fold
sedeo, -ere	I sit	*Sirius, -a, -um*	of Sirius
sedes, sedis f.	seat, home, palace, dwelling	*sisto, -ere*	I place
		sitis, -is f.	drought
segnis, -e	slow	*situs, -us* m.	inactivity
semel	once	*sive ... seu*	whether ... or
semifer, -eri m.	half-beast	*socer, -eri* m.	father-in-law
semihomo, -inis	half-human	*socio, -are*	I unite, join
seminecis, -is	half-dead	*socius, -a, -um*	allied
semita, -ae f.	path	*socius, -i* m.	comrade, ally
semper	always	*sodalis, -is* m.	friend
semustus, -a, -um	half-burnt	*sol, solis* m.	sun
senatus, -us m.	senate	*Sol, Solis* m.	the Sun God, Sun
senecta, -ae f.	old age	*solacium, -i* n.	consolation
senectus, -utis f.	old age	*solamen, -inis* n.	consolation
senex, -is	old	*solidus, -a, -um*	solid
senex, -is m.	old man	*solitus, -a, -um*	usual
seni, -ae, -a	six, six each	*sollemnis, -e*	customary
senior, -oris	elderly	*sollicito, -are*	I disturb
sensus, -us m.	sense	*solor, -ari, -atus sum*	I console
sententia, -ae f.	decision, purpose, opinion	*solum, -i* n.	ground, earth, soil, foundation
sentes, -ium m.pl.	brambles	*solus, -a, -um*	alone, only
sentio, -ire, sensi, sensus	I realise, feel	*solvo, -ere, solvi, solutus*	I free, untie, let loose, relax, loosen, absolve, exempt
septemplex, -icis	sevenfold		
septenus, -a, -um	sevenfold		
sequestra, -ae f.	guarantor		
sequor, sequi, secutus sum	I follow	*somnus, -i* m.	sleep
serenus, -a, -um	clear	*sonitus, -us* m.	sound, noise
sermo, -onis m.	speech	*sono, -are*	I sound
serpens, -entis f.	snake	*sonorus, -a, -um*	roaring, clashing
Serranus, -i m.	Serranus	*soror, -oris* f.	sister
serus, -a, -um	late, too late	*sors, sortis* f.	lot, fate
servo, -are, -avi, -atus	I keep alive, protect, watch over, look after, keep, save, heal, preserve	*sortior, -iri, -itus sum*	I seek, share out
		sospes, -itis	safe, unhurt
		spargo, -ere, sparsi, sparsus	I scatter
		sparus, -i m.	hunting-spear
setius	less	*spatium, -i* n.	space, place, course
seu, sive	whether, or		
sibilo, -are	I hiss	*spectator, -oris* m.	spectator
siccus, -a, -um	dry, parched	*specto, -are*	I observe, watch over
Siculus, -a, -um	Sicilian		
sidereus, -a, -um	starry	*specula, -ae* f.	view-point
sidus, -eris n.	star	*specus, -us* m.	cave
significo, -are	I signal	*spelunca, -ae* f.	cave
signo, -are	I mark	*sperno, -ere*	I reject
signum, -i n.	sign, standard, token, signal	*spero, -are, -avi, -atus*	I hope, hope for
		spes, spei f.	hope

spiculum, -i n.	arrow	*sucus, -i* m.	juice
spina, -ae f.	spine	*sudor, -oris* m.	sweat
splendens, -entis	gleaming	*suffundo, -ere, -fudi, -fusus*	I stumble
spolia, -orum n.pl.	spoils	*summoveo, -ere, -movi, -motus*	I remove
spolio, -are, -avi, -atus	I despoil, rob, deprive	*summus, -a, -um*	the top of, highest, topmost, the tip of, most important
spolium, -i n.	booty		
sponte	by one's will	*sumo, -ere*	I take, exact
squama, -ae f.	scale	*super*	over, above, from above
stabulum, -i n.	stall		
stagnum, -i n.	pool	*super* + abl.	at, upon, about
statio, -onis f.	sentry duty	*super* + acc.	over, through, on top of
statuo, -ere, -ui, -utus	I place		
status, -us m.	state	*superbus, -a, -um*	arrogant, proud, magnificent
stella, -ae f.	star		
sterno, -ere, stravi, stratus	I strike down, flatten, cover, overthrow	*superi, -orum* m.pl.	the gods
		supero, -are	I overcome, cross, cross over, pass, prevail
stimulus, -i m.	goad, spur		
stirps, -is m/f.	stem, trunk, lineage	*superstes, -stitis*	surviving
		supersum, -esse	I am left, survive
sto, stare	I stand, stop	*superus, -a, -um*	above, of heaven
strepitus, -us m.	din	*supplex, -icis*	humble, as a suppliant
strideo, -ere	I hiss		
strido, -ere	I hiss, whirr	*supplicium, -i* n.	punishment
stridor, -oris m.	buzzing	*suppono, -ere*	I place beneath
stringo, -ere, strinxi, strictus	I graze, skim	*supra*	above
struo, -ere, struxi, structus	I build, arrange for battle	*supra* + acc.	beyond
		supremus, -a, -um	last, greatest
studium, -i n.	enthusiasm	*sura, -ae* f.	calf (of the leg)
stupefactus, -a, -um	astonished	*surgo, -ere, surrexi, surrectus*	I arise, rise
stupeo, -ere	I am amazed	*sus, suis* m/f.	pig, boar, sow
Strymonius, -a, -um	of the Strymon	*suscipio, -ere*	I take up, catch
suadeo, -ere, -si, -sus + dat.	I urge, persuade	*suscito, -are*	I rouse
sub + acc./abl.	under	*suspensus, -a, -um*	raised
subdo, -ere	I send into	*sustineo, -ere*	I hold up
subduco, -ere	I remove	*tabum, -i* n.	corruption, decay
subeo, -ire + dat.	I creep up on, come up to, approach, rise	*Taburnus, -i* m.	Mt Taburnus
		tacitus, -a, -um	silent
subicio, -ere, -ieci, -iectus	I place under	*taeda, -ae* f.	pine wood, torch, pine-torch
subigo, -ere, -egi, -actus	I force, compel, induce		
		taenia, -ae f.	band, ribbon
subito	suddenly	*talis -e*	such
subitus, -a, -um	sudden	*tandem*	at last
subiungo, -ere, -iunxi, -iunctus	I attach, subdue	*tango, -ere, tetigi, tactus*	I touch, move
sublabor, -i, -lapsus sum	I undermine, slip under	*tantum*	only, so greatly, so much
sublimis, -e	high, tall	*tantus, -a, -um*	so great, such great
sublustris, -e	dim		
subnecto, -ere	I clasp	*tapes, -etis* m.	rug
subremigo, -are	I paddle below	*Tarchon, -onis* m.	Tarchon
subrideo, -ere	I smile	*tardus, -a, -um*	slow
subsidium, -i n.	aid, relief	*Tarpeia, -ae* f.	Tarpeia
subsisto, -ere, -stiti	I stop, halt, stand still	*Tartara, -orum* n.pl.	Tartarus
		taurus, -i m.	bull
subvecto, -are	bring up, transport	*tectum, -i* n.	roof, building, house
subveho, -ere, -vexi, -vectus	I convey up	*tegmen, -inis* n.	covering
subvenio, -ire	I help	*tego, -ere, texi, tectus*	I protect, cover, conceal
succedo, -ere + dat.	I approach, go to, draw near (to)		
		tellus, -uris f.	land, earth, ground
succido, -ere, -cidi, -cisus	I cut down	*telum, -i* n.	weapon, missile, dart
succingo, -ere, -cinxi, -cinctus	I tuck up		

temere	by chance, for nothing	*transcribo, -ere*	I transfer
tempestas, -atis f.	storm	*transeo, -ire, -ii, -itus*	I pass through
templum, -i n.	temple	*transverbero, -are*	I pierce
tempto, -are	I try, test	*tremefacio, -ere, -feci, -factus*	I shake
tempus, -oris n.	time, temple	*tremo, -ere*	I tremble
tenax, -acis	gripping	*tremor, -oris* m.	trembling
tendo, -ere, tetendi, tensus	I extend, hold out, proceed, offer, go, head	*trepido, -are*	I tremble, bustle about
tenebrae, -arum f.pl.	darkness	*trepidus, -a, -um*	anxious, excited
teneo, -ere	I hold, keep, occupy	*triginta*	thirty
		triplex, -icis	triple
tepefacio, -ere, -feci, -factus	I make warm	*tristis, -e*	sad, bitter, grim
tepeo, -ere	I am warm	*triumphus, -i* m.	triumph
tepidus, -a, -um	warm	*Troia, -ae* f.	Troy
ter	thrice, three times	*Troianus, -a, -um*	Trojan
terebinthus, -i f.	terebinth	*Troiugena, -ae* m.	a Trojan
teres, teretis	shapely	*Troius, -a, -um*	Trojan
Tereus, -eos (acc. *-ea*)	Tereus	*Tros, Trois* m.	Trojan
tergeminus, -a, -um	three-bodied	*truncus, -i* m.	torso, trunk
tergum, -i n.	rear, back, hide	*trux, trucis*	grim, fierce
terra, -ae f.	land, ground, earth	*tuba, -ae* f.	trumpet
terreo, -ere	I frighten	*tueor, -eri, tuitus sum*	I look after, look at, observe
terribilis, -e	dreadful, terrible	*Tulla, -ae* f.	Tulla
terrificus, -a, -um	frightening	*tumeo, -ere*	I swell
terror, -oris m.	terror	*tumidus, -a, -um*	swollen, swelling
testor, -ari, -atus sum	I call as witness	*tumor, -oris* m.	swelling
Teucri, -orum m.pl.	Trojans	*tumultus, -us* m.	uprising, commotion
textum, -i n.	fabric	*tumulus, -i* m.	mound, tomb
thalamus, -i m.	bed-chamber, bedroom, wedding	*tunc*	then
		tundo, -ere, tutudi, tunsus	I beat
thiasus, -i m.	Bacchic dance	*tunica, -ae* f.	tunic
thorax, -acis m.	breast-plate	*turba, -ae* f.	crowd, crush
Thracius, -a, -um	Thracian	*turbidus, -a, -um*	wild
Thybris, -is m.	river Tiber	*turbo, -are, -avi, -atus*	I trouble, bewilder, confuse, cause havoc
Tiburtus, -i m.	Tiburtus		
tigris, -is (acc. *-im*) f.	tigress	*turbo, -inis* m.	tornado, whirlwind, twisting force, whipping top
timeo, -ere	I am afraid		
timor, -oris m.	fear		
tingo, -ere	I dip		
Tirynthius, -i m.	Hercules	*turma, -ae* f.	cavalry squadron
tolero, -are	I endure	*Turnus, -i* m.	Turnus
tollo, -ere, sustuli, sublatus	I raise, remove, get rid of	*turris, -is* f.	tower
		tus, turis n.	incense
tormentum, -i n.	torture, siege-weapon	*tutus, -a, -um*	safe
		tyrannus, -i m.	ruler, tyrant
torqueo, -ere, torsi, tortus	I spin, turn, twist	*Tyrius, -a, -um*	Carthaginian
tortilis, -e	twisted	*Tyrrhenus, -a, -um*	Etruscan
torus, -i m.	bed	*Tyrrhidae, -arum* m.pl.	the sons of Tyrrheus
tot	so many		
totidem	the same number (of)	*uber, -eris* n.	fruitfulness, udder
		udus, -a, -um	damp, moist
totiens	so often	*ullus, -a, -um*	any
totus, -a, -um	all, the whole (of)	*ulterius*	further
traho, -ere, traxi, tractus	I drag, draw, pull, prolong	*ultor, -oris* m.	avenger
		ultrix, -icis f.	avenging
traicio, -ere	I pierce	*ultro*	spontaneously
trames, -itis m.	path	*ululatus, -us* m.	wailing
trano, -are	I fly through	*umbo, -onis* m.	shield boss
trans + acc.	across	*umbra, -ae* f.	shade, shadow, shelter, darkness
transabeo, -ire, -ii	I pierce		

umbrosus, -a, -um	shady
umerus, -i m.	shoulder
umidus, -a, -um	damp, dewy
umquam	ever
una	together
unda, -ae f.	wave, water
unde	from where
undique	on/from all sides
ungo, -ere, unxi, unctus	I caulk
ungula, -ae f.	hoof
unus, -a, -um	one, alone
urbs, urbis f.	city
urgeo, -ere	I encourage, press, attack
usquam	anywhere
usque	all the way
usus, -us m. + abl.	need, use
ut + indic.	as, when
uterque, utraque, utrumque	both
utor, uti, usus sum + abl.	I use, enjoy
vaco, -are	I am left open
vacuus, -a, -um	empty
vado, -ere	I go
vadum, -i n.	shallow water, sea
vagina, -ae f.	sheath
vale	farewell
valeo, -ere	I am able
validus, -a, -um	strong
vallis, -is f.	valley
vallum, -i n.	rampart
vanus, -a, -um	vain, empty
varius, -a, -um	various
vasta do, dare,	I lay waste to
vasto, -are	I lay waste
vastus, -a, -um	huge, vast, extensive
vates, -is m/f.	prophet, poet, prophetess
vecto, -are	I carry, convey
veho, -ere, vexi, vectus	I convey, carry
vehor, -i, vectus sum	I am conveyed
vel	or
vello, -ere	I pick up
velo, -are, -avi, -atus	I veil, cover
velox, -ocis	swift
velum, -i n.	sail
veluti	just like, just as
venator, -oris m.	hunter
venatrix, -icis f.	huntress
venenum, -i n.	poison
veneror, -ari, -atus sum	I venerate
venia, -ae f.	permission
venio, -ire	I come
ventosus, -a, -um	windy
ventus, -i m.	wind
Venus, -eris f.	Venus
verbena, -ae f.	sacred foliage
verber, -eris n.	whip
verbum, -i n.	word
vergo, -ere	I sink down
vero	indeed, however
verso, -are	I twist, writhe
vertex, -icis m.	head, summit, top
verto, -ere, verti, versus	I turn, overturn, apply
verum	but
verus, -a, -um	true
vesanus, -a, -um	mad
Vesta, -ae f.	Vesta
vester, -tra, -trum	your
vestigium, -i n.	tracks, prints, footstep
vestigo, -are	I investigate
vestis, -is f.	clothes
veto, -are, -ui, -itus	I forbid
vetus, veteris	old
vetustas, -atis f.	old age
vetustus, -a, -um	old, ancient
via, viae f.	journey, way, road
vibro, -are	I quiver
vicissim	in turn
victor, -oris	victorious
victor, -oris m.	victor
victoria, -ae f.	victory
victrix, -icis	victorious
video, -ere, vidi, visus	I see
videor, -eri, visus sum	I appear, seem
vigilo, -are	I am awake, stay awake
viginti	twenty
villosus, -a, -um	shaggy
vincio, -ire, vinxi, vinctus	I bind
vinclum, -i n.	chain, bond
vinco, -ere, vici, victus	I conquer, win, defeat, overcome
vinculum, -i n.	chain
vinum, -i n.	wine
violentus, -a, -um	violent
violo, -are, -avi, -atus	I violate, harm
vipereus, -a, -um	of a snake
vir, viri m.	man, husband
vires, virium f.pl.	strength
virgineus, -a, -um	of a maiden
virginitas, -atis f.	virginity
virgo, -inis f.	maiden
virgulta, -orum n.pl.	shoots
viridis, -e	green
virilis, -e	male, of a man
virtus, -utis f.	valour, courage
vis, vim, vi f.	force, violence, power
viscera, -um n.pl.	innards, insides, entrails
visus, -us m.	vision, stare, sight
vita, -ae f.	life
vitta, -ae f.	head-band
vivo, -ere, vixi, victus	I live
vivus, -a, -um	living, alive
vix	scarcely
voco, -are	I call
Volcanus, -i m.	Vulcan, fire
Volcens, -entis m.	Volcens
volito, -are	I fly to and fro, fly about

volo, -are	I fly, dash	*vomo, -ere*	I spew out, pour forth
volo, velle	I want, wish		
Volsci, -orum m.pl.	the Volsci	*votum, -i* n.	vow, prayer
volubilis, -e	spinning	*vox, vocis* f.	voice, word
volucer, -cris, -cre	swift, flying	*vulgo, -are*	I publish
volucris, -is f.	bird	*vulgus, -i* n.	mass, multitude
voluntas, -atis f.	will, wish	*vulnificus, -a, -um*	causing wounds
voluto, -are	I roll about, ponder	*vulnus, -eris* n.	wound
		vultus, -us m.	face
volvo, -ere	I roll, turn, throw down, coil	*Xanthus, -i* m.	river Xanthus
		Zephyrus, -i m.	West Wind

INDEX